Sweden's Age of Greatness
1632-1718

Each volume in the 'Problems in Focus' series is designed to make available to students important new work on key historical problems and periods that they encounter in their courses. Every volume is devoted to a central topic or theme, and the most important aspects of this are dealt with by specially commissioned essays from authorities in the relevant fields. The editorial Introduction reviews the problem or period as a whole, and each essay provides an assessment of the particular aspect, pointing out the areas of development and controversy, and indicating where conclusions can be drawn or where further work is necessary. An annotated bibliography serves as a guide to further reading.

PROBLEMS IN FOCUS SERIES

PUBLISHED

Britain after the Glorious Revolution 1689–1714
edited by Geoffrey Holmes

*Britain Pre-eminent: Studies of British World Influence in
the Nineteenth Century*
edited by C. J. Bartlett

Popular Movements c. 1830–1850
edited by J. T. Ward

The Republic and the Civil War in Spain
edited by Raymond Carr

Financing Development in Latin America
edited by Keith Griffin

The Hundred Years War
edited by Kenneth Fowler

The Reign of James VI and I
edited by Alan G. R. Smith

Sweden's Age of Greatness 1632–1718
edited by Michael Roberts

VOLUMES IN PREPARATION INCLUDE

Industrial Revolutions
edited by R. M. Hartwell

The Conservative Leadership 1831–1937
edited by Donald Southgate

Sweden's Age of Greatness
1632–1718

EDITED BY
MICHAEL ROBERTS

St. Martin's Press   New York

AFFILIATED PUBLISHERS: Macmillan Limited, London –
also at Bombay, Calcutta, Madras and Melbourne

Contents

Acknowledgements   vii

Preface   ix

Introduction   1
   MICHAEL ROBERTS

1 The Experience of Empire: Sweden as a Great Power   20
   SVEN LUNDKVIST

2 The Swedish Economy and Sweden's Role as a Great
      Power 1632–1697   58
   SVEN-ERIK ÅSTRÖM

3 Estates and Classes   102
   STELLAN DAHLGREN

4 The Swedish Church   132
   MICHAEL ROBERTS

5 Charles X and the Constitution   174
   STELLAN DAHLGREN

6 Magnus Gabriel De la Gardie   203
   GÖRAN RYSTAD

7 The *reduktion*   237
   KURT ÅGREN

8 The Swedish Army, from Lützen to Narva   265
   ALF ÅBERG

Bibliography   288

Notes and References   296

Notes on Contributors   304

Index   305

Acknowledgements

Chapter 3, 'Estates and Classes', by Stellan Dahlgren, is translated with slight modifications from the author's '1600-talets ståndssamhälle', which forms part of the collective work *Kultur och samhälle i stormakt-stidens Sverige* (Stockholm 1967). It is reproduced here in English by kind permission of the publishers, Wahlström & Widstrand.

Preface

WHEN I was invited to edit a volume of essays on seventeenth-century Sweden it was not without some misgivings that I accepted the commission. To put one's Problems in Focus is no doubt a useful service, or a salutary exercise, according as to whether one is the reader or the writer; but it does presuppose that both have some idea about what the problems are. And it does suggest a concentration of studies within a limited space of time or a fairly sharply defined range of topics. Neither of these conditions seemed to apply to a book of essays about Sweden. The English reader could not be expected to be able to keep abreast of contemporary controversy among Swedish historians. And although it would not have been difficult to assemble teams of Swedish experts to contribute to symposia on, let us say, the Form of Government of 1634, or the nobility's claim to the indeterminate revenues on alienated crown lands, or the Polish policy of Charles XII, it is a question whether such a volume would have commanded a very widespread appeal.

What was needed, it seemed to me, was a volume which should give some indication of the state of Swedish historical thinking on topics with which, by reason of their obvious importance, students of history in English-speaking countries had already some slight acquaintance, but which they were debarred by the language barrier from pursuing further. It followed therefore that the spread of the book must be a good deal wider than is usual in volumes in this series; and it followed also that there was no point at all in including essays dealing with periods or personalities on which something more than a modicum of information was already available in English: hence the omission of anything upon Gustavus Adolphus at the beginning of the century, and upon Charles XII at the end of it; hence too the absence of any general survey of Swedish parliamentarianism during the period. It is hoped that the present volume conforms to this plan, and that it will be found (as I have tried to indicate in the Introduction) to have a real inner logic of its own which links its apparently disparate chapters together.

The tragic and untimely death of the scholar who had undertaken to survey the achievement of Charles X, followed by the unavoidable withdrawal, at something a good deal later than the last possible moment, of the contributor who had agreed to write what would obviously have been a crucial essay on Axel Oxenstierna after 1632, deprived us of two studies which would have been particularly welcome. In this emergency Dr Stellan Dahlgren most generously agreed, at very short notice, to contribute an examination of Charles X's constitutional relations with council and *riksdag*; an offer for which I was particularly grateful, since it provided the book with its only study of constitutional history. It proved impossible, in the time available, to find anybody who was willing to take on Oxenstierna; and I had no other resource, in the circumstances, than to produce a chapter of my own. And since attempts to persuade any Swedish ecclesiastical historian to write a chapter on the church had proved vain, it seemed that the best thing I could do was to try to supply that deficiency myself.

At the very outset it was only the timely promise of a generous subsidy from the Swedish Institute for Cultural Exchange that saved the project from perishing of inanition before it had well begun, and gave it a chance to get off the ground. As so often before, I should like to express my deep appreciation of all that the Institute has done, and is doing, to facilitate the study of Swedish history in this country.

For the translations of the essays in this volume I am entirely responsible, though each was of course submitted to the author for his approval. I can only hope that in an attempt to make the versions run smoothly I have not obliterated personal idiosyncrasies of style.

M. R.

Introduction

SWEDEN'S career as an imperial power lasted exactly a century. It was the capture of Riga by Gustavus Adolphus in 1621 that first impressed Europe with the realisation that a new great power was arising in the inner recesses of the Baltic; it was the peace of Nystad in 1721 that made it plain to all observers that the intervening display of political and military pyrotechnics was over, that the astonishing rocket had exhausted itself, and that all that remained was to pick up the stick. It is true that there were foreign observers who had long ago foreseen this conclusion: the peak of the parabola had been reached already in 1661, and in the four decades that succeeded it was easy to infer that the curve was already trending downwards. But at the last moment a booster had appeared, in the person of Charles XII; and in the first decade of his reign he had showered stars and detonations on eastern Europe in such profusion that only an exceptionally rash prophet would have predicted that this portentous display would shortly burn itself out.

If the British Empire was acquired in a fit of absence of mind, this was certainly not true of the Swedish. The Swedish empire was founded, and grew, by deliberate acts of royal policy. It was not the product of spontaneous economic expansion, nor of private enterprise which sought access to exotic raw materials or looked for a market for its own wares. It was not, as the Habsburg empire had been, a haphazard agglomeration produced by dynastic inbreeding. The discovery of new lands and the opening-up of new trade routes played no part in it, as in the empires of Portugal and Spain. It was equally destitute of Pilgrim Fathers and of East India Companies. No doubt religion had a share in it: one of its salient characteristics was a monolithic Lutheranism; and Gustavus Adolphus was after all (at least in one aspect) the Protestant Hero. The tradition that Sweden was the European champion of the Protestant cause was accepted by contemporaries, continued vigorously by Charles XII, and was still plausible as late as 1757. But in the seventeenth century religion and politics were inextricably commingled; and even in the time of Gustavus political considerations, no less than religious, supplied the dynamic which was to make Sweden a great power.

The first lodgement on the further Baltic shore had occurred as long ago as 1561, and had been expanded until by the end of the century Sweden was master of all Estonia. The logic of expansion imposed itself as the only means of securing what in the beginning had been an essentially defensive outpost; since that outpost, economically no less than militarily, was scarcely tenable without its natural hinterland. And such outposts were felt to be necessary to the security of Sweden itself: for Sweden, the Baltic coasts and their harbours were what the Channel ports were to England; positions which could not be left without anxiety in the hands of a hostile power, whether that power were Russia, or Poland, or Denmark, or the Habsburgs. The empire was not built by neo-Viking marauders; nor was it a product of the *Ubermensch* mentality: the cult of the ancient Goths, which reached its final expression in Olof Rudbeck's *Atlantica*, was not a creed of imperialism; it was the flattering unction which a self-consciously poor and backward country laid to its collective soul: as peripheral to the Swedish imperial experience as Kipling to the British.

Nor is there much sign that the expansion of the empire was a thing in which the nation as a whole was much concerned. It offered a military career, and the prospect of donations, to some of the aristocracy; but for the rest it was a process which increased the taxes and demanded cannon-fodder. Expansion came by the personal decision of successive monarchs, personally assessing political (or possibly economic) needs, and adroitly enlisting the support of council and *riksdag* for their policies – sometimes, as Dr Dahlgren shows in the case of Charles X, by confronting them with a virtual *fait accompli* (see below, p. 186). The process was neither continuous nor consistent, and it almost always aroused misgivings in some: in Axel Oxenstierna himself before 1630; in his opponents after 1634; in Gustav Bonde and some of his colleagues in 1654; in the counsellors of Charles XII after Narva. As early as 1634 the council was complaining that 'the branches expand, but the tree withers at the root'; and the whole reign of Charles XI is marked by a caution which arises, partly from satiety, but also from exhaustion.

This empire, then, which a possibly malign destiny conspired to thrust upon Sweden, was first of all based upon considerations of strategy and national security; and Sven Lundkvist in his essay makes clear the military functions which the overseas provinces were supposed to discharge, and which, on the whole, they did discharge (see below, p. 29). But the strategic value of the provinces depended upon command of the sea: the empire was essentially a maritime empire, bound together by the Baltic. At times the binding came unstuck; for the Baltic is a treacherous and tempestuous sea for sailing-ships; and in the arctic seventeenth century – at least until Charles XI moved the main naval base to Karlskrona – the Swedish navy and transports might find themselves icebound in their ports at a moment of crisis. There was indeed only one power in the Baltic able to engage the Swedish navy on terms of equality, and that was Denmark; but one power was quite enough. Swedish statesmen were determined that there should not be another. Hence the exultation of Gustavus Adolphus when the peace of Stolbova shut Russia off from the sea; hence the immediate reaction to the prospect of a Habsburg fleet under Wallenstein's command; hence the Swedish occupation of Courland in 1658. Danes and Swedes at least agreed in maintaining their joint monopoly of the *jus classis immitendae*, the sole right to keep a naval force in the Baltic: it was in order to preserve that right that the Danes did a Pearl Harbour on the Polish fleet in 1637. The trouble from Sweden's point of view came when the Danes under the stress of war temporarily abandoned this principle and called in the aid of the Dutch. It was the Dutch fleet which tipped the balance against Sweden in 1658–9, and again in 1676; and it was with the idea of preventing this happening that Sweden had framed the terms of the peace of Roskilde, and that Johan Gyllenstierna was to launch his programme for reconciliation with Denmark in 1679.

From a strategic point of view the Swedish empire certainly made sense. But historians have nevertheless been inclined to argue that the motives which lay behind its creation were not primarily strategic; that its purpose was aggressive rather than defensive; that it represented not so much the response to threats as a long-range plan for acquiring control of the trade of the Baltic Sea, and especially the lucrative transit trade from Russia to the west. They see the whole adventure as an aspect of Sweden's poverty, and the motive power of imperialism as economic rather than political. Without going to the extremes of the ingenious Friedrich Bothe – who half a century ago sought to explain Sweden's intervention in the Thirty Years War as an attempt to secure a vent for Swedish copper and attract German capital for Swedish trading ventures – we can recognise that such an approach presents an important aspect of the truth. But the antithesis between political and economic motivations must not be pressed too hard. Whether the empire was conceived as a means to national enrichment for its own sake, or whether the wealth which might come from conquest was seen as an indispensable necessity for safeguarding Sweden's vital political interests, is perhaps mainly a question of emphasis. And it is difficult to resist the impression that, as a matter of history, the emphasis is not always constant. There is remarkably little in the correspondence of Gustavus and Oxenstierna, for instance, to suggest that economic motives played a major part in the king's policies. In his triumphant speech on the conclusion of the peace of Stolbova, Gustavus was concerned to emphasise the political rather than the economic advantages which the peace had brought – so much so, that Artur Attman (for whom the economic interpretation of Swedish policy was the only admissible one) regarded the peace as a Swedish reverse. It is a fact that in 1622 Gustavus would have been ready to surrender all his conquests in Livonia (including Riga) in return for a firm peace. For him (as for Oxenstierna too) the Prussian 'licences' were valuable mainly as serving political and military ends; and in 1635 the council (which felt much less strongly about those ends) purchased the truce of Stuhmsdorf by surrendering them. Oxenstierna never seems to have given more than tepid support to the idea that Sweden relinquish her claims in Pomerania in return for the cession of Prussia, with all the economic advantages which would have resulted from the exchange.

By the 1650s, however, it is clear that we have to deal with a policy of conscious economic imperialism. In 1651, in his great Instruction for the new College of Commerce, Axel Oxenstierna laid down two main principles: that Sweden should aim at channelling the trade of the Baltic through Swedish-controlled ports; and that she should seek to build up her own mercantile marine. Neither of these policies was new; and the former of them had certainly a very long history. It lay behind Tyrgils Knutsson's foundation of Viborg in 1295, Gustavus Vasa's foundation of Helsingfors in 1550, and Gustavus Adolphus's foundation of Nyen in 1632; it prompted Eric XIV's dream of a Göta canal. From time to time attempts had been made to plug the gaps through which the Russian trade could evade the Swedish customs houses or the Swedish navy: from the reign of John III to that of Charles XII, Sweden made occasional ineffectual snatches at Archangel. In the seventeenth century government policy varied between an attempt to enforce a rigorous application of staple-rights at Swedish-controlled ports, and Axel Oxenstierna's more 'free trade' tactic of tempting the foreigner to use them by the lowering of tolls and the relaxation of controls; but either way the objective was the same. But perhaps it was only in Charles X's reign that the economic and political aspects of expansion fused into a single policy – a policy which culminated in the grand design of solving political difficulties, and securing a permanently stable financial situation, by the conquest of Denmark and the seizure of the Sound tolls.

The attempt failed. Swedish imperialism was never able to realise the programme set out in the Instruction of 1651. The mercantile marine did indeed develop, especially in the last decades of the century; and Sweden obtained a markedly increased share of the Russian transit trade. But the grand design, or (it might be better to call it) the favourite device, never really became effective. Moreover, despite a general control of economic policy from Stockholm the empire was never an economic unit. There were many factors militating against economic unity: different and anomalous rates of duty as between, for instance, Riga and Reval; customs barriers between one overseas province and another, or between the provinces and the motherland; a confusion of weights and measures and currencies; entrenched privileges and ancient jealousies between town and town, noble and burgher, seaports and upland, which defied efforts at rationalisation. Had Charles XI lived as long as Gustavus Vasa, had the Northern War not broken out in 1700, it may well be that more progress in solving some of these problems might have been made. But throughout the whole period any planned economic policy for the empire was liable to be disturbed by the pressing needs of temporary emergencies, and the difficulty of meeting them which was a consequence of Sweden's poverty: grain exports to the west from the Baltic provinces (a main source of revenue) might have to be prohibited in order to feed the armies – or indeed, in the 1680s and 1690s, to ease the pressure of shortages in Scandinavia; in response to urgent demands for cash the tolls would be sharply raised, to the prejudice of the long term objective of attracting western traders; purely political considerations might entail the alienation of the vital Dutch middlemen, and produce unpleasant economic consequences.

The effects of these *ad hoc* policies were certainly prejudicial to the welfare of the Baltic provinces, whose livelihood depended essentially on the exportation of grain. High tolls were bad enough, but violent oscillations in the level of tolls were worse, and periodical total bans upon export westwards were worst of all. The involvement of the provinces in Sweden's wars depressed trade, and on occasion (as under Charles X) exposed them to terrible devastations by invading armies: indeed a recent Soviet historian (A. Lyublinskaya) is disposed to see in the disturbed political conditions of the Baltic region the most obvious cause of that general depression of trade in north-west Europe which set in around 1630. In view of all this it may well be asked whether the conquered provinces derived any material advantage from their inclusion in the empire. To such a question it may be answered that there were real compensations to offset the inconveniences. The Baltic ports had, after all, the same economic interest as the Swedish government in the elimination of rivals, and they looked, not in vain, to Stockholm to fight their battle. The influx of the great Swedish landlords into Estonia and Livonia seems to have led to better farming, to an extension of the land under cultivation, and to an increase in grain-growing.

Whatever the economic importance of the Swedish connection for the provinces, there can be no doubt of the economic importance of the empire to Sweden herself. No doubt the economic development of the country might have come without imperial expansion, for that development rested on copper and iron, and upon the industries associated with them; and Dutch capital in search of investment would probably sooner or later have been attracted by cheap labour, abundant fuel and water power, good water communications and liberal royal inducements. Nevertheless the empire did something to accelerate this process, if only because its defence made such developments necessary. But it was also economically important in more direct ways. Riga, after all, was the first city of the empire in wealth and population; the Baltic tolls, though they might be disappointing in comparison with the high expectations entertained of them, were a major source of revenue. From the crown's vast grants of land in the conquered provinces the high aristocracy – the Oxenstiernas, De la Gardies, Königsmarcks and their kind – drew much of the income which went to build Makalös, Läckö, Skokloster, Jakobs-dal, Tidö and all the other ornaments of *Suecia Antiqua et Hodierna.* Yet it would be rash to jump to the conclusion that it was the prospect of such riches which influenced the nobility to support an expansionist foreign policy. It was Gustavus Adolphus, not the council, who decided on the German war; it was Charles X, adroitly manoeuvring council and *riksdag*, who committed the country to aggression in 1665; it was Charles XII, against his council's wishes, who embarked on the campaign against Poland.

Nevertheless it is clear that when the *reduktion* came, the transference of the extensive noble estates in the Baltic provinces into crown hands was among the more important gains of the monarchy, and contributed substantially to bringing about the situation of 1693, when the king, for the first time since 1560, could truly boast that he was able to 'live of his own'. Ever since 1648 it had been the aim of Swedish statesmen to make the provinces financially self-sufficient. Before 1680 this objective was scarcely attained; but by the 1690s the picture had been transformed. The provinces were not merely self-sufficient, they

were running at a profit; and that profit was an important factor in
balancing the budget of the mother-country (see below, pp. 23–4).
Anything less like the financial arrangements of the British Empire can
scarcely be imagined.

Just as the empire was something less than an economic unit, so too
it was never a unit administratively. Acquired piecemeal, it remained
to the end a collection of disparate elements and uncoordinated practices (see below, pp. 39–43). The essential link that bound them all
together was simply the crown. There was nothing to correspond to
Spain's Council of the Indies; there was nothing like the Dutch East
India Company exercising what was virtually a proconsular authority
over wide-spreading territories. The council of state did indeed discuss
imperial affairs, and orders concerning the Baltic provinces were issued,
like all other orders, through the Chancery; but in Bremen–Verden and
Pomerania the king ruled as duke, and these provinces were scarcely
more under the control of the central government in Stockholm than
George I's Hanover was under the control of Westminster. There was
no supreme judicial authority for the whole empire; instead a Supreme
Court for the Baltic provinces was set up at Dorpat, and another for
the German provinces at Wismar. Local judicial systems, local privileges
and peculiarities, were everywhere retained; and Swedish law did not
run in any province save Ingria. On military and naval matters, indeed,
the appropriate Colleges in Stockholm took the appropriate decisions,
and tried to see that they were put into effect – though even here provincial uncooperativeness might be a nuisance; but apart from this the only
central authority which habitually looked at imperial policy as a whole
was the College of Commerce, which acted as a sort of analogue to the
English Committee for Trade and Plantations. After 1680, indeed, there
are many signs of change: the provinces conquered from Denmark in
1660 are fully integrated, by threats and cajolery, into the Swedish state;
there are signs of a wish to make the administration of Finland unilingu-
ally Swedish; and Charles XI, by his tough attitude to the Baltic
nobility, his destruction of their Estates, his determination to override
local differences and privileges in the general interest of the monarchy
as a whole, is plainly moving towards an empire more in the style of
George Grenville. But by the end of the century the process had still not
got very far.

One of the obstacles to integration, as Dr Lundkvist shows, was the
difference in constitutional tradition and situation between one province
and another; a difference which was especially marked between the

Baltic and German halves of the empire. The difference was no less obvious in other ways. Bremen–Verden and Pomerania, though relatively backward among the states of Germany, had certainly no need to fear comparison with Sweden in regard to living standards, cultural life and general civilisation; but the Baltic provinces, once you passed beyond the great ports, were retarded and barbarous to a degree which initially at least) shocked Swedish observers. A brutalised and self-sufficient rural nobility which treated its peasantry as little better than rightless beasts; a church impoverished, degraded and ignorant, conducting its ministrations in a language which was the language of the noble oppressor, and not the native tongue of its neglected congregations; a land devastated by wars; justice in the hands of the exploiting and privileged classes; virtually no education at all: such were the Baltic provinces when they came into Swedish hands. Gustavus Adolphus, Johan Skytte, Johannes Rudbeckius, contemplated with a sense of outrage a state of affairs which fell so far below their notion of what was tolerable. In 1627 a commission was sent to Estonia and Livonia to investigate these matters. It met with compact resistance from the local nobility, who explained, with exasperated iteration, that the Swedes did not know the local background; that they had not appreciated the legacy of past history; and that they were naïve in supposing that the Estonian or Livonian peasant was capable of being educated, or could be trusted to be diligent without firm discipline. It was a line of argument which cut no ice with Rudbeckius, and little with Skytte. In the Baltic provinces, certainly, Sweden stood – at least in principle – for enlightenment, reform, higher standards of administration, better justice between man and man; and was entitled to feel, as Austria–Hungary was later to feel in regard to Bosnia, that she was discharging (or at least attempting to discharge) a civilising mission.

And indeed a good deal was actually accomplished. The church was slowly reformed, and parsons began to preach in Estonian or Lettish instead of German; the judicial system was purged of some of its abuses; and above all a successful effort was made in the field of education: the first *gymnasia* were established at Dorpat, Reval and Riga. At Dorpat the terms of the foundation provided that the school was to be open to boys of all classes (not, as the nobility would have wished, to nobles only); and its curriculum offered the first attempt to cater for education in the Baltic languages. A year after the opening of the school at Dorpat Gustavus decided to transform it into a regular university; and from his camp at Nuremberg in 1632 he issued its charter, granted its privileges and provided for its endowment. Though Dorpat's history in this century was chequered by the interruptions of war, its creation was a landmark in the cultural history of the region which it served. Here, certainly, the Swedish conquest meant a glimmering of light in what the English Puritans called 'the dark corners of the land'. Nevertheless the main social evil proved too deeply rooted for easy eradication. Serfdom remained. The resistance of the local nobility proved stronger than the government's will to destroy it; the incoming Swedish landholders themselves quickly conformed to the customs (they would have said, to the economic facts of life) of the lands into which they came, and there is little to suggest that they treated their peasants less arbitrarily, or more benevolently, than the brutal Balts (see below, p. 46). But here too there were signs of change before the century ended. The great *reduktion* of the 1680s swept away a great part of the noble estates in Livonia; the crown, which was the beneficiary of the change, showed greater concern for its labour-force than the nobles it had displaced; by the end of the 1690s it seemed to have broken the back of noble resistance; and it appeared at least possible that the Baltic peasant might achieve a status more nearly approaching that of his brother in Sweden. But the change came too late: the death of Charles XI, the impact of the Northern War, came before the process of liberalisation had succeeded in making much difference, and the Russian conquest ended all hope of betterment.

The imperial adventure left its marks not only on the conquered provinces but also upon the imperial power. The most obvious of these was the heavy burden which expansion and defence entailed upon the Swedish and Finnish populations, and the drain in manpower (and hence in wealth) from losses in war. Professor Aström's study of the Swedish economy gives us some idea of the heaviness of those burdens and of the meagreness of the reserves which were available to meet such strains; while Dr Agren's chapter provides a salutary reminder that they fell also upon those who by birth and privilege were nominally exempt from taxation – i.e. upon the nobility. There were, all the same, some compensations for the fortunate few. The empire offered opportunities for a career: a career in the army, with all the chances of enrichment and of rising in the social scale which that implied; civil employment for Swedes or Finns in the administrations of Ingria and Estonia; jobs in the schools and universities; jobs for jurists in the new Supreme Courts (as the career of Georg Stiernhielm reminds us); while the cleric in search of preferment might be willing for a time to exile himself to what W. S. Gilbert once described as 'the congenial gloom of a colonial bishopric'. But admittedly such opportunities were limited. There was little real emigration from Sweden to the provinces: the trend indeed was very much the other way, since the Swedish connection offered many careers open to provincial talent. There was no colonial pressure-group to compare with the West India interest at Westminster; no nabobs returned home enriched, to interfere in domestic politics; no Dundas emerged to organise the non-existent patronage of a non-existent India.

Nevertheless the total imperial experience left a deep and permanent impression. In the sixteenth century Sweden had been a second- or third-class power, pent in the remotest recesses of the Baltic, rude, poor, backward; a power which only with difficulty had maintained its political independence, and which economically had only recently emancipated itself from the position of being a Hanseatic colonial-land. The seventeenth century changed all this. It brought Sweden out of her backwater, culturally, economically, politically; it raised her standards of life to meet those of continental Europe. From the conquered provinces themselves she learned nothing, or at least nothing that was good. The Swedish church turned for theological stimulus – in so far as it felt the need for such stimulus at all (see below, p. 135) – not to the German provinces but to Helmstedt or Wittenberg or Jena, as it might happen: Syncretism and Pietism did not filter into Sweden from Pomerania or Bremen–Verden; Cartesianism did not come from Germany at all. But certain other, more tangible, cultural influences followed from the Thirty Years War. The Swedes had a Napoleonic eye for cultural loot, and a well-grounded feeling that their library holdings could do with reinforcement: hence the plunder of Marienberg and Prague; hence the presence of Ulfilas's Bible in *Carolina* (see below, pp. 231–2). The cultural efflorescence of Christina's court, with its ballets and operas and its vaguely *libertin* atmosphere, though it existed side by side with ruder and more barbarous diversions, was real enough; and Christina's removal from the scene did not mean the end of it, as Göran Rystad's essay on Magnus Gabriel De la Gardie makes plain. The immigration of foreign artists and scholars continued after she had gone: De la Vallée, Tessin, Ehrenstrahl, Krafft and the rest. This kind of development may indeed have been an imported exotic: but it was at least an exotic that struck root. The artists and the architects, or very many of them, settled down in Sweden; and that says something. Their summoning was itself an aspect of Sweden's great-power status: the co-guarantor of Westphalia could not afford to present to the world the sort of image which had served well enough for the grim piety and brutal violence of Charles IX. The rustic, provincial Swedish nobility returned from the great wars not only with booty but with wider cultural perspectives, changed ideas about what became a nobleman, heightened demands on life; they sent their sons on the Grand Tour – to Paris and Saumur to learn polite accomplishments, to Dutch universities to study law, to Italy to see that classic civilisation which their Gothic ancestors had subjected long ago. No doubt only the very greatest of the magnates, enriched by Livonian or German donations, could afford to build Läckö or Skokloster; but continental fashions in furnishing and architecture were seeping downwards to more modest social levels; and even if we discount the too flattering pencil of Erik Dahlberg, it is clear that after the war many middling nobles were building country houses of a standard which much exceeded that which had obtained in earlier years. The Sweden which Magalotti saw in 1674 was very different from the land described by Charles Ogier forty years earlier.

On the other hand the great wars also had social effects which were anything but desirable. The church felt some of them, in the shape of turbulent regimental chaplains who came home when peace was made, hungry for a living, and obtained a pastorate for which their moral and intellectual standards did not always fit them, and for which they might have no diocesan qualification, by the favour of noble patrons whom they had known in the army. The nobility itself was confronted by a massive influx of foreign families – soldiers of fortune such as Hamilton and Douglas, Fleetwood and Ramsay, Wrangel and Königsmarck; financiers and entrepreneurs such as De Geer and Momma – Germans, Balts, Scots, Dutch: men who had risen to the top as a result of the wars, and whose wealth, pretensions and political importance now overshadowed that of men of older and more honourable lineages. Upon those numerous members of the middling and lesser nobility who were dependent on the emoluments they earned in the king's service if they were to live as became a gentleman, the strain which war imposed upon the national finances could inflict real hardship, for it might mean that their wages were unpaid, or in arrear. Among the high nobility, on the other hand, contact with German and Baltic serfdom threatened a corruption of standards and a consequent erosion of the immemorial freedom of the peasantry; and this produced in the lower Estates the fear of what they termed 'a Livonian servitude'. The menace, as Kurt Agren suggests (see below, pp. 257–60), may have been exaggerated for political purposes, but it had a basis in reality.

But indeed the empire was from start to finish a structure which not merely set up tensions, but was itself increasingly under strain. It had grown up as a solution to a fundamental geopolitical problem; but the solution had removed one hazard only to beget others: the complications of German politics which followed Sweden's membership of the German Diet; the international obligations which were laid upon her as a guarantor of the Westphalian settlement. As Professor Aström makes clear, Sweden lacked the natural resources, the capital, the commerce and the manpower which would have been necessary to sustain securely a position as a great power. She did indeed escape most of the financial problems which beset those states which felt the full impact of the price revolution; for Sweden, to a far greater extent than any major power, remained an economy based on payments in kind rather than in cash. In spite of all her difficulties, Sweden managed to avoid Spain's 'bankruptcies', or the desperation finance of Richelieu and Mazarin, or the economic collapse of the closing years of Louis XIV. There was no selling of offices; there were no *traitants*. Money might be tight, taxation heavy, wages unpaid; but formally, at least, the state remained solvent, and thanks to Charles XI's reforms for a time really became so. But it was a solvency based on very exiguous resources, rather than (as in the case of France) an insolvency which disguised high economic potential, and was made possible by it; and it was a solvency which could not long survive involvement in a major war if the Swedish people were left to bear the sole burden of paying for it.

One possible answer to this difficulty lay in the paradox that security and solvency might be found in what to Sweden's victims appeared to be aggression. War might be made to sustain war, and might bring rich rewards besides: a war economy, rather than a peace economy, was what suited Sweden's needs. During the Thirty Years War this seemed to be true. Nobody is going to argue that Gustavus invaded Germany as the only means of paying the arrears due to the Prussian cavalry, but nevertheless it is true that his financial difficulties, which neither his attempted corner in copper nor the yield of the Prussian 'licences' had really solved, did vanish after Breitenfeld (see below, pp. 92–4). The German war became virtually self-supporting, as long as the armies continued victorious; its enormous cost was borne by the 'contributions' of the occupied areas, exacted as far as possible in cash, and carefully gauged so as to ensure that the economic life of the country was kept going, and that the goose that laid the golden eggs was not killed. It was a system which worked well when things were going well; but it broke down in the face of military disaster. When in the mid-1630s the Swedes were fighting desperately with their backs to the Baltic, the area from which contributions could be drawn shrank so much that this financial system could not function properly. Then, and only then, French subsidies became important and necessary, enabling fresh recruits to be enlisted, mutinous troops to be paid, lost ground to be recovered, contributions once more to be exacted. French gold having as it were primed the pump, the automatically functioning machinery could start work once more.

With the end of the great war in Germany the situation changed. The native army whose size and composition was laid down by the Form of Government of 1634 was never by itself sufficient to carry on imperial wars: in the later stages of the Thirty Years War it formed only an insignificant proportion of the Swedish forces. And in every emergency after the war the native army had to be reinforced by the enlistment of mercenaries. Sweden could not from her own resources afford to keep a mercenary force in being for very long – nor, indeed, afford the heavy outlay involved in the recruitment of one. The only solution was to recruit on credit; transfer the army as quickly as possible to foreign soil; and hope that contributions, and the income from captured toll revenues, would take care of the soldiers' wages and suffice to pay off the creditors. Thus when danger threatened, war almost inevitably followed: what might be a legitimate measure of precaution could be endured only if someone else paid for it; mobilisation entailed war. Charles X exploited this situation, as Stellan Dahlgren shows us (see below, p. 186), to drag Sweden into war in 1655; it supplied one of the motives for the attack on Denmark in 1658; and it received its classic exemplification in the events of 1675 (see below, p. 215). From 1648 to 1680 the constant nightmare of Swedish foreign policy was how to be secure without becoming bankrupt.

The reign of Charles X saw the last great attempt to solve this problem by expansion and aggression. It failed: Charles's grab at the Sound in 1658 was answered by a Dutch fleet, a European coalition and a dictated peace. His reign, which saw the culmination of Swedish power and the expansion of Sweden to her natural limits within Scandinavia, is a kind of watershed; and Charles himself seems to stand with a foot in two different worlds: on the one hand the martial, triumphant world which leads up to Roskilde; on the other the new world of Charles XI, with its strengthening of royal power, its *reduktion*, its *indelningsverk*. After 1660, certainly, new methods became necessary, and it was no easy task to devise them. It fell to Magnus Gabriel De la Gardie to make the first attempt. Henceforward Sweden was a power whose prime interest was the maintenance of peace. No prospect now of policies in the style of Axel Oxenstierna and Charles X: for the first time for nearly half a century Sweden was confronted with the task of securing her interests on the basis of a peace economy. It proved extraordinarly difficult. The obligations which Sweden had incurred, as *pars principalis paciscens* at Westphalia, as one of the three co-guarantors of that settlement, threatened always to involve her in unwelcome entanglements. But it seemed to De la Gardie that Sweden's obligations might just conceivably be turned to her advantage; that he might use them to keep Sweden *out* of continental quarrels, and establish her as the mediator, the pacificator and (with luck) the arbitrator of international disputes. The Westphalian settlement was now the public law of Europe: Sweden's safety, and Sweden's prestige, might alike be secured by seeing that it was applied. De la Gardie's considerable diplomatic skill was therefore devoted to the conscious effort to establish the principle of a European balance of power.

In vain. And this partly through miscalculation, partly through ill-luck; but mainly because as soon as Sweden settled into peaceful habits, as soon as her armies ceased to strike fear into her neighbours, the real inadequacy of her resources became increasingly apparent. Something more than diplomatic skill was necessary if Europe were to swallow Sweden's pretensions to holding the balance between Bourbon and Habsburg. The military and naval power which would have been required to give credibility to such a policy was no longer there: the country could not afford it. Indeed it was far from certain that Sweden's armed forces were now adequate to her own protection, let alone to imposing international settlements upon others. Deprived of the extraordinary revenues which in the past had been the result of successful wars, De la Gardie had no option but to seek financial assistance by way of subsidies from foreign powers: of all the resources which Axel Oxenstierna had had at his disposal, over and above what the country could provide, only the French subsidies now remained. De la Gardie might protest that subsidies were to be no more than 'accessories'; but they were accessories which were now indispensable. They fettered Sweden's freedom of action; they made nonsense of De la Gardie's attempt to elevate Sweden into the position of impartial mediator; and in 1675

they dragged her into the disastrous war which it had been De la
Gardie's especial care to avoid. After Charles X the maintenance of
Sweden's position as a great power by means of expansion and war had
ceased to be possible. After De la Gardie the alternative solution through
peace seemed to have become impossible too. A peace economy was
proving more disastrous than a war economy; a war economy was no
longer an option that was open to them.

This was the problem which Charles XI had to solve, and which
(within limits) he did solve. But it was not his only problem; and its
solution went hand in hand with the settlement of other great questions
which had long troubled the Swedish state. The absolutism of Charles
XI, from 1680 to 1697, concentrated into one sharply focused image
the military, financial, constitutional and social problems of the last
half-century. It is the point upon which all the streams which run
through earlier Swedish history seem to converge; it is the watersmeet
where they commingle and become one. And it is really what this book
is about. In essay after essay, authors who have set out from widely
separated starting-points, and who are discussing widely differing topics,
find themselves writing about Charles XI at the last. How indeed could
they help it, when every major problem of state was here brought to a
head? The desperate need, in 1680, for a stronger army and navy; the
need to liberate Sweden's foreign policy from dependence on foreign
paymasters; the consequent necessity to provide the crown with adequate
financial resources – these all imposed that *reduktion* which Charles X
had begun, but which his martial preoccupations had precluded him
from bringing to a conclusion. They lent added incisiveness to the in-
quisition into the finances of the regency, and to the proceedings of the
Great Commission, which brought not only harsh retribution to the
regents and the council of state, but huge financial plunder to the
exchequer. The *indelningsverk* for the army solved the problem of
maintaining adequate defensive strength without recourse to mercenaries, through a native army organised upon an automatically functioning and immutable financial basis (see below, pp. 269–71). The Swedish
fiscal system swung back from that concentration upon a cash revenue
which had been the policy of Axel Oxenstierna in the days of expansion
to the traditional emphasis upon payment in commodities, which
assorted best with a peaceable foreign policy. The gains from the *reduktion* and the Great Commission made the *indelningsverk* possible; and
after a decade of swingeing taxation they made possible also a balanced
budget and the normative estimates of 1696. Buoyant customs dues

permitted the accumulation of royal hoard on lines which recall Gustavus Vasa. The problem of financing security was apparently solved: Sweden, it seemed, could after all be safe without being bankrupt. Bengt Oxenstierna could pursue a foreign policy which was essentially analogous to that of Magnus Gabriel De la Gardie, and attain success where De la Gardie had found failure; for he had at his back resources, military and financial, which De la Gardie had never been able to command.

But these achievements were possible only because they also provided a resolution to tensions which had long been building up within Swedish society. The jealousy which the council of state had felt for the regents; resentment by the middling and lesser nobility of the social pretensions of counts, barons and the high aristocracy from which the regents and council were both recruited; competition for places in the public service, in which all the plums seemed to go to a narrow ring of council families, some of them recently ennobled and recently naturalised; discontent with a situation in which the crown could not be relied upon to repay its creditors – all these things produced a climate of opinion in which a majority of the House of Nobility was ready to start the landslide of the *reduktion*. They were soon to regret that they could not stop it. In 1655 the Nobility had been able to attempt to bargain with Charles X; in 1680 they were so divided that Charles XI was able to frame the *reduktion* to suit himself. And what suited him suited (for the moment at any rate) the three non-noble Estates too. For them the *reduktion* of 1680 was the successful issue of a long campaign, going back in the case of the Peasants at least to 1611; a campaign which had reached its first great climax at the *riksdag* of 1650. In 1680 the hopes, the fears and the rancours of 1650 united them solidly in the demand for a *reduktion* and in support of the king's measures. It may well be that Kurt Agren's investigations into the position of the peasants on land alienated to the nobility will turn out to have a general application, and that the old commonplaces about noble oppression will have to be discarded; but there can be little doubt that in 1680 disillusionment with aristocratic rule, and dislike of the nobility as a class, was strong among Clergy, Burghers and Peasants alike, and that for them the *reduktion* was seen not only as a financially necessary measure, but as a triumphant reversal of the failure of 1650. And for the peasantry, however small a part the consideration may have played in the king's strategy, it meant a final safeguarding of their liberties, their property rights and their unique position as one of the Estates of the Realm. Here, certainly, Charles XI and his advisers were working with the grain of history and not against it.

This could hardly be said of the constitutional consequences which followed in the years after 1680. Since 1660 the trend had been rather towards parliamentarianism than towards absolutism. The claim of the *riksdag* to a share in decisions, its aspiration to provide constitutional checks, which had been so apparent in the 1630s, had gathered strength during the regency for Charles XI, and had appeared strongly in 1675. The transformation of Sweden into an absolutism, which by 1682 was almost complete, was thus not an obvious development. Yet it too had deep roots in Swedish history. The champions of constitutionalism had for centuries been the council aristocracy. But after 1680 that aristocracy was shattered, disgraced, plundered and powerless, and from them no effective stand against the prerogative was now to be expected – at least for the next generation or so. The three lower Estates, on the other hand, had always looked to the monarchy as their natural ally and protector; and even in the 1660s had supported the regents, as the temporary custodians of the prerogative, against the king-yoking magnates of the council. Hence, when in 1680 regents and council were alike discredited by the disastrous outcome of their government and the strong suspicion that they had used their tenure of power to line their own pockets, it is no wonder that the lower Estates turned once again to the crown, or that they were ready to abandon for a while the constitutional aspirations of the *riksdag* in the hope of efficient government and the redress of social grievances. Charles X in his day had demonstrated how much play a monarch might find within the letter of the constitution; Charles XI would show that an absolutist régime might be fitted into a framework of legality by judicious interpretations of the Land Law.

Thus the perennial problem of Sweden's security which had precipitated the crisis of 1680 found at least a temporarily stable solution in a strong monarchy and an efficient administration. The Form of Government of 1634 had given Sweden a bureaucratic framework which had stood the test of time; and that framework was now stiffened and extended. With the king at its head the bureaucracy captured the state, and retained its hold upon it in the king's despite after the revolution of 1719–20 had swept the absolutism away. Through the bureaucracy the king was for the first time able to extend his effective control to spheres which hitherto had successfully resisted royal interference: as, for instance, the church (see below, pp. 168–70); or the recalcitrant nobility of Livonia (see below, pp. 44–6). Efficient administration of the country's manpower resources, better management of the greatly improved finances, enabled him to rebuild the navy and reform the army. The *indelningsverk* provided him with a standing force of 75,000 men, self-supporting, self-recruiting, highly organised, well disciplined, ready to mobilise with clockwork precision to the defence of any threatened frontier (see below, p. 286). The old equation between mobilisation and war no longer held good.

It was in many respects a remarkable achievement; and it seemed to meet many of the main difficulties. But it was based essentially on a foreign policy of caution and peace: the empire was now clearly on the defensive. Its weakness lay in the fact that it could not alter that geopolitical situation which had led to the empire's creation, and perhaps had made it necessary. Sweden was still ringed round with actual or potential enemies: indeed with neighbours who only waited the opportunity to settle old scores. Poland, indeed, had since 1660 been a friend; but a friend who was almost a liability: a vacuum of power into which traditional foes – Russia, for instance – might easily penetrate. And the innocuousness of Poland had been more than compensated by the arrival on the scene of a new enemy, Brandenburg, which had never forgotten or forgiven the loss of western Pomerania. And however the patterns of international alliances might shift and dissolve, the perennial threat from Denmark and Russia remained. In 1697, as in 1610, Sweden was menaced simultaneously on two fronts: Denmark, humiliated and despoiled in 1660, thwarted of revenge in 1679, still awaiting her opportunity; Russia, reviving under Ordyn-Nashchokin the claim of Ivan IV to regard the Baltic provinces as the Tsar's 'manors'. When the Russian onslaught came at last it would come in concert with Denmark, who for seventy years past had been manoeuvring to obtain Russia's assistance. In this situation Charles XI's policy of limited commitments and deliberate fence-sitting, his virtual renunciation of Sweden's role and responsibilities as a great power, however necessary it may have been, was seen to involve the consequence of cooling possible friends without disarming certain enemies. The Maritime Powers might indeed be willing to intervene to prevent a Danish *revanche* which would put both shores of the Sound into Danish hands; but the same commercial considerations which produced this policy made them relatively indifferent as to who owned Riga – provided their trade were not interfered with.

Thus the cycle of destiny fulfilled itself. Urgent political dangers had led to Eric XIV's lodgement in Reval. An irrefutable political logic had forced Gustavus Adolphus to doom Sweden to an international position which her own resources were inadequate to sustain. Charles X's final bid to make the empire economically viable, and therefore defensible, had failed in 1660. The narrow realism of Charles XI could neither ward off the coming storm nor fit Sweden to ride it out when at last it came upon her, for his reforms were neither intended to apply to a long period of war, nor flexible enough to be adapted to one. And the rigid logic of Charles XII finally condemned the whole imperial structure to ruin. All of them were right, according to their lights; all made choices which seemed to them inescapable. Gustavus Adolphus, Charles X, Charles XII, all sought to solve their problem by seeking a 'final' or 'radical' solution; all were drawn step by step to look for the one last victory which would set everything right. But all were pursuing an illusion; for in truth the problem that confronted them admitted of no permanent solution. Without the empire the history of Sweden would assuredly have been very different; and perhaps in the balance it brought as much good as ill. But it was an expedient which was possible only in the short run; and though the brash arrogance of Gyllenborg and the Hats might seek to turn the clock back in 1741, and the rash opportunism of Gustavus III might renew the attempt in 1788, such heroics could not disguise the fact that Sweden was not – and perhaps had never been – sufficiently strong to build a permanent dam against the Muscovite flood. When Charles XII fell at Fredrikshald, and Frederick I succeeded him in 1720, the clock did indeed move; but it moved forwards rather than backwards; forwards, in the words of the famous epigram, from XII to I.

> Vad i sin period den högsta punkten sett
> skall snart därpå sitt förra Intet röna.
> Kung Karl vi nyss begravt, Kung Fredrik nu vi kröna:
> så har vårt svenska ur då gått från XII till I.

Which may perhaps be rendered:

> The glory of the Age is past and gone;
> We to our former Nothingness are fated.
> King Charles is dead, King Frederick consecrated;
> And Sweden's clock has moved from XII to I.

1. The Experience of Empire: Sweden as a Great Power

SVEN LUNDKVIST

THE Thirty Years War made Sweden a great power. From being a relatively unknown country on the periphery of Europe, she became – and was by the peace of Westphalia formally recognised to be – one of the leading states of the continent. In the first decades of the eighteenth century this position began to crumble; at the peace of Nystad in 1721, when large portions of the empire were lost, it was for ever destroyed. And with that Sweden resumed her former less conspicuous place in the European community.

The period of greatness presents a wide range of interesting problems, and can be considered from many points of view. Some of these problems are sufficiently familiar; others, in the present state of our knowledge, are still inadequately explored, or can scarcely be said to have been explored at all. In the following essay we shall try to examine a few of them. All are bound up with Sweden's experience of greatness; and they can be formulated as follows:

1. What effect had Swedish administration upon the conquered provinces, and particularly on the Baltic provinces?
2. What effect had those provinces upon Sweden, economically, strategically, and from the point of view of foreign policy?
3. How was the imperial connection regarded in the various parts of the empire? How did it look from Stockholm and Riga, Stettin and Bremen?
4. What effect had the peace of Nystad upon Sweden?

In trying to find answers to these questions we shall not be concerned with the territories which Denmark was forced to cede in 1660, and which are now part of the Swedish state; for here the problems are somewhat different from those presented by the other provinces, and any attempt to treat them would lead us too far afield.

Finland had been linked to Sweden proper since the early twelfth century; but within the Scandinavian peninsula Sweden attained her present frontiers through a series of peace treaties in 1645, 1658 and 1660, whereby Denmark and Norway were forced to surrender portions of what is now southern and western Sweden; though in the far north a precise delimitation of the boundary had to wait until the eighteenth century. In Germany, the treaties of 1648 brought the acquisition of western Pomerania, a part of eastern Pomerania, and Wismar, Bremen and Verden; though most of eastern Pomerania was lost to Brandenburg in the 1670s. By the peace of Stolbova in 1617 Sweden came into possession of Ingria; and in the next decade steadily extended her conquests in the eastern Baltic. A series of truces with Poland reinforced her hold upon them; and they were finally confirmed to her by the peace of Oliva in 1660 and the peace of Kardis (with Russia) in 1661. The great settlement which followed the death of Charles XII, however, swept away the greater part of these conquests; and after 1721 there remained only Sweden and Finland, together with some territories in Pomerania and around Wismar.

I

The problems which confronted Sweden as a great power can be appreciated only if they are seen against the background of her manpower and other national resources, as compared with the corresponding resources of other leading European states; and this is made difficult by the lack of any reliable population statistics for the period. Nevertheless it is possible that the Swedish empire in 1700 may have had somewhere between 2·4 million and 3 million inhabitants – admittedly not a certain figure, but at least of the right order of magnitude. (For a slightly different estimate, see below, pp. 60–1.)

When we come to the rest of Europe, the basis for calculation is of very variable quality, and some figures cannot be much more than a guess. France, the dominant power in the second half of the seventeenth century, is said to have had about 21 million inhabitants in 1700; England and Wales, in the same year, is put at 5·2 million; Spain in 1723 at 6·1 million.

For all their defectiveness, these figures do show convincingly that the Swedish empire rested on a very slender population basis in comparison with (for example) France, where the available resources were of a quite different order. This must also have been true in regard to revenue and economic potential. And there can hardly be any doubt either but that many of the continental powers were considerably more advanced than the Swedish realms in many types of industrial development.

One essential precondition for the rise of the Swedish empire was the financial methods which were devised in the course of the Thirty Years War, mainly by Gustavus Adolphus in the years immediately after 1630. During his wars in Russia, Livonia and Poland, the main problem had been how to transport the resources at his disposal to the seat of war. The army for long remained quite small – between 15,000 and 25,000 men – and it was recruited at home. With the coming of the intervention in Germany this situation was transformed. The field army grew rapidly until in 1632 it reached about 150,000 men, most of them mercenary units raised elsewhere than in Sweden. Gustavus Adolphus had thus transformed a small native army into a hired continental army of considerable size. He had also succeeded in mastering the great financial problems of earlier years in such a way as to be able to raise that army and maintain it. Sweden herself had no longer to pay for it: the main burden now fell on the conquered and occcupied areas in Germany. It was only comparatively small sums which came from tolls and subsidies: the main share was derived from 'contributions' and similar sources of revenue. War sustained war; and this – with fluctuations produced by victory or defeat – remained the normal pattern until the peace of 1648, and the basis upon which the Swedish empire rested. The means for making war were taken from the areas in which war was to be fought; and those means provided the wherewithal to maintain the large armies which were needed to support Sweden's political pretensions and her status as a great power.

The coming of peace, and the demobilisation of the armies, brought a new situation. The areas from which contributions could be extracted became smaller, and those that remained could no longer be utilised in the same way as the occupied areas which in former years had been stripped bare in the name of *jus belli*. The result was a sharp drop in available revenue. It proved, moreover, that the garrisons scattered through the empire were not adequate to form the nucleus of an army which could be used in a crisis as an *ultima ratio*, or at least as a threat, against refractory opponents. The problem of the relationship between available means, requisite means, and political objectives, provided many of the difficulties – and many of the instructive lessons – of the Age of Greatness. Some of them will be discussed in what follows.

One of the guiding principles of Swedish statesmen after 1648 was that each of the provinces of the empire should be financially self-sufficient, and if possible should yield a surplus which could be applied to expenses elsewhere. This was an ideal, however, to which reality obstinately declined to conform: between 1660 and 1675, for example, the Swedish empire was more or less at peace; but despite that fact the finances of the states were overstrained, and stringent economy was necessary. In the provinces, the financial situation varied according to circumstances. After the devastations of the wars of the 1650s, some of them were faced with the need for large-scale reconstruction. But at the same time considerable sums were needed for their garrisons; and in general their budgets were dominated by military expenditures. If their accounts were to balance, cuts had to be made somewhere; but even so there were cases – particularly that of Ingria – where the mother-country had to come to the rescue with financial contributions. Revenue could cover expenditure only on the supposition that peace was preserved: any major military enterprise would infallibly upset the balance.

Charles XI's reforms, and the long period of peace between 1680 and 1700, permitted the finances to settle down into a more regular pattern; and in that pattern the provinces played an important part. In 1699 the total ordinary revenues of the state amounted to 6,576,724 silver *daler*, divided as follows:[1]

TABLE I: REVENUE IN 1699

	Silver daler	%	
Sweden	3,597,847	54·7	} 63·4
Finland	570,617	8·7	
Livonia	930,094	14·2	} 21·1
Estonia and Osel	263,746	4·0	
Ingria	191,000	2·9	
Pomerania	427,970	6·5	} 15·5
Bremen and Verden	579,875	8·8	
Wismar	15,575	0·2	
	6,576,724	100·0	

Thus the greater part of the revenue came from Sweden–Finland; the Baltic provinces and Ingria provided 21·1 per cent, and the German lands 15·5 per cent. It is clear, nevertheless, that the provinces ran at a profit. This is particularly noticeable in Estonia and Livonia. In 1699 Estonia yielded 397,139 silver *daler* in revenue, while the expenses were 63,742; in 1700 the budget for Livonia was put at 947,693 silver *daler* on the income side, and 543,095 for disbursements, so that the surplus available 'for the further disposal of His Most Gracious Majesty' amounted to 404,598 silver *daler*. In 1700 Osel also showed a surplus of 28,541 silver daler.[2] And the same was true of all the other provinces, though the largest sums came from the Baltic lands: in 1704, after they had been overrun by the Russians, a member of the council, Fabian Wrede, could state that it was they which had provided the greater part of the treasury's surplus. Our statistics underline this fact: a good 10 per cent of the budget consisted of the surplus from the Baltic lands.

It can be considered as established, then, that any surplus in the Swedish treasury came mainly from the provinces. It is also the fact that the economic position of the Swedish empire was far from brilliant, and could not in itself provide a solid basis for a career as a great power. Undoubtedly this was connected with the fact that its resources in population were too small. Swedish statesmen were always struggling with an economic problem, and only a period of peace could produce a budget with a favourable balance. And when the Great Northern War broke out in 1700 the whole set of circumstances within which the country operated was in fact totally altered. The sources of revenue changed in character – a fact which was underlined when some of the former provinces were lost; so that either the basis for military control and military effort had to be recast in another mould, or the whole position as a great power had to be abandoned. And this brings us to another facet of the question: the purely military problem.

II

In 1632, as we have seen, the field army of Gustavus Adolphus had a strength of about 150,000 men. At the close of the Thirty Years War it amounted to about 40,000 in the field and something like 30,000 in garrisons dispersed throughout Germany; to which may be added the garrisons at home and in Finland, and in the Baltic provinces. Thereafter the numbers tended to fall; but a new expansion began during Charles X's wars from 1655 to 1660. After his death in the latter year, and the peace settlements that followed it, there came another reduction. During the summer of 1660 there were discussions in the council of state as to how necessary it was to keep up a strong army. There was general agreement that the very existence of the Swedish empire depended in the last resort on its military strength: as one member put it, 'Sweden's greatness hangs upon her sword'.[3] And since she could not from her own limited resources of population produce the forces that were required, there was no alternative but to rely on hired troops. But it soon became apparent that the cost of such hired troops would be too great to bear; so that in 1661 the council was forced to get rid of troops of which they really stood in need. Only the national regiments, each based on its province, together with some few mercenary units, now remained: the army had been put on a peace footing.

The weakness of this peace establishment, however, was revealed on a number of occasions, which demonstrated that the army was not capable of coping with an emergency without a large intake of new recruits. This was true, for example, during the crisis with Bremen in 1668, and above all during the war with Denmark between 1675 and 1680. It therefore became one of Charles XI's main tasks to create an army which should be equal to the demands upon it; and this was the more necessary in view not only of recent experiences, but also of the military situation in other countries where standing armies had now been established. The chief of these was France. In 1667 Louis XIV had at his disposal more than 72,000 men; in 1672, 120,000; in 1678, 279,000. The standing army of Denmark–Norway had by the end of the century reached a figure of 25,000 men, mostly mercenaries. The corresponding figure for Brandenburg in 1700 was 30,000; for Russia, 36,000. From the point of view of the war office these standing armies implied the need for a higher degree of military preparedness all round, and for increased speed in arming, mobilising and taking the field, whenever war should break out.

Charles XI therefore confronted a situation which made itself felt over the whole range of policy: the country's position as a great power depended in the last resort upon his finding a solution to these problems. And, as before, the difficulty was to fit the means that were available to the means that were required in such a way as to produce an acceptable answer. How were the necessary economic resources to be created? The way for which he and his advisers opted was a solution which was natural, and (in peacetime) ingenious. The resolutions of the Diets of 1680 and 1682 had opened the way to a *reduktion* of lands earlier alienated by the crown; and these lands, now once more under the crown's control, would provide (among other things) for an expansion of the army. Here the king was building upon the earlier type of standing army which had existed from the time of Gustavus Vasa to that of Gustavus Adolphus. The result was a logically developed allotment system (the so-called *indelningsverk*) in which all items of expenditure had definite and permanent sources of revenue assigned to them. The *reduktion* meant that the state now had the means to support its armed forces:

crown- and tax-farms were assigned in the various provinces, each one to the support of its own cavalrymen; officers – for infantry no less than for cavalry – were provided with special houses to live in. Each province concluded with the king a contract whereby, in return for exemption from conscription, it promised instead to provide a fixed number of men. Men of military age were grouped into 'files'; and each 'file' undertook to furnish one man, who was then provided with a cottage and a small plot of ground for his maintenance. The result was a native army, strongly bound to the soil. In peacetime the man in the ranks worked as a labourer for the peasant on whose farm he lived; in wartime he became a soldier. And every so often his agricultural labours were interrupted by a call to join his unit for training and manoeuvres. (For the *indelningsverk*, see below, pp. 269–71). Thus Sweden acquired a standing army of respectable proportions: at the beginning of 1700 the standing force of cavalry numbered 11,459 troopers; the infantry, 25,211 men; a total force of 36,000, maintained by the new method. In addition, there were about 25,00 hired soldiers in the Guard, the artillery, and the garrisons in the fortresses, together with a fleet of 38 ships of the line with over 15,000 men: in all, about 77,000.

Thus, within the limits of what the country's resources made practicable, Charles XI solved the military problem. And in peacetime his solution worked. In wartime, however, it was found to creak at the joints. Its weakness was the indissoluble tie between the source of revenue and the item of expenditure; and in wartime it proved impossible to maintain it. Moreover the system made inadequate provision for filling gaps in the ranks. It is also clear that Charles XII fell back on Gustavus Adolphus's maxim that war must sustain war: it is scarcely possible to interpret otherwise the comprehensive system of contributions which was developed during his campaigns in Poland and Russia; though this is a subject which is still insufficiently explored. Nevertheless Charles XI's reforms had provided not only a standing army, but also the facilities for equipping it and transporting it across the seas to the theatre of operations, which had always been a difficulty in the past. For if war was indeed to sustain war, the country must not only possess forces ready to move to foreign soil; it must also be capable of transporting them thither, and it must be able to ensure that they would have a bridgehead from which the army could launch itself towards its objectives. And this brings us to the part played by the provinces in Sweden's imperial strategy.

III

For centuries it had been Sweden's lot to face enemies on two fronts: Russia in the east; Denmark in the south and west. Her emergence as a great power made no change in this situation; but it involved her, through her German possessions, in a third front on the continent. In the worst event, Swedish statesmen had now to reckon with the possibility of war on all three fronts simultaneously; and this actually happened under Charles X. Frontier defence was now divided into five distinct strategic areas: the south-eastern frontier of Finland, the Estonian–Livonian theatre, the German possessions, the western frontier of Sweden proper, and the southern coastlands. It was also essential to command the seas which separated the motherland from its possessions on the other side of the Baltic, whether in Germany or in the Livonian region. To these general considerations all Swedish strategy must pay attention.

The lessons to be drawn from this situation appear with particular clarity in the time of Charles XI. His planning was based on the assumption that the core of the army, its striking force, would be the units maintained by the new system. The mercenary regiments were to be used to provide garrisons and to protect the frontier areas: behind the cover they afforded the mobilisation and concentration of the native army could proceed undisturbed. The weakness of the plan lay partly (as we have seen) in the lack of any satisfactory provision for reserves; but also in the amount of time it took for the army to concentrate, which was a result of its provincial basis and of the great size of the country. And in fact quite early in Charles XII's war special measures had to be taken to provide reserves, either by increasing the demand for men at home, or by further recruitment of mercenaries. What happened can perhaps best be shown by some statistics. As we have seen, the army provided by the new system in 1699 numbered 36,660 men, while the mercenary forces amounted to about 25,000; by the end of 1700 the corresponding figures were 56,837 and 32,052, which represents an increase of 54 per cent for the native army and 29 per cent for the others. Thus the total peace establishment had been augmented by 43 per cent.

The wide-spreading network of fortified positions on the frontiers might at first sight seem to indicate a commitment to a defensive strategy, and an intention to fight upon the interior lines: the troops stationed in the overseas provinces would fight delaying actions around the fortresses until the main armies should have time to arrive. But a defensive interpretation of this sort takes no account of another factor to which reference has been made already, namely the financial necessity of securing supplies in wartime from foreign territory. The need to be able to establish bridgeheads, and to expand them quickly, had been convincingly demonstrated at the time of Sweden's entry into the Thirty Years War in 1630. Bridgeheads were indeed the obvious prerequisite for a successful campaign. In order to be able to seize them, the country needed adequate military forces, and also a sufficiency of suitable transports; and we have seen what measures were taken to ensure this. The bridgehead concept, however, envisaged not defensive but *offensive* warfare; and in its application to the overseas provinces it implied that they were regarded as suitable bases for further military activity, if that should prove necessary. In peacetime their business was to produce sufficient revenue to maintain the necessary garrisons. No doubt it would have been highly desirable for them to support large standing armies too; but this, as we have seen, was not possible, for the cost was too great. Whenever the situation became acute, therefore, and the presence of a standing army in the provinces became necessary, it was essential to move it swiftly into some other area large enough to support it.

The more we look at the course of events during Sweden's Age of Greatness, the more clear it becomes that the experiences of Gustavus Adolphus's time exerted a profound influence on her statesmen's strategic thinking. That experience had convincingly shown that success could be obtained only by a swift expansion of bases and the occupation of large areas of country which could be made to provide the necessary subsistence to the troops and the necessary finance for the campaign.[4] The pattern is repeated throughout the whole course of the Thirty Years War: great tracts of Germany were overrun; and the war to a large extent paid for itself. And when the next cycle of wars came along, under Charles X, the same problem elicited the same answer. At the council meetings in December 1654, the king and his advisers resolved that their objective should be the occupation of the coastlands from Prussia to Pomerania.[5] At the same time, the forces in Livonia were mobilised and bases in Swedish hands were made ready for action. But it was to Prussia that the main army was transported; and it was Prussia which came to serve as the bridgehead and starting-point for operations against Poland. It was the same line of thought as in the time of Gustavus Adolphus: the essential was still a swift offensive and the early occupation of important supply areas; and it was those areas still which were to pay for the war.[6] Charles XII's campaigns in many respects conformed to the same pattern. From the Swedish bases in the overseas provinces, rapid offensive thrusts were directed against hostile territory; great areas of enemy country were occupied by the Swedish armies; and from them flowed the means to pay the troops.

Looked at from this angle, then, one function of the conquered provinces was to provide springboards for Swedish attacks. On the one hand was the purely military advantage of having sally-ports and facilities for defence in depth; on the other was the military-financial advantage of being able to sustain war by transferring it as soon as possible to somebody else's country. In order to provide the numbers which an adequately large army demanded, it was necessary to enlist foreign troops; and these too, like the money and the supplies, could to a large extent be obtained from occupied territory. But it is obvious also that the overseas provinces served one other strategic purpose. They acted as a shield for the mother-country. Their garrisons were Sweden's first line of defence; and when at last they succumbed, Sweden herself would taste the experience of foreign attack: this actually happened after Charles XII's death in 1718, when Russian forces harried the Swedish coasts. The newly-won provinces in the south – Skåne, Blekinge, Halland, Bohuslän – fulfilled this function too: after their acquisition the Danish armies could no longer simply walk across the frontier; they had to be shipped across the Sound with all the difficulties attendant upon that operation.

Thus the overseas provinces came to provide Sweden with a flexible wall of defence. During the Great Northern War after 1700 her armies could move freely within the area which they covered: not until 1710 did the Baltic provinces fall entirely under Russian control; not until 1716 did Sweden lose her last foothold in Germany.

IV

If we are to grasp the problems which confronted Sweden as a great power, and understand how those problems bore upon her relations with the overseas provinces, we must take a survey of her foreign policy. And of necessity it must be rather a lengthy survey, in view of the long period under review and the many variations in the pattern of European international relations.

At the moment of the accession of Gustavus Adolphus in 1611, Swedish foreign policy was dominated by three problems: the problem of Denmark, the problem of Poland, and the problem of Russia. The

country was at war with all three of them. In the last resort, the struggle
with Denmark was to decide which was to be the leading power in the
north. From the Swedish point of view Danish policy appeared acutely
dangerous, since it seemed to threaten Sweden's encirclement: in the
south and west the Danes controlled the coastal provinces which Sweden
was later to incorporate; the only opening westward to the sea was a
narrow strip of land around the site of the modern Göteborg (Gothen-
burg); and at the beginning of 1612 even this fell into Denmark's hands.
When peace came in 1613, it had to be bought back at heavy sacrifice.
And lastly, the ring of Danish possessions was completed by Denmark's
ownership of the islands of Gotland and Osel.

The war with Poland was bound up with the dynastic struggle between the Swedish and Polish royal houses, for Sigismund had been
driven from the Swedish throne at the turn of the century, and since then
had been waging – mostly in Livonia – a war of varying fortunes,
punctuated by occasional truces which brought no permanent solution.
Among the terms of peace which the Poles sought to extort was the
cession of the Swedish portions of Estonia.

The war with Russia had its roots in ancient controversies and long-
standing Swedish ambitions. Among them was a strong interest in the
possibility of dominating the trade routes between Russia and western
Europe. This was no new idea: during the sixteenth century it had
provided one of the main motives for Swedish attempts to establish
control of the Baltic provinces and the Scandinavian Arctic, and to put
a stop to the direct trade between England and Russia by way of Archangel. Then, at the beginning of the seventeenth century, Russia was
convulsed by the Time of Troubles, and a new opportunity for intervention presented itself. The Russian crown was offered to Gustavus
Adolphus's brother, Charles Philip, after he had declined it for himself.
The restoration of order after 1613 did indeed knock the bottom out of
these plans; but when peace was made at Stolbova in 1617 Sweden
succeeded in gaining, by the cession of Ingria and the fief of Kexholm,
large territories round the innermost end of the Gulf of Finland, so that
henceforward there was a continuous land route from Stockholm to
Reval. This meant that Sweden now dominated some of the end-ports
for the Russian trade. Logically her next objective must be Riga; and
in 1621 that city duly passed into Swedish hands. Its capture represented
one more step on the road towards control of the Russian trade, since
in that trade Riga played a major part. Thus, in the Baltic provinces,
commercial ambitions and dynastic struggles went hand in hand: on

the one hand the coastal towns were desired for economic reasons, on the other they could provide bases for the war against Poland. These successes, however, served only to whet the Swedish appetite; and that appetite was shortly to be presented with fresh opportunities by the course of events in Europe.

In the latter half of the 1620s Sweden's security began to be threatened by developments in Germany. In Vienna, Swedish expansion was viewed with disquiet; already Imperialist troops had clashed with Swedish forces in Prussia, which since 1626 had become the main centre of operations in the war against Poland. Sweden's successes in that war entailed a corresponding revision of her objectives: by 1630 they had come to include a *dominium maris Baltici*. Intervention in the Thirty Years War now appeared as a logical corollary to what had gone before. Thereafter, for the remainder of the war, Sweden's war aims varied with circumstances – there was even a moment when Gustavus Adolphus seems to have thought of the Imperial crown – but in the end they defined themselves as a cash indemnity and territorial acquisitions within the Empire.

But the peace of Westphalia in 1648 did not mean that the objectives had been attained. The Courland ports were out of reach of Swedish control, and the Prussian ports had had to be abandoned in 1635. The Vistula was still in Polish hands. A *dominium maris Baltici*, which alone would give the Swedish empire the security it sought, was not possible unless the command of the sea was used to turn the Baltic into a *mare clausum*, dominated by the Swedish navy and barred to the fleets of the western European powers. For after all, the creation of the Swedish empire had been made possible only by the weakness and divisions of Sweden's neighbours; and of those neighbours Russia in particular had great resources to fall back upon. The day would come when she would be in a position to bring those resources to bear; and then the situation within the Baltic would be transformed.

Charles X sought to push further along the line his predecessors had followed. For him too commercial considerations were of essential importance; for him too the old problems of Denmark, Poland and Russia demanded a solution. But, like Gustavus Adolphus, he had also to take into account new factors; among others, the German princes, among whom Brandenburg in particular was emerging as a power to be reckoned with. There was moreover a number of powers – the United Provinces, France, England – concerned to neutralise and control a Sweden which had become too powerful. And it was these new factors which provided the basis for the complex foreign policy which the acquisition of the new provinces, and the attainment of great-power status, now brought in its train.

The collaboration between Sweden and France during the Thirty Years War had been based upon a common hostility to the Austrian Habsburgs. After the peace of 1648, however, their interests tended steadily to diverge. France's German policy continued to be character-ised by opposition to the Emperor, and it aimed at engineering a league of princes to keep him in check. Sweden did not share these objectives. Her newly acquired German provinces were not in the first instance threatened by the Emperor, but rather by other German princes – such as the elector of Brandenburg – who coveted the territories which had fallen to Sweden at Westphalia. It was therefore natural for Sweden to be on good terms with Vienna.

In the same way, the acquisition of the new provinces affected rela-tions with the Dutch. By her territorial gains from 1617 to 1648 Sweden had become one of the most important riparian states in the Baltic. Around 1650, about 40 per cent of all ships passing westward through the Sound were carrying freight loaded in harbours belonging to Sweden, as against 35 per cent from Polish ports; and most of these ships were Dutch. Sweden sought to counteract this Dutch predomin-ance, and by doing so came into conflict with the United Provinces. In this situation it was natural to seek the friendship of Holland's rival, England; while the Dutch on their side turned to Denmark. And this produced various diplomatic alignments which affected Swedish foreign policy.

For Charles X, the situation at his accession in 1654 presented a number of threats to Sweden's Baltic empire. The successes of Russia in her war against Poland opened up the possibility of Russian expan-sion to the Baltic coastlands, which would imply not only an imminent threat to Sweden's actual position, but a bar to the prosecution of any plans for the establishment of a *dominium maris Baltici*. A Swedish attack on Prussia must now be on the cards. Simultaneously, it became a matter for urgent consideration as to what to do about Denmark; for though Denmark alone presented no difficulty, Denmark in alliance with another power – the Dutch, for example – was another matter. The war that followed reflected this problem in all its complexity.

The conflict began in 1655 with a Swedish attack upon Poland. Bran-denburg collaborated with Sweden for as long as the Swedish arms were victorious, but thereafter manoeuvred to obtain the maximum advantage at Sweden's expense; Austria came to Poland's aid; and in 1656 the Russians launched an attack against Sweden. By the summer of 1656 a Dutch fleet had appeared in the Baltic, the United Provinces having concluded an alliance with Denmark to assist Danzig, which was threatened by the Swedish armies. In the face of an allied declaration demanding freedom of trade to the Baltic ports, Sweden was forced to relax her demands and lower her customs dues: the trading interests of the western powers could not acquiesce in a situation in which a single power dominated the end-ports of eastern Europe. Denmark did her best to exploit the opportunity, but without much success. It was rather Charles X who seized his chance, and used it – despite his lack of a powerful fleet[7] – to acquire Skåne and Blekinge. Henceforward he was in control of one shore of the Sound; and he sought to compel Denmark to agree to close the Sound to foreign ships of war – that is, to turn the Baltic into a *mare clausum*. But neither France nor England, who by this time had appeared as mediators, could swallow a proposal of this sort. In the meantime, Denmark had been seriously weakened; and it was with a view to taking advantage of her weakness that Charles launched his second attack upon her in the summer of 1658. (For the constitutional implications of this, see below, pp. 191–4). But once again it proved that the weak Swedish navy was not able to prevent the intervention of a Dutch fleet; and after the failure of the attemped storm of Copenhagen in February 1659 the issue of the war against Denmark became increasingly dependent upon the policy of the great powers. Attempts to secure the support of England were unsuccessful; in the end France intervened, in her own interest, to put an end to the conflict in the north. For France needed Sweden's support against the Emperor; and the Emperor, with Brandenburg and Poland, had sought to take advantage of Sweden's difficulties, and had backed Denmark.

The negotiations and wars of Charles X's reign provide an excellent illustration of what was said earlier as to the dilemma of Swedish foreign policy. To the eastward, the gaps in the system still remained after Charles X's death in 1660: the bastion against Russia had not been strengthened; and Poland and west Prussia remained a latent threat, since it would be easy for a foreign power – Russia, or the Emperor, or Brandenburg – to establish a strong influence there. Denmark felt and feared Sweden's grip on her throat – a grip manifested in the Swedish possession of her former provinces beyond the Sound – while the Swedish alliance with the duke of Holstein-Gottorp threatened her with a stab in the back. But the war had also demonstrated how dependent Swedish policy now was on the state of France's relations with the Emperor; and France's strong interest in Germany must necessarily have its effect on Swedish policy, since Sweden was one of the guarantors of the peace of Westphalia.

Sweden's career as a great power, as we have seen, was characterised by a lack of correspondence betweens ends and means which set its mark upon the foreign policy she pursued. In the period which followed Charles X's death this was more clearly the case than ever before. Foreign policy now became decidedly pacific: alliances were sought as a means of protecting exposed positions, but they were not to lead to military commitments. Sweden attempted, therefore, to pursue a policy of maintaining the balance between the Habsburg and Bourbon blocs. But in the long run this was not a policy calculated to inspire respect. Contemporaries very soon discerned the military weakness and the lack of economic resources which made the country dependent upon subsidies from foreign powers. For this state of affairs the only remedy lay in the expansion of the fleet and the maintenance of a standing army on German soil; and this became the more necessary when at the beginning of the 1670s the regrouping of the powers produced a changed situation in Europe. In this situation Sweden in 1672 allied herself with France in return for a French undertaking to pay her army in Germany, and a French guarantee against Danish attack: economically and diplomatically Sweden was now dependent upon French aid. It is true that the association with France was not designed to lead to war: its object rather was the exploitation of the alliance by peaceful means. (See the discussion of Magnus De la Gardie's foreign policy, below, pp. 213–15). But France's reverses in Germany brought a total change in the position. It was now France who demanded the aid of Sweden. Yet it was typical that the Swedish attack on Brandenburg was made necessary by the difficulty of maintaining the army. Within a short time Sweden was also involved in hostilities with the Emperor and the Dutch; and Denmark's attack upon Holstein-Gottorp – the Swedish ally in her rear – was tantamount to a declaration of war. This renewal of conflict engaged Sweden in war from 1675 to 1679. She suffered reverses in Germany which left the field open to speculators in Swedish territorial booty; the German provinces had to be abandoned to their fate; the Dutch and Danish fleets knocked out the Swedish navy and for the rest of the war were the masters of the Baltic.

Thus the military situation had reached a point at which Sweden had lost her German lands, and could only with the greatest difficulty defend those of her southern provinces which had formerly been Danish possessions. The prospect of recovering her German empire now depended upon the resources of diplomacy. Louis XIV was by this time once more in a stronger position, and at the congress of Nijmegen (1678) was able to play off his enemies against each other. The Emperor and the Dutch had no particular interest in weakening Sweden territorially; Denmark, Brandenburg and Lüneburg, for their part, were very ready to partition Sweden's German possessions, but they could not agree on how to do it; so that Sweden, thanks to French mediation, obtained a series of separate peaces which restored the *status quo*, the only exception being the cession to Brandenburg (by the peace of St Germain, 1679) of a part of eastern Pomerania.

The war had shown quite clearly that militarily Sweden was now too weak. If she were to preserve her position as a great power, she must now depend either on the help of France or of some other major state. The peace had been made almost over her head; and it was obviously only the fact that it suited France's game to have a relatively strong Sweden that had permitted her to preserve her former international status. Yet there was one other way to amend the situation in which she now found herself; and for a moment in 1680 it seemed that it might be taken. This was to go hand in hand with Denmark. Together, it seemed, they would have greater weight in international affairs, and a more solid basis to build on, than if each continued on its way alone. But this was an idea which proved to have no future.

In the course of the 1680s the connection with France came to an end, and Sweden turned instead to the Dutch. From the point of view of commercial policy this implied more or less a capitulation; but it gave security against Denmark, among other things, and it provided aid for the duke of Holstein-Gottorp, Sweden's bastion in Denmark's rear. After 1689, the union of England and Holland in the person of William III brought Sweden into alliance with the Maritime Powers, and this meant naval protection for Sweden's communications with her provinces on the other side of the Baltic. By this time, however, Sweden had an increasingly powerful fleet of her own, and in the 1690s this enabled her on occasion to strike out an independent line. One instance of this was her collaboration with Denmark in defence of freedom of trade; and this despite the fact that Denmark (like Brandenburg) had drawn closer to France since Sweden had moved towards Holland in 1681. By 1690, however, the situation had changed again: Brandenburg had returned to her anti-French position, and Denmark's attempts at expansion in Germany had begun to alarm the German princes. In 1689 the duke of Holstein-Gottorp (whom the Danes had evicted some years before) was restored to his dominions, and by the treaty of Altona was guaranteed in his possession of them by England, Holland and Lüneburg. The Swedish encirclement of Denmark was an accomplished fact.

With the turn of the century came a new phase. And once again the Swedish provinces played an important part in bringing it about; for it was they who acted as a bait to Poland, Russia and Denmark. The importance of the Baltic for the nations of western Europe had greatly increased during the latter half of the century; and Peter the Great was determined to break through to the sea, and to unite the harbours which handled the export trade with their hinterland. Poland had not forgotten her ambitions in Livonia, and her former possession of that province. Denmark hoped to get possession of Holstein-Gottorp, and so eliminate the threat to her rear. To the west, Sweden now had a dependable alliance with Lüneburg and the Maritime Powers, the guarantors of Holstein-Gottorp; but to the east the situation was much less satisfactory: in this quarter her isolation was total.

The Danes had no success with their attack on Gottorp, and the peace that followed took care of Sweden's interests. But on the other hand the annihilation of Denmark was no more an interest of the Maritime Powers in 1700 than it had been forty years earlier. Charles XII's crossing of the Dvina, and the subsequent course of his campaign in Poland, made it clear that he hoped to extend the Swedish dominions to include Courland. The peace which he imposed on Poland in 1705 was entirely in line with the traditional Swedish plans for a *dominium maris Baltici*; and its commercial implications were unmistakable. His foreign policy had, indeed, strong expansionist features; of which a hint had appeared already at the time of the settlement with Denmark in 1700.

Swedish operations against Poland, and later against Saxony, had left a clear field for the Russian armies, which now pressed forward to the Baltic. The disaster at Pultava in 1709 gave Tsar Peter a free hand both in Poland and in the Swedish Baltic provinces. The Swedish empire in the east thereupon collapsed. And at the same time the Swedish system of alliances in the west had been undermined. Denmark and Augustus the Strong had drawn closer to the Maritime Powers, which were no longer as concerned to prop up Sweden as they had been in earlier years; for they had come to fear the commercial implications of Sweden's maritime predominance. Peter's advance to the Baltic, moreover, had created a new situation in which it was possible to purchase the important commodities which Russia exported without having to deal with Swedish middlemen. And Russia, Poland and Denmark were careful to avoid provoking the Maritime Powers by attacks on Sweden's German possessions: instead Denmark proceeded to a direct onslaught against Sweden, and Russia continued her offensive against Livonia and Finland. Charles XII's attempts to checkmate Russia with the help of the Turks proved a failure; while his effort to mount a Swedish invasion of Poland by an army based on Pomerania not only came to nothing, but resulted in the German provinces' being dragged into the war. By 1716 everything was lost; and Prussia, Hanover and Denmark divided the spoils.

The Maritime Powers did not find that a Russian predominance appealed to them any more than a Swedish. England was therefore anxious to mediate in the Northern War; but Charles XII would have none of it. But the coalition of Sweden's adversaries was not solidly united; and in any case the peace of Utrecht produced a shift in the relations of the great powers. The Maritime Powers and France drew together; and with that the old alternative in Swedish foreign policy disappeared. The new choice lay between Russia and Prussia on the one hand, and England and Hanover on the other; and for the rest of Charles XII's reign Swedish foreign policy sought to exploit their conflicting interests in the hope of playing off Russia against England–Hanover and Denmark; the idea being that territorial cessions to the one party might purchase support for the extraction of corresponding cessions from the other.

The death of Charles XII in 1718, and the constitutional changes which followed it, altered the whole basis of Swedish foreign policy. Its pattern would now be determined by the issue of the struggle between that party which favoured Charles Frederick of Holstein as successor to the throne, and that which favoured Frederick of Hesse. The Holsteiners were inclined towards Russia; the Hessians leaned to England and Hanover. And it was this latter policy which produced the peace treaties with Hanover (1718) and Prussia (1720), whereby Sweden abandoned Bremen–Verden in return for a sum of one million *riksdaler*, and ceded much of Pomerania in return for two million more. Denmark received no territorial compensation; but she did rid herself of the threat from ducal Holstein. Thus Sweden had sacrificed most of her positions in Germany, and relinquished her grip on Denmark, in the hope of saving the Baltic provinces when it came to making a settlement with Russia.

The plan was that peace with the Tsar should be concluded under English mediation; but when it came to the point, England was unable to carry out her undertakings. Sweden was left – without an ally, and without an army fit for battle – to negotiate directly with the Russians. By the peace of Nystad, in November 1721, she was compelled to cede Livonia, Estonia, Ingria, portions of Karelia and the fief of Viborg, together with the islands of Osel and Dagö. The Swedish empire was at an end.

Swedish foreign policy during the Age of Greatness had had to contend with formidable difficulties. A fundamental one was the discrepancy between ends and means. The overriding objects – a vigorous navigation policy, and *dominium maris Baltici* – were determined by the realities of her situation, and in that situation the conquered provinces played a part of crucial importance. But the strength of the country was never sufficient for more than a piecemeal attainment of these objectives. The brutal truth was that there were not, as a rule, enough men and money for the kind of army which could provide Sweden's aspirations with a solid basis of power. The aim of foreign policy came therefore to be to compensate for this disadvantage by diplomatic manoeuvre in such a way as to make it possible for the country to maintain its position with the help of alliances and the economic support which they might furnish. The time came when this game could be played no longer, and when rivals who had earlier been enfeebled – notably Russia – re-entered the struggle for the overseas provinces and the mastery of the Baltic, and proved too strong to be resisted. And when that day dawned, the conditions which made a Swedish empire possible disappeared for ever.

Yet though the weakness in the Swedish empire was inherent, it was possible to overcome it. Gustavus Adolphus managed to do it by his expansive policies and offensive tactics, and by so doing he laid the empire's foundations. The burden of his policies was swiftly transferred to other lands, since it could not be borne by his own; and this transference produced the resources in men and money without which they would never have been conceivable: Sweden's inadequate potential ceased to matter. The same pattern unfolded itself under Charles X and Charles XII: they too sought to find a solid bottom for their policy beyond the frontiers of the realm. Charles XI, on the other hand, tried to create it at home. And for that the necessary precondition was peace: without it, an offensive was the only resource. A defensive strategy, based on the home country and the provinces, was simply not practicable, since in the long run they lacked the resources to produce the dynamic thrust that was required. Looked at in this way, Sweden's career as a great power was built on war and the possibilities which war created. The question is how far this was equally clear to men like Charles X and Charles XII. Were they dragged into war by the chain of circumstance, or in response to an instinctive appreciation of the basic structure of Sweden's greatness? In the present state of historical scholarship this is a question impossible to answer. But at least it is a question which must be posed.

V

The development of the conquered provinces, and the problems they presented, did not conform to a single pattern. And this for various reasons, one of which was the differences between them in their constitutional position.

The status of the German provinces was based upon the peace of 1648. By article 10 of the treaty of Osnabrück, the Emperor Ferdinand III handed over Pomerania, Wismar and the secularised bishoprics of Bremen and Verden to the Swedish crown as hereditary Imperial fiefs. They formed a part of the Swedish empire in virtue of a personal union; and the Swedish Estates had no power to meddle with them. Sweden was also granted, as far as they were concerned, the *privilegium de non appellando*, and had in consequence to erect a Supreme Court in Germany. In virtue of its Imperial fiefs, the Swedish crown had a seat and a vote in three Circles of the Empire: the Upper Saxon Circle (for Pomerania), the Lower Saxon Circle (for Bremen and Wismar) and the Westphalian Circle (for Verden). In regard to the *town* of Bremen the text of the treaty was ambiguous, since it laid it down that the 'existing' state of affairs was to be respected; which among other things meant that the town could claim to be a Free Imperial City. Sweden was consequently unable to obtain a clear acceptance of her interpretation of the treaty as giving her full sovereignty over the town: it was a situation which was to lead to wrangles – and indeed to hostilities – in 1653–4 and 1666.

In the Baltic provinces the situation was more complex. Estonia had entered the Swedish empire by treaty; Livonia had been conquered by arms. The latter was true also for Ingria and the province of Kexholm. The dubious constitutional position was to give rise to conflicting attitudes, or at least to an attempt to maintain that it was possible to take more than one view of the question.

The distinction between the constitutional position of the German and the Baltic provinces was essential. In the former the Swedish monarch was a German prince, and was free to deal with his lands in that capacity; and, as we shall see, this was to entail some tension between him and the German Estates. In the Baltic provinces the basic assumption was that they were crown property, even though there might thereafter be room for debate about their constitutional rights within that framework. This difference was reflected in Swedish policy and Swedish thinking in regard to the overseas territories.

Among the higher officials of the Swedish central government there were during the Age of Greatness two main lines of thought about the provinces. According to one of them, they ought to be incorporated into, and made uniform with, the remainder of the Swedish realm: their inhabitants should be absorbed into the Swedish system of Estates, and be represented in the Swedish Diet; they were to be subject to Swedish law and have the benefit of Swedish privileges. In 1630 Johan Skytte, a member of the council of state, and at that time governor of Livonia, Ingria and Karelia, defined the objective as '*unus rex, una lex et grex unus*'. The other main line of thought started from the same premiss as to the implications of incorporation, but deduced from it that incorporation was undesirable. The leading representative of this school, and chief adversary to Skytte, was the chancellor, Axel Oxenstierna. Skytte and Oxenstierna accepted the same basic assumption: incorporation implied uniformity. But when it came to deciding what line to take with the provinces, they came to totally different conclusions. What lay behind these diametrically opposite viewpoints?

Skytte's attitude looked back to the policy of previous monarchs, and in particular to that of Charles IX. As Charles had fought out his battle against Sigismund, the high aristocracy and Roman Catholicism, he had sought to establish his authority on the broad basis of the support of the Estates. He had pursued the same line in the Baltic provinces. In the Baltic provinces, uniformity with Sweden would entail a serious loss of power by the nobility and a curtailment of their privileges; but it would bring advantages to the clergy and peasants, as well as strengthening the power of the state. Uniformity, therefore, was Charles IX's policy, though he never in fact succeeded in carrying it through. In the 1620s it became an issue once again in Ingria and the Baltic provinces; and when Skytte became governor there in 1629 he adopted it as his programme. One of the characteristics of that programme was its strong attachment to the authority and interests of the crown.

Behind Axel Oxenstierna's attitude lay the interests of high aristocracy. (For the definition of this dictinctive Swedish category, see below, pp. 119–22). A policy of uniformity entailed measures directed above all against the landed nobility; and the high aristocracy of Sweden, as represented by such families as the Oxenstiernas and De la Gardies, had managed to possess themselves of large estates in the conquered provinces: around 1650 no less than two-fifths of the land of Livonia was in such hands. In 1640 Axel Oxenstierna reminded a deputation from the provincial council of Estonia that 'there were some Swedish gentlemen, as the marshal [Jakob De la Gardie], the chancellor himself, Herr Johann De la Gardie, etc., who have in this matter as great an interest as they, and are not minded that any of the province's privileges shall fall out of use'.[8] He was opposed also to any representation of the provinces at the Diet, or in the council. In 1643 he put this point when he said that those were not entitled to 'honores' who did not also bear 'onus'. The remark was directed against the nobility of Livonia, who were seeking incorporation into Sweden, among other reasons because they lacked binding guarantees of their privileges, since the country had been won *jure belli*. But it was not only that the chancellor objected to their obtaining posts; he also had another motive. If the Livonians were to be regarded as part of 'the Estates of the Realm for such matters as concern Livonia (since it often happens that wars must be fought there), [they] will try to thwart me'.[9] This can only mean that Oxenstierna was also opposed to an incorporation because it might mean a diminution of his authority. It was the interest of the high aristocracy of Sweden on the one hand to preserve the great privileges which the nobility of the Baltic provinces enjoyed, and on the other to keep membership of the Estate of Nobles and the Swedish council of state as a close preserve for themselves.

Thus from the point of view of the Swedish government and from the standpoint of constitutional theory, the position of the subject provinces gave rise to two conflicting principles. The one had a history going back to the 1560s. The other became dominant from the time of Sweden's intervention in the Thirty Years War. In the Form of Government of 1634, the dualism between Sweden and the provinces was laid down by law: only those noblemen who were resident in Sweden proper, or in Finland, were to have a seat and a vote in the Estate of Nobility; and only those members of the other Estates who were similarly qualified had a right to participate in meetings of the Diet, or 'other decisions of state', unless special permission to do so had been obtained. It is obvious that this application of the second of the two principles reflects the shift in domestic politics from a strong monarchy to the ascendancy of the high nobility. In the time of Charles X there was once more a tendency to uniformity; but it was not until about 1680, and the establishment of Charles XI's authority, that a real change occurred. It began with the old Danish provinces in the south. Here uniformity was enforced, in the first place upon the clergy and burghers, with the opposition coming mainly from the nobility. The coming of absolutism also brought about a change in the relationship between the central government and the Baltic provinces, in the shape of a return to the programme for the provinces which the monarchy had pursued in former years.

The above account is of course no more than a general outline of what was an involved and complex story. But if we look a little more closely at what happened in the Baltic provinces it is possible to obtain a somewhat sharper impression.

The history of Estonia in the Swedish period (1561–1710) falls into two distinctive halves, with the coming of the Form of Government of 1634 as the dividing-line between them. During the first period the administration was essentially decentralised and formless. The Swedes took over the existing local divisions of the region, replaced the former officials with Swedish successors, and gave Swedish names to their offices. In the 1620s the frontiers of the provinces were altered, partly because Ingria and Livonia now became part of the Swedish empire. Local administration was reorganised, and the result of the reorganisation appears in the Form of Government of 1634, and in a new Instruction for Provincial Governors of 1635. The consequence was a stabilisation and centralisation of the administration. At its head was a governor (from 1673, governor-general) who combined military duties with civil functions which were both administrative and judicial. Livonia too had its governor-general, with much the same sort of organisation as Estonia, though differences in local circumstances led to some variations in the distribution of offices. At first the governor-generalship consisted of Livonia and Ingria; but after 1642 it was divided into two, one half comprising Livonia and the other Ingria and the province of Kexholm. The administrative organisation remained relatively stable until 1710, when the Swedes quitted the country, and in general it was entirely in accord with the policies which set in after 1634.

This description, however, does no more than reflect the formalities of the position. What was equally important was that from about the middle of the century practically all the lands of the crown had been

assigned to members of the nobility. The result was that the crown had
no local administrative officers of its own. Its rights passed into the
nobility's hands, and it had no real occasion to meddle with local affairs
at all – a fact which was to influence what happened in connection with
the *reduktion* in the 1680s and 1690s.

Both in Estonia and in Livonia the Swedish administration found its
freedom of action curtailed by the Estates; that is, by the nobility
organised in provincial diets and provincial councils, and by the towns
through their autonomous magistracies, which in the case of Reval and
Riga inherited the traditions and privileges which they had enjoyed as
independent members of the Hansa. In Estonia, as we have seen, the
transference to Sweden had been effected *per pactum*, while in Livonia
it had been *jure belli*; and the course of events was influenced by this
difference. It is interesting, however, that the powerful nobility of
Livonia managed to contrive that many of their former rights remained
intact. From the 1640s onwards we can see them strengthening their
position, favoured among other things by the support of high-aristocratic
circles in Sweden. The Form of Government of 1634 set the seal on this
policy. In Ingria, on the other hand, events took a different course.
Almost immediately after the conquest of the territory a series of
Swedish administrative institutions was introduced into it. The Swedish
legal system with its various types of court and its decisions according
to Swedish law was transferred without further ado to the new province. The local administrative divisions became entirely Swedish. In
Estonia and Livonia nothing of this kind occurred, even though the
institution of a Supreme Court in Dorpat (modern Tartu) in 1630 could
be considered a step in that direction.

The explanation of this difference has been sought, among other
things, in the fact that Ingria, in contrast to Estonia and Livonia, did not
possess a strong nobility or an independent burgher class. But the
distinction must also be seen against the background of difference in
constitutional position which we have already mentioned. Ingria had
been taken at the sword's point, and its constitutional position had been
promptly defined at the peace of Stolbova in 1617. It is true that Livonia
was also a conquered territory, but here the final constitutional settlement was deferred until 1660, and in the meantime the situation had
developed in such a way as to favour a relatively independent position
and to preclude any incorporation in the interests of uniformity. Add to
this the existence of strong groups of nobles and burghers, who effectively ran the country and who were extremely unwilling to relax their

grip on their privileges. The course of events here presents marked parallels with what happened in the provinces conquered from Denmark: by the terms of the treaties by which they were acquired Sweden was forced to permit them to retain their old laws and privileges; though in 1683 they did voluntarily agree to permit the introduction of the Swedish judicial system.

However, a new and considerably tougher attitude towards the Baltic provinces became apparent in the 1680s and 1690s, with determined attempts to eliminate provincial peculiarities and reduce provincial practice to the Swedish norm. The judicial system, and the administration in general, were to be made uniform and to be centralised. The opposition of the Estates was crushed. The cause of the change has usually been considered to be the fact that after the peace with Denmark in 1680 Charles XI had leisure to devote himself to the running of the Baltic provinces. The attitude of the king and his advisers towards the movement for uniformity had altered; the old lukewarmness had been abandoned. Yet the question does remain why they were now so vehemently anxious to introduce uniformity. Is it to be seen simply as a return to older royal policies, in circumstances which (thanks to the establishment of absolutism) offered a better hope of success than before; or must we look for other reasons? Information scattered throughout the available literature tends to suggest that the movement towards uniformity was tied up with the *reduktion* which had been sanctioned at the Diets of 1680 and 1682, and which was also extended to the provinces. What connection was there then between the two?

In the first place, it is quite clear that uniformity in administration was going to make the *reduktion* easier to carry out. But this was not all. In the Baltic provinces the greater part of the land had before the *reduktion* been in noble hands; and among those who possessed large estates were members of the high nobility in Sweden. As a result of the *reduktion*, great masses of land passed once again to the crown, which consequently was in urgent need of civil servants of various kinds to take over and administer these lands and estates. This brought the landowning nobility into conflict with the crown, since they must now both provide it with resources and share their rights with it – for instance, in the administration of justice, where the crown now had an interest in the condition of the peasantry. The crown wanted a uniform, centralised administration; and naturally enough its agents tended to have recourse to the central rather than to the local government. The result was a situation in which local and central interests were in conflict; and it is in part against this background that we must see the violent reaction of the Livonian nobility. Their opposition was not primarily an expression of any national feeling; it is to be thought of rather as in the main a simple clash of interests, in which the crown represented strong central authority, and the nobility stood for local and decentralised interests and the integrity of their privileges.[10]

VI

So far we have mainly been considering the Swedish empire from the point of view of the central government. But it had another aspect too, which we may call the local aspect; and from this viewpoint we can command other perspectives, and discern different centres of interest. How did the Swedish empire look to observers stationed at different places within it?

We may begin our survey with the Baltic provinces, and in particular with their attitude to the policy of assimilation.

Charles XI sought by every means to limit the authority and curtail the activity of the provincial diets. The Livonians, on the contrary, strove to create a situation in which a representative body should be in permanent session, as an organ for safeguarding the interests of the nobility. And they did in fact succeed in bringing this about. In 1692 this standing committee addressed a memorial to the king on the condition of affairs in Livonia, which contained expressions stigmatised by him as constituting an incitement to revolt. The signatories were tried and adjudged guilty of high treason. Among them was Johan Reinhold Patkul, destined after his flight into exile to play a part in the international intrigues which preceded the Great Northern War.

These events were linked to the policy of assimilation which was being pursued by the Swedish government, whose attitude and motives in this matter have been touched on already. Assimilation took the form, for instance, of requiring that every candidate for office in Livonia must have studied for at least two years at the University of Dorpat, where the professors were Swedes; or of preferring Finnish or Ingrian priests rather than Germans, for appointment to Livonian livings. It was hoped also to provide a scheme of general education in the language of the people (as against the German of the upper classes); and the institution of serfdom came under attack. It was ordered that Swedish law should run in the province, and a Swedish system of appellate jurisdiction was projected.

These measures were unpopular in Livonia – or rather, the surviving source-material, which mostly reflects the attitude of the aristocracy, shows that the nobility were opposed to them. Since they were mostly of German extraction they felt themselves menaced; and they proceeded to a counter-attack. The definitive breach came in 1694; but before that date we can trace minor grievances arising from the assimilation policy. Among other things, there were complaints that sermons were delivered in Swedish rather than in German; and that Livonian nobles were passed over in favour of Swedes in appointments to government posts. Nor were the nobility anxious that the judicial system should be remodelled on Swedish lines: they wanted rather to retain the local manorial and provincial courts, and other privileges. Negotiations which took place in 1719 between representatives of the monarchy and the Livonian nobility for a revision of their privileges revealed the same attitude. The Livonians insisted that uniformity must imply that the local nobility should participate in legislation. As far as they were concerned there was no hostility to the Swedish connection as such, provided only that they were able to retain their privileges; but if those privileges were infringed they would oppose it. Thus the conflict had resolved itself into a dispute about privilege, in which groups with differing interests stood opposed to one another. But it was not a question of resistance to an imperialist oppressor. It is also a fact of some interest that there is no trace in Estonian constitutional documents of the kind of restrictions which occur in Livonia; nor was there any opposition from the Estonian nobility. It is obvious that Estonia's position, as a province acquired *per pactum*, was what determined the position here; and that the Swedes in consequence took a softer line. But this did not prevent Charles XI from getting what he wanted.

The position of the peasants under Swedish rule in the Baltic provinces has provoked some discussion. The general trends of agricultural development in this part of Europe entailed the consequence that their position became increasingly servile, and their freedom of movement grew less. Towards the end of the seventeenth century there were various attempts at reform which have received a good deal of attention; but other matters intervened, and they did not lead to any result. It is worth emphasising that peasants on the estates of Swedish noblemen were not any better off than the others. At the turn of the century the population was hard hit by famine. The king could give no help, and some of the measures taken by the government – as for instance its shipping of grain to Finland and Sweden – aroused criticism. Some modern Soviet historians have contended that the population now rose in revolt against

Swedish rule in consequence of the harsh measures of the government, and that it took an active part in the fight against Swedish 'colonialism' during the Great Northern War. But the surviving evidence is too complex to permit a generalisation of this sort: there is in fact testimony of a directly opposite tendency, to the effect that the population avoided the Russians, and tended rather to associate itself with the Swedish 'colonial' power. In the present state of our knowledge the question must be left open pending more exhaustive enquiries.

As to the burghers, it is symptomatic that we have no traces of any opposition of any significance from, e.g., Riga. The Riga burghers took no part in the opposition of the nobility, nor did they support their programme; though it must be added that their own privileges were not in question. It is characteristic too that the burghers of Reval and Riga did not yield their towns to Russia until further military resistance had become impossible; Riga, in particular, stood a long siege with no sign of a break in morale. Their attitude is bound up with another aspect of the question; namely trade and commercial policy. One element in the expansion of the Swedish empire was the driving force of commercial aspirations, the dream of being able to control the important trade routes within the Baltic and those which linked the Baltic to more distant lands. From this point of view Stettin turned out to be a failure: control of the mouth of the Oder was not followed by the routing of an important long-distance trade through Swedish territory, for Brandenburg carried off the prize with her system of canals. Nor did much trade come from the acquisition of Reval (the modern Tallinn); for since the middle of the sixteenth century Reval had traded mainly on a local basis in the produce of Livonia and Estonia, and above all in grain. Narva had a long-distance trade in Russian goods, but it was of limited dimensions and of no great importance. But at one point at least the Swedes did succeed in securing that a really important trade route should pass through Swedish territory; and that was in Riga. All the traffic down the Dvina came to Riga, and there was no possibility of diverting it before it got there. Riga was important above all for the great quantities of flax and hemp which came from its extensive hinterland, stretching deep into Russia. These commodities were vital to navigation, and their indispensability to ships of war gave them also political importance. And this was true too of timber exports, and in particular of masts.

The statistics for the trade of Riga show an unmistakable upward trend in the latter part of the seventeenth century; and the importance of the town steadily increased. Militarily, however, it was in an exposed position: the principle of making use of the river mouths here revealed its weakness. The Dvina ran through Swedish territory for only a quite small stretch of its course; then, as one ascended it, it became the frontier between Swedish territory and Courland; and further up still was outside Swedish control altogether. The link with Sweden did indeed bring the benefits of the transit traffic; but it did not provide depth and solidity. During the Northern War the trade of Riga was powerfully affected by changes in the military situation: local trade flourished, but the long-distance trade suffered severely. Swedish plans after 1700 reveal a clear intention to obtain control of Courland and Königsberg, Riga's chief rivals. Representatives of Riga were given the opportunity of putting forward their views at the peace negotiations with Poland, where precisely these important objectives of commercial policy were on the *tapis*. One of the Swedish negotiators had for many years been a Syndic in Riga's service, and through him the town had some security that its interests would not be lost sight of. And in fact the results were such as to satisfy the burghers: they obtained guarantees which gave them certain economic advantages, but which above all were aimed at providing them with a hinterland which should be both ample and secure.

Thus Swedish rule, as seen from Riga, had its advantages. The policy of expansion on the side of Russia and Poland was in the town's interest as well as in that of Sweden, since it could bring important gains in the form of security and the elimination of such rivals as Courland and Königsberg. The city fathers also had the possibility of getting their views brought before the Swedish central government; and, what was even more important, the government listened to them, since in fact on questions of importance it agreed with them.

The Russian conquest of the Baltic provinces, and the foundation of St Petersburg in 1703, brought about an important shift in commercial politics. The centre of gravity of the Russia trade was now transferred to Peter's new foundation, which became in ever-increasing measure the port for Russian exports. It was obvious that towns such as Narva and Reval were now in danger of being entirely eclipsed; and this was true not only for the trade with the west, but also for local trade within the Baltic. But Riga too was similarly threatened. Its future under Russian rule would to a great extent depend upon how far the Tsars were prepared to go in favouring the trade of St Petersburg. And in fact from 1710, when Riga passed into Russian hands, until the middle of the century, its trade was not in a flourishing condition. This may in part have been a consequence of the war, but it was probably to a still greater degree the result of a deliberate Russian policy.

The interests of the Baltic towns were therefore linked to those of Sweden in various ways: Sweden could eliminate rivals and provide protection; and after 1703 collaboration with Russia could entail risks for their own trade and prosperity. For as long, therefore, as their Swedish rulers made no attempt to curtail their privileges and their trade, but on the contrary were content to see them flourish, there was no reason for opposition to the Swedish connection as far as Riga was concerned. From the horizon of Riga the Swedish empire seemed to offer considerable advantages. But for another section of Livonian society – the nobility – the situation looked very different: to them, Swedish rule appeared as a threat to their position.

The German provinces, as we have seen, were Imperial fiefs; their Swedish rulers were princes of the Empire; their link with Sweden was purely personal. This fact set its mark on their development, and also upon their attitude to the connection with Sweden and their position within the Swedish empire.

While the Thirty Years War lasted, it was natural that the Swedes should introduce into the provinces their own methods and personnel; and the provinces acquiesced in this, as a necessary war measure. But with the coming of peace came a change. In Pomerania, with its capital at Stettin, the situation defined itself in the classic terms of opposition between the Estates and the duke – the queen (and afterwards the king) of Sweden was duke of Pomerania – and it lost nothing in sharpness from the fact that the two parties were of different nationalities. The Swedes proceeded upon the assumption that it was a matter of the relations between sovereign and subjects, and that the sovereign must prevail. The Estates on their side maintained that it was a question of the relationship of *Landsfürst* to *Land*, where neither was superior to the other but each had equal rights. Thus both the dukes and the Estates thought in dualistic terms. But neither side was prepared to push its point of view to the extreme of absolutism on the one hand, or of parliamentarism on the other; and this reciprocal moderation made possible a certain measure of unity when it came to applying a constitution as to whose main features there was general agreement. But when it was a question of the competence, constitution and composition of the organs of government which were acceptable to each, or of the cost of administration, then differences of opinion became evident, and the basic divergences at once came to the surface. The Estates demanded a say in all decisions of importance. This was conceded; but the duke-king reserved the right to decide which questions belonged to that category, and claimed also that any meetings of the Estates must take place only with his leave and under his supervision. To that the Estates would not agree. The duke also maintained that appointments to offices should be made by himself alone, while the Estates demanded that they should be consulted in regard to filling the higher offices in the *collegia* and the courts of justice.

Princes and Estates in Germany in this period habitually quarrelled about questions of this kind. Of greater importance for Pomerania's position within the Swedish empire was a difference of opinion in regard to another matter. The Swedish government demanded that the duke should have the right to maintain a standing army in the province; the Estates insisted that the existing system of defensive arrangements be preserved. This would have meant in fact that they washed their hands of Sweden's problems and declared their indifference to Sweden's needs; only when their own country was directly concerned would they be prepared to make a serious effort. It was characteristic of their attitude that they should have demanded that Pomerania should remain neutral in all wars which Sweden waged 'for her own ends'. From the Swedish point of view it is obvious that such a demand could not be admitted.

The dispute continued all through the 1650s, and it was not until 1663 that a settlement was reached. It was essentially a compromise. The Estates carried their demand that the basic principle of dualism should be incorporated into the constitution; but on the other hand they were forced to agree that the duke-king had the right to maintain a standing army in the duchy, and that the new taxes (and especially the excise) which had been introduced to meet the cost of the war should continue to be levied.

In Stettin then, despite the duchy's position as a part of the Swedish empire, it was possible to take an optimistic view of the way things were going. The Estates retained their influence, and were not, as in so many other German territories, forced to capitulate to the authority of the prince. The government did not become an absolutism: not even under Charles XI; though in the 1680s and 1690s the king pursued a policy which, if it had succeeded, would have extended the limits of the ducal authority, and correspondingly diminished that of the Estates. But on the whole the Estates were able to maintain their position. There were disputes about the *reduktion*, about attempts to reduce the authority of the Supreme Court at Wismar, and about the respective spheres of action of duke and Estates; but there was no Caroline absolutism in Pomerania. Charles XI made no attempt to impose it by using the military resources which were available to him. And the reason for this lies, among other things, in the fact that Pomerania was far too important as an actual or potential base of operations to be treated with undue harshness.

The ability of the Estates to maintain their rights was to have consequences of the greatest importance for Pomerania's future history; for the constitutional principles which they had defended remained intact throughout the whole eighteenth century. Thus the rule of Sweden contributed to the preservation of ancient institutions and of a degree of independence which is really surprising in a mere province. The history of Bremen–Verden followed a parallel course to that of Pomerania. Here too absolutism failed to impose itself. And the fundamental reason for this must probably be sought in the fact that the government was never quite clear what it wanted – an explanation which becomes the more plausible when we contrast the way things developed in Livonia, where the reign of Charles XI saw the defeat and capitulation of the Estates.

Viewed from the *town* of Bremen (as against the duchy) the Swedish empire had very different implications, and presented very different problems from those which applied to Stettin and Pomerania. The basic situation also differed from that in the duchies of Bremen and Verden, if only because of the controversy about the town's constitutional status. The town claimed to be the Emperor's immediate vassal; it claimed membership of the Diet of the Empire. From the beginning the Swedish authorities handled Bremen with great caution: neither in 1632 nor in 1645, when the issue became a live one, did they enforce the acceptance of a Swedish garrison; and the town made capital out of this during the negotiations which preceded the peace of 1648. The Emperor moreover had in 1646 confirmed Bremen's status as a member of the Diet. The Swedes, on their side, refused to recognise the validity of this declaration, and regarded themselves as the successor to the sovereign authority of the last archbishop of Bremen. They interpreted the treaty of Osnabrück in this sense; Bremen put forward a directly contrary interpretation. Such controversies were not unusual in seventeenth-century Germany: other German princes prosecuted comparable disputes with other recalcitrant cities desirous of winning the status of immediate vassals of the Emperor. Nevertheless the special position which Bremen demanded posed problems for the Swedish crown. It meant a weakening of Sweden's military position in the duchies, and it put an obstacle in the way of the extensive commercial plans which were being formulated in Stockholm in the years around 1650. Swedish policy therefore proceeded on the line of trying to isolate Bremen in order to make the town more amenable. But the pressure which Sweden now brought to bear produced a strong anti-Swedish sentiment in Germany, which manifested itself in diplomatic action. The successes of Swedish arms, however, and Swedish diplomatic counter-measures, led to a settlement at the close of 1654 which postponed a decision on Bremen's status. The result was undoubtedly a success for Sweden. Bremen acknowledged the king of Sweden, and paid a partial indemnity for his military expenses; and though it retained its own government it had to pay something in the way of contributions.

In the years that followed each side clung to its interpretation of the treaty of 1648. In 1663 Bremen was admitted to a seat and vote in the Diet at Regensburg, and was thus publicly accepted as an Imperial Free City. The Swedish government retorted by demanding that the town should once again acknowledge the sovereignty of the king of Sweden; and when this was refused proceeded to military action. But as on the previous occasion this provoked opposition from various quarters in Germany, whose princes had no desire to see the town in Swedish hands. Confronted with this military and diplomatic opposition, Sweden was compelled to abandon her demand for Bremen's capitulation. It was agreed that after the conclusion of the present session of the Diet Bremen should refrain from taking her seat until the year 1700, unless some other settlement had been agreed upon in the meantime. But since the Diet continued in permanent session at Regensburg until the old Empire came to an end, the agreement never became operative, and Bremen continued to take her place among the Imperial Cities.

Thus Bremen was successful in her resistance to Swedish authority. But it must be observed that this was not in the first instance a conflict between Sweden and one of her provinces, but a struggle in which a town sought to secure the status and independence which attached to the Emperor's immediate vassals. For the duchies, however, the affair was not without its consequences. It had fallen to them to finance the army which was collected to subdue Bremen. In 1666 and in the years that followed this army was of great importance for the Swedish empire: as we noted earlier, a force of this kind was necessary to the maintenance of Sweden's international position. The course of events was to demonstrate the fact, already well known to the inhabitants of the duchies, that the right of their Estates to exert influence, and to be consulted, became illusory in the face of military force. In other words, they had to pay in a number of ways for the attempts of the town of Bremen to establish its independence. Their trade suffered moreover from the blockade of the Weser, which the Swedes instituted in order to put pressure on Bremen, and this too produced hard feelings.

The Baltic provinces, like the German, were called upon to bear a heavy economic burden; not only for their own support, but for that of the empire as a whole. The government in Stockholm was firmly of the opinion that it was the duty of the provinces to contribute to the safety of all the king's dominions. And as we have seen, this caused problems not only for Bremen–Verden, but also for Pomerania. The idea was not a Swedish invention: it was applied also elsewhere, as for instance in Brandenburg; but it goes without saying that it caused bad blood. The demands were frequent; they were considered to be excessive; and there was a feeling that each province ought to be left to run its own affairs, and not be called upon to assume responsibility for those of other territories. In short, there was here a clear conflict between the wishes of the provinces and those of the mother-country.[11]

One question upon which it is extremely difficult to arrive at more than very general conclusions is what the provinces thought of Sweden's ability to protect them. What did it mean to the German territories, when in the 1670s they were abandoned to their fate? How did the Baltic provinces feel about the Russian harryings in the years after 1700? Did they begin to be afraid that Sweden was not going to be able in the future to give them any better assurance of the security that they needed? And if so, what part was played by this feeling in preparing the way for a loosening of the ties between the home country and the provinces? Such questions may be asked, but in the present state of our knowledge it is not possible to give a definite answer to them. The immediate impact was small. But it is interesting to note that in 1709 Peter the Great, in his great manifesto to the inhabitants of the Baltic provinces, raised just this question.

Another field which would repay more intensive investigation is the relation between the central and local organs of government. It is quite clear that the coming of absolutism induced in certain subordinate officers a timidity about taking the initiative and devising new methods for dealing with situations which were not provided for in their instructions. This can be seen in the 1690s, when Axel Julius De la Gardie, as governor-general of Estonia, did not venture to act on his own responsibility in a time of severe famine, but referred important decisions to the king in Stockholm. Difficulties of communication meant that it took a long time for instructions to reach him, and in the meantime nothing was done, though the situation was grave. In the light of this case it becomes a question whether the absolutism, and the remoteness of the provinces from Stockholm, may not have adversely affected their administration in some ways; and, if so, in what ways. But in the present state of our information no general answer can be given.

Another aspect of the question as to how the connection between the provinces and the mother-country was regarded is the recruiting of candidates for the various offices and jobs within the Swedish central government. How large was the foreign element in the senior positions, civil and military, in Sweden and Finland?

It is in the first place a fact that we can point to a long list of names which bear witness to the cosmopolitan character of the Age of Greatness. Names such as De Geer, Wrangel and Wachtmeister are evidence that some of them reached the highest positions in the kingdom and played an important part in shaping policy. More interesting than this general observation, however, is the question whether it is possible to establish any quantitative criterion. And it seems that it is possible. In an essay on 'Finnish Office-holders and the Swedish Realm in the Eighteenth century', Sten Carlsson has provided important statistics about the extent of foreign infiltration; and an adaptation of his figures affords information essential to the consideration of this question.[12] If we divide the higher civil servants in Sweden and Finland in certain years between 1640 and 1735 according to their places of origin, we get the following percentages:[13]

TABLE 2: HIGHER CIVIL SERVANTS 1640–1735

Place of origin	1640	1660	1680	1700	1720	1735
Sweden	65·1	70·6	76·3	74·1	78·5	79·1
Finland	11·5	9·6	9·7	15·6	9·6	10·3
Baltic provinces	4·5	2·0	3·2	1·5	5·1	5·6
Germany	5·1	3·6	4·2	2·6	2·6	1·6
Other	–	1·0	–	0·3	0·3	–
Unknown	13·8	13·2	6·6	5·9	3·9	3·4
	100·0	100·0	100·0	100·0	100·0	100·0

The tendency for Sweden proper to provide the greater part of these office-holders is clear. More interesting in this connection is the size of the Baltic and German elements. Germany reaches a peak in 1640 and during the Thirty Years War, and afterwards falls away, except for another peak in 1680. For the Baltic provinces the picture is rather different. Here too we find a peak in 1640, followed by a decline and then another peak in 1680; but then comes a difference: after 1700 the percentage goes up, and stays at about the same level in 1735.

An analysis of senior military officers belonging to units of Swedish or Finnish origin arranged in the same way for certain years between 1660 and 1729 gives the following percentages: [14]

TABLE 3: SENIOR MILITARY OFFICERS 1640–1735

Place of origin	1640	1684	1698	1719	1729
Sweden	39·2	54·3	53·8	45·7	57·0
Finland	16·5	8·0	6·3	10·3	8·1
Baltic provinces	16·5	22·5	22·6	31·4	23·7
Germany	9·8	9·2	10·5	10·0	9·1
Other	18·0	6·0	2·8	2·6	2·1
	100·0	100·0	100·0	100·0	100·0

Thus even in Swedish native units the foreign element is considerable. This is particularly true during the Thirty Years War and the Great Northern War. The German element remains relatively constant throughout. The Baltic element, on the other hand, is large, and tends to get larger until 1719, declining a little thereafter. The Balts in fact had clearly a very strong position in the native Swedish and Finnish regiments: on closer examination, indeed, it appears that in 1719 they formed almost 54 per cent of senior officers in Finnish units; and even as late as 1729 the figure was almost 43 per cent.

These statistics show how large was the share of the provinces in the higher posts of the civil and military establishment. It was both possible and usual for provincials to make a career for themselves in the service of the imperial power, since that power needed them to help to man its civil service and its army: the recruitment of foreigners is particularly marked in wartime. But the high figures for the Baltic provinces for years when those provinces had already been lost to Russia demand some explanation. When in 1710 the Tsar established his authority over these areas, he proclaimed emphatically that he intended to accept the validity of their old privileges and concessions. The reason for this was that he needed trained personnel to run the administration and carry on the economic life of the provinces. As we saw, the Swedish government, in its negotiations with the Livonian nobility in 1719, was forced to make far-reaching concessions in regard to their privileges, under the impression of the effect produced by the prospects which the Tsar was holding out. We know too that many of the Baltic nobility, confronted by the prospect of the detachment of their old homeland in Livonia from their new homeland in Sweden, designated one member of the family to be a Russian subject, and so safeguard their family interests across the water. Yet despite the peace, and the loss of the provinces to Russia, it is interesting to find that the Baltic element in the Swedish service remains at the same high level. And this can only mean that the Balts felt themselves at home in Sweden, and were accepted there – which is the more remarkable, since in the years around 1720 there was keen competition for army appointments, now that the country was on a peace footing. This must imply that the Swedish administration had expanded to such an extent, and had so fully assimilated the new men, that they were considered to be necessary in their new positions. And this leads us to the fall of the Swedish empire and its consequences.

VII

The peace settlements which were concluded between 1719 and 1721 imposed upon Sweden great cessions of territory; they deprived her of between half a million and one million inhabitants; and from a financial point of view they swept away a surplus which in the past had accrued to the central government. The revenues of the reduced estates, which had previously been assigned to defray the cost of the administration in Stockholm, were no longer available for that purpose. And as we have seen, the peace of Nystad had important consequences for the fortunes of private individuals. The economic relations between Sweden and the former provinces were in general adversely affected, though the important imports of grain were able to continue as before, among other reasons because one clause in the peace treaty stipulated that Sweden should be permitted to import grain up to an annual value of 50,000 roubles duty-free. Nevertheless, as Eli Heckscher made clear, the effects of the change were very small when seen in relation to the size of the territorial losses. But this is only one side of the question. There remains the problem why it was that the peace meant the definitive ending of Sweden's career as a great power.

We have seen that the Swedish empire was too weak, demographically and economically, for the part it was called upon to play. In an attempt to solve this problem, the Swedish government had recourse to devices of various kinds: on the one hand it tried to ensure that the economic burden of war was transferred as soon as possible to the territory of other states; on the other it recruited its armies in wartime to a large extent from foreign mercenaries. Attempts to deal with the problem on a domestic basis entailed a solution which was really only valid for times of peace. The provinces beyond the sea functioned as strategic bases to protect the home country, but above all as starting-points for offensive campaigns against foreign territory. But after 1721 the former possessions on the other side of the Baltic (with the exception of western Pomerania, Rügen and Wismar) had been transformed into potential bases for an assault on Sweden. Sweden had been forced back to a defensive position.

In the present state of our information, we can go no further than simply to state that the Swedish empire's resources were inadequate to sustain its position in the long run. Attempts to solve the problem through using the provinces as instruments of an offensive policy, whenever the general interests of the empire should demand it, proved no sure way out of the difficulty. Such a policy, if it were to be successful, demanded not only a good army, but statesmanship which was not daunted by difficulties, and an effective administration in the new territories. The wars of the 1740s and 1750s showed this; and they showed too that Sweden's adversaries, Russia and Prussia, had by that time acquired greater resources than in earlier years. Sweden's position as a great power was the result of the favourable accident of having weak neighbours, and of *ad hoc* solutions with resources too small for the great objects in view. When one of these conditions vanished, and the other was partly destroyed as a result of the weakening or removal of the basis upon which it rested, the day of Sweden as a great power was over for good.

2. The Swedish Economy and Sweden's Role as a Great Power 1632–1697

SVEN-ERIK ÅSTRÖM

THROUGHOUT the greater part of the seventeenth century Sweden appeared upon the European stage in the character of a great power. Her entry into the German war had been preceded by political and military activity directed against Poland, Denmark and Russia; whereby the geographical limits of the realm had indeed been extended but its economic resources stretched to the uttermost. New frontier fortresses entailed maintenance of defence works and garrisons; the transport of troops, the struggle for the command of the sea, demanded a fleet in being. From the reign of Gustavus Adolphus to the death of Charles XI in 1697, despite periods of apparent peace (which might even, as between 1680 and 1697, be of considerable duration), this condition of strain remained as a permanent feature of the Swedish economy. The grand finale of the reign of Charles XII, filled as it was with practically uninterrupted war, was but the echo of an old song. For in contrast to the active intervention of Gustavus Adolphus and Axel Oxenstierna in the general politics of the continent, Charles XII operated for the most part in eastern Europe: Sweden's career as a great power ended, as it had begun, in the east. And despite the attention which contemporaries (and posterity) devoted to Charles's campaigns, the year of his accession, 1697, marked a dividing-line. After Narva, Altranstädt and Pultava those preoccupations with the east which had marked Swedish policy in the sixteenth century appeared in ever-clearer contrast to Sweden's involvement in the affairs of Europe from 1632 to 1697. The great struggle of the opening of the eighteenth century concerned the Spanish succession. And in that struggle, despite the baits held out, Sweden took no part.

Within the period 1632–97 too we can discern significant lines of division. Until Charles X's death in 1660, Sweden waged wars that were offensive, even though they might be punctuated by periods of more or less inescapable defensive wars, waged to maintain her position on the continent. The government of Charles XI attacked Brandenburg as the *quid pro quo* for those French subsidies which from the early days of Sweden's greatness had reinforced the state's finances. Charles XI's war against Denmark was a clearly defensive war waged to consolidate the acquisitions made in the years before 1660.

The ability to sustain the part of a great power is at bottom essentially a question of economic potential; and the problem to be discussed must therefore be how far Sweden possessed these necessary resources, and how they were utilised to maintain her great international position. Social questions too were involved. To what extent was Swedish society adaptable to a foreign policy of the kind which was pursued until the end of the seventeenth century? What were the resources, material and human, upon which the country could draw in order to maintain a great empire? How could she conjure into existence the soldiers, diplomats, administrators, propagandists, entrepreneurs, financiers, which a war economy demanded?

I. RESOURCES
(i)

It is important to draw a purely geographical distinction between the various constituent elements which formed the Swedish realm. Climatically, its newest portions (the Danish and German provinces, Livonia, Estonia) were most closely akin to central and eastern Europe. Politically, it was a fact of cardinal importance that the old parts of the empire – Sweden and Finland (excluding the province of Kexholm) – were dominant. Only they were represented in the *riksdag* and the council of state throughout the whole period. That the first Estate, the Nobility, received during the period of expansion a strong admixture of foreign (especially German) elements does not alter the picture; for an aristocrat of Baltic or German origin could enter the council or the *riksdag* only as a Swedish nobleman. There was indeed a considerable foreign element in the Estate of Burghers too; but the Clergy and the fourth Estate, the Peasants, were wholly Swedish or Finnish. So when the government appealed for, or demanded, grants for fresh war efforts, it was to the core of the country's population, Swedes or Finns, that it must address itself. The great magnates – Bielkes, Bondes, Brahes, Oxenstiernas – were all members of great families linked by ties of blood to the crown, and drawn from the Swedish heartlands; or they were German or Danish families – Fleming, Gyllenstierna – who had become acclimatised in Sweden long ago in the Middle Ages; or families from

Finland – Creutz, Horn, Kurck – of ancient lineage, often enough members of the council of state. Sweden's great-power status gave rise both to a lively internal social mobility, and to an immigration of foreign experts – soldiers such as Pontus De la Gardie, financiers such as Momma-Reenstierna, diplomats such as Hugo Grotius, armaments kings such as Louis De Geer. But it was typical of the period of Swedish expansion that one of the 'great' Swedish commanders, Duke Bernard of Saxe-Weimar, should never have set foot in Sweden at all.

The distant, hyperborean great power attracted enterprising adventurers from the thickly populated river valleys of central Europe and the bleak highlands of Scotland – but not the social élite of German feudal society. With the new men came new weapons, new ideas of administration, new techniques of production for Sweden's staple commodities of iron and tar. Eli Heckscher emphasised this point in various connections, above all in his monumental *Sveriges ekonomiska historia från Gustav Vasa*; but Heckscher, himself the son of an immigrant, had less feeling for the importance of the purely native elements: the statesmen in the council, the representatives of the 'voice of the people', the Swedish–Finnish members of the Estates – clergy, burghers, and above all peasants; to say nothing of the government's agents scattered over the countryside – the petty justices, the bailiffs, the constables. Nevertheless it was with justice that he wrote:

> The immigrants came to a land with a strong central power, and probably the most effective administrative machinery that any country could show in that age. They were therefore integrated into a society which from a cultural and economic point of view was certainly backward but which politically was unusually solid, a society in which there was no room for particularism, or for foreign interests seeking to assert themselves in opposition to the government. In this society they settled, and with a kind of inevitability became as good Swedes as those of native origin, rather than foreigners who took possession of a colonial land to exploit it and subsequently returned with their accumulated fortunes to the land of their birth.[1]

But the basis of that society was the people, and it was astonishingly thin on the ground. It seems that the population of the whole Swedish realm grew during the period, but this process was mainly related to the expansion which added new provinces to Sweden. At the death of Gustavus Adolphus the population may have been $1\frac{1}{2}$ million people, of which perhaps 900,000 lived in Sweden, 375,000 in Finland and the rest in the newly acquired provinces. Up to the middle of the 1690s the population in the central parts of Sweden (with Finland) did not show much growth, but the addition of Danes, Norwegians, Germans and others to 'Sweden' means that the population before the hunger years 1696–7 may be estimated at about 2½ million. And thanks to the stress of circumstances – a worsening of the climate, wars, years of shortage, epidemics – its numbers were virtually stationary. If they did in fact show an increase, this is to be attributed to relatively good harvests in the Baltic provinces, and to the gradual incorporation of the old Danish provinces – Jämtland, Härjedalen, Halland, Bohuslän, Skåne, Blekinge – which represented the tangible gains of an aggressive economic policy. The objective of incorporating the whole southern coasts of the Baltic into the empire, the much-desired *dominium maris Baltici*, was never attained. Danzig retained her independence, Courland remained a vassal-state of Poland, East Prussia of Brandenburg. The lands of the dukes of Holstein-Gottorp could indeed be reckoned as under Swedish influence. Two queens came from Holstein-Gottorp; but they brought no hereditary possessions with them. Eastern and western Pomerania, however, where the old line of dukes died out in 1637; and the tiny territory of Zweibrücken, the succession to which fell to Charles XI in 1685; can be considered as incorporated in the Swedish realm in virtue of dynastic ties. But the connection was superficial, and the population remained German – as it did in Bremen–Verden, another of the territorial gains from the Thirty Years War. The population of Skåne and the other southern provinces was Danish. In Riga, Reval, Narva, nobles and burghers spoke German; while the peasantry spoke a variety of Finno-Ugrian languages, or Lettish. Finnish was the language too in the sensitive frontier zone of Kexholm and Ingria, whence after the war of 1655–6 such of the population as was of the Greek Orthodox faith (and hence under Russian influence) emigrated across the frontier to be replaced by colonists mostly from Finland.[2]

(ii)

The Swedish realm was based upon a social structure, and upon economic resources, of a quite peculiar kind, which differed widely from the circumstances prevailing in neighbouring countries.

At the beginning of the Age of Greatness, Finland's relative importance was greater than at its conclusion, for by that time the former Danish and Norwegian provinces had begun to be affected by the slow

process of economic and social assimilation, and their combined population was not much less than that of Finland. But in the years from
1632 to 1697 Finland had made a contribution of far greater value
than its share of the population of the heartlands (about a third) might
have led one to expect. With its unfavourable climate and sparse population, Finland can be compared with Sweden north of Stockholm. Its
agricultural techniques were primitive: all over the interior, and on
the eastern borderlands, burn-beat cultivation was the rule. It was a
form of agriculture which was extremely extensive (as against intensive),
even though in good years and on virgin soil it might give a harvest of
as much as tenfold of the seed corn. Gerd Eneqvist's investigations of
the yield on permanently cultivated ground in the lower Lule valley in
Norrland give a figure of 1 : 2·7; and her results seem in the light of what
we know about Swedish agriculture to be a fair reflection also of the
situation in large tracts of northern Sweden north of a line running
through the Göta river and the Mälar area.

The commonest grain-crop was rye; but in Finland, as also in Norrland, barley also had considerable importance, though it seems to have
diminished towards the end of the century. Wheat growing occurred
only in patches, usually in connection with a noble household; oats were
significant on the Swedish west coast. There was in general a correspondence between the choice of crop and manner of cultivation on the
one hand, and the kind of farm animals on the other. Land of old
cultivation, well manured and of good quality where ox traction was
the rule, implied cattle; burn-beat cultivation mainly went with horses,
among other reasons because they provided quicker transport over
long distances.

The high aristocracy managed their farms on lines which differed
from those used by peasants: better planned, more rational lines. There
is something to be said for the argument used by members of the
council in opposition to the *reduktion*, that the land was more productive
if it were in noble hands – though this was of course something that
varied from one case to another. Those ramshackle rookeries which
some of them dignified with the name of manor, but which they often
enough took good care not to live in, are not to be compared with estates
such as Count Hans Wachtmeister's Johannishus, with its sixty-five
tenant farms on the domain and its accounts and supervision in the
hands of Countess Wachtmeister herself: she was a countess in her own
right, and like her husband belonged to that new aristocracy which had
been ennobled for civil or military service. Nor did these great estates

vanish with the *reduktion* (see below, Chapters 6 and 7). The great noble families who had enjoyed their golden age under Charles XI's regency could, if all went well, re-establish their economic, if not always their political, position by means of well-judged marriages. Consolidation or exchange of scattered possessions could lead once more to the creation of *latifundia*; and this made it possible for certain family groups which had been great in the Age of Greatness – as for instance the De Geers – to play a major part in politics until the age of industrialism.

At the beginning of the Age of Greatness about one-fifth of the peasantry of Sweden proper were tenants of the nobility on land which was anciently noble. At the time of Gustavus Vasa's death in 1560 over 20 per cent of all farms in Sweden were in noble hands; in Finland, something over 2 per cent. This meant that in the more important half of the kingdom – that is, in Sweden – the number of independent tax-paying peasants was less than twice as many as in Finland. And even though during the wars with Russia and Poland in the years before 1629 there was a steady growth of noble holdings, especially in Finland, the rate of increase (as Sven A. Nilsson has shown) was nevertheless relatively slow. It was not until the great land grants and the creation of counties and baronies in Christina's time that Finland was seriously affected (see below, pp. 77, 87); and it was not until the Thirty Years War was over that the alienation of land to the nobility set in in real earnest.

(iii)

The task of the peasant, however, was not simply to cultivate the soil, to produce consumption goods. He could and must be fitted in directly into the war economy. For example, the Finnish light cavalry came from areas where the methods of cultivation were primitive, noble estates few, and the land in peasant hands. A very ancient method of exempting the land from tax consisted in furnishing a cavalryman and his horse; and this was used by 3,000 of Finland's 30,000 peasants. The horses which were accustomed to draw their primitive ploughs and brush-harrows over Finland's stony soils were no bigger than a modern pony. But the light cavalry which they furnished had a technique of its own: it rode to the front, but it fought on foot. Under Torsten Stålhandske it garnered laurels on the extreme right wing at Breitenfeld; under Johan Galle it ensured victory at Lund; under Carl

Gustaf Creutz it had perforce to surrender its standards after Pultava. And between the family farms of these three generals the distance was no more than twenty miles as the crow flies. It is perhaps an unhistorical parallel, or an eccentric exaggeration, to say that at the opening of the Age of Greatness the Finnish cavalry formed a kind of analogue to the Cossacks. But there is truth in it nevertheless. It is illuminating that in eight of the twenty engagements fought by Gustavus Adolphus in Germany from June 1630 to November 1632, the Finnish cavalry was placed in the front rank on the right wing, and on two other occasions in the front rank on the left. It is significant that whereas the proportion between horse and foot was 1 : 4 for Sweden, it was 1 : 2 for Finland. From the 1640s onward, the lightest cavalry of all, the dragoons, were recruited from the most easterly part of Finland, scraped together from farms which had fallen out of cultivation. Their day of glory came at the battle of Lund on 4 December 1676, at a moment when the human and economic resources of the country were stretched to the uttermost. An east Finnish dragoon regiment under Colonel von Burghausen had been stationed on the extreme left. When the battle ended, victory had indeed been won, but the regiment was virtually annihilated. The colonel was killed; the lieutenant-colonel, major and all the captains save one were wounded: of a strength of 483 men before the battle, only 44 troopers survived.

While Finnish cavalry units were standing fast against the well-equipped heavy cuirassiers of the Imperial, Bavarian, Polish and Danish armies, Finnish foot were garrisoning that girdle of defensive bastions which stretched from Kexholm, by way of Narva, Reval and Riga, to Stralsund. The Osterbotten regiment, for example, was permanently stationed in Riga to a strength of 1,000 men, which meant that every tenth adult male in Osterbotten was a member of the Riga garrison, and so formed a part of the most vital, and the strongest, link in the chain of fortresses surrounding the Baltic.[3] The burghers of the Baltic ports, it is true, showed no obvious disposition to be disloyal to their Swedish sovereign; but all the same the presence of troops from Sweden and Finland offered a better guarantee of security than could be provided by garrisons composed of German-speaking mercenaries. Garrisons, however, like pitched camps, bred epidemics, and the resulting losses bore heavily on an exiguous population, and especially on the more sparsely-populated Finland.

Though these examples have been taken from Finland, they show in general how intensively the Swedish–Finnish realm was compelled to use its limited human resources. It may well be questioned whether Sweden alone, without the conquered Danish–Norwegian provinces (which after all were acquired fairly late), could have attained, and maintained, its position as a great power. It is therefore the more necessary to emphasise the importance of Finland for the country's economy, and hence its war potential; and from this point of view these salient examples from Finland have a general relevance to the whole picture.

(iv)

To the mercantilists, the wealth of a country was to be measured partly by the size of its population but above all by its resources of precious metals. And in the silver mine at Sala and the great copper mine at Falun, Sweden possessed resources of this kind, though by the close of the Age of Greatness they were beginning to show signs of being exhausted. Gustavus Adolphus and the regents in Christina's time could still count on support for their policies from the produce of Sala. Copper was used for coining the famous massive *kopparplåtar* under Christina and Charles X; and in the same period Sweden enjoyed from time to time a monopoly of the European copper market, despite some competition from Japanese copper imported into Europe by the Dutch. It is not easy to arrive at a conclusion on the importance of Swedish copper for Sweden's policy as a great power. One thing, however, is certain. Sweden's supplies of copper were important during the Vasa period for the financing of war, and they were one of the preconditions for the support given to Sweden by foreign entrepreneurs. But towards the end of Charles XI's reign the minting of copper came to an end. England's extrication of herself from the copper monopoly, and Japanese copper imports into Europe, combined with the increasing difficulty of winning the ore from the deeper seams at Falun, in the end reduced the significance of copper – as had already happened with silver – in the Swedish finances.

In their place came a third metal: iron. Iron mining in Sweden had a very long history, but a real iron industry began to emerge only in the sixteenth century when imported experts – at first Germans, later Walloons – transformed the technique for the production of bar iron. 'Walloon iron' was not only a mass product; it was a quality product too, and it was stimulated by the Dutch and above all the English demand for an iron of high quality, which reached a decisive point in the increasingly important English market around 1660.

TABLE 4: EXPORTS OF BAR IRON TO ENGLAND
FROM STOCKHOLM AND GÖTEBORG 1648-1700[4]

(English tons)

	Stockholm		Göteborg
1648	373	1649	188
1652	750	1655	930
1659	3,443		
1661	(5,733)*	1661	1,193
1669	(8,133)*	1667	525
		1672	1,473
1681	9,042	1681	(2,255)*
1685	7,859	1685	2,058
1687	12,684	1687	2,585
1691	8,536	1691	2,190
1694	9,251	1695	3,554
1698	10,608		
1700	9,863		

* Sources are defective; figures approximate.

Stockholm and Göteborg were the ports of export for the Bergslag (applying that term in its widest sense as the generic name for the mining district of central Sweden). There were furnaces and foundries all over central Sweden, as well as in western Finland and Småland: in the main, therefore, it was the Swedish heartlands which produced the bar iron which was so important to the balance of payments, while southern Sweden, like eastern Finland, was a grain-producing area.

A precondition for an iron industry was not only the existence of ore, but an abundance of wood. There was no ore in Finland, but it was readily available in the skerries outside Stockholm, and it was thence that the Finnish ironworks drew their raw material: boats plied to Stockholm with cargoes of finished iron and victuals, and took back ore as a return freight. Stringent legislation protected the timber resources in areas where ore was abundant, and attempted to hold a balance between the competing demands of the iron industry's need for charcoal, the cultivation of the waste by burn-beat, and the needs of the tar burners.

Together with copper, iron was Sweden's leading export commodity. The advance of iron is shown in Table 5, which indicates the main (legal) export commodities. It is easy to understand, in the light of these statistics, how great an object of concern the iron industry was to the authorities of the period.

TABLE 5: PERCENTAGE VALUE OF EXPORTS
FROM SWEDEN AND FINLAND ACCORDING
TO COMMODITIES 1637 AND 1685[5]

	1637	1685
Iron and steel	35·4	57·0
Copper and brass	27·3	23·5
Pitch and tar	7·9	8·1
Wood products	4·1	2·4
Grains	16·0	0·1
Hides and skins	2·4	0·1
'Russian goods'	–	3·9
Dried and salt fish	0·1	0·5
Unspecified	6·8	4·4
Total	100·0	100·0

Next in importance after iron and copper came timber and timber products. Tar and pitch, the country's third great staple, was produced above all in northern and eastern Finland. Exports from the northern area were channelled through Stockholm. In the south-eastern area tar burning was already on the decline, mainly as a result of regulations creating a monopoly for the Tar Company located in Stockholm, and by a policy of forest conservation in the interests of the metallurgical industries. Thus national legislation essentially designed to safeguard commercial interests in Stockholm and the flourishing iron industry of central Sweden had damaging side-effects in Finland. And when tar prices fell, the cost of transport over the stretch from the source of production to the coast became a decisive factor. In the lake region of south-eastern Finland around Lake Saima the tar was still able to bear the low cost of transport by water to Villmanstrand; but the threshold of payability was reached in the Villmanstrand–Viborg region, where in winter the tar barrels had to be drawn on sledges by peasant teamsters.

Tar manufacture was therefore more lucrative in the river valleys of Osterbotten, where the barrels were taken by boat to the nearest market town, and there loaded on to hoys for transport to Stockholm.

For English, Dutch and Swedish skippers sailing from Stockholm to western Europe a main cargo of heavy bar iron, tar as ballast, and plank as a possible extra, provided an excellent combination. Such traders on their inward voyage brought to Sweden textiles, salt, fancy goods and wines – a mixture designed to cater both for the general customer and for those social categories who represented the governing classes of a great power – nobles, clergy, burghers, officials, soldiers. The commonalty might be clothed in homespun and coarse linen; the upper classes wore cloth. Fine cloths were permitted only to gentlemen; cheap varieties were used as a form of payment, and as uniforms for the indispensable instruments of greatness, the army and navy. No one was more interested than Charles XI in securing the standardisation of regimental uniforms, in the continental style: it was only in his time that a native cloth industry was developed in order to meet the needs of an increasingly well-organised army. As to luxuries, the only one vouchsafed to the ordinary man was tobacco.

From the point of view of providing for the nation's supplies, whether in war or peace, the trade in grain was of special concern. Both Sweden proper and Finland were in this respect areas of deficiency, in part for purely climatic reasons. The country's requirements in the way of meat and animal products were rather better covered. Yet in years of good harvests, or when the price of grain on the international market was high (and here Amsterdam prices offered the main and best indicator), export of grain did occur (see above, Table 5).

(v)

Estonia, Livonia, Ingria and the province of Kexholm can be considered, economically and politically, as colonies of the Swedish–Finnish motherland. In Estonia and Livonia the social structure was purely feudal. Their ancient aristocracy, organised as a knightly corporation, was German in language and ways of thought. This was true also of the burghers in the most important trading entrepôts, in stable Riga, stagnating Reval and flourishing Narva. For these old Hansa outposts Lübeck had been the mother-city, and German commercial techniques and traditions permeated their economic and social life. Governors-general and governors, with their little courts and staffs of officials and servants from Sweden and Finland, administered the duchies on behalf of the Swedish crown; garrisons from Sweden and Finland formed the basis of their authority.

The Estonian and Livonian nobility lived on their estates, encompassed by an enserfed peasantry which spoke another tongue than that of their masters. Upon the nobility lay the obligation to provide, by way of knight-service, a trained force of cavalry; and they also performed the important function of furnishing commanders for the Swedish armies. In this way they came to be integrated into the Swedish aristocracy, and in course of time to be naturalised as Swedish nobles. Nevertheless it was also the case that a large part of the noble lands in these Baltic provinces passed by royal alienations or donations into the hands of the high Swedish nobility, and especially to families such as De la Gardie, Stenbock and Tott, who were connected by marriage with the royal house. Other large estates were in the hands of the families of provincial governors, such as Horn, Fleming and Cruus. The great family of Oxenstierna was strongly entrenched all over this region: it is significant that even after the great *reduktion* Charles XI's foreign minister Bengt Oxenstierna drew his salary partly from silver paid in customs dues at Stockholm, and partly from taxes paid to the crown in Ingria.

Ingria's history was peculiar, in that the original Greek Orthodox population, as we have seen, left the country in the years before and after the peace of Kardis in 1661. The vacuum was filled by 'colonists' from eastern Finland. It is interesting to see the Russian baptismal names and surnames, as recorded in the tax lists, being replaced by Finnish. But the social structure remained unaffected by the change. And though serfdom never took root in Ingria, the peasants were subject to their lords or their lords' bailiffs, a motley collection of very mixed provenance. The whole country was parcelled out into estates which the crown had now either pawned, sold or given in fief, but which originally had been villages with an Ingrian or Vatjak population and had subsequently been the property of Russian boyars.

The province of Kexholm had been handed over to Sweden by the treaty of Stolbova in 1617. Its northern portion was a pioneer area, where tax was levied on the number of bowmen in any one district; its southern was already feudalised, with Russian boyars, Orthodox monasteries and the Great Dukes of Moscow as overlords; and the first Swedish lord-lieutenant therefore attempted to fix its fiscal obligations, as in Estonia, on the basis of the unit of cultivation. The same demographic and religious pattern which marked the history of Ingria was applied throughout the whole of Kexholm. The Finnish element in the population was strengthened; the Lutheran clergy imposed their liturgy. The population of this God-forsaken region remained unrepresented in the Swedish *riksdag*. The estates in the possession of fief-holders, and the later crown tenants, were to all intents and purposes self-sufficient units. Yet the agrarian population increased in the fertile areas around Lake Ladoga, and in consequence this became a surplus area for grain – a not unwelcome supplement to the grudging soils of the mother-country.

The customs accounts for Stockholm for the year 1685 reveal how much the Baltic area contributed to the provisioning of the capital. In that year Estonia, Livonia and Ingria sent the following quantities of foodstuffs to Stockholm (a Stockholm *tunna*, or *rikstunna*, equalled 156 litres):

	tunnor
Rye	62,840
Malt	24,350
Oats	10,110
Meal	720
Wheat	150

To this must be added butter, pork, salt and dried meat in considerable quantities. It should, however, be noted that the import of supplies in 1685 was exceptional, on account of the bad harvest in central Sweden. The value of these imports amounted to 470,000 silver *daler* or, expressed in a currency of constant value, 235,000 *riksdaler*. And this did not include the province of Kexholm, whose export surplus is probably concealed in the export figures for Viborg, which amounted in value to 35,000 *riksdaler* and of which perhaps one-third, or roughly 10,000 *riksdaler*, may be presumed to have gone to Stockholm. This means that if we also include imports from Pomerania and Wismar, Stockholm in 1685 imported something like 300,000 *riksdaler* worth of commodities, mainly foodstuffs. Even so, this omits supplies from Norrland and the rest of Finland, since they were not subject to customs. It would appear therefore that Stockholm attracted to itself, from various parts of the empire, foodstuffs to a value of at least half a million *riksdaler*. Such proportion of this import as was not consumed by Stockholm's growing population passed through middlemen to areas of deficiency in Sweden proper, or was exported abroad. When Swedish harvests failed, the government intervened to prohibit grain exports from the Baltic territories to foreign countries. The Baltic provinces were indeed literally Sweden's granary during the Age of Greatness, as Arnold Soom has pointed out.[6] One of the few favourable articles in the peace of Nystad in 1721 was that Russia pledged herself to permit Sweden to import annually from Livonia and Estonia, free of duty, grain to the value of 50,000 roubles.

Such commodities as were imported into Sweden were on account either of the crown, the high aristocracy or the great merchants. The figures we have been considering are for the year 1685 – that is, for a date five years after the counties and baronies had been resumed to the crown at the *reduktion*. It is therefore hardly possible to form any idea of how great was the flow of goods and capital which before the *reduktion* passed through the hands of the stewards in the great palaces which the nobility built for themselves in Stockholm and its new suburbs, or in the high brick houses of the merchant aristocracy which faced the quays at Skeppsbron.

(vi)

During the long period between 1680 and 1697, when Sweden contrived to preserve her neutrality, her mercantile marine expanded vigorously. The volume of trade was growing, and native shipping increased to take its share in the increase of imports and exports. From traffic between the ports of Sweden and Finland proper all foreign vessels were excluded; and the country's shipping resources were reinforced by the incorporation of the merchantmen of the former Danish provinces. Most of the country's high-seas shipping was, however, concentrated in Stockholm. In 1695 the great Stockholm shipowners had 75 vessels of over 100 *läster*, to a total of 13,600 *läster* in all (one *läst* is equivalent to about 2½ tons); Ystad had only one, and Hälsingborg only three, which carried freight to southern Europe. Second to Stockholm came Göteborg, whose merchants in 1695 owned ten ships of over 100 *läster* (or 1,510 *läster* in all). The towns of Finland confined themselves to a passive trade: in 1695 only Viborg possessed ships of more than 100 *läster*; and even the great city of Riga in that year had only a dozen or so vessels trading to Spain. On the other hand there were plenty of small craft in certain regions. So for instance in Osterbotten; so along the south coast of the Gulf of Finland, where a parish such as Björkö (just outside Viborg) had some dozens of coasters, and the ironworks at Nyland and the great noble estates had their own barks trading to Stockholm; so again the small towns and landing-places on the Swedish west coast, from Kristianstad to Strömstad; and the Mälar area, where the high aristocracy used small craft to move victuals from their country houses to their palaces in Stockholm. Metals also formed an important element in the Mälar traffic. Wismar and Stralsund were real centres for transport vessels and passenger yachts, maintaining a traffic between Germany and the harbours of southern Sweden. Bremen–Verden's importance from the point of view of commerce was reduced by the fact that the town

of Bremen itself lay outside Swedish control; but Stade had nevertheless a dozen or so ships of middling tonnage, big enough at least to
trade with other harbours on the North Sea.

One aspect of Sweden's war economy which has hitherto received
insufficient investigation is the connection between sea traffic and her
great-power status. Its significance appears on several levels. In the
first place it was sea traffic that bound the various parts of the realm
together and linked it with western and southern Europe, including
England and Scotland. The route from Stockholm to Nyen (site of the
present Leningrad) or to Narva provided the line of contact with
eastern Europe. Danzig, the leading emporium of the Baltic, was
accessible from Sweden only by sea. In the existing state of traffic
techniques, transport by sea was in summer-time the cheapest method
of moving goods. In winter most of the Baltic was frozen over; and
then only southern Sweden could maintain contact with continental
Europe and Sweden's bastions in north Germany, Pomerania and
Wismar. This had its implications for naval strategy. When in 1680
Charles XI shifted the base of Sweden's battle fleet from Stockholm to
his new foundation of Karlskrona, in the southern province of Blekinge,
he thereby made it possible for his navy to get to sea early in the year,
and keep the seas until far into the autumn. During the war with Denmark from 1674 to 1676 Sweden had seen the nucleus of her high seas
fleet virtually destroyed; but by 1697 she had 37 ships of the line and
9 frigates and smaller craft, with crews totalling 11,700 seamen and
1,800 soldiers, in addition to officers and dockyard staffs. This meant
that the Swedish fleet, when reinforced by armed merchantmen and
other vessels trading in the North Sea or the Baltic, took fourth place
after the navies of England, Holland and France. It was no wonder if
kings of Denmark, in the struggles that lay ahead, preferred to keep
themselves snug in their fortress in Copenhagen, rather than emulate
their predecessor Christian IV by stationing themselves by the main-
mast of the ship that flew their admiral's flag. The fleet of 1643, with
Stockholm as its base, had in contrast numbered only 4 ships of the
line (royal ships), 11 ships roughly corresponding with the frigates of
a later day, 30 vessels of lesser tonnage and 150 transports.

When the Great Northern War broke out in 1700, the entire resources of the Baltic in small craft were mobilised: without them the
Swedish armies could never have been moved swiftly from one theatre
of war to another. Thus the vast extent of the Swedish empire,
economically and geographically, implied no anomaly in an age when

sea transport by small vessels, or horse-drawn traffic over frozen seas, lakes and marshes, offered a more serviceable form of communication than could be provided by wheeled traffic over execrable roads.

(vii)

Despite all her attempts to present a splendid appearance to the world, Sweden was during her Age of Greatness a poor country, with her exiguous population, her diminishing mineral resources (except of course for iron) and her costly ventures into German politics. She could not easily support the expensive aristocratic style of living of her upper social strata, or the grandiose splendours of her court. And hence when she was free to choose between a war or a peace economy it was not difficult to choose the former. For a war economy worked to the advantage of the ruling classes, and not only the generals, but also those – the regents, the high aristocracy – who above all found their advantage in an active foreign policy. This depended on the fact that Sweden waged her wars not with her own armies or at her own expense, but (at least in part) with German mercenaries paid by French subsidies. The gap in the war budget between the amount received in subventions from abroad, and available resources at home, was filled by the alienation of revenues in return for immediate cash aid, a process which the ruling élite pushed so far that the budgetary situation became chaotic. For who was it that really controlled the machinery of government? Certainly not the crown. Gustavus Adolphus fell at Lützen in 1632. His daughter Christina attained her majority in 1644, but abdicated in 1654. Charles X died in 1660. Charles XI officially came of age and assumed the government in 1672, but in reality not until some years later. He died in 1697. The list of names of members of the council of state is to a very large extent also a list of the men to whom the royal revenues had been alienated, either by way of hypothecation, or exchange, or sale. For almost half the period from 1632 to 1697, indeed, the country was governed by regents and by their supporters and opponents.

Who were these people? What was their background, what did they stand for? Were they Swedes or foreigners? Before 1675 they are to be found in the narrow circle of aristocrats who provided the members of the council of state. At a lower level, they are the host of those involved in the war economy in one way or another, men of middling station in society, lesser nobles, army officers, higher or lower officials of the chancery or the exchequer, military entrepreneurs. The visible sign of membership of this group was a patent of nobility: outside the symbolic ring-fence constituted by membership of the peerage stood only the bishops and a handful of educated persons, whose sons as a rule could expect to be ennobled too. The nobility and the bureaucracy constituted the thin upper crust, the 'bishops' on the chess-board, who with the help of the 'knights' – the cavalry, the garrison troops in the fortresses, the sailors in the 'floating bulwarks' of the navy – sustained the burden of great-power status. To push the comparison further, we may say that the peasantry were the pawns who, as in chess, formed the country's first line of defence. And, as in chess, the rules permitted a pawn which succeeded in reaching the other side of the board to be converted into any other piece – except a king. It is an image which reflects the vigorous social mobility which was characteristic of seventeenth-century Sweden, where peasants' sons became bishops, majors and senior civil servants. In contemporary Europe, where the peasantry had neither seat nor voice in such parliamentary institutions as existed, it was a situation which probably had no parallel.

At the time of Gustavus Adolphus's death (1632), the elements in the population which formed the key groups in Swedish society may be summarised roughly as follows:

	Nobility, civil servants, clergy with their households	Native soldiers and sailors
Sweden proper	15,000	30,000
Finland	5,000	18,000
Totals	20,000	48,000

At the close of the period, in 1697, the country was at peace. The population had grown, the bureaucracy had expanded, the number of parishes, and with them the number of clergy, had increased. The army had become mainly a native army. The fleet, Hans Wachtmeister's creation, was now stationed at its new base at Karlskrona. Fortresses were more numerous, their garrisons greater. In the intervening years the Scandinavian portion of the empire had been extended by the incorporation of Danish and Norwegian provinces whose population, after half a century of Swedish rule, was beginning to feel loyalty towards its new fatherland. A rough estimate of the same population groups at the close of the reign of Charles XI (1697) gives the following results:

	Nobility, civil servants, clergy with their households	Native soldiers and sailors
Sweden proper	40,000	45,000
Finland	10,000	15,000
Totals	50,000	55,000

The military forces drawn from Sweden and Finland had a vital tactical importance even during periods where the main theatre of war lay far away in southern Germany and the Emperor's hereditary dominions. The garrisons in Livonia and Pomerania formed the strategic reserve which was called upon during the Thirty Years War, during Charles X's Polish and Danish wars, and finally during Charles XI's humiliating war with Brandenburg. The losses of these national units were disproportionately great. Garrison service in the crowded 'quarters' or barracks in the fortress towns of the Baltic, and the fact that native troops were thrown in at the most dangerous crises in the field, or in defence of fortified positions, produced losses which are difficult to estimate. Military historians such as Julius Mankell do indeed tell us how many soldiers were recruited and how many of them reached their units; but we look in vain for figures which will tell us how many of them came back. The fortunes of the great are remembered; the fate of the little man is easily forgotten.

(viii)

Despite the opposition – which at times became explicit – of the un-privileged Estates, it was in the first instance the nobility (or those of them who had Swedish patents of nobility) who stood for the might, honour and glory of their country. An officer who reached the rank of major could count on ennoblement; every colonel was in fact ennobled. And the same process applied to the corps of civil servants. Entrepreneurs, financiers, merchant magnates, entered almost automatically into the peerage. But it is worth while to take a closer look at the 'titled' nobility – those, that is, who were counts or barons; the men who stood nearest the throne, and who during the long regencies were responsible for the foreign and economic policy of the country.

The titled nobility had been created by Eric XIV (1560–8), on the occasion of his coronation; but until Christina's reign only a very few noble families had been elevated in this way above the level of their peers. The second class of the nobility – those descended from former members of the council of state [7] – played only a subordinate part, economically, politically and socially, in the country's affairs: on one side of them stood the titled nobility, the counts and barons, divided among themselves into family coteries or political cliques; on the other, the general mass of the nobility, with its various divisions depending upon wealth, family alliances or regional interests. Among the high nobility were families whose ancestry may well have stretched far back into the Middle Ages, but which had first emerged into prominence under the Vasa kings and had profited from the wars in the eastern Baltic or established their fortunes on the battlefields of central Europe. As the apparatus of government became more bureaucratised – a process in which the stages are marked by the administrative methods of Gustavus Vasa and his sons, the Form of Government of 1634, and the formalism of Charles XI's absolute régime – the permanent civil servants too moved to the top of the social ladder. Sweden's involvement in the great game of European politics opened the way to diplomatic talents, as the exigencies of war finance did for economists, and the new metallurgical industries for expert technicians; while the territorial expansion of the empire offered a career to men capable of governing a duchy, leading an expedition and commanding a fleet.

Table 6 shows the geographical origin of the high nobility.

TABLE 6: PLACES OF ORIGIN OF TITLED NOBILITY
INTRODUCED INTO THE RIDDARHUS 1560–1697[8]

			Counts						
	Sweden	Fin-land	Baltic pro-vinces	Ger-many	France	Scot-land	Eng-land	Nether-lands	Total
Eric XIV (1560–8)	I								I
John III (1568–92)	I								I
Charles IX (1600–12)									–
Gustavus Adolphus (1612–32)					I				I
Regency (1632–44)	I			I					2
Christina (1644–54)	8	2	2	3		I		I	17
Charles X (1654–60)									–
Regency (1660–72)	2								2
Charles XI (1672–97)	10	2	5	4		I			22
	23	4	7	8	I	2	–	I	46
	27								

TABLE 6: PLACES OF ORIGIN—*continued*

	Sweden	Fin-land	Baltic pro-vinces	Barons Ger-many	France	Scot-land	Eng-land	Nether-lands	Total
Eric XIV	1	1							2
John III	1				1				2
Charles IX	1								1
Gustavus Adolphus	2			1		1			4
Regency (1632–44)									–
Christina	20	5	13	5		1	2	1	47
Charles X									–
Regency (1660–72)	3		3	1		1		2	10
Charles XI	17		13	13			1	1	45
	45 6		29	20	1	3	3	4	111
	51								

Until Christina's time, as will be seen, the native element is conspicuous. And in spite of all that had been said to the contrary, it was predominantly the old noble families of Sweden and Finland to whom Christina herself gave titles: the foreigners were fewer in number, but they attracted a disproportionate amount of attention. It was clearly not only personal preference which produced this state of affairs. Despite her German mother and grandmother, Christina was herself a member of a Swedish noble family which in the later Middle Ages had come to be recognised as one of the leading families in the kingdom. A large part of the old nobility was related to her, more or less closely. It was natural for a monarch confronted with a Europe dominated by aristocracies to give counties and baronies to her connections, even though in many cases politics might play a part. In Christina's time the court in Stockholm felt the need for a titled aristocracy capable of meeting the social demands implicit in Sweden's rising international status.

But Christina also raised into the ranks of the high nobility a large number (29) of foreigners, mainly German-Balts; and her example was followed, paradoxically enough, by Charles XI, who gave patents of nobility (9 counts, 26 barons) to Balts or Germans who enjoyed his confidence. They were men whose mother-tongue was German. Against this, there were only 12 counts and 17 barons from Sweden and Finland. Nevertheless the counsellors with whom he preferred to work were members of the high nobility, zealots for the *reduktion*; men

from Finland – such as Creutz, Fleming or Wrede; or men from
central Sweden whose families had only recently risen in the social
scale, as the following list makes clear:

Counts	Social position of father
1687 Erik Lindschöld	Blacksmith and town
Court chancellor, marshal of	councillor in Skänninge
Estate of Nobility	
1693 Erik Dahlberg	Provincial treasurer in
Field-marshal, governor-general	Uppsala
of Livonia and Estonia	
1693 Lars Wallenstedt	Chaplain to the court,
Member of king's council, one of	bishop of Strängnäs
regents for Charles XII	

Barons	
1687 Olof Thegner	Peasant in parish of Vist
Member of commission of enquiry	
into regents for Charles XI,	
lord-lieutenant of Uppland	
1687 Erik Lovisin	Assessor in Supreme
Secretary in Great Commission,	Court, Stockholm
lord-lieutenant of Östergötland	
1687 Johan Lejonberg	Town councillor in
Court chancellor, diplomat	Stockholm
1691 Lars Eldstierna	Burgher of Norrköping
Member of *Reduktion* College,	
lord-lieutenant of Östergötland	
1692 Anders Lindhielm	Secretary in Exchequer
Member of *Reduktion* commission,	College
lord-lieutenant of Viborg	
1692 Mårten Lindhielm	(Younger brother of
Colonel of the Nobility's cavalry	preceding)
regiment in Sweden and Finland,	
lord-lieutenant of Jönköping	
1694 Johan Bergenhielm	Burgomaster of Uppsala
Court chancellor, diplomat	
1697 Nils Lillieroth	Parish priest of Vifolka
Court chancellor, diplomat	

Unlike his brother-in-law Christian V of Denmark, Charles XI did not
germanise the bureaucracy or the army; and his court, unlike that of
Denmark, never became germanised either. He wrote his diaries (as
indeed Christian V did too) in his native tongue, laconic and unadorned.
And with this in mind we can understand how it was that in his time

positions of importance fell to men who came directly from a bourgeois or peasant background, or had grown up in the class of subordinate officials in Stockholm or the provinces.

Social mobility was rapid at a time when the empire was expanding, or in periods of transition from aristocratic rule (as under the regencies) to absolutism; and it was then that the new men came to the front. Of III barons created in this period, almost half (48) were the founders of their families and had begun life as commoners. And here too the reign of Charles XI – in part, of course, because of its length – is conspicuous: that no fewer than 36 of the 67 new counts and barons he created fell into this category implies a clear change of system in comparison with the practice under Queen Christina.

This high nobility, whether of ancient or more recent origin, did not only give prestige to a parvenu great power. For it fell to them, sometimes alone, sometimes as the props of the monarchy, to bear or to share the responsibility for governing the country, in peace as in war.

II. THE PROBLEMS OF A PERMANENT WAR ECONOMY

(i)

The Danish and Polish wars at the beginning of the seventeenth century, and still more the campaigns of Gustavus Adolphus in Prussia and Germany, necessitated a mobilisation of the financial resources of the country. The basic element in the fiscal system was provided by the ancient taxes on land, later known as the 'ordinary revenue'; but these were supplemented, on lines which were now long established, by temporary aids – for royal marriages, equipment of the armed forces, or the payment of war indemnities in order to recover fortresses of strategic importance such as Alvsborg, which twice had to be redeemed in this way – once under John III, once under Gustavus Adolphus. But as a state of war became more or less permanent, certain additional taxes tended to become regularised; they formed the so-called 'extraordinary revenues'. Among this new type of taxes was for instance a poll-tax (*mantalspengar*) which was assessed not upon the land but per capita. It affected the whole labouring population, men and women, between the ages of fifteen and sixty, with the exception of paupers, vagabonds and disabled persons, together with certain privileged groups such as the citizens of Stockholm, the nobility, their servants, the soldiery, and the population in the Baltic and German provinces, who were not represented in the *riksdag*.

After 1623, when the Dutchman Abraham Cabiljau drew up the first national balance-sheet, using double-entry book-keeping, it is possible with some adjustments to arrive at something approaching a national statement of accounts in the modern sense of the expression. With the 1620s the estimates (either general or particular) which then began to be prepared provide us with the first approaches to something like a modern budget. The administrative reforms of the 1630s had far-reaching effects, and facilitated national and provincial accounting. In the martial reign of Charles X it was deemed inexpedient to draw up any national balance-sheet; but thereafter the practice was resumed, and the latter portion of the reign of Charles XI entailed a revision of budgetary procedure (see below, pp. 97–9). The council of state and the Exchequer College were now excluded from the preparation of the budget; and the king's administration operated not on one single estimate for the country as a whole, but on separate estimates for each of the main regions of the empire, and for particular services such as the navy. As L. M. Bååth rightly observes of the estimates after 1680:

> The national estimate did not include all the normal revenues, since there were other incomes, not included in it, in distinct funds, drawn mainly from surpluses and special grants. These moneys were not under the control of the Estimates Office (*Statskontoret*), nor did they appear in the national audit. Their use, especially for purposes of defence, was considered to demand secrecy. In the period 1686–97 they amounted to about 10 million silver *daler* [5 million *riksdaler*], or twice as much as the normal ordinary budget. These moneys were paid into the so called reserve accounts, of which one was directly under the king's immediate supervision, since the money was kept in the vaults of Stockholm castle, while others were scattered about in various castles and fortresses in the custody of lords-lieutenant, commanders and provincial receivers of revenue.[9]

(ii)

Charles XI and his collaborators can scarcely have been naïve enough to rely blindly upon the expectation that their military and financial organisations would be immune to disturbance. The work of Wacht-meister in building up the fleet, Dahlberg's efforts as governor-general of Livonia to maintain and strengthen the Baltic fortresses, were carried out with an eye to the possibility of a 'rupture' which might endanger the navy and Sweden's eastern frontiers. All the secret estimates for the admiralty, and the numerous special estimates for fortifications, were drawn up, with the king's approval, with such a contingency in mind. The course of the war after Charles XI's death, when Stockholm was threatened with a Russian invasion, provides the justification for the provision in those estimates for defensive works which should surround the capital with a girdle of fortifications.

Lastly, as a final financial measure undertaken in the closing years of Charles XI's reign, came the establishment of a reserve of treasure. Already in 1693 it was suggested that such a reserve be established, and the possibilities for creating it were under discussion. From such accounts as have been preserved, however, it would seem that it was not until 1695, in consequence of an order issued in that year, that accumulation began in a vault of Stockholm castle called 'The Elephant'.[10] This hoard of silver attained its maximum size in 1696, when it is calculated to have amounted to 20 metric tons. The accounts for it for the years 1695–9 are as follows (in *riksdaler*):[11]

	Deposited	Withdrawn
1695	400,000	–
1696	100,000	–
1697	–	–
1698	50,000	417,500
1699	–	132,500
	550,000	550,000

It is worth noting, in the first place, that the amount deposited in 1695 corresponds exactly with the amount derived from French subsidies in those years in the 1630s in which such subsidies were paid. The absence of deposits after 1696 may be connected with the great harvest failures and famines of 1696–7. The deposit and withdrawals of 1698 and 1699 are duly signed 'Carolus', as required by the regulation; but by now it was no longer Charles XI. The king's funeral, Charles XII's coronation, a royal wedding (Charles's sister Hedvig Sofia married the duke of Holstein-Gottorp), and the preparations for war resulted in the fact that when hostilities broke out in 1700 the reserve of silver in Stockholm castle had already been consumed.

Thus Charles XI's attempts in his closing years to accumulate a hoard of silver to meet the needs of the central administration may be said to have ended in failure. That such a hoard could be created at all was an aspect of the budgetary surpluses of the 1690s. The financial allocations for that decade show that most of the income which went directly into the king's pocket came from customs dues in Stockholm – the safest, most substantial and most readily accessible source of cash revenue. In 1690, for instance, some 250,000 *riksdaler* of customs dues (which were paid in silver) was assigned to the crown's personal expenses. It was this increasing source of revenue which made it possible, after the household expenses of the court had been paid, to build up a standing reserve of precious metals under the king's supervision. Its modest dimensions reflect a foreign trade which even yet was relatively small. But the real basis for this highly personal policy of economy and insurance was the export trade from Stockholm in iron and tar.

(iii)

If revenues which did not appear in the estimates could thus be hoarded up in various ways (especially towards the close of the period), that does not preclude us from making a comparison of national revenues and national expenditures for various years and in different historical situations. For this purpose we have chosen the years 1633 and 1677 – both years of crucial importance, politically and economically, for Sweden's international position. The first of them is the financial year that followed Gustavus Adolphus's death, when Sweden's position in central Europe was in jeopardy. The second was a year of crisis in that it brought war to the former Danish provinces, and a threat to central Sweden which was beaten off only with difficulty. Bremen and Verden, Pomerania and Wismar, were in the hands of the country's enemies. Sweden's faithful satellite, the duke of Holstein-Gottorp, had been eliminated from the contest, and his duchy was occupied by the Danes. It is against this background that we must see the two accounting years we have selected.

TABLE 7: STATE INCOME AND EXPENDITURE 1633 AND 1677
(in *riksdaler*)[12a]

Income	1633	1677
Sweden and Finland		
'Ordinary' revenue	1,229,920	925,759
'Extraordinary' revenue	573,872	546,006
Customs and excise	22,040	808,796
Loans	59,384	770,437
Grants and contributions		165,607
Revenues from Queen Christina's lands		77,500
French subsidies	400,000[12b]	750,000
Other income		517,226

TABLE 7 : STATE INCOME AND EXPENDITURE—*continued*

Estonia, Livonia, Ingria		
Ship tolls and customs	125,299	169,365
Other income	238,937	385,706
Pomerania		
Ships tolls and customs		6,343
Other income		196,620
Prussian ship tolls	614,000[12c]	
	————	————
Total	3,263,452	5,319,365

Expenditure

Sweden and Finland		
Queen Christina's allowance		83,144
Court expenses	15,753	240,175
Salaries of council of state	55,752	18,111
Judicial salaries	3,059	29,715
Chancery and foreign affairs	5,233	83,178
Exchequer and financial administration	1,351	4,988
Army and army administration	358,524	502,772
Navy and naval administration	84,202	383,257
Local government	96,769	64,812
War expenses		861,967
Debts paid	107,123	1,117,789
Other expenses	350,882	422,741
Estonia, Livonia, Ingria	304,462	204,265
Bremen–Verden		65
	————	————
	1,473,120	4,089,553
Deductions from revenue	753,789	1,158,863
	————	————
Total expenditure	2,226,909	5,248,416
Total income	3,263,452	5,319,365
	————	————
Surplus	1,036,543	70,949

Peace came in 1648, and again (after the last fragments of the German possessions had been lost) in 1679. The years 1633 and 1677 have been chosen deliberately as providing cross-sections which on the one hand reveal the insecurity of Sweden's position in Germany, and on the other illustrate the economic pressures on the heartlands of the empire and the Baltic provinces. A Russian attack against the latter in the 1670s would have been fatal. But the death of Alexis, the still primitive character of Russian diplomacy, the disturbed state of Russian politics, and the Turkish danger, combined, as Klaus Zernack has shown,[13] to restrain Moscow from action.

The importance of the Baltic provinces' contributions to the war-chest emerges clearly both in 1633 and 1677. Income from indirect taxation is indeed more conspicuous in 1677 than in 1633, but even in 1633 it is apparent that the Baltic ship tolls and customs provided a large proportion of this type of finance. The fiscal policy of Axel Oxenstierna had preferred customs revenues to the older form of taxation in kind, though this latter, in contrast to the methods which had prevailed under the earlier Vasas, was already in process of being converted from goods to cash; and this made possible a more flexible type of finance, even though taxes in grain and other commodities continued to be collected and magazined throughout the whole period: in years of bad harvest, or when armies were being mobilised, such a procedure was indispensably necessary. The fact that the 'ordinary' revenue was less in 1677 than in 1633 is of course a reflection of the increased alienation of crown lands and revenues.

Of cardinal importance in 1633 were the Prussian ship tolls and the French subsidies: it was these which produced the apparently favourable balance. Neither appears in the national statement of accounts; and it is plain that they were applied to meet war expenses. In 1677, on the other hand, the accounts do include the item 'French subsidies': without them, indeed, they would have shown a considerable deficit.

If we turn now to expenditure, one striking feature in 1677 is the increased share claimed by court expenses. The expansion of the diplomatic service also necessitated larger allocations. The military sector appears greatly inflated, but we have to remember that the Thirty Years War, in contrast to the defensive war of the 1670s, was waged in distant lands and to some extent paid for itself. We still lack a full elucidation of how the Thirty Years War was financed, but for certain periods at least we can get some idea of what happened. A study carried out by the Military History Section of the Swedish Defence Staff shows that only between 3 and 5 per cent of the disbursements from the exchequer in 1646 went directly to pay for the war in Germany.[14] On the other hand the same analysis indicates that almost 35 per cent of the revenues of the state in that year were spent on military requirements, or on defence.

In this connection one item stands out, though it is difficult to put a precise figure upon it, or bring its importance to the economy into sharp focus. In 1646, besides provision for maintaining the navy and keeping garrisons up to strength, 6,630 men were armed and equipped for transport to the theatre of war in southern Germany. Their transport entailed the supply of provisions, fodder, equipment in the form of cloth, arms, standards and banners, and a small armada of 73 ships. The conscripts were paid wages; but the accounts have nothing to say as to the value of the labour resources which were thus withdrawn from the country. The high rate of wastage in manpower is well attested: in siege operations and on the battlefield losses could be so high that towards the end of the war there was a general tendency towards a tactic of manoeuvre, as a means of safeguarding the armies against losses. The contingent which crossed the Baltic in 1646 played an active part in the closing phases of the war. When it reached the scene of operations, it was able, on the whole, to live off the country: it was here that the future Charles X, as generalissimo of the Swedish armies, learned the tactic of surprising a superior enemy on his own territory by rapid marches and unexpected diversions; and it was here too that he learned to emulate his uncle Gustavus Adolphus's methods of maintaining his armies at the enemy's expense.

(iv)

The army commissaries were not less important than the generals: indeed the most enterprising and unscrupulous of them might act in both capacities at once. After the disaster at Nördlingen in 1634 Erik Andersson,[15] the army commissary for the Lower Saxon Circle, put himself at the head of the storm-columns which vainly attempted to capture Minden. Another typical case was that of Hans Christopher von Königsmarck, who led the attack upon Prague in 1648 – the last great battle of the Thirty Years War – and at his death left a fortune of more than 1 million *riksdaler*. The nature of his assets at his death is not without interest.

Credit	riksdaler
Cash	183,478
Capital out at loan	1,140,201
Landed property	406,100
Total	1,729,779
Less outstanding debts	114,000
Balance	1,615,779

The capital on loan consisted for the most part of sums due from the crown, and the landed property of fiefs in Bremen and Verden.[16] But the foundation of Königsmarck's great fortune is above all to be sought in rewards of various kinds (large profits as a commander, military entrepreneur and administrator) and in the sums which accrued from holding towns to ransom. All this makes it plain that when it came to making war and paying for it, Sweden at the height of her power used methods which did not differ from those employed by her opponents. Fritz Redlich's study of the military entrepreneurs makes no great use of Swedish material, but it does show that the phenomenon made good its footing in the Swedish armies.[17] A military élite was emerging, with rising claims to wealth and influence.

III. THE CONCENTRATION OF RESOURCES IN THE HANDS OF THE RULING ÉLITE AND THE GROWING INDEBTEDNESS OF THE STATE

(i)

The élite which participated in the creation of the Swedish empire did not offer its services for nothing. The leading men in the administration, the commanders on sea and land, the governors-general and lords-lieutenant, the expert diplomats or financiers, all were of course highly paid servants of the state. Before 1680 members of the council of state had moreover, by way of 'supplements' to their salaries, incomes arising from fines in provincial or county courts. As the leading personages in one of the great powers, they had an obligation to add lustre to its position and represent it with appropriate splendour. They shaped their habits of life and measured their requirements by the standards of central Europe. When the great chancellor Axel Oxenstierna made his peregrination at the close of the previous century, he had been accompanied by a handful of followers, and had even moved from one European university to another on foot. His son Johan, proceeding in his great carriage with a numerous escort, was treated wherever he went as a prince.

In the middle of the century – the years after the peace of Westphalia – the council aristocracy formed a closely interwoven group, whose intimate family connections and relationship to the royal family gave them authority, prestige and community of interest. The conferment of the title of count or baron in the majority of cases brought with it territorial fiefs in the form of counties and baronies. Finland, where tax- and crown-farms predominated, the provinces of Kexholm and Ingria which constituted a conquered region with no provincial nobility of its own, and Estonia and Livonia where the lands of the Knights of the Sword and the episcopate had fallen into the hands of the crown, were the areas where compact baronies of this kind could most readily be created. And at the other end of the scale from the great fiefs of the high aristocracy were fiefs consisting of a single farm which provided sustenance for the relics of lieutenants whose husbands had perished in the wars, or parsons' widows left with large families.

There is unfortunately no detailed study based on treasury accounts of the extent and distribution of such fiefs in Sweden proper. For Finland, Carl von Bonsdorff's investigation (1889) into alienation of crown lands at the time of Christina's abdication, and Mauno Jokipii's study (1956–60) of counties and baronies, gives us a more homogeneous and complete picture than for any other part of the realm. Both these specialists in the 'quasi-feudalism' which grew up in the shadow of Sweden's greatness based their researches on primary material and were not content with the extracts which were compiled by contemporaries and of which the objectivity must remain an open question. Bonsdorff's lists, compiled parish by parish, make it clear that it was in Aland, in parts of Nyland, Tavastland and Karelia, and above all in Savolaks, that the fief system was least successful in obtaining a foothold: this was why Aland could provide sailors for the navy, and eastern Finland light cavalry for the army (cf. above, pp. 63–4).[18]

Yet about the year 1654 there were in Sweden twenty-two counties and baronies, while in Finland and the province of Kexholm there were twenty-four; and it is clear that for the recipient of royal donations Finland and the province of Kexholm constituted the Promised Land.

These donations were located along the shores of the Gulf of Bothnia and Lake Ladoga; and their geographical situation was connected with the fact that it offered good transport facilities to Stockholm, or provided access to Europe's biggest lake, Ladoga, and thence by way of the Neva to the eastern end of the Gulf of Finland, where the little town and fortress of Nyen (the present Leningrad) afforded facilities for the export of the produce of the great estates of the high council nobility. The donations of Korpo (owned by the Bielkes), Kimito (Oxenstierna) and Raseborg (Leijonhufvud) all lay on the coast of the Gulf of Finland, and all were centres of large-scale fisheries and the coasting trade. Among the most unfavourably situated of these Finnish baronies were those of Elimä and Libelitz, owned respectively by the Wredes and the Flemings; and one wonders whether this has anything to do with the fact that their owners were among the leading champions of the *reduktion*.

It was only at the *reduktion* Diets of 1680 and 1682 that these alienations of crown lands – first of all the great donations, later the smaller ones – were resumed into the king's hands. The situation in Finland, as it was in the years 1653–4, has been analysed as follows: *

	mantal
Land anciently noble	1,278
Counties and baronies	3,735
Unconditional donations	1,198
Conditional donations	6,110
Land given in noble tenure for life or at pleasure	150
Crown lands sold	1,778
Crowns lands exchanged	74
Deductions from royal revenues, in *mantal*	14,323
Total *mantal* in Finland	24,539

Thus in round figures three-fifths of the *mantal* (and hence of the 'ordinary revenue', for which the *mantal* formed the unit) were in hands other than the crown's. This fiscal blood-letting was the more alarming from the point of view of the state's finances because large categories of the peasantry situated on the lands of nobles and donation-holders enjoyed special advantages in taxation and the provision of recruits. By Eli Heckscher's calculation, some two-thirds of the *mantal* in Sweden and Finland at this period were to a greater or lesser extent exempt from taxation.[19]

The *reduktion* cannot be understood without some consideration of the events that led up to it. Already in the 1640s attacks upon the great alienations were being made at meetings of the *riksdag* – mainly from the lower civil servants, the burghers, the clergy and the peasants' representatives at the Diet. But the storm of 1650 was weathered; and the partial *reduktion* of Charles X (which was never pushed home) gave a breathing-space. During the regency of Charles XI the financial crisis became permanent. At the time of Charles X's death the state was indebted to an amount of about 5 million *riksdaler*, that is, to about as much as its gross anual revenue. By 1682 the debt is said to have risen to 7·5 million *riksdaler*.

The decision to carry through a *reduktion* must be seen against this background. One important factor, however, was that the alienated revenues of the crown were collected into the hands not only of a small

* The figures are expressed in whole *mantal*, i.e. in official units corresponding to the (notional) fiscal farm; but since farms were divided and not assessed on a uniform basis, they give no indication of the real number of units of cultivation.

group of aristocratic clans, but also of a small group of families within those clans. In terms of hard cash, as Heckscher has shown, some twenty families disposed of capital assets which had been transferred from the crown in one form or another to a value of over 5 million *riksdaler*.[20] At their head, if Heckscher's calculations are correct, stood the Oxenstiernas, De la Gardies, Brahes, Banérs, Horns, Skyttes, Vasaborgs – most of them related to the royal house, as were also the Leijonhufvuds, Stenbocks, Totts and Gyllenhielms. A special position was occupied by the commanders in the field – Wrangel, Wittenberg, Torstensson – and the financiers such as De Geer, Leijonsköld and Cronstierna, whose character as businessmen appears clearly from the large number of royal revenues which they had acquired as mortgages.

Since Charles X during his short reign was much less disposed to make grants of this sort (and this was true too of the ensuing regency), Heckscher's calculation shows the culmination of the policy of alienation. In Finland, for instance, by the extinction of a family's male line, by exchanges, or by the operation of Charles X's partial *reduktion*, no fewer than fourteen counties and baronies vanished from the map between 1674 and 1679, leaving only thirteen (including those in the province of Kexholm) to be dealt with by the great *reduktion* of Charles XI. In the province of Kexholm, and in Ingria, the effect of that *reduktion* was to transform them into estates leased from the crown whose rent was collected by powerful crown tenants. Estonia and Livonia did not begin to be seriously included in the plans for a *reduktion* until the 1690s. Nevertheless the process continued, side by side with the punitive measures against the former regents, for the whole of the later portion of Charles XI's reign: not until the outbreak of war in 1700 did it come to a halt.

By that time the greater part of the crown's alienated revenues had been resumed, and thereby its main objective – the stabilisation of the finances – attained, at least for the moment. But on the other hand the new bureaucratic nobility which had carried through the *reduktion* and the attack upon the regents had itself contrived to create a new complex of *latifundia*, whose last remaining traces may still be seen, despite all reforms of land tenure, not only in central Sweden but also in the former Danish provinces, and in southern Finland. Descendants of Barons Wachtmeister, Wrede and Creutz still possess, in the outer fringes of the former kingdom, huge estates which stand in marked contrast to the small-scale agriculture of the surrounding districts, or the urbanised communities which lie at their gates.

(ii)

Despite the *reduktion*, despite the harrying of the regents during Charles XI's minority, there still remained at the time of his death loans which were unpaid, as the king himself admitted. Nevertheless by the beginning of the 1690s the crown felt itself to be in a position to master the financial situation without the imposition of any taxes additional to the regular revenues: at the *riksdag* of 1693, the last of the reign, no aids were demanded. And this was something unusual for Swedish seventeenth-century Diets: as a rule, they functioned not only as a forum for important political decisions, but also as an instrument for exacting supplies. But in 1693 the speech from the throne was able to report that the finances were in a healthy condition. The budget was balanced, the army and fleet reorganised, trade and shipping were expanding, any deficits could be met out of ordinary revenue. F. F. Carlson – whose great work on the history of Sweden under the Palatine dynasty is a kind of Swedish analogue to Macaulay – summed up his view of the situation in the laconic judgement, 'The picture was brilliant'.[21]

Nevertheless the long-term economic prospects were not reassuring, either to contemporary critics or in the judgement of later historians. The stabilisation of the economy had been won at the price of a bureaucratic rigidity which would take its toll in the period of political strain and fresh economic demands which was to follow. The military reorganisation was still incomplete (but see below, Chapter 8). The boom in Swedish exports and shipping had been a bonus resulting from Sweden's neutrality. Stockholm had been increasingly given a specially favoured trading position by the government, and the export of the basic staples, iron and tar, had been deliberately concentrated in the capital. Copper, as we have seen, had lost the importance which during the earlier part of the century had made it the treasury's most reliable support. The minting of silver had indeed much increased in consequence of the favourable balance of trade; but it was no longer based on native production, but on the sums which the great customs in Stockholm and Göteborg, and the ship tolls in Riga and Narva, brought in from abroad. The increase in the volume and value of foreign trade depended much less upon native merchants than upon the English who came to buy iron in Stockholm, or the agents who bought masts in Riga, or traded at Narva in flax and hemp.

The national debt had indeed been cut down, but at high cost. By repudiating state loans of ancient date, by harsh proceedings against financial operators who had stood by the crown in difficult times (e.g. Börje Cronberg, the brothers Momma-Reenstierna, Joel Gripenhielm and others), the crown had diminished its chances of raising loans in the crisis period which lay ahead.[22] At the beginning of 1692 the crown still acknowledged indebtedness, partly in the form of forced loans or unpaid salaries to its servants, amounting to a figure of 1,375,000 *riksdaler*, and this excluded sums raised on mortgage. And there is nothing to show that these debts had been paid – at least, not entirely – before the *riksdag* of November 1693.

The acknowledged national debt at the beginning of 1693 was made up of 387 items. Something over a million *riksdaler* was due to persons and institutions who had come to the crown's assistance with sums of over 5,000 riksdaler apiece: [23]

Creditors	Amount (riksdaler)
2 private persons	500,000
19 private persons	250,000
18 large shipping concerns	215,000
5 towns, etc.	30,000
Total	995,000
10 small shipping concerns	30,000
333 smaller lenders	330,000
Grand total	1,355,000

The two large lenders were Etienne de Mollie, through whose hands the French subsidies passed, and the receiver of revenue at the Exchequer College, Jakob Sneckenberg. Among the other unlucky creditors are to be found senior state servants (some members of the council and provincial governors, assessors in the central offices of government, and diplomats, including the Swedish envoy in London, Johan Paulin Olivecrantz), together with big Stockholm merchants and English and Scottish iron exporters such as Thomas Cutler and William Smith. They even included the archbishop and the king's personal physician. Most of the shipping partnerships seem to have been located in Stockholm: Finland is represented by the *Charitas* of Abo, which had been lost in the crown's service during the war of 1674–6. Her owners had still received no compensation in 1693.[24] Among the small lenders appear a mass of civil servants in the central government, with such titles as assessor, secretary or notary.

The schedule indicates a notable attempt on the part of the crown to reach a settlement with creditors who in some cases had been waiting twenty years for what was due to them. In comparison with other absolute monarchies in the early modern period of European financial history the Swedish régime did take a rather different attitude to its creditors, whether native or foreign. But it did not help much to try to reach a settlement with the small lenders, when the big ones had been frightened off by repudiations, and the heavy-handedness of the *reduktion*. There was also the fact that the injections of foreign capital which had rescued Sweden in earlier crises of liquidity – the Prussian ship tolls, the German 'satisfaction' at the close of the Thirty Years War, the French subsidies down to 1679 – were no longer in view. It is possible to hold different opinions as to the economic importance of these items when it came to making war or (in the case of the 'satisfaction') peace. But it is not possible to exclude them from any description of Sweden's economic position during her Age of Greatness.

IV. PRUSSIAN SHIP TOLLS, FRENCH SUBSIDIES AND GERMAN 'SATISFACTION'

(i)

A European state such as seventeenth-century Sweden, with its peripheral geographical position and its limited human and natural resources, could play an active part in war and diplomacy only with the support of capital which its own economy was in no condition to mobilise. The military successes had to be used to provide the economic underpinning necessary to consolidate her gains and to open the way to more. An excellent example of this blend of military and economic tactics is provided by the Prussian ship tolls which were collected from 1628 to 1635.

As a consequence of the truce of Altmark, concluded between Poland and Sweden in 1629, Danzig, Brandenburg and Courland agreed to permit the Swedish authorities to levy a toll in the 'Prussian' harbours. Of these the most important was Danzig, the centre of the grain trade, the greatest port in the Baltic. In the years 1632–5 the yield of these licences was as follows (in *riksdaler*): [25]

1632	626,154
1633	662,632
1634	812,118
1635	676,755

Deducting the cost of collection, which remained constant at well under 10 per cent of the recorded proceeds, the Prussian licences brought in an annual sum which amounted to between a sixth and a fifth of the total recorded revenue of the country, and in the peak year 1634 even more. Even though a part of the proceeds was swallowed up in the expense of garrisons, fortifications and administration in occupied Prussia, the major portion was available for use in the German theatre of war, for repayment of war debts and for the needs of the central government. This last item – the fact that money was transmitted from Prussia to Sweden – is surprising, in view of the heavy cost of the German war effort. Unfortunately it is not possible, from the accounts which have survived, to trace how it was employed. The national accounts for 1633, for example, simply omit the revenue from the Prussian licences on the credit side, in contrast to the revenues from licences in the Baltic provinces and Pomerania. The administration of the Prussian licences was under the special supervision of Axel Oxenstierna; and the sums realised were probably applied to the fitting-out of new troops, the strengthening of the navy and the provision of transports. It is impossible to suppose that in the years of crisis after Gustavus Adolphus's death sums amounting to hundreds of thousands of *riksdaler* simply disappeared into the pockets of the regents. The Oxenstierna family may indeed have occupied a dominant position in the conduct of the war and the administration of the country, but the mere fact that Swedish auditing was by contemporary standards of high quality makes any such idea incredible.

When at the close of 1635 the Prussian licences had to be surrendered, this entailed a severe though not irreparable sacrifice to the neighbouring territories of Poland and Brandenburg. By the treaty of Stuhmsdorf (1635) Sweden abandoned her Prussian base area and the levying of ship tolls at the Prussian harbours and at Danzig, but in exchange obtained security for her possession of Livonia and the licences at Livonian ports, e.g. Riga. It is curious that the French mediator, d'Avaux, sympathised with the delegates of Holland and England on the question of the abolition of the Prussian licences; for while Holland and England were directly interested in the trade to Prussia, and indeed had much the largest share in commerce with the Prussian region and its Polish hinterland, France had no direct trading connections of her own to defend: the licences had mainly hit Dutch and English shipping. But as Swedish historians have pointed out, it happened that from the close of 1634 to the beginning of 1638 there was no political alliance between Sweden and France, a circumstance which depended upon the fact that in these years there were no objectives – political or economic – which were common to the two powers. And this meant that at Stuhmsdorf France gave Sweden neither economic nor political support. In 1632 and 1633 on the other hand, France had provided Sweden with subsidies, though not indeed to an amount which can be compared with the Prussian licences. After 1637 they were resumed, and this time became of more permanent importance: their effect upon Sweden's financial situation was indeed at times such as to make her virtually a French satellite – a situation which lasted until 1679.

(ii)

France was of course not the only state which financed Sweden's wars. But the small subsidies occasionally available from Holland, England, Spain and some German states were of quite subordinate importance. The French subsidies on the other hand – both in this century and the next – became a permanent feature, and one which all too easily dragged the country into campaigns which subserved French rather than Swedish interests. They compelled Sweden moreover to maintain, or if need be to raise, armies which became the direct instrument of French foreign policy in central and eastern Europe. In the seventeenth century these subsidies were paid in 1632–3, 1637–48, 1657–66 and 1672–8, to varying amounts, as shown in Table 8. At no time did they amount in value to the maximum attained by the Prussian licences in 1634. From Sweden's point of view, the mulcting of the Baltic trade was to be preferred to dependence on French subsidies; and one can understand Axel Oxenstierna's anger when the Swedish negotiators at Stuhmsdorf failed in their attempt to preserve the licence system. Licences provided a source of income which, geographically speaking, was handier than subsidies; and though both licences and subsidies entailed the maintenance of armies and fortresses, the income from licences could be used as might be most convenient, without pressure from outside. The Swedish army of the Rhine, fighting far away from its home base, had to a large extent to look to foreign resources to supply it with recruits, cash and provisions. Once the Prussian licences were lost, the Swedish Rhine army, nominally paid by the crown, was driven to live off the country, with the help of French *louis d'or*. And when, in the period 1638–48, French and Swedish war aims once again coincided, and both sought to end the war in Germany, the French

TABLE 8: FRENCH SUBSIDIES 1632–1678[26a]

(in *riksdaler*)

1632	159,012	1656	–
1633	(400,000)[26b]	1657	210,000
1634	–	1658	180,000
1635	–	1659	200,000
1636	–	1660	100,000
1637	400,000	1661	–
1638	400,000	1662	100,000
1639	400,000	1663	100,000
1640	200,000	1664	100,000
1641	480,000	1665	100,000
1642	480,000	1666	100,000
1643	480,000	1667	–
1644	480,000	1668	–
1645	480,000	1669	–
1646	480,000	1670	–
1647	480,000	1671	–
1648	206,555	1672	466,666
1649	–	1673	(300,000)[26c]
1650	–	1674	729,368
1651	–	1675	595,700
1652	–	1676	723,766
1653	–	1677	773,348
1654	–	1678	502,784
1655	–		

subsidies reached their first peak: 480,000 *riksdaler* annually for each year from 1641 to 1647.

(iii)

The war-weariness of the combatants at last produced the peace settlement of Westphalia. That peace gave Sweden a part, at least, of the territorial satisfaction she had sought so long, and so enabled her to consolidate her strategically important conquests in Germany. But it also did something to provide for what was called 'the satisfaction of the soldiery', without which, indeed, the German armies could hardly have been disbanded and paid off.

The amount of cash which Sweden received by way of satisfaction falls under the following heads (in *riksdaler*): [27]

Holy Roman Empire	5,000,000
Bohemia, Moravia, Silesia	200,000
Palatine Electorate	81,346
	5,281,346

Of this amount the cavalry and infantry from Sweden and Finland received something over 1·5 million *riksdaler*, the Swedish high command 500,000 *riksdaler* (divided among twenty-three field-marshals and generals, led by the queen's cousin, the future Charles X), and Swedish diplomats about 100,000 (divided among six persons, with Axel Oxenstierna at their head). The remainder of the money went to pay off the German troops (1·5 million *riksdaler*), to evangelical princes and towns (Nuremberg, for instance, got 100,000 *riksdaler*), and to the payment of sundry outstanding debts.[28] Thus the direct cash gains to the crown from twenty years' participation in the Thirty Years War were nothing to write home about. The real gains came from the territorial cessions in north Germany. It was unfortunately the case, however, that these were mostly thinly populated areas which economically yielded only a meagre profit, and from this point of view cost more than they were worth. (For other implications of the German acquisitions, see above, pp. 27–9, 49–53.)

Sweden's own resources did not permit her attempts to expand to the south and east to be followed up. The only permanent acquisition was the provinces won from Denmark and Norway in 1645 and 1660. And during the seventeenth century the full value of these conquests could not be realised: not until Sweden had ceased to be a great power were they completely assimilated. But in the long run Charles X's Danish wars did more for Sweden than Gustavus Adolphus's campaigns in Russia, Poland, Prussia and Germany.

The sudden irruption of Gustavus Adolphus into the politics of Europe was something which Sweden and Finland could achieve only through a system of finance based on a money economy. But the country's resources were geared to, and indeed presupposed, a natural economy: necessarily so, since that economy, apart from a small export sector – at first copper, later iron and tar – was essentially agrarian. And when the problem of liquidity was temporarily solved during the period of peace which lasted from 1680 to 1700, it was solved by taking this fact into account. The financing of the army and administration was to be supplied by imposts on the land paid in kind, and among them those 'extraordinary' taxes which had been occasionally levied in the earlier part of the century, but which now had become permanent and, like other taxes, were based on the land. The state was supported in the first place by these land revenues in kind, which were proportioned to the productivity of all those farms which the *reduktion* had now placed at the king's disposal, and in the second place by services in the form

of militia levies. It was only in the third place that account was taken
of the yield of taxes in hard cash. Taxation in the form of customs dues
now no doubt provided some possibility of laying up a national reserve
of precious metals; but its volume was never very large.

V. THE TEMPORARY SOLVING OF THE PROBLEM OF LIQUIDITY: 'ESTIMATES' AND THE ALLOTMENT SYSTEM

(i)

In itself, the *reduktion* (and the harsh proceedings against the regents
and the crown's creditors which were associated with it) provided no
solution to the country's financial problems. In some respects indeed –
for instance, by its long-term effect in limiting the possibility of raising
loans – it even made the situation worse, especially if the country should
again be involved in war (cf. above, p. 92). On the other hand it brought
great changes to the administration of the finances. In 1655 two-
thirds of the land, as assessed for taxation, had been in the hands of
the nobility. When the *reduktion* was stopped by the outbreak
of the Great Northern War, the proportion (excluding the overseas
provinces) had dropped to a quarter. And if we take into account the
measures of *reduktion* in the Baltic provinces also, whereby the
Swedish nobility lost almost all its earlier grants from the crown, it is
clear that the agrarian basis of the royal finances had been very greatly
broadened.

The period from 1680 to 1697 was marked by a feverish effort to
provide, for every economic need of the state, an 'authority to pay'
which would permanently cover it. This entailed the drawing-up of
regular estimates for every branch of the country's administration. In
itself this was not new: what was new was the logical consistency, the
precision, the demand for planning and for permanence, which now
characterised it. A new office of state, the Estimates Office (*Statskontoret*) began its work in 1680. Its president was also to act as head of
the Exchequer College. But despite this personal union, it was the king
himself who really supervised the estimates: the presidents, in this
initial stage, were officials who to an especial degree enjoyed Charles
XI's confidence – Klas Fleming and his brother-in-law Fabian Wrede.
The papers of the Estimates Office have not all been preserved, so that
it is difficult to form a judgement as to how far it was successful in
mobilising Sweden's economic resources. But on the whole it is possible
to agree with Arne Munthe's verdict, when he writes:

When Charles XI died, his financial system had more or less been codified and applied: the *reduktion* was practically complete, the terriers of the reduced estates had been drawn up, the military *indelningsverk* had been scrutinised and provided with its guarantee of immutability, a norm for the national estimates had been laid down, with revenues from every farm assigned to specified types of expenditure; the greater part of the national debt had been either paid off or written off; and the Estimates Office could work on a balance-sheet which showed a dazzling surplus. The whole system was the expression of a typical peace economy, and was based on the principle – already beginning to be outmoded – of payment in kind.[29]

Whether it was indeed 'outmoded' is of course a matter of opinion. It was not until the nineteenth century that Sweden's economy became industrialised in any modern sense, or that cash payments clearly gained the upper hand. In the agrarian society of the seventeenth century it was just not possible to achieve numerical uniformity in the modern style. Moreover the fact that the budget included a number of different funds – the 'ordinary' revenues, the 'extraordinary' revenues, the assigned revenues and personal expenditures, the funds for the fortifications and the admiralty – reflected the cameral diversity of the incomes of the state. Even an absolute monarch such as Charles XI was limited by the right of the Estates to give their consent to any new taxation, a right which could be set aside only in the event of a sudden outbreak of war. Moreover Sweden as a great power was confined within an approach to finance which held that every item of expenditure must be furnished with a corresponding source of income which in contemporary eyes could be plausibly related to it. The first priority was the strengthening of the country's defences, and the secret reserves of specie were amassed with that end in view. These were controlled by the king himself, or by trusted servants in charge of the various depositaries. They did not feature in the nation's accounts, for tactical reasons: there were good grounds for denying to the country's enemies any inkling as to the extent of its resources.

The new finance system brought with it a degree of control which had not previously existed. One task of the Estimates Office was the preparation of a budget or, to use the terminology of the age, the drawing-up of 'states', where requirements were specified, and assured sources of income allotted to cover them. Its second task, termed 'assignment', was to see that the 'authorities to pay' proposed in the budget were actually applied. No alteration of these arrangements was permitted: if any new need arose, payment to cover it could be made only if authorised by the king's personal signature.

This rigid control, in which the king himself functioned as a kind of auditor-general, was made possible because government offices and government servants were compelled to send in, at regular intervals, precise accounts of their receipts and expenditures. Thus the famous Form of Government of 1634 was in point of financial administration completed by the budgetary reforms of Charles XI. The Form of Government had reorganised the central administration of each province by giving it a lord-lieutenant with a staff of officials to deal with different types of business; it had given the country a military organisation which raised its recruits and paid its officers on a provincial basis; but it was not until the instructions issued to the Estimates Office in 1680 and 1685 that this territorial organisation was firmly applied in the economic sphere also. While Gustavus Adolphus and his successors had operated almost at random, and met demands from whatever source was most readily available, the bureaucracy of the period of absolutism strove to find the most appropriate and the most secure source of income for every purpose. And seen from this angle, as Fredrik Lagerroth pointed out, the 'allotment system' (indelningsverk), which is usually thought of simply as a form of military organisation, acquires a wider significance. (For the indelningsverk, see also pp. 269–71 below.)

(ii)

It is plain, then, that in the event of war Sweden's strength rested upon other resources than the royal hoard of silver. The long-drawn-out history of the Great Northern War makes this clear. However that war had been fought, the Swedish economy would not in the long run have been able to withstand the shock, and the pressure of the superior resources of four neighbour states. However well the indelningsverk functioned militarily and administratively, when mobilisation occurred in 1700 fresh taxes had to be raised, merchantmen had to be used as transports, recruits had to be drafted to fill the gaps in horse and foot, garrisons had to be reinforced, dragoon regiments had to be hired. As time went on, revenues assigned to civil purposes had to be diverted to cover military needs – which meant, for example, that the state could not pay its servants' wages. At the outbreak of the war the army of Charles XII, native and mercenaries together, is estimated to have totalled nearly 80,000 men. To keep this force in being was a severe test of economic strength, particularly when it is remembered that – in contrast to the situation during the Thirty Years War – fresh recruits had mostly to be raised from the heart of the empire.

Thanks to an administrative apparatus which by contemporary standards was of high quality, the challenge was to a certain extent met. But with no hope of raising new regiments in Finland (thanks to the Russian occupation), with no ship tolls and grain supplies from the Baltic provinces, with no subsidies from a France which was herself heavily engaged in a struggle to defend her international position, the 'Swedish lion' had by degrees to bow to the inevitable. Sweden had risen to be a great power in very different conditions from these, and in a world where Russia still counted for nothing as a Baltic state. Once the Russian economy was mobilised for war, Sweden had no choice but to give up the game. She did indeed retain her original territories, augmented by those frontier provinces which she had taken from Norway and Denmark and to which she was linked by social and linguistic affinities. But their united resources, together with later injections of French subsidies, could not between them avail to rebuild her former greatness. All attempts to do so (the Russian wars of 1741–3 and 1788–90, the Prussian campaigns of 1757–62) came to grief on the fact that Sweden now had neighbours in the Baltic who economically were stronger than herself, and could never be cut back to the economic potential they had possessed between 1632 and 1697. And the peace settlements which ended these ventures, as well as the wars themselves, entailed still further erosion of the country's economic and territorial position.

VI. EPILOGUE

The sunset of Swedish power had consequences also for the international politics of Europe. Karl Marx discerned, with penetrating insight, the new politico-economic situation which Sweden's eclipse as the leading economic Baltic power left behind it. In his posthumously published book *The Secret Diplomatic History of the Eighteenth Century* he contended that it was Great Britain who was the main loser – economically and politically – from her failure to stand by the Anglo-Swedish defensive treaty of 1700. He lamented that Britain broke her promise to come to the aid of Sweden – who formed the barrier against Peter the Great's expansion – and permitted Russia to occupy the Baltic provinces. For those provinces gave the undeveloped Russian state

German experts in the fields of administration, military organisation and technology. Marx condemned the errors of British diplomacy (and the Russia Company as a 'pressure group') in strong terms: when in 1719 and 1720 British policy changed course, it was too late; Russia's economic grip on the Baltic was already a fact.[30]

It is natural enough that Marx's views on economic history should not be free from misconceptions; since he wrote his study of the genesis of Anglo-Russian relations new material has come to light which has raised new questions. Marx shared with the sources upon which he relied a preoccupation with what were called 'naval stores'. It is of course true that hemp and flax came from Russian-controlled areas, and were in part (as he emphasised) exported through Swedish-controlled ports, especially Riga and Narva. But from the British point of view the most important Baltic commodities (in a strictly economic sense) were iron and tar, which were produced, the one in Sweden, the other in Finland, and were shipped by way of Stockholm and Göteborg, the two main export centres of the Swedish mainland. When the Swedish empire collapsed Sweden did indeed lose her position in the European iron and tar trade. But the fact that this change was the result of the granting of a premium to American tar, and to the geographical redistribution and increased productiveness of the English iron industry, was something which Karl Marx, a self-taught economic historian, could hardly be expected to know.

The correlation of economic and political factors can indeed be a tricky business, as an attempt to analyse Sweden's status as a great power, and her subsequent collapse, sufficiently reveals. In many cases it is best simply to present the quantifiable material, and allow the reader to draw his own conclusions as to its relevance and reliability. And this means that the discussion of some problems is necessarily insecurely based, simply because the quantifiable material which is needed to test the model is now missing – or has never existed.

3. Estates and Classes

STELLAN DAHLGREN

IN the course of the last few centuries of the Middle Ages, feudal society was transformed, as far as the greater part of Europe was concerned, into a society organised upon a basis of Estates. In Scandinavia the preconditions for such a transformation differed from those which prevailed elsewhere, for the northern countries were never feudalised in the same way as the great states of the continent; but here too the idea of a society of Estates was developed, and became a political reality.

In Sweden, as elsewhere, the habit of thinking in terms of Estates first became evident in regard to parliamentary institutions. As early as the fourteenth century men were beginning to talk of representation through four Estates as a natural arrangement; and in the fifteenth the idea became a fact with the coming into existence of the Diet of four Estates. But another two centuries were to elapse before the principles of representation, and the forms of procedure of the Diet, were regulated by Gustavus Adolphus's *riksdagsordning* of 1617.

The division into Nobles, Clergy, Burghers and Peasants was not something which contemporaries confined only to the Diet: they applied it also to society as a whole. It was a differentiation which was to a very large extent based upon differences of a juridical nature. Every Estate, apart from the Peasants, had its own particular privileges; every Estate had its own particular function which only it could discharge. The political thinking of the Age of Greatness was permeated by the concept of Estates; and preservation of the distinction between them was considered fundamental to the harmony of society.

Among historians too it has been usual to start from the assumption that the Estates in seventeenth-century Sweden corresponded to a social reality: that is, that they embraced the great majority of the population, and that the lines of demarcation between them followed the critical lines of division, social and economic, between one class and another. But it cannot be too strongly emphasised that it would be unwise to exaggerate the social relevance of the Estate structure of the Age of Greatness. Table 9 illustrates some of the difficulties.

TABLE 9: THE ESTATES AND THE SOCIAL STRUCTURE

Occupation	Nobles	Clergy	Burghers	Peasants	Outside the Estates Non-noble 'persons of standing'	Others
Landowners	★				★	
Civil servants	★	★	★		★	
Military	★				★	
Entrepreneurs, works owners	★		★		★	
Merchants	★		★			
Craftsmen			★	★		★
Stewards and bailiffs in private employ				★	★	★
Professions	★				★	★
Farmers				★		
Cottars, labourers, workmen						★

Some comment is needed if this table is not to be misunderstood. One interesting category in it, for our purpose, is that of the 'non-noble persons of standing' (ståndspersoner). By this expression is meant those persons who, in spite of not falling within any particular Estate, enjoyed, in virtue of their incomes, or of the education which they had contrived to obtain, a social standing equal to that which they would have had if they had belonged to the Clergy or the Burghers. A noble-man naturally took precedence over Clergy, Burghers and stånds-personer; while the Peasantry, though standing lowest among the Estates, was still above the true working classes in town and country. The table suggests that the Nobility and the Burghers were particularly heterogeneous in their occupations; and it also shows that large groups were not included in the Estate system at all. It is clear too that the Clergy was the most homogeneous of the Estates, in virtue of the fact that in general it followed only one occupation. But in one respect the table is entirely misleading; for it gives us no information about the relative numbers engaged in each occupation within each Estate. The homogeneity within the Nobility was greater than might be inferred from the table, since the Estate mainly consisted of landowners, civil servants and officers; and often the same person combined landowner-ship with the civil service. The Burghers comprised mainly merchants, craftsmen and members of town governments, that is, persons in the magistracy; but apart from these, only those who had obtained burgage rights – that is, had been approved by the magistracy, taken the burgher oath, and secured right of domicile – were accounted Burghers. It is moreover clear that certain occupational groups were distributed among several Estates, and that some others were completely unrepresented in the Diet, to which of course only the four Estates were admitted. It is also plain that this distribution of employment between Estates entailed clashes of interest within them, and that groups in different Estates might act together when they had a common interest to defend.

During the second half of the seventeenth century Sweden and Finland, taken together, may perhaps have had about 1½ million or at most 2 million inhabitants. Of these, according to Professor Sten Carlsson's calculations,[1] about 95 per cent belonged to the Commonalty (peasants, cottars, servants and other members of the working class); while the figures for the Nobility are at most 0·5 per cent, for the Clergy about 1 per cent, for the Burghers perhaps as much as 2 per cent, and for the *ståndspersoner* between 1 and 2 per cent. Probably not more than a few per cent of the population lived in the towns, though Stockholm expanded vigorously from about 10,000 inhabitants in the 1620s to 50,000–55,000 at the close of the century. By that date, the next largest towns – Falun, Norrköping and Göteborg – had no more than 4,000 to 6,000 apiece. Not all those who lived in a town belonged to the Estate of Burghers, nor did they all follow urban occupations. The size of Stockholm is largely to be explained by the fact that so many officials (and, not least, officials drawn from the nobility) lived there. These noble officials often built great town houses, where they provided employment for a large staff of servants; so that the settlement of the nobility in Stockholm also helped to swell the numbers of the city's lower classes. Everywhere there was a large group of such town dwellers below the Burgher level: it has been calculated that in the smaller towns the Burghers constituted no more than a third of the population, and in Stockholm considerably less.

Any attempt to describe the economic and social situation of the various groups in seventeenth-century Swedish society can only deal in approximations. It is impossible, for instance, to make any overall judgements about the distribution of wealth or the relative size of incomes. In order to do so, we should require a wide spread of documentation bearing on the economic circumstances of individuals; and such material does not exist for this period. What we lack above all is something corresponding to the tax registers of our own day, which may indeed be defective, but which do at least give some basis for an economic classification. The direct taxation of the seventeenth century was directed at visible manifestations of wealth, and in particular at land; and in regard to land its valuations, based on a conventional assessment, were unrealistic and often misleading. Taxes on land hit the peasantry above all; but they also bore on the noble landowners. The clergy were taxed in relation to the tithe they collected from their parishioners. After Charles XI became absolute, he began also to tax the pay of officers and civil servants. The nearest equivalent to a modern type of tax was the 'grant' of the Burghers. This was apportioned in each town according to a calculation of the individual burgher's ability to pay made by the town government or by specially appointed tax officials. The absolute monarchy also established a tax on servants; but this was probably mostly paid by their employers.

In the absence of evidence which could provide comparable figures, we can do no more than discuss the economic and social conditions of different groups in general terms. For some of the generalisations which we shall be making the evidence elicited by research is still scarcely adequate to support a conclusion; but at least they can be considered as the most probable interpretations of the tenuous material which is available to us.

I. THE PEASANTS

If we begin by looking at the position of the peasants, it is at once apparent that their economic and social situation could vary very widely. There were considerable differences between the size and productivity of peasant holdings from one district to another, and even within the same parish or village. Enterprising and thriving farmers expanded at the expense of others, added neighbouring holdings to their own, cultivated the waste, and so created large farms. Some of these more substantial peasants might also engage in trade, become constables and innkeepers, perhaps bailiffs and petty justices, or act as foremen or stewards to a nobleman. They formed an upper class within the Estate of Peasants, from which *ståndspersoner*, and even in a few cases noblemen, might be recruited. After 1680 wealthy peasants of this sort were often selected to be *rusthållare*, which meant that they undertook the responsibility of fitting out a cavalryman with horse and equipment in return for fiscal concessions and other advantages from the crown. (On *rusthållare*, see below, p. 270).

But while some peasants moved up, others found their circumstances getting worse. Landless peasants probably increased very considerably in number in the course of the century. They worked as servants, or maintained themselves by hunting and fishing; in many cases they kept cows, despite the fact that they 'lived in' with someone else and had no farm of their own. In the mining areas some of them supported themselves by working in the mines or the forges. The severe Statutes of Labourers of 1664 and 1686, and other similar ordinances, aimed at giving the crown control over these people so that it might be able to use their labour and their taxable capacity in a way which would be advantageous to the state, and (not least) to the noble landowners. But with the social problem presented by the really asocial elements – the beggars, the infirm – the state never made any serious effort to come to grips. Such people lived in squalor, and suffered grievously when the harvest failed or epidemics were raging. It is true that ordinances were issued – in 1642, 1686, 1698 – which enjoined that the poor be maintained by the municipalities or the parishes; but since the government did not venture to force them to levy a rate for this purpose, poor-relief continued to be defective and dependent upon the initiative of individuals.

As to the peasants, there was a further great difference between various categories, depending upon who owned the land which they cultivated. The 'tax-peasant' was a freeholder, paying taxes to the king, while the farm of a crown-peasant was the property of the crown, and that of a *frälse*-peasant was owned by his noble landlord.* Both crown- and *frälse*-peasants could be given notice to quit; but the crown-peasant is considered to have have had more security of tenure, since the nobleman was more likely than the crown to concern himself with getting a tenant to suit him. As to the freehold farm, it appears that on the average it was larger than the crown-farm; and as a rule the 'tax-peasant' enjoyed a higher social standing than other peasants – no doubt for the simple reason that he was his own master.

In the course of the seventeenth century, the crown's great need for revenue (particularly in cash), and also its need to pay its servants and officers, resulted in the sale, pawning and donation of a large number of farms to the nobility. At the time of Queen Christina's abdication in 1654, about two-thirds of all the farms in Sweden and Finland were

---

* *Frälse*-peasant': from *frälse*, literally 'deliverance', in this context 'exempt' (from taxation), or the privilege of such exemption, total or partial: the nobility enjoyed *frälse*; they were the *frälse*-Estate; their land was *frälse*-land, their peasants *frälse*-peasants.

in noble hands. In this way many crown- and tax-peasants passed under the control of noble landlords. The tax-peasants did indeed retain the right of ownership to their farms, but like other peasants under the nobility they now paid the greater part of their taxes to the nobleman, and did their labour services to him. At meetings of the Diet the non-noble Estates – and especially the Peasants – clamoured for the crown to carry through a *reduktion* and resume these alienated farms, pointing out that the burdens upon those crown- and tax-peasants whose farms had not been alienated grew heavier, as their numbers became fewer. They spoke hard words about the way the nobility oppressed their peasants with impositions – and in particular with labour services – which were too heavy for them to bear; and they alleged that the nobility were trying to rob the tax-peasants who had come under their control of the freehold rights. These accusations reached a climax at the Diet of 1650, when Christina was forcing through the election of the future Charles X as hereditary prince. The Peasants demanded that the crown should take back the alienated estates, and laid great stress on the danger that those who were under the nobility might lose their independence: as they put it in 1650, in words which were long remembered, 'We know that in other lands the Commonalty are slaves, and we fear that the like may happen to us, who are yet born a free people'.[2] And when Christina at a confrontation with the peasant members declared that she would punish noble oppressors, they told her that 'they have no one to complain to, when they suffer injustice: between noblemen it is nothing but "Brother, brother", and there is no good in complaining to one brother that another is doing wrong'.[3]

The attitude taken up by the Peasants at the Diet of 1650 was typical of their attitude throughout the century, and to some extent it was a tactical move, designed to secure advantages of one sort or another. Yet it cannot be doubted that the Estate of Peasants was on the whole entirely in earnest in its fight to curb the Nobility by depriving them of much of the crown and freehold land which had passed into noble hands; and their view of the situation appears to have been that the peasant who was under a nobleman was not so well off as the peasant who was under the crown.

Recent research, however, suggests that economically speaking the peasants of the nobility – and even freeholders who had come under noble control – were no worse off than peasants who remained under the crown. Noblemen do not as a rule seem to have oppressed the peasants who were under them with heavier taxes and burdens than the crown exacted of its own peasants. They often refrained from collecting all the taxes to which they were entitled. Nor did they show much sign, when the Diet met, of being very ready to vote new taxes, despite the fact that they would have been entitled to put a part of the yield into their own pockets. There were cases – most of those which have been unearthed so far come from Finland – where freehold peasants, alienated by the crown, were forced to surrender the title to their farms to a nobleman. Usually they were peasants so poor that they were not able to meet their arrears even by handing over all their chattels; and in return for the surrender of their freeholds they were allowed to write off some of their indebtedness. But this was a development which was by no means always agreeable to their noble landlords. It could happen, however, that a nobleman might be interested in extending his property: this was particularly the case if he wished to lump several farms together within his demesne and so increase the land which he farmed himself by means of his servants. But such facts as we know do not suggest that there was any general desire on the part of the nobility to acquire peasant freeholds; and those peasants who possessed them could in fact feel themselves relatively secure.

And there was one other very favourable circumstance to be added to this picture of the relatively tolerable situation enjoyed by peasants under the nobility. The most dreaded of all the burdens which the crown imposed was that of conscription. A certain proportion of the population of the country had necessarily to be taken for the army, and in wartime that proportion of course increased. The method by which it was done was to group the peasants, and the male labourers and servants who lived with them, into 'files', each of (e.g.) ten men, from each of which one man was taken for a soldier. Upon the peasants of the nobility, however, the burden fell less heavily, since by the terms of the nobility's privileges their peasants were bound to supply only half as many men as the corresponding number of tax-peasants and crown-peasants. It must be said, however, that in time of war the nobility often permitted a larger quota. (For further discussion of the grievances of the peasantry, see below, pp. 259–61.)

As a speciment of the 'good' landlord's attitude towards his peasants, we may take the words which Axel Oxenstierna put into his last will and testament. He wrote:

> My late wife and I, like our parents before us, have always felt a
> warm sympathy for our subjects and tenants, refraining to the best

of our ability from troubling them with great and exorbitant burdens and contenting ourselves for the most part with what was customary and reasonable, as our dear children may find set out in the terriers, old and new. . . . And we have done what in us lay to ensure that we, while enjoying in some measure that which is our own, might yet preserve our subjects; distinguishing in this between those afflicted with poverty, and those who are contumacious. . . . Whereby we have thriven better than many another (as well in Livonia, as in Sweden and Finland) who has shorn them close and often.[4]

We do not know how far the benevolent attitude expressed in Oxenstierna's testament tallied with his practice; nor do we know how many noble landlords shared it. But it does appear that the chancellor had seen examples of what he regarded as violent and oppressive treatment of the peasantry. It is also obvious that despite his professions of goodwill he regarded the peasants as his 'subjects', and considered that he was entitled to impose taxes upon them above the ordinary rate, and to mete out special treatment to the recalcitrant. For a seventeenth-century peasant, despite the benevolent phrases, Oxenstierna's attitude cannot have had much appeal. It reveals, all unconsciously, some of the reasons why the Estate of Peasants demanded a restriction of noble ownership, even though the noble might be (as he often was) a good landlord. Peasants under the nobility were to some extent at the mercy of their masters: this was so, for instance, in regard to labour services, which for large groups of peasants of the nobility were not regulated by law or custom and could be particularly oppressive in cases where there was a good deal of building activity at the lord's manor. The right of trial and punishment which the nobility in some places exercised against their peasants was much resented. The insecurity of tenure of *frälse*-peasants was a considerable disadvantage. The risk (for there was a risk) that freehold peasants who had passed under noble control might lose their rights of ownership to their farms, was another reason for the peasants' attacks on the first Estate. A pamphleteer of the mid-century put it like this: 'And in this complaint all the freeholders [under noble control] have joined (although some of them have nothing to allege against their lords) solely on account of the danger in which they perceive themselves to stand by the example of what has befallen their brethren.'[5] Moreover it is certain that those peasants who still remained under the crown wanted the burden of taxation to be spread more broadly; and this must have played a part in this connection. But for those peasants who had some political consciousness one point must have weighed more heavily than all the rest: the danger that the Nobility might become so dominant, economically and politically, that the other Estates, and not least the Peasants, might be in danger of being reduced to impotence.

The *reduktion* carried through by Charles XI led to a drastic diminution of noble landholding. Many noble farms became once again crown-farms or tax-farms. But for many peasants this meant that henceforward they would pay their dues to a noble who served the state in a civil or military capacity, and who – as a consequence of Charles XI's 'allotment system' (*indelningsverk*) – had had their taxes assigned to him as his pay. (On the 'allotment system', see below, pp. 269–71). It was a situation which gave rise to many conflicts. In many cases the peasant was actually worse off after the *reduktion* than before it, since the crown was less disposed than the nobleman it had displaced to adjust its demands to what the peasant could pay. Nevertheless it does seem to be agreed that in spite of everything the *reduktion* did mean for the peasantry an advance towards greater independence and greater political influence.

II. THE BURGHERS

In the struggle of the Estate of Peasantry to push back the advance of the Nobility they could count on the steady support of the Estate of Burghers. From the middle of the century the Estate played an important part in the parliamentary battle, and was at times very active. This was the case at the Diet of 1650, when on a number of occasions it took the lead in the attack upon the Nobility. When at the Diet of 1682 the scope of the *reduktion* was extended, among those who did a good deal to bring about that result was the leader of the Burghers, Olof Thegner, who was in close touch with Charles XI. There is a suggestive passage in the notes of a conference between the king and the Secret Committee taken by a clerical diarist: 'When the Clergy made to take their leave, His Majesty went across to Thegner; but what he whispered in his ear I could not catch.'[6]

The growing political influence of the Burghers was of course connected with the increased economic importance of the towns as the century progressed. The advance of the copper and iron industries provided many new means of livelihood to merchants and craftsmen. Merchants could make large profits by satisfying the large demands of the metallurgical industries for advances of capital and commodities.

Craftwork of various kinds, the textile industry, and other manufactures also, all underwent an expansion – especially in the latter half of the century – which in its turn led to increased trade. The development of the mercantile marine led to the emergence of a considerable group of shipowners in the business world of Stockholm and Göteborg.

In general these shipowners belonged to the richest section of the burghers. It often happened that rich merchants combined in their own hands various types of economic activity: they put money into shipping, they gave credit to forges and foundries, they set up works of their own, they bought shares in trading companies. Even in the small towns of the mining district it was usual for burghers to run their own ironworks. Wealthy merchants frequently secured landed estates for themselves, partly because land was a safe investment, partly because by doing so they raised their social status. It was merchants of this sort, for the most part, who advanced money to the crown, or arranged credits for it from abroad. Such merchants tended to be concentrated mainly in Stockholm and Göteborg; hardly any of them lived in the smaller towns. Towards the end of the century their numbers increased, and they became particularly prominent after the nobility had been hit by the *reduktion*, which forced many noble financiers to go out of business. The process can be traced, *inter alia*, in the record of deposits in the state bank: at first the nobility predominated; by the end of the nineties almost all the customers were burghers.

It might be supposed that this class of wealthier burgers would have produced its own style of living, as it did in the nineteenth century. But this was not the case. Despite the fact that the Estate of Burghers was politically the opponent of the Nobility, its members took as their ideal a way of life which was strongly under noble influence. In Stockholm, no doubt, the proximity to the court and the large numbers of noblemen in the town must have had an effect: the burgher was permitted to be present as a spectator at the great court festivals and banquets; and the unending series of grand aristocratic weddings and funerals presented him with spectacles which he might aspire to imitate in so far as his resources permitted, and the ordinances against luxury allowed.

If a burgher could obtain ennoblement for himself or his children he considered himself to have scored a great social success. This did not indeed happen with any great frequency: most of the commoners who were ennobled belonged rather to the *ståndspersoner*. All the same, there was quite a number of ennobled burghers, and a few of them had children who succeeded in climbing to very exalted positions. The richest burger in Stockholm in the 1630s, Erik Larsson, was one of these: in 1631 he was ennobled under the name of van der Linde; both his sons were created barons; one of them became a member of the council of state, the other became the governor of a province. In 1698 another rich Stockholm merchant was ennobled under the name of Törnflycht: his sons were raised to the rank of count, two of them entered the council, and all his daughters took members of the council for their husbands.

Only a small minority of the burghers who engaged in trade were really wealthy. Most of the remainder were petty retailers, often with relatively small incomes, and with interests which diverged widely from those of the great wholesalers – for instance, in the matter of taxes and duties. This clash of interest was partly a reflection of the fact that the retailers were to a high degree dependent upon imports, while the wholesalers were mainly concerned with exports. In the larger towns the two groups were often in conflict, and sometimes they carried their struggles up to the Diet. It often happened, moreover, that the petty traders and the merchants stood for the interests of the smaller towns, while the wholesalers were identified with the interests of the larger. But there were occasions, of course, when all the merchants in any one town united in a common fight against outsiders; as happened when the burghers of the upland towns attacked the merchants of the coastal towns for invading the upland markets and competing with their trade.

An example of the opposition between retailers and wholesalers is provided by a petition to the king in 1673 from the lesser burghers of Göteborg. In this they complain of

the ill custom and pernicious abuse . . . that when any ship or vessel comes to the town, whatever be its cargo, the *kommerspresident* gathers his friends and cronies together, and forthwith they engross the entire cargo to their sole profit, that they may insatiably exploit the poor townsfolk and raise the prices against them, whereby is caused not only misery and want, but the lesser burghers are prevented from ever improving their condition by trade. Wherefore they beseech Your Majesty most humbly, not only that such proceedings and unlawful trading and oppression may be restrained and corrected, but also that our *kommerspresident* (who incidentally is a nobleman) be enjoined either to abstain from trade, or to quit his office.[7]

This is a case, then, of the retailers complaining because the wholesalers appropriated the *import* trade to themselves, and so put themselves in a position to make large profits at the retailers' expense. The particular target for their attack was Abraham van Eijck, who held the municipal office of *kommerspresident*. It emerges incidentally that the noble status which he had acquired in 1672 was a source of offence to the burghers in general, who were always very actively concerned to reserve to themselves all bourgeois occupations, and often attacked nobles and peasants for engaging in trade. A burgher who was ennobled tended to find himself in opposition to his former colleagues within the Estate; and since the nobility on their side did not welcome peerages for burghers, new creations might well find themselves isolated as a result of their elevation. Our quotation also reveals a cleavage between the town's officials and its burghers, taking the form in this case of a covert accusation against the official that he used his position for business purposes. It was no part of the duties of the *kommerspresident*, they considered, to engage in commerce.

More important than this was a division of interest of another type. Town officials formed a part of the magistracy, which both governed the town and functioned as a court of law. The most important of such officers were as a rule the burgomaster and the town councillors. The larger towns had several burgomasters, while Göteborg had a special organisation consisting of a burgrave, presidents and councillors. To a great extent the members of the magistracy were recruited from the ranks of the rich merchants, less frequently from those of the retailers, and only very rarely from among the craftsmen. As the seventeenth century progressed, however, it became increasingly usual to appoint persons with a legal or other academic training to the magistracy, which thus came to include a growing number of persons who were not burghers at all, but had made their career in the civil service – in a government office, for instance, or in one of the supreme courts, or (in the case of smaller towns) in local administration, as royal bailiffs or petty justices. This development was largely the work of the crown which, acting very often through provincial governors, tended more and more to appoint the magistrates, and above all the burgomasters. There was probably a certain connection between this development and the tendency which can be discerned for the magistracy to identify itself with the crown's interests. By doing so, they came more and more into conflict with the burghers. After 1680 the pressure exercised by the state upon the burghers, not least through the magistrates, came to be extremely burdensome. Sometimes the opposition between burghers and magistrates reached a point at which the burghers attempted to take certain kinds of business out of the magistrates' control, and to put them in the hands of their own representatives.

The largest group within the burghers was that of the craftsmen, who in general were worse off than the magistrates, had a lower social status, and exercised less political influence. The life of the craftsmen was dominated by the gilds. The gilds were societies of master craftsmen, and their main purpose was to keep up the price of craft products by keeping down production and limiting the number of masters. They were bound together by a strong corporate feeling. It was considered a slur on a master's honour to accuse him of underselling other masters of the same craft. Craftsmen outside the gild were harried unmercifully, unless they happened to be in the service of a nobleman or of the crown. Entry to a gild could be obtained by a journeyman only when he had executed a 'masterpiece' in conformity with the gild's regulations, paid the stipulated fee and given a donation to the poor.

As a rule craftsmen had few or no employees, though members of a few of the bigger crafts – for instance, the masons – might have a considerable number. In so far as masons were also architects, however, they rose above the craftsman level; and in that case they were reckoned as *ståndspersoner*, and fell outside the Estate of Burghers altogether. Most architects were foreigners, or at least of foreign ancestry, as Nicodemus Tessin the elder was, for example; and their social status was very considerably above that of the craftsmen. Tessin was ennobled; and his son, Nicodemus Tessin the younger, the creator of the royal palace in Stockholm, finished his life as a count and a member of the council.

Side by side with the burghers were various groups of people engaged in business activities, who stood outside the pattern of Estates, but who often enjoyed considerable social prestige. Such were the various types of entrepreneur, often immigrants from abroad. They made great contributions in the industrial field, as for instance in regard to textiles, but above all in the metallurgical industries. The great expansion in the exploitation of Sweden's mineral resources in this century was made possible only by a heavy investment of capital. A good deal of it came from the Swedish nobility and from the burghers in the towns; but many of the works in central Sweden were founded and run by immigrants, and it was the contacts of these men with the continent which provided Swedish exports with better market facilities than they had previously had at their disposal. Many of these people were ennobled, as for example Louis De Geer (the greatest of them all), Gillis De Besche, the Kock-Cronström family, the brothers Momma-Reenstierna. Such peerages were often not only the reward for their services to Swedish industry; they can also be considered as the crown's expression of gratitude for the credits they had made available to it and as an encouragement to make fresh loans. They could often also entail important economic gains, since they brought with them the advantages inherent in noble status – e.g. partial exemption from taxation – and so enhanced the attractiveness of buying and working industrial enterprises. But there were of course many families of works owners who were not noble: the first generation of them had often acted as managers or lessees of a works belonging to a nobleman, and had worked their way up until they were able to start a works of their own.

III. THE CLERGY

In the struggles between the Estates during the seventeenth century, the Clergy played a part of some importance. And the reason for this was certainly that of all the non-noble Estates it was they who were equipped with the best education. Hence it was among them that were usually to be found the persons best qualified to fight the battle against the Nobility. It was the Clergy moreover – at times supported by the lesser nobles – who as a rule provided the leadership of the lower Estates in the attack upon the high aristocracy which provided the members of the council and filled the great offices of state. In this connection it was important that the Clergy, more than any other Estate, had the confidence of the Peasants. It is true that friction between peasants and clergy was not infrequent, both at a local and a national level. Usually it had to do with the clergy's stipends; for the clergy collected from their parishioners tithe, offertories, fees for services, mortuary fees and other items; and it is not surprising that from time to time they should have been accused by the peasants of squeezing them unreasonably. They also often functioned as agents of the crown in connection with tax assessments, conscription and other distasteful royal demands; and in this capacity too they were exposed to the peasantry's resentment. But on the other hand clergy and peasants had very much in common. The clergy lived in their parishes (non-residence was virtually unknown in Sweden), and they had the condition of the peasants constantly before their eyes. They were the trusted agents of their parishioners not only in spiritual but also in worldly matters. As *ex officio* occupants of the chair at parish meetings they were necessarily involved in all civic questions. And the fact that economically they were dependent on their parishes meant that the welfare of the peasantry was bound up with their own.

With the Peasants they shared a common hostility to the Nobility. In many cases noblemen had the right of patronage in the parishes within which their manor-houses lay. This, in Sweden, meant no more than that they were entitled to *propose* a candidate; but in fact they often attempted, by various means, to put in their own man without further ceremony. This produced many clashes between the Nobility and the Clergy. It often happened also that nobles would refuse to pay tithe and other parochial dues, and would extend this refusal to the peasants under their control, or at least to those of them who lived on the demesne. As the number of noblemen grew, and with it the number of farms in noble hands, there was therefore a real risk that the incomes of the clergy would decline. The parson came increasingly to be at the mercy of the nobleman's steward when it came to getting in his tithe from *frälse*-peasants. The political side of the question was also obviously of enormous importance; and in this the Clergy had an interest in common with the Peasants and the Burghers. Archbishop Lenaeus gave expression to it at the Diet of 1650, when he said:

> When the Nobility get all the peasants under them, the Estate of Peasantry will have no *votum* at the Diet. And when the Estate of Peasantry goes under, the Burghers and the Clergy may well go under too, and the country will be left with only the king and one single Estate, namely the Nobility. And since the Nobility now have all the land in the country in their hands, where would the king's authority be then? For he who has the lands and estates rules the roost. And thereby a *servitus* would be introduced into the country.[8]

The Nobility did, however, win over a section of the Clergy to their side by giving them appointments as domestic chaplains, or presenting them to livings in the parishes where they were patrons. But for a politically conscious parson this would only be another argument for attacking the Nobility's position, since any dependence upon the nobility entailed a weakening of the influence of their own Estate Bishop Samuel Enander of Linköping entered his protest on this point at a meeting of the clergy of his diocese in 1656:

It was declared also [by the bishop] that the nobility in our parishes should not all without distinction or weighty reason have their own chaplains, but it was rather held to be proper that apart from the ordinary pastor and *comminster* there should be no other priest in any parish, seeing that a multiplicity of priests within the one congregation is attended by many evils, such as want of reverence for the churches, contempt for the clergy, and other ill consequences, even to the disregard for, and diminution of, ordinary rights.[9]

Enander further warned his clergy against allowing themselves to be used as the nobility's bailiffs and clerks. He exhorted them to maintain the respect due to their office, to refrain from undue and unnecessary familiarity with their parishioners, and not to permit the bailiff or the constable to take precedence of them at table or walk before them in processions.

Another bishop of Linköping provides an example of how difficult it could sometimes be for the clergy to preserve their independence against the aristocracy. At the Diet of 1650 the Clergy, like the other non-noble Estates, made energetic attempts to bring about the resumption by the crown of lands alienated to the nobility. One result of their activities was a memorial from the three Estates to the queen, which became known as their Protestation. Among the members of the Clergy who signed it was the bishop of Linköping, Andreas Prytz. He had no sooner done so than he regretted it and asked that his name should be deleted. He also wrote to the chancellor, Axel Oxenstierna, with excuses for his signature. The Protestation, he explained, had been against his conscience: in this matter God had taken His hand from over him; and 'I most humbly beseech that I may once more be taken into the favour of my gracious lord, and of Your Excellency's dear children'.[10] The form of words reveals that Prytz had got wind of the fact that his attitude had aroused the chancellor's displeasure. It is not irrelevant to note that Prytz had been tutor in Oxenstierna's service, that the revenue of a farm had been assigned to him by the chancellor's good offices, and that he had been favoured by him in various other ways. The episode sheds light on how the political conduct of the clergy could be influenced by a desire to preserve good relations with influential nobles who were in a position to do them a good turn.

And it was in fact the bishops and the higher ranks of the clergy who in most cases were on a friendly footing with aristocratic circles. Indeed in certain respects the bishops could approximate to the nobility's level. It is true that they could not themselves be ennobled;[11] but it happened fairly frequently that their children were, and they often acquired land with the same sort of exemptions as the nobility enjoyed. The friendship for the nobility which certain bishops showed, or were suspected of feeling, from time to time produced friction between the higher and lower ranks of the clergy. This did not alter the fact that members of the aristocracy could treat them with great arrogance, especially in times of political strife. As an example of this we may quote Axel Oxenstierna's outburst in the council, in 1650, when Archbishop Lenaeus contended that 'academic persons' were accorded wide privileges in all Christian countries. 'What is an academic person?' asked the chancellor ironically. 'A gown, a pair of breeches, and a handful of books!' [12]

Behind this negative attitude there lay, of course, a certain fear of the clergy. Magnus Gabriel De la Gardie expressed the view of many of his noble brethren in a memorial of 1655: 'The spiritual Estate is perhaps inclined to assume to itself a little too much in *politicis* and matters of government, and seems disposed to constitute itself as *regi et reipublicae graves*': the clergy, he thought, should be relieved of 'their needless care for the secrets of state and important government business'.[13]

Within the clerical Estate there existed not only a split between higher and lower clergy which was perhaps based mainly on social position, but also economic differences. To some extent of course the two lines of division coincided. At all events it was mostly the bishops who became known for their great riches – as for example Queen Christina's tutor, Johannes Matthiae. But there were also other members of the Estate who could be considered wealthy. Many parsons had well-endowed livings which afforded them large incomes. Sometimes they grew richer by lending out money to their parishioners, or engaging in trade, or some form of innkeeping. On the other hand there were priests who had poor congregations and small incomes. The worst off were probably those priests who had no living of their own but served in dependent chapelries or as curates, or had no regular employment at all and drifted about from parish to parish and from one manor to another.

As a rule the Clergy and the monarchy were very well disposed to each other. The king could in general count on the Clergy's support in any attempts to strengthen his position and repress his most important domestic rival, the Nobility. Nevertheless when the king became absolute after 1680 the Clergy were to find that a monarchy which had become too powerful might endanger the church's position. In 1686 Charles XI forced through a new statute for the church which in important respects curtailed its liberties; and with the support of the law he greatly extended his opportunities for interfering in clerical appointments, and his general control of church affairs. (For further discussion of this, see below, pp. 167–70). As a result the absolutism produced an ecclesiastical opposition, whose foremost representative was Jakob Boëthius, the rural dean of Mora. In a memorial which he drew up immediately after Charles XI's death in 1697 he declared that a king who assumed sovereignty over the church made himself an Antichrist. For this performance Boëthius was consigned to prison for thirteen years. But he was certainly not alone in his opinions. The clergy might indeed salute the absolutism in their sermons as something instituted by God; but their concealed dislike of it became manifest after Charles XII's death, when the absolutism came to an end: with few exceptions they gave their hearty support to the new constitution and actively opposed the monarchy's attempt to recover its authority.

IV. THE NOBILITY

From an early period of the Middle Ages, Sweden had possessed a magnate class, endowed with great political influence and great economic privileges. Among the most important of their rights was that of freedom from taxation. In the course of the sixteenth century the Vasa monarchy forced the nobility on to the defensive, but after 1600 its influence once again increased strongly. The great imperial expansion of the seventeenth century was led by the monarchy and the aristocracy in collaboration; though even so considerable tension between them could develop from time to time. The monarchy was indeed dependent upon the nobility for the simple reason that it was only the aristocracy that possessed the financial resources required to give its children the kind of training which was needed for service in the corps of officers or in the higher civil administration.

It was from the highest office-holders, civil and military, that the king recruited his council of state. This was a body which had existed since the Middle Ages. The duty of its members was to assist the king with their advice; but it had more than once happened that they had taken the care of the country's destinies into their own hands. In the seventeenth century the council had a great part to play, especially during the minorities of Christina and of Charles XI when the regents who conducted the government were drawn from among the council's leading members. The most important of those members in this period was the chancellor: Axel Oxenstierna was chancellor for more than forty years, and from 1632 until Christina took over the direction of affairs in 1644 he was the dominant figure in the government. During the minority of Charles XI, Magnus Gabriel De la Gardie tried to play a similar role; but he met, both in the council and at the Diet, with stronger opposition (see below, pp. 211 ff.). When Charles XI made himself absolute, the position of the council was weakened, particularly in regard to domestic affairs, though on matters of foreign policy it could often exert a good deal of influence; and individual members might likewise strongly influence the king's attitude both in internal and external matters.

The basis for the nobility's grip on the administration, and for its political weight, was the economic power which arose from its vast landed property. Most noblemen owned land. As we saw, around 1654 they owned about two-thirds of all the farms in Sweden and Finland. They lost some of them as a result of Charles X's *reduktion* and his restrictive policy about donations. How the situation developed in the years after his death is not clear; but it is clear that it was not until Charles XI's *reduktion* that the crown succeeded in stripping the nobility of any sizeable proportion of their holdings. It has been calculated that by 1700 their share of the land had fallen to about one-third.

When we speak of the nobility as landowners, however, it is important to remember the restrictive conditions upon which some of their land was held. It might happen that they had received land as a donation; or the crown might have pawned it; or they might merely have been assigned the revenues from it by way of wages. Sooner or later such land would have to revert to the crown according to regulations which had been laid down in the deed of conveyance, or in official ordinances, or as a matter of common practice. Some of the land they held, as we have seen, was really the property of freehold peasants who (as a result of the crown's action) were now paying a great part of their dues and services to their noble landlord.

Most of the land in noble possession was made up of farms cultivated by peasants on their own account; and it was the peasants' labour services which provided much of the work on the demesne round the noble's family seat, the produce of which was appropriated entirely to his own needs. The exemption from taxation enjoyed by noble land was entrenched in the privileges of the Nobility, whose history goes back to the early Middle Ages. In the seventeenth century the most important grants of privilege occurred in 1617 (a revision of that of 1612) and in 1644; and their effect was that while the crown drew tax at only a fraction of the ordinary rate from most of a noble's land, the land included in the demesne was almost entirely exempt. The monarchy and its agents, however, did their best to extract additional tax from the nobility by forcing them to agree to exemptions from their privileges, and by demanding from them personal contributions; and Professor Sven A. Nilsson has shown that in the course of the seventeenth century the burden of taxation upon the Nobility increased relatively to the increase of the burden upon other Estates. In this way the monarchy to some extent compensated itself for what it lost by the increase in noble landholding.

The land in the nobility's possession was very unevenly distributed. Much of it, probably most of it, was in the hands of the upper ranks of the aristocracy. The high nobility may be defined as the counts, the barons, and the descendants of members of the council, who constituted the first two classes in the House of Nobility, while all the lesser nobility were grouped together in the third class. It was from the high nobility, in large measure, that members of the council, and the highest officers of state, were recruited; and this gave them in consequence a very strong grip upon economic and political power. But the high nobility was by no means a closed caste. In the course of the century many noble families were raised to the dignity of count or baron (see above, pp. 75-8). As a rule they were person of the old nobility of Sweden, or the Baltic provinces, or foreign countries. Before 1680 it was rare for anyone who had been ennobled, or whose family had entered the peerage only in the previous generation, to move into the high nobility. Among the few exceptions were Johan Skytte and Johan Adler Salvius (both members of the council, created barons in 1624 and 1651 respectively); Mårten Leijonsköld, who was director-general of the customs and a great lender of money to the crown (created baron 1654); Henrik Cronstierna, also one of the crown's great creditors (baron 1653); Charles XI's tutor, Edmund Gripenhielm (baron 1673); and Field-Marshal Simon Grundel-Hemfelt (baron 1673) – the two last being also members of the council. Of those who became counts before 1680, only one was not a member of the old nobility. This was Anton von Steinberg, one of Christina's courtiers, whom the queen created a count in 1654; but he came near to being thrown out by his fellow counts when he came to be inducted into his new dignity. Under the absolutism it came to be more usual for newly ennobled families to be received into the high nobility. The monarchy rewarded some of its most faithful servants in this way. Among the barons we may note the leader of the Burghers and zealot for the *reduktion* Olof Thegner, royal secretaries and servants such as Lovisin, Lindhielm, Edelstierna and Cronhielm, and among the counts the royal councillors Gyllenborg, Polus, Piper and Tessin.

The great size of the estates of the high nobility may well to some extent have been a consequence of the fact that so many of these aristocratic families were drawn from the old Swedish nobility, and so had been accumulating land for decades, or even longer. But for the most part these vast holdings were the fruit of the policy of the crown in the sixteenth and seventeenth centuries. As members of the council, or as holders of great military or civil offices, the high aristocracy were given great donations by successive sovereigns. The greatest of them were the counties and baronies, which from the time of John III to the coming of the absolutism were handed out to newly created counts and barons. And in addition to the donations there were the lands which the crown sold, and which also for the most part came into the hands of the high nobility: as an example of the extent to which they benefited by royal alienations, we may note that considerably more than half of the lands donated between 1632 and 1654 went to families of this sort. Nor should it be forgotten that as compared with the lower nobility the high aristocracy comprised considerably fewer families and individuals, so that every family among them had therefore on an average many times as much land. And as far as we can see it was among the higher nobility that the country's greatest accumulations of wealth were to be found. It is, however, almost impossible to form any concrete idea of the size of their incomes, since these consisted to so large an extent of food products and commodities which they received from their peasants by way of tax, to say nothing of the income in services which arose, e.g., from the peasants' day-work. Their expensive way of life and their extensive building activities do, however, suggest that their incomes were very considerable. Professor Eli Heckscher once calculated that Magnus Gabriel De la Gardie's budget for 1679 amounted to a sum equal to about one-twentieth of the king's, which to our way of thinking seems gigantic.[14] But De la Gardie, of course, had the reputation of being the greatest builder of the century and the greatest patron of the arts apart from the king.

The landed families of the lesser nobility, as has been suggested, lived as a rule in more modest style than this. Often enough they owned only a handful of farms, one of which served them as a manor. There were, however, exceptions; among them several businessmen and works owners, who after ennoblement managed to amass considerable properties in the shape of country seats, farms and industrial installations. One of them was Louis De Geer, who among other things purchased from the crown the ironworks at Finspång, Leufsta, Osterby and Gimo. Other wealthy members of the lower nobility included several persons who successfully combined a business career with the administration of government funds. Among them we find several directors-general of the customs: Mårten Leijonsköld (afterwards a baron), W. Drakenhielm, B. Cronberg and – perhaps the best known and most venturesome of them all – Joel Gripenstierna. Of these the largest landowner was probably Leijonsköld.

In one sense it is true to say that a very large proportion of the landowning nobility engaged in trade, in that they or their stewards sold the produce which they obtained from their peasants at markets in the towns. These small-scale dealings naturally did not qualify them to be considered as businessmen or entrepreneurs; but in fact very many of those belonging to old families or the high nobility did own a forge or a foundry, or have some other industrial interest side by side with their activities as landowners. One such person was Jakob De la Gardie, who was the possessor of large tracts of land in the mining districts of Västmanland and was also engaged in the manufacture of cannon at Julita in Södermanland. His daughter Maria Sophia – one of the many noblewomen of this period signalised by their independent spirit and enterprising character – was also the possessor of several ironworks, as well as textile mills, paperworks and many other manufactories at Tyresö, to say nothing of coal mines in Skåne. But the state looked with disapproval on noble-owned ironworks, and their owners were hard hit by the *reduktion*.

Since the landowning nobleman received a great part of his income in commodities, many of them were compelled to borrow money on the security of their estates in order to meet their cash expenses. They borrowed from each other, from merchants, from the Palmstruch bank for as long as it lasted (1657–64), and later (from 1668 onwards) from the Bank of the Estates. Members of the high aristocracy and the upper ranks of office-holders were among the most enthusiastic users of the credit facilities which these institutions provided. For a Swedish nobleman, being in debt can be said to have been a more or less normal state of affairs. Even persons of wealth with a highly developed business sense might be debtors for quite large sums. As long as they had assets equal to, or in excess of, their liabilities, they were not unduly perturbed about it. When Axel Oxenstierna drew up his will in 1650 he still had debts unpaid; but this did not mean that he was not a wealthy man. Holders of high offices, moreover, displayed a surprising readiness to mortgage their own estates in order to be able to lend money to the crown. There were of course always noblemen who became indebted beyond their capacity to pay, and went bankrupt. But before the *reduktion* they were the exception.

In other European countries, and even in a country as close to Sweden as Denmark, it was frequently the case that the landowning nobility found itself passing through a period of acute economic crisis. How far this was true of Sweden also is a question which cannot yet be said to have been thoroughly explored. But from such research as is available on the problem, one gets the decided impression that there is no trace of any such crisis in the period before 1680 as far as the Swedish nobility is concerned. One circumstance which seems to indicate that they were doing reasonably well is the fact that so very many of them, not least those belonging to the higher aristocracy, took advantage of opportunities to invest money in business ventures of various kinds, or in shipping, or in the trading companies. The Africa Company, which was formed to trade in slaves from West Africa (among other commodities), gives a good example of this. According to a list from 1656, the company's share capital amounted to 193,000 silver *daler*. Of this, members of the council had contributed 41,000, or 21 per cent; royal secretaries and holders of similar posts, 12 per cent; the executors of Louis De Geer, no less than 47 per cent; other businessmen and entrepreneurs 14 per cent; and miscellaneous investors 6 per cent. The profit to be expected was estimated at 37 per cent 'if the four ships that have been sent out come safe home again'. Hopes were high, it seems; but they were scarcely justified, for the company soon came to grief. Speculative enterprises of this kind, however, were by no means unusual in seventeenth-century Sweden, and occasionally they were rewarded with large profits. The interesting thing about the Africa Company, from our point of view, is that so many persons from the high aristocracy ventured their money in the concern, and also the striking fact that some secretaries could amass so much money that they could afford to speculate.

It was not until after 1680 that the Swedish nobility was confronted with a crisis, and when it came it was the result of political decisions rather than economic factors. It was brought about by the *reduktion*, when the nobility lost a great part of the land which it possessed or which it had in the course of centuries received from the crown. The principles governing these resumptions (which were extremely complicated) were laid down at the Diets of 1680, 1682 and 1686 under strong pressure from the monarchy; but many of the regulations were promulgated by Charles XI without consulting the Diet at all. It is thought that what the nobility lost was above all the detached farms which lay outside the demesne. For the *reduktion* gave the nobleman the right to satisfy the crown's demands with whichever farms might be most convenient to him; he naturally preferred to preserve the demesne intact and hand over property which lay outside it. The result was that the manors remained to a surprising extent in noble possession; and even when they were taken by the crown their former owner was often allowed to keep possession of them in return for providing and maintaining one cavalryman with full equipment. It is possible, however, to exaggerate the extent to which they succeeded in saving their manors: during the eighteenth century as much as two-thirds of the land of the nobility seems to have lain outside the demesnes. The hardest hit by the *reduktion* were the high aristocracy, since it was they who had acquired most from the crown; and its effects were reinforced by the commission of enquiry into the administration of the regency. This was almost exclusively directed at the high nobility, since it was they who had provided the members of the council who had governed during Charles XI's minority and who were now called upon to make restitution either in person or through their heirs. The commission fixed upon them pecuniary responsibility for the financial mistakes which the regency was considered to have committed; and the crown in consequence made enormous demands for cash compensation which proved ruinous to a number of leading families. Yet even so it appears that the high nobility recovered surprisingly quickly from these blows – to some extent by making advantageous marriages, which enabled certain great families to reassemble the lands they had lost. And some of the leading servants of the crown succeeded also in using the drop in the price of land which was a consequence of the *reduktion* to acquire great landed estates for themselves. (For further discussion of this question, see below, pp. 255–6.)

One important feature of the *reduktion* was the rigorous measures taken against those who had lent money to the crown in earlier and more expansive times. A typical instance of this, and also the most notorious example, is the case of Joel Gripenstierna. Gripenstierna had earlier held various appointments which involved the handling and administration of the king's revenues, and he had made handsome profits out of his dealings with the crown. After 1680 he was accused of misappropriation of funds and sentenced to reimburse the state to an enormous amount. He himself contended that he was in reality a man of high patriotism, who was undeservedly persecuted by his enemies in the civil service. However that may be, punitive measures of this sort naturally weakened the crown's credit. Charles XI, it is true, had no need to trouble himself about such consequences, since in his time the land had peace, and the crown could meet its expenses with the aid of new taxes and the resources acquired by the *reduktion*. Charles XII was not so fortunate. The Great Northern War almost at once swallowed up the reserves which his father had accumulated, and it became necessary to raise money by loans. In order to recover the confidence of lenders, Charles XII was forced, in a famous ordinance of 1700, to bring the machinery of the *reduktion* practically to a halt, and to promise to restore lands which had been taken in contravention of the terms of the *reduktion* ordinances.

Nevertheless one result of the *reduktion* remained, in the shape of a considerable diminution of the lands of the nobility; and this provides at least a part of the explanation for their weakened political position in the eighteenth century, and for the levelling process within the Estate which occurred in the same period. The lower nobility, who in general were more dependent upon the emoluments of service than the higher, were presumably gainers by the *reduktion*. This is clearly especially true for the very large number of families who had been ennobled after 1680, and had not to any considerable extent acquired land from the crown.

A very large proportion of the nobility served the state, in one capacity or another. They were especially strongly represented among the officers in the army. Sten Carlsson calculated that in 1700 every tenth nobleman was an officer; which would mean that more than half of the whole Estate of Nobility was at that time either wholly or partially maintained by military service. But there were also, of course, very large numbers of non-nobles holding commissioned rank: at the turn of the century they formed about two-fifths of the corps of officers in Sweden and Finland. At the Diet, noble and non-noble officers were jointly represented under the name of the 'Army Command'. The Army Command had no right to participate in decisions of the Diet, but it played its part in the formulation of complaints from the army, and was politically active in other ways, usually in support of the Nobility and at the Nobility's request.

In general, no officer who was not a noble could rise beyond the rank of captain: if he got past that barrier, he was given a peerage. Almost all the higher commands in the army were in noble hands. There has unfortunately been no investigation into the extent to which men who were not of noble birth acquired noble status and climbed to high rank in the army. In the seventeenth century it was probably relatively common, since the army was less concerned with birth than the civil service was. During Charles XII's war, moreover, all the ordinary rules went by the board, and many attained high military rank without being ennobled.

In the civil bureaucracy too there was an element of non-noble *ståndspersoner*, but only at the lower levels: when a man reached a certain stage in his career, he was ennobled. Even so it was extremely difficult for such men to reach the highest positions. Before 1680 there are only a few isolated instances in which it was done. One of those who got furthest was Johan Bengtsson Schroderus. Son of a burgomaster, he was ennobled under the name of Skytte, raised to the rank of baron and member of the council by Gustavus Adolphus, and made a name for himself as one of that king's outstanding ministers. Another parvenu was Johan Adler Salvius, whom Christina made a member of the council despite the protests of his future colleagues. The high steward Per Brahe made it an objection against Salvius that every man ought to be given office according to his Estate; Axel Oxenstierna declared that Salvius's nomination was in conflict with law and privileges; but Christina carried her point, incidentally citing Skytte's case as a precedent. A third commoner who attained the rank of council member was Matthias Mylonius, ennobled as Biörnklou, who was the son of a miller. All these were among those who opposed the high-aristocratic majority which desired to weaken the monarchy to the advantage of the council. After 1680 it became rather more common for persons not of noble birth, and peers of recent creation, to enter the council; and membership of that body became, what it had hardly been before, the final phase of a career in the civil service.

Non-noble civil servants, then (unless they were ennobled), got no further than the lower ranks in the service. They belonged to that group of *ståndspersoner* which might occupy really important positions but nevertheless was unrepresented in the Diet. Obviously they did not relish the position. In 1719 their discontent found expression in a petition to the Nobility from a group of non-noble office-holders, whose attitude is probably equally representative of that of similar groups during the previous century. In their petition they contended that they had acquired, through their official positions and their training, an insight into the affairs of state which fitted them to participate in the proceedings of the Diet. They also asserted the democratic principle 'that all *membra* who by their pains, labour and trouble have reciprocally contributed to preserve that body which is the state, ought also to be partakers in those general resolutions which affect its welfare, on which the welfare of each and all of us doth hang'.[15] They also pointed out that the Estates of the Diet had not all been constituted at the same time, but one after another, and suggested that a fifth Estate ought now to be instituted for the educated members of the non-noble population.

The petition gives evidence of considerable self-assurance in these *ståndspersoner*, with their belief in the importance of their potential contribution to the Diet's debates. But in 1719 the Diet was far from being ready to take the question of altering the basis of the representation into serious consideration. The problem was shelved by the ennobling in 1719 and 1720 of massive numbers of lower civil servants and their like. Of the twenty who signed the petition in 1719, eleven had been ennobled before the year was out, and three were ennobled later.

Within the Estate of Nobility, those lesser nobles who were in state service played a part of great importance. It was often they who led the opposition of the lower nobility to the higher. An example of this is provided by G. H. Taubenfelt. Taubenfelt was one of the secretaries to the chancery, and at the Diet of 1672 he came forward to defend the monarchy against the council in connection with the drawing-up of Charles XI's Accession Charter: among other things, he was anxious to prevent too strong an aristocratic influence upon appointments to the services. His action caused extreme resentment in the council. On this occasion, as on so many others, it became obvious that the king and the lower ranks of the civil service had a common interest in weakening the high aristocracy's position.

Within the offices of government those civil servants who were drawn from the lower nobility often occupied key positions. This was certainly true of the secretaries to the chancery. It would admittedly be difficult to prove that any of them during the seventeenth century exercised a decisive influence on the government for any long period. But the chancery secretaries controlled the channels through which the leading ministers could be approached; and this enabled them to play an important part as intermediaries between the outside world and those in authority, and as spokesmen for those who desired to negotiate some personal or political advantage. It was therefore extremely important, even for influential members of the council, to stand well with the secretaries, or at least with some of them, if they wished to have their suits presented and recommended to the king or the chancellor.

Civil service salaries were paid in some cases in commodities, in others in cash. At the beginning of the century it was quite usual for civil servants to have the revenues from one or more farms assigned to them as their wages. As the century progressed, this type of emolument tended to disappear, though examples of it persisted even under the absolutism. A method of payment which was in some respects similar to it was the so-called allotment (*indelning*), which applied above all to army officers and local government officials, who were paid out of the taxes levied on particular farms – the distinction from the earlier system being that the *indelning* was linked not to the office-holder but to the office, and was not given for life, or for some shorter period, but was supposed to be irrevocable. It was this system of payment to which Charles XI gave general application under the name of *indelningsverk*.

Before the establishment of the absolutism and the success of the *reduktion* the crown had not possessed sufficient farms to make the *indelningsverk* possible. And the trouble about wages which were paid in cash was that the demands on the treasury were such that the state often lacked the resources to pay them. It constantly happened, and above all in wartime, that half or more of an official's wages would be withheld, and the money applied to meeting more urgent needs. For many, this irregularity must have had disastrous consequences. Not, however, to the extent that might be supposed. And the explanation for this lies partly in the fact that many officials had private means of their own – donations from the crown, for example – and partly in the fact that a large number of offices afforded an income in addition to their official emoluments.

It is not easy to draw a line between legitimate and illegitimate earnings in seventeenth-century Sweden. This is true, for example, of the many officials who handled government funds, and made a fortune out of it: among them, as we have seen, a long line of directors-general of the customs. Such men had opportunities to use the funds and credits which were at their disposal in such a way as to ensure that whatever happened they should not be the losers. Often enough they lent money to the crown – sometimes, it was alleged, out of the crown's own pocket. After 1680 the commission of enquiry would deal drastically with such persons and their heirs.

Other offices enriched their holders with fees: this was the case with many places in the Colleges which brought their holders into touch with the general public. Earnings of this kind were considered, up to a point, to be unexceptionable. It was felt to be a natural thing to pay a fee on receiving one's letter of appointment to an office, or a deed of donation, or a contract. But there were complaints from time to time that officials in the Colleges, and especially the secretaries, demanded – in the words of a complaint by the Nobility at the Diet of 1654 – 'large gratifications, beyond what a man's resources will bear'.[16] At that Diet, indeed, there were violent attacks upon the secretaries' exorbitant demands for fees. Secretary Anders Gyldenklou, against whom the fiercest onslaughts were directed, was accused of extorting no less than 14,000 *riksdaler* for his good offices to a comparatively small number of persons. It was alleged that a patent of nobility involved a fee of 100 *riksdaler*, which was a considerable sum: a secretary would not need to draw up many such patents before he had amassed as much in fees as the amount of his nominal salary. And several secretaries did in fact become wealthy men, Anders Gyldenklou among them: he was in a position not only to buy numerous farms from the crown, but also to make large loans to it.

Those who held the highest positions in the kingdom, the members of the council, the generals and so on, were also able to make a good thing of their offices. By their influence in the government they could secure donations, or make advantageous agreements with the crown in the matter of leasing its revenues or buying its land.

After 1680 the opportunities for such additional earnings diminished. The fee system did indeed continue, but greater efforts were made to control it. The alienations ceased, and a sharp eye was kept on the rights of the crown when it came to leases and other contracts. The drop in bonus earning was compensated for by the fact that after 1680 ordinary salaries and wages were paid in full, and (as a result of the *indelningsverk*) to a large extent in commodities. The king hoped also to pay certain officials in the Colleges by *indelning*, but this project was never realised. Nevertheless the *indelningsverk*, as Charles XI established it, was to last until far on in the nineteenth century.

As we have seen, the three upper Estates probably did not comprise between them more than 3 to 4 per cent of the population of Sweden and Finland at the close of the seventeenth century. And we may well ask whether they are fairly entitled to as much space as we have given to them. In any social survey of this kind, would it not rather be reasonable to concentrate attention upon the broad mass of the population?

One possible answer to this objection lies in the fact that the three upper Estates were of course much more important in the structure of society than their share in the total population would suggest. The fate of the masses, as should now be clear, was largely determined by circumstances over which the ordinary man had no control. For example, the changes in the nobility's landed possessions, and in its political power, were of decisive importance to the peasantry. And the attitude of the clergy to the peasants, in the parishes no less than in the Diet, is further evidence of how the position of the Commonalty was affected by the social status of the higher Estates.

Nevertheless it may be frankly admitted that it would have been more satisfactory to give an account of the position of the lower classes in somewhat less general terms. But our picture of seventeenth-century Sweden can be based only on the information which is available to us. Of such historical writing as is concerned with social analysis, the greater part has been devoted to the three upper Estates. Historians have found great difficulty in achieving an overall view of the agricultural population, partly because it was so large and partly because conditions differed so widely from one part of the country to another. The source-material which has survived for the seventeenth century is not of uniform nature, and in many respects it is meagre. Before we are able to pronounce with confidence upon what was of general application and what was not, much detailed investigation will be required.

4. The Swedish Church

MICHAEL ROBERTS

IN the year 1663 the regency which was conducting the government during the minority of Charles XI put out a proclamation in which it congratulated itself (and thanked God) that Sweden had for so long a time been 'free from the infection of all false and heretical dogmas and hurtful novelties, and thereby attained to a unity and harmony in doctrine and practice such as no Christian congregation . . . and no Christian government . . . can boast of'.[1]

Broadly speaking, their complacency was justified. Throughout an age of sectarian division and theological strife the Swedish church remained singularly tranquil, and in the monolithically Lutheran fabric of the state scarce a hair-crack was to be detected. Swedish statesmen had no doubt of the importance for their country of this happy state of affairs. In 1636 Axel Oxenstierna told his colleagues on the council that religion 'is the great *vinculum communis affectus et societatis humanae*; and there is no greater or stronger *nexus concordiae ac communitatis* than *unitas religionis*'.[2] The Form of Government of 1634 had made the same point, and Johannes Loccenius – Sweden's first great jurist – was to lay it down that unity of religion was a fundamental law of the land.

It is true that clashes between the ecclesiastical and lay powers did occur; that the limits of the rights of each were a constant subject of controversy; that the Estate of Clergy on occasion came into sharp conflict with the Nobility on the one hand and the Peasantry on the other. But on the whole Swedish statesmen believed that theological problems were best left to the decision of the professional theologians; and the professional theologians on their side manifested no great propensity to heresy and schism. Of amateur theologians there were indeed plenty: Christina and Charles X carried on the tradition of interest in theology which John III and Charles IX had established in the previous period; Axel Oxenstierna was so learned a theologian that he could be called *sacerdos sine sacerdotio*; and a long succession of Swedish statesmen – Johan Skytte, Per Brahe, Johan Adler Salvius, Magnus Gabriel De la

Gardie, Matthias Björnklou, to mention only some of the more conspicuous – were, and considered themselves to be, well qualified to
engage in theological debate: indeed a Swedish pamphleteer could
write that 'without a thorough grounding in theology, no man can be a
politicus'.[3] Yet even they did not stray from the paths of orthodoxy: on
the fundamentals of Lutheran doctrine all were agreed. With the exception of Christina, all Swedish sovereigns from 1611 to 1718 had a deeply
ingrained piety; and though they might chafe at the pretensions of the
episcopate, they had a healthy respect for the spiritual authority of the
clergy. Gustavus Adolphus responded to Rudbeckius's censure of his
moral lapses by promoting him to the see of Västerås; Charles XI meekly
accepted Jesper Swedberg's strictures on the *reduktion*, when once it
was pointed out to him that they were grounded upon the Scriptures.[4]

Things had not always been so harmonious. John III had pursued the
will-o'-the-wisp of reconciliation with Rome (and duly landed himself
in a political bog); Charles IX had been suspected by his clergy of
crypto-Calvinism, with results which were scarcely much better; and
both reigns had witnessed divisions within the church and acute tension
between crown and clergy. But with the accession of Gustavus Adolphus
in 1611 the church for the first time for many years could feel itself
secure from danger; the crown abandoned its attempt to impose its own
doctrinal whimsies; *jus subditorum* prevailed over *jus reformandi*, and
as far as doctrine was concerned continued to hold its ascendancy for
the remainder of the century. Over wide fields of action church and
state collaborated in harmony, each complementing the efforts of the
other. The civil power was invoked, not in vain, to lend its aid in the
enforcing of church discipline and the bringing to book of contumacious
sinners (stringent statutes in 1665 and 1687 fulminated against the
misuse of God's name, the profanation of holy days and absence from
church); the Form of Government of 1634 ordered provincial governors
to support episcopal authority; and the constable usually accompanied
the bishop as he went upon his arduous visitations. The council of state
itself devoted an impressive amount of its time to sympathetic and in-
formed consideration of such matters; and lay and ecclesiastical jurisdictions tossed cases to and fro between them with surprising lack of
friction. In Charles IX's time elements of Mosaic law had been en-
grafted upon the Swedish legal system in order to provide norms for
dealing with certain categories of offences which lay on the borderline
between sin and crime, or perhaps partook of both – categories for
which King Christopher's Land Law had made no provision; and it

was now something of a toss-up whether such cases were decided by the
bishop and his diocesan court or by the *hovrätt* (Supreme Court); by
the Estate of Clergy assembled for a *riksdag* or by the council of state.
Often enough, indeed, a case might come before them all. In practice
this overlapping of jurisdictions caused less difficulty than might have
been expected, for all shared a common approach to these problems;
and though the *hovrätt* might take a different line from the bishop, the
Estate of Clergy and the council usually managed to sort things out on
the basis of a shared commitment to all godly ends.

If the state thus buttressed with its sanctions the authority of the
church, the clergy on their side were in virtue of their office committed
to the support of the state. In 1654 this commitment was made explicit
in the oath which they swore upon the accession of Charles X, for in
that oath they pledged themselves to 'exhort all of the commonalty who
anciently have been, and still are, liable to taxation, to give and render
their yearly dues to His Majesty, with goodwill and without fraud'.[5]
They complained indeed of the heavy unpaid administrative labours
which they were required to perform, especially in regard to the operation of the fiscal system and the machinery of recruiting, and of the
odium which this entailed. But they formed too large a proportion of
the educated population for the crown to be able to dispense with their
services. The 'clerking and summing' [6] had to go on; the pulpit remained
the necessary medium for the dissemination of royal propaganda, the
communication of governmental orders and regulations, and the calming
of public opinion. The parish was the basic unit of local government;
large sections of what would now be a part of the social services were
almost wholly in the clergy's hands – education, hospitals and poor-
relief, in particular; and here the church, continuing the traditions of
the Middle Ages, was rather concerned to maintain its control than
anxious to disburden itself of a duty. The crown was well aware that
the parson had an influence over his congregation which was of high
political importance; as Gustavus Adophus put it, in his farewell speech
to the Estates in 1630, it was the clergy's duty

> to adjure your congregations, whose hearts are in your power to
> twist and turn as you will, to be faithful and true to their governors,
> and to do their duty cheerfully and obediently, confirming them in
> all unity and concord, so that they be not let astray by evil men.
> And you shall not only exhort and persuade them thereto, but shall
> also yourselves show them the way, by your decent and modest

bearing; so that they keep themselves quiet and conformable not only by reason of your learned sermons, but by the example of your behaviour.[7]

In a country of large size and difficult communications it was vital to the lay power to feel that even in the most inaccessible backwoods it had an ally on whom it could rely to support the established order and persuade to acquiescence in government policies and fiscal burdens. Hence the state could never afford seriously to quarrel with the clergy – least of all during a minority, when the personal prestige of the sovereign was for the moment in abeyance. This is true even of such a monarch as Gustavus Adolphus, upon whom (as we shall see) the clergy inflicted a serious political defeat; it is true of Charles X; and it held good even under the absolutism of Charles XI: indeed it is just from the 1680s and 1690s that we have the most striking example of the clergy's acting as the executors of a political decision, for it was in the first instance through the church that the programme for the full integration of Skåne into the Swedish state was put in hand, by the holding of services in Swedish, the deprivation of Danish clergy, and the instruction of the young in Swedish hymns and the Swedish catechism.

The remarkable solidarity of Swedish Lutheranism, and its relative immunity to the grievous theological controversies which distracted the Lutheran churches of Germany, reinforced Sweden's claim to be the especial protector and champion of the Protestant cause everywhere. Botvidi had imposed Swedish ecclesiastical organisation upon conquered Germany; Rudbeckius had come like a new Reformer upon the degraded churches of Estonia and Livonia. The triumph of Westphalia, when contrasted with the decline of Denmark and the ignominy of electoral Saxony, had given Sweden a political predominance in the Protestant world and made Swedish statesmen and ecclesiastics unwilling any longer to take their cue from Wittenberg, Jena, Rostock or Helmstedt. The days were past when, as Terserus complained, Swedish theologians 'trembled like frightened schoolboys about the judgement of German theologians upon their orthodoxy';[8] and Axel Oxenstierna, for one, was determined that they should not come again. It was in an attempt to bolster up these new pretensions by scholarly prestige that this same Terserus embarked upon his heroic but ill-fated attempt to produce, single-handed, a new translation of the Bible based on the original texts – an attempt which got no further than the Pentateuch.

But essentially Sweden's position in the Protestant world depended upon political success rather than learned exegesis. And with that political success the church wholeheartedly identified itself. It would not be true to say that its influence affected foreign policy: decisions were royal decisions, and there was no question of their being deflected by clerical pressure for a Protestant crusade. But where the king led, the church gladly followed, not doubting that it was the work of God that was going forward in Germany or Poland or Russia. Bishop Enander saw Charles X's victories in terms of the Book of Kings; Dryselius in 1706 pointed out that God had cast down Augustus II of Poland because he had renounced the true religion for a kingly crown. After all, Haffen-reffer [9] (who was Sweden's preferred theological authority, and whom Charles XII is said to have had almost by heart) had laid it down that it was one of the duties of a king to defend his subjects by war when that was necessary to the preservation of their tranquillity and liberty. Moreover the armies of Gustavus Adolphus were (as far as he could make them so) godly armies; and the field chaplains who accompanied them were often men of high character and ability who later rose to eminence in the church: Rudbeckius, for instance, or Botvidi, or Matthiae, or Terserus – men of tough physical and moral fibre, able to impress their standards on the soldiery, as they were later to do upon their dioceses. Haqvin Spegel continued the line under Charles XI; and at the end of the century Jesper Swedberg noted, with reminiscent satisfaction, that when he was an army chaplain his regiment was more afraid of him than of the enemy. And the tradition of the godly army lived on too, in the armies of Charles XI and Charles XII. Specially designed *Manuals* of devotion were issued to the troops. Charles XI's proclamation of 28 September 1685 ordered that the regiments under the new allotment system were to be instructed in the creeds and cate-chism by their local incumbents, as long as they were living on their farms; or by the regimental padre when they gathered for their annual manoeuvres, 'since we find that one of the best, most necessary and most useful things in our army is that they be brought up in the fear of God; and particularly that the common soldiers, who cannot be well in-formed of these things, be diligently instructed in the elements of Christianity, whereby they may be brought from self-will and loose living to a true knowledge of the Most High'.[10] And when, after the catastrophe of Pultava, some 30,000 Swedes found themselves prisoners of war in Russia and Siberia, it was this tradition of godly discipline which enabled them to hold together through the long years of captivity, to create their own ecclesiastical organisation and to build their own church at Tobolsk.

I. DOCTRINE AND DISCIPLINE

The church of Sweden, in common with Lutheran churches in general, insisted that, though purged of error and superstition, it was still catholic. Its leaders might have said, with Archbishop Bramhall: 'We do not arrogate to ourselves a new church, or a new religion, or new Holy Orders. . . . Our religion is the same it was; our church the same it was; our Holy Orders the same they were, in *substance*; differing only from what they were formerly as a garden weeded from a garden unweeded.'[11] And indeed Swedish Protestantism still bore ample evidence of the older faith. Its episcopate believed itself to have preserved the Apostolic Succession; its cathedrals continued to retain their chapters; its congregations clung to customs, ceremonies and abuses inherited from pre-Reformation times. Laurentius Petri's Church Ordinance of 1571, strikingly conservative in its regard for tradition, took a genially tolerant line over *adiaphora* such as vestments, frontals, images and bells; permitted exorcism and the use of the cross in baptism, as conformable to long tradition; allowed large urban churches to have more than one altar; prescribed the singing of the canticles alternately in Swedish and Latin; contemplated the possibility of a return to vicars-choral; and listed a score of saints' days and festal days, including Candlemas, the Annunciation and Visitation of the Virgin Mary – so many of them in fact that in the next century the peasantry were to complain that their work was unduly interrupted. The Puritanism of Charles IX restricted some of this luxuriance; but it is hardly surprising that Bulstrode Whitelocke, when he visited Sweden in 1654, should have noted:

> In the Choir [sc. of Skara cathedral] are many pictures of saints and other images; and at the east end of it a high altar, with a rich carpet of velvet embroidered with gold, and a stately crucifix upon it: there are also divers other and lesser crucifixes in several places of the church and Choir. In the vestry . . . chalices and pyxes, with pieces of wafers in them; and none could see a difference between this and the Papists' churches.[12]

This latitude in matters of ceremony was long matched by a marked lack of definition of dogma. It had been no part of Gustavus Vasa's design to impose a doctrinal straitjacket upon the church: provided he could assert effective royal control and appropriate the wealth of the clergy, his religious feelings were satisfied by ensuring that there should be a godly preaching ministry. At the time of his death in 1560 the doctrinal position was still quite vague: the church called itself Lutheran no doubt, but it had adopted no formal confession. Sweden escaped the Zwinglian influences which England experienced; and though there was some alarm about Calvinism under Eric XIV, it was not sufficiently serious to drive the church to a formulation of its beliefs. That was effected only by the High Church ecumenism of John III. John's attempt to impose his own religious ideas upon his subjects, followed as it was by the supposed threat of re-catholicisation under Sigismund, forced the church to declare itself unambiguously. At the Uppsala Council of 1593 Sweden committed itself for the first time to the unaltered Confession of Augsburg which, with the three creeds, Luther's Bible and the Church Ordinance of 1571, was henceforth to be the basis of Swedish Lutheranism – with the addition, by the Form of Government of 1634, of Luther's Catechism. Thus in the definition of dogma Sweden was a whole generation behind England, and two generations behind Germany. But once the step was taken, it inevitably involved some participation in the theological debate which was raging on the continent. The philippism of Wittenberg, with its emphasis on a common Protestant front against Rome, commanded the sympathy of Charles IX. The rigid 'integrism' of the gnesio-Lutheran school of Jena [13] found its Swedish analogue in 'Norrland orthodoxy', which made the doctrine of ubiquity the shibboleth to distinguish friend from foe. In 1593 the Uppsala Council was still sufficiently Melanchthonian to take the Loci communes as its guide; but the grinding religious strife between king and bishops which darkened the reign of Charles IX had the effect of pushing the church away from philippism. And this meant, as the event proved, that henceforth there would be little chance of a 'continuing Reformation', which was certainly one of Charles IX's ideals: the church would take refuge in an orthodoxy increasingly narrow; theological debate would be reduced to expository exercises and learned glosses upon the Augustana and the Bible; and the dynamism of the Reformers would fade into a Protestant scholasticism not less arid than its medieval predecessor.

This process degraded the Bible into a quarry for texts appropriate to the demolition of theological opponents and the silencing of innovators; the *sufficientia et perspicuitas* of Holy Writ provided a clinching retort to end an argument. It was a development which coincided with (and indeed was related to) a closing of the shutters against the fresh breezes of Ramism, and a retreat into the vitiated atmosphere of neo-Aristotelianism. A knowledge of the Scriptures, it was held, was a *precondition* of that faith which is necessary to salvation. Thus the Scriptures stood as it were in the place of Christ as the agent of redemption. It was therefore unfortunate that the Swedish Bible of 1541 (a translation of Luther), besides having the defects of its original, had others of its own; and was besides far too bulky and expensive for the ordinary man. In 1630, indeed, Johannes Matthiae obtained a privilege to print the Bible in a more handy and portable format; but even so, it seems clear that there were plenty of churches in which no Bible was to be found.[14] Yet, accessible or not, the Bible was the foundation of orthodoxy – at least for the clergy: Swedberg took a modest pride in the fact that he had read the Bible so often that he could find the place in it with his eyes shut, and wished that all Bibles might be printed with the same pagination in order to render this feat easier. The need for a new edition had been realised as early as the reign of Charles IX, and a committee set up by him had provided, in the *Observationes Strengnenses*, some of the prolegomena to a critical text; but the initiative was never wholeheartedly pursued. Gustavus Adolphus's Bible of 1618 was little more than a corrected reprint of that of 1541; the *Observationes Strengnenses* gathered dust in the archives until Jesper Swedberg disinterred them ninety years later. It was left to the enterprise of individual churchmen to provide the new translation that was required: Terserus, Haqvin Spegel, Jesper Swedberg, all tried their hand at it. But their versions were either incomplete or considered too innovating; and in the end Charles XII's Bible (the work of a commission which was determined to have no nonsense about going to the original texts) proved to be little better than that of Gustavus Adolphus, with some misprints removed. In these circumstances the ordinary layman could never attain to that expertise in the game of bandying texts which was almost a national sport in Cromwellian England. Portions of Holy Writ did indeed become familiar to them from hearing the Epistles and Gospels, Sunday after Sunday; and it was also usual to read one lesson from the pulpit. The *Manual* issued to the army contained suitably martial selections from the Old Testament. But essentially the Scriptures were administered to the faithful through the vehicle of the sermon, which was designed primarily to teach rather than to edify:

for lack of cheap Bibles, the parson became, quite as much as in pre-Reformation days, the mediator between man and God, or at least the indispensable helper to grace.

Thus the Bible was not, as King James's Bible was, a book of the people; it did not become so, indeed, until the rise of the Bible Societies in the early nineteenth century. Its place was taken by Luther's Lesser Catechism in its Swedish translation, and by the various more or less official 'Explanations' of it which appeared from time to time. The catechism was readily available in a handy volume which included, besides the Epistles and Gospels for the day, those vivid if rugged Lutheran hymns which everybody knew: the tunes which the herdsman whistled as he grazed his beasts, and the housewife sang as she went about her domestic business. Hymns and catechism together provided the solid bedrock of popular piety: it is significant that when the Pietist movement began to challenge the church at the end of the century it sought to secure its foothold by the publication of its own 'Explanation' of the catechism, and by the production of new hymn-books with such typical titles as *Songs of Moses and the Lamb.* As Johannes Terserus put it in 1663, the catechism 'may be called the little Bible, since everything that the great Bible contains . . . as needful to be known to a man's salvation, is all in this little book; so that those who cannot read, or do not possess the great Bible, or lack the time to read it through, have from this little Bible all that they require'.[15]

It was therefore the duty of every pastor to see to it that his flock were instructed in the catechism: sermons were supposed to 'land on' some point in it; congregations were divided into 'files' (as for army recruiting!) for purposes of catechetical instruction. In this matter Sweden retained more of the spirit of Luther than did Lutheran Germany, where by the seventeenth century the practice of catechising had greatly decayed.[16] The Swedish parishioner must know his catechism by heart, though he might not be able to read, and still less understand it: if he fell short in this respect he might find himself excluded from communion, and the parson might refuse to marry him. For those who were capable of being instructed in the art of reading, catechism classes formed the bottom rung of the educational ladder and played an important part in the spread of literacy: thanks to the measures taken by Charles XI,[17] a quite high proportion of Charles XII's armies seems to have been able to read.

In one respect at least the Swedish church was for long doctrinally out of line with German Lutheranism, inasmuch as it did not include among its *symbola* the *Liber Concordiae* or the Formula of Concord which formed a part of it. It might perhaps have been expected that the moment of definition – at Uppsala in 1593 – would have provided the opportunity for its inclusion. If so, the opportunity was missed; and for nearly a century thereafter controversy raged as to whether the omission ought or ought not to be repaired. In the circumstances of 1593 the decision was intelligible. For the Formula of Concord (1580) had been an attempt to reconcile philippists and integrists in the face of the double threat of Calvinism on the one hand and resurgent Catholicism on the other; and in Sweden at that date the Calvinist overtones of philippism were less well appreciated than on the continent. The situation altered, however, upon the accession of Charles IX in 1600; for Charles's religious policy seemed to his bishops to make explicit all the latent dangers of philippism and to expose them to the pestilential influence of Geneva. It was natural enough, therefore, that in 1611 the Clergy should have demanded of Gustavus Adolphus the inclusion of the Formula among the articles of faith. They asked in vain; for Gustavus – perhaps from his father, certainly from his tutor Johan Skytte – had inherited a type of broad churchmanship which was averse to over-rigorous definitions. As long as he lived, the church's confidence in him, and his moral authority as the Protestant hero, sufficed to prevent the question's being seriously pressed; and in the Form of Government of 1634 the Formula of Concord was not mentioned. But in the later years of the regency, and in the reign of Christina, the demand for its acceptance became of importance once again. That demand was undoubtedly provoked by the Unionist activities of John Durie and his Swedish sympathiser Johannes Matthiae (see below, p. 148), but also by the influx of Calvinist Walloons in the wake of Louis De Geer. In 1647 the Clergy signed a declaration that they 'have held, and do hold, *Librum Concordiae* for the sign and rule of our true religion, and the further explanation of the confession of Augsburg', and asked Christina to pledge herself to see to it that *all* Estates 'take it for their true confession of faith and *Libro Symbolico*'.[18] By this time the tide of orthodoxy was already setting strongly; and Whitelock was justified in his comment that the attitude of the Swedish church was 'somewhat strict, and may be construed as an assumption of infallibility':[19] in 1647 Jonas Magni of Skara, in a sermon before the queen, had said that 'He who refuses to recognise *Formulam Concordiae* as a symbolic book cannot be accounted a Christian'[20] – a dictum which reflects the attitude of those

German Lutherans such as Hutter who did not hesitate to declare that *Liber Concordia* was inspired by the Holy Ghost.

In 1650 Christina appointed a small commission of clerics and laymen to draft an amended Church Ordinance; and the question of the Formula inevitably made a part of their discussions. The arguments they used on that occasion shed some light on the difficulty which Swedish churchmen felt in making up their minds. On the one hand the champions of the Formula insisted that it was a necessary bulwark against the danger of Unionism – a *'limes et maceries inter nos et Heterodoxos'*;[21] on the other it was urged that it would be disreputable to accept the private work of foreigners for a *symbolum* (if the *Liber Concordiae*, why not Haffenreffer too?); that Calvinism had hitherto been effectively kept at bay without it; that it was far too long, too polemical and too difficult to understand to be suitable as a *symbolum*; that many of the clergy had scarcely heard of it, still less read it; and finally, that so important an addition to the national confession must await the sanction of the *riksdag*. Axel Oxenstierna, who intervened weightily in favour of acceptance, was apparently influenced by the desire to preserve good relations with Lutheran allies in Germany, and probably also by his distrust of Calvinist Brandenburg. In the end moderation prevailed, at least for the time being: the committee would go no further than to accept the *Liber Concordiae* as a recommended *explanation* of the Confession of Augsburg. The ordinance on religion of 1663, and the draft Church Ordinance of 1682, really went no further than this. The orthodox movement within the church, which reached its culmination in the early sixties, was already moderating in the seventies, and laymen were growing less sympathetic to clerical rigour; and though Charles XI by his Church Law of 1686 did at last give to the Formula a quasi-symbolic character, the advent of more liberalising influences in the church made the ultimate result less important than might have been the case if it had come forty years earlier.

Few Protestant churches can have been so little troubled with sectarianism as the Swedish. Apart from a brief appearance of Anabaptism in the early years of the Reformation, there had never been, and in this period there never was to be, any religious movement which questioned the foundations of the ecclesiastical or the social order. From Socinianism, Familism and Quakerism the Swedish church had nothing to fear: perhaps because the social strata most congenial to such developments were in Sweden so thinly represented, and the level of literacy (at least to begin with) so low. In a country where Bibles were so scarce and expensive, and where so few could read for themselves, the Apocalypse offered no temptation to chiliastic speculation. And in any case Calvinism, with its apparently greater theocentric emphasis, was perhaps more vulnerable than Lutheranism to such divagations. However that may be, in Sweden they were certainly of minimal importance: the occasional 'enthusiast' got short shrift and attracted few disciples. Linderhielm could not find a single case of personal 'conversion' in the first half of the century;[22] and as to 'revelations', the average parson would have agreed with Petrus Gyllenius when he tartly observed: 'We have, thank God, revelations enough in the Word of God, and further visions are superfluous.'[23]

Attacks on the church establishment were almost unknown, and were certainly not linked, as in England, with attacks on the royal prerogative. Laurentius Petri's Church Ordinance had stated firmly that the institution of bishops is 'useful, and undoubtedly proceeds from God and the Holy Spirit, and so is universally approved and accepted throughout Christendom, and has always so been; and so must remain, for as long as the world shall stand'.[24] Apart from Gustavus Vasa himself, no Swede ever really questioned that statement. Certainly resistance to episcopal authority never assumed Puritan forms: the type of opposition to the episcopate represented by Johannes Baazius in the 1620s was a protest movement by a section of the lower clergy, which never came near to dissent; and though there were some bishops (Matthiae, Emporagrius, Stigzelius) who favoured the institution of some form of presbyterian organisation at the parochial level, they had no idea thereby of limiting their own authority, but were concerned rather to enlist the laity's aid in the maintenance of church discipline: in any case their suggestions met with little response. It never occurred to anybody to pursue the Brownist or congregational line; and a Rule of the Saints would have seemed as outlandish and incongruous in the Swedish context as a *Fronde princière*.

If episcopacy went unquestioned, so too did the authority of the parson in his parish. It was only an extreme statement of generally accepted doctrine when Litherius told his parishioners of Hagebyhöga that he was 'as it were in the place of God, as a spiritual Moses and as a Daniel', and demanded that they should show 'respect for his office, as being an ambassador, which indeed he is'.[25] Indeed one 'Explanation' of the catechism went so far as to categorise the clergy as 'Angels of the Lord God of Sabaoth'.[26] The Puritan demand for a godly preaching ministry would have fallen strangely upon a Swedish ear; for if there was one duty which every Swedish parson discharged with remorseless zeal it was the duty of preaching. The clergy's position as mediators with God was assumed as a matter of course. Luther himself had never given the idea of the priesthood of all believers much practical application, and in the Sweden of Rudbeckius it had as little place as the notion of the Inner Light or the idea of the Invisible Church; not until the Pietist movement at the beginning of the next century do we find anyone denouncing the clergy as 'priests of Baal'.[27] Bishop Enander, upon his appointment to Linköping in the 1650s, found a certain amount of unauthorised preaching in his diocese; but it was mostly by candidates for ordination who were anxious to get their hand in. There was some Paracelsian mysticism, and also some Rosicrucianism, in the time of Gustavus Adolphus and again in the 1650s; there were occasional judaistic aberrations too; and in the 1690s Finland produced a couple of radical Pietists whose exploits recall the more scandalous excesses of early Quakerism. But such problems were much less serious than the relics of paganism, the flourishing of superstition, and the great witchcraft epidemic of the 1660s and 1670s.

Nevertheless the church was taking no chances; and the limits of toleration, on paper at all events, were exceeding strait. The Succession Pact of Norrköping (1604) had debarred all non-Lutherans from the throne; Gustavus Adolphus's Charter of 1611 excluded 'papists, Calvinists, Anabaptists, or any other than Lutherans' from holding office, and particularly forbade their employment as schoolmasters. It had indeed taken care to add that 'for economic and military reasons, any private persons who are not subjects of this realm, and are of a different religion, shall not be denied the right to remain in the country and lawfully to pursue their avocations, provided they behave themselves peacefully, do not disseminate their errors, nor by word or deed attack or defame our religion and worship'[28] – and this provision remained a constant qualification throughout the period. But such persons were prohibited from holding services in private houses; and by later regulations were obliged to have their children baptised into the Lutheran faith and forbidden to educate them in their own religion. And even these concessions applied to laymen only. Even so, there was to be no persecution simply on grounds of opinion: the Charter of 1611 went out of its way to declare that 'no sovereign has power to control or govern a man's conscience'; and even the proclamation of 1667, at a moment when intolerance was at its height, contained the provision that 'no one, simply on account of his religion, shall be prosecuted or harassed, provided he conform to our laws, statutes and ordinances'.[29] These reservations, however, did not apply to Roman Catholics. For them there could be no toleration, even if they abided in peace under the laws; for the mere holding of Catholic beliefs was considered by the authorities to imply that sooner or later overt action was to be apprehended. For Gustavus Adolphus, as for Elizabeth, Catholicism was not merely a religious but a political menace. The Roman church was seen as the natural ally of the senior line of Vasa which sat upon the Polish throne, hopeful of reconquering its hereditary realm of Sweden with the aid of Spanish fleets and Wallenstein's armies. Hence the extreme rigour of the Statute of Orebro (1617) which required all papists to quit the country in three months; deprived Swedes lapsing to Roman Catholicism of all civil rights as though they were naturally dead; equated attempts at conversion with sedition; and outlawed any student resorting to a Catholic university. The operation of the statute was indeed limited to the duration of the war with Poland; but that war, as it turned out, lasted (with intervals of truce) till the Peace of Oliva in 1660. However, there was never any real danger from Catholicism after 1600: the Catholic 'plots' of the 1620s were trivial episodes; the conversion of Christina entailed her abdication, and was not an example which found many imitators. In 1653 Johan Ekeblad, in a familiar letter to his brother,[30] could write 'Catholic' as a colloquial equivalent for crazy. From time to time there was anxiety about services held in the private chapels of foreign embassies; there were occasional sensational lapses to Catholicism, such as Lars Skytte; but it all amounted to very little. Perhaps it was a realisation of this fact which restrained the government, even in the intolerant 1660s, from any re-enactment of the Statute of Orebro: in 1671 the rights of foreign embassies were restricted and a proclamation of the same year forbade the admission of Jesuits to Sweden in any circumstances, but that was all.

The case of the Protestant dissenters was not quite so straightforward, and in practice the law was much more flexibly applied. Gustavus Adolphus had after all married a Calvinist; his brother-in-law, John Casimir of the Palatinate, though a Calvinist too, was given high office: his exclusion from the regency after 1632 was a matter more of political jealousy than of religion. The truth was that Calvinists were too useful to the country to be restricted to the limits of 1611. Gustavus's most faithful allies in Germany were Calvinists; the new town of Göteborg was settled by a Dutch Calvinist community to whom the episcopal authorities found it politic to allow a good deal of latitude; Dutch financiers such as Abraham Cabiljau, Dutch entrepreneurs such as Louis De Geer, even an Anabaptist shipwright such as Francis Sheldon, rendered to their adopted country services which entitled them to special consideration, despite the rumblings of the Estate of Clergy. The massive influx of foreigners into the Estate of Nobility – from Scotland, Germany or the Low Countries – reinforced the expediency of connivance with considerations of privilege; for noblemen were apt to resent the attempts of clerical zealots to enforce the law. Those attempts nevertheless could be successful on occasion. In 1655 the Estate of Clergy denied Christian burial to the stepdaughter of a heretic nobleman;[31] and in 1668 the jealousy which the lesser native nobility felt for these foreign incomers, and the resentment at their frequent success in the highly competitive scramble for offices, produced a resolution of the *riksdag* depriving of civil rights all those who educated their children in heresy, even though they might be noblemen.

But from the thirties to the fifties the needs of the state ensured that it should often avert its gaze from breaches of the law. The Walloons whom De Geer brought to work in his manufactories were virtually autonomous religious communities, with their own schoolmaster imported from Flanders: they attended Lutheran services no doubt, but they probably paid more attention to their schoolmaster's reading from the *postilla* when the formal service was over; and it is unlikely that compulsory baptism into the state church left many traces upon most of them. Under Charles X, however, and still more under the regency that followed him, there was a sharp reaction, for both had strong political reasons for keeping on the right side of the Estate of Clergy. A statute of 1655 punished those who celebrated heretical services (though not, apparently, mere prayer meetings), or who imported heretical teachers, with a fine of 100 silver *daler* for the first offence, imprisonment for the second, and expulsion from the realm for the third. An ordinance of 1667 required all heretics already resident in the country to report immediately to the nearest parson: neglect to do so would entail loss of toleration, and a presumption that the offender harboured designs against the state. But it may be doubted whether there was much more in this than an attempt to appease clerical indignation. The Scots community in Stockholm in 1661 presented an address of thanks to the crown for the liberal toleration they enjoyed; and though there might be complaints in the Estate of Clergy at the prevalence of Calvinist heresy, their debates do not suggest that the government made much effort to do anything about it. The foreign influx was in any case dying away; the second generation of Walloons was becoming assimilated to the Swedish environment, and there was not much sign that they were infecting the community with their erroneous ideas about the eucharist, or winning a popular following for their views on predestination. By the 1680s alarm had so far subsided that Charles XI's Church Law could permit the holding of Calvinist services in private houses, provided they took place behind locked doors.

One particular aspect of the struggle to safeguard the Church from error was the problem of student peregrination. In the sixteenth century, when the University of Uppsala had for long periods been virtually moribund, all Swedes in search of higher education (whether theological or not) had been forced to resort to the universities of the continent, and especially of north Germany; and even after the munificence of Gustavus Adolphus had put Uppsala on its legs again, the habit continued. It was reinforced by the desire of the aristocracy to acquire the civility and social graces appropriate to the élite of what had now become a great power: the practice of sending sons of the nobility on the Grand Tour began to take root. Poor students, too, continued to go abroad, often with *stipendia* from their dioceses, and spent months or years wandering from university to university as their fancy took them, attracted by the reputation of this or that eminent professor; not much deterred, it seems, by the hazards of the Thirty Years War. Inevitably some of them came home with unorthodox opinions. The Statute of Orebro did effectively deter them from frequenting Catholic universities or going to seminaries such as Braunsberg or Olmütz; but the peril of Calvinist influences remained: indeed it rather increased, as the trend of peregrination set increasingly towards Holland, and even towards England. From the time of John III the authorities at home made repeated attempts to exercise a supervision over such students by ensuring that they were firm in the faith before departure, and by examining them when they came back to make certain that they had not in the interval absorbed any dangerous ideas. The responsibility for this supervision was laid, now upon the bishops, now upon the university, but it was never continuously or systematically applied, and it does not seem to have been very effective. The nobility, not unreasonably, tried to draw a distinction between its own sons who fared abroad to learn fencing and French at Saumur, and the needy ordinand who went to improve his theology and drifted into perilous company at Helmstedt; and they resented the church's interference as an infringement of their privileges. The distinction was acknowledged in 1661, when peregrination became free; henceforward sanctions were to be applied only to those theologians who upon their return were found to be infected, and even this was probably retained only in the hope of keeping the Swedish church out of the syncretist controversy then raging in Germany.[32] By 1686 the last element of compulsion had been abandoned: Charles XI's Church Law of that year was content to *exhort* those about to travel abroad to take care that they were well grounded in the faith before setting out.

Thus the attempt to control peregrination failed. Yet from the point of view of the orthodox the history of the Swedish church certainly suggested that the attempt had been necessary. For the main threat to Lutheran orthodoxy throughout the period came, not from any indigenous dissent, but from dangerous notions imported from abroad.

The first of these was Unionism. Already by the opening of the seventeenth century a revulsion from the ceaseless squabbling of Protestant theologians had led to a desire for conciliation, and indeed for reconciliation. It found perhaps its most popular expression in the *Irenicum* of Pareus. Pareus was a Lutheran turned Calvinist, and his book was a plea for the reunion of the two main Protestant confessions in a common effort to fight the reviving power of Rome. It had thus something in common with the theological views of Charles IX, and was akin to the broadly tolerant outlook of Gustavus Adolphus. But the Unionist movement really made its first appearance in Sweden with John Durie. Durie, a Scots Calvinist who took Anglican orders, devoted most of a long life to propaganda for the cause of reunion. He made his first contact with Axel Oxenstierna at Elbing in 1628, pursued him round Germany in the years that followed, and eventually appeared in Sweden in 1636 at the invitation of Louis De Geer. Durie sought to reunite the Protestant churches by concentrating on certain fundamental dogmas common to them all, and treating all the rest as *adiaphora* – an approach which, however sweetly reasonable it might at first sight appear, was foredoomed to failure as soon as it became necessary to decide which was which. More constructively, he pleaded for a 'practical theology' as against the scholasticism of contemporary polemics; and sought to divert some of the ardour expended in controversy into the more rewarding field of pastoral ministration. Oxenstierna encouraged him for a time in the mistaken belief that he spoke for Laud, and that a willingness to go along with him might persuade Charles I to intervene in Germany as Sweden's ally; but when this turned out to be a misapprehension he made no great difficulty about gratifying the indignant Swedish episcopate's demand for Durie's removal.

But though Durie thus vanished from the scene, his influence remained. In Johannes Matthiae Gothus (whom Durie had met in Würzburg in 1631, and with whom he renewed contact in 1636) he found a receptive audience for his ideas, or at least for some of them. Matthiae was an enlightened educationist who won the friendship of Comenius; a brilliant linguist, more especially in oriental languages; pious, learned, humane and tolerant; an inveterate snob whose *savoir-vivre* put him on easy terms with the aristocracy: in many respects, indeed, a natural Anglican. He was also tutor to that trying infant prodigy Queen Christina, and was one of the few Swedish divines for whom she had any respect: as long as she remained on the throne his influence in the church was considerable. Matthiae gradually emerged as a convinced Unionist. He prepared the way for reconciliation by the production in 1646 of his *Idea bonae ordinis*, which drew heavily on the Church Ordinance of the Bohemian Brothers; and also by his suggestions for amending the Swedish liturgy along lines which were alarmingly reminiscent of the Anglican Morning Prayer.

About the same time the University of Helmstedt, under the leadership of George Calixtus (1586–1656), had produced that movement for reconciliation which its enemies termed syncretist. Calixtus disavowed any idea of reunion; but he agreed with Durie in the plan of fundamental doctrines, as contrasted with those doctrines which were rather matters of theology than matters of faith; on these latter, he believed, Protestant churches should be content respectfully to differ, appealing for guidance to the early Christian church, to whose authority he attached much importance. By the end of the 1640s, Lutheran Germany was torn in two by the syncretist controversy; and it was not very long before the quarrel spread to Sweden: already at the *riksdag* of 1655 Archbishop Lenaeus was warning the clergy of the danger. Matthiae's *Idea bonae ordinis* had aroused the deep suspicion of some of his colleagues; and their alarm was not allayed by the production in 1656 of his *Rami olivae septentrionalis*. Christina was known to have intended that he should draft the revision of the Church Ordinance; and with Charles X he was in high favour. It was no wonder if orthodox bishops such as Laurelius saw in him not so much an errant sheep as a wolf in sheep's clothing.

In reality the flock was in no great danger: Unionism had virtually no following in Sweden. Syncretism, however, could command rather more sympathy. The orthodox grouped them both together, transferring Calovius's attacks upon Calixtus to Matthiae, and on the other hand fixing upon syncretism the stigma of doctrinal appeasement, betrayal of the faith and crypto-Unionism. Hence the demands in the fifties and sixties for the acceptance of the Formula of Concord as a *symbolum* which might be used not only as a preservative against Calvinism but as an offensive weapon against dissident Lutherans. Hence too the resistance to that demand by the lay authorities; for though they felt no inclination towards Calvinism, they felt just as little desire to brand Helmstedt as heretical and so exacerbate the divisions in the Lutheran camp. Fortunately these views were shared by the theological faculty at Uppsala, which did its best to exercise a moderating influence upon the excessive zeal of a section of the clergy. After 1660, indeed, the regency, under heavy pressure from the clerical Estate, was driven to the conclusion that the easiest way to escape the *odium theologicum* which was poisoning the air of Germany was to sacrifice Matthiae; and he was duly removed from his bishopric of Strängnäs in 1662. At the same time the government constrained Terserus to resign his see of Abo; for Terserus, in an effort to win the Walloons to a genuine Lutheranism, had published a catechism of syncretist temper which concentrated on essentials and played down theological difficulties. In 1664 the regents formally condemned the writings of Matthiae and Terserus, lumping both together in the same document; which was less than fair to Terserus. But this was a matter of tactics rather than of conviction, a device to clear the Swedish church of the imputation of appeasement, and above all to avert schism; and it represented no more than the regency's determination not to be dragged into the syncretist controversy and not to quarrel with the clerical Estate. As such it was successful. Matthiae ended his days comfortably provided for, and on excellent terms with his noble friends; Terserus was speedily rehabilitated, and in 1671 became bishop of Linköping. The unity of the church was preserved, no more was heard of syncretism, and the cause of orthodoxy seemed to have triumphed.

Already, however, that triumph was threatened from other quarters. It was in 1663 that Cartesianism first made its appearance at Uppsala: typically enough, in the faculty of medicine, where Professor Hoffwenius lectured in terms of the New Philosophy, to the scandal of a university where for nearly half a century neo-Aristotelianism had held an almost unchallenged ascendancy. Cartesianism was offensive, not merely to the philosophers, but above all to the theologians, since it seemed to attack the verbal inspiration of Scripture and propounded views of the soul which were irreconcilable with Lutheran (but not with Calvinist) theology. In 1664 the Estate of Clergy demanded that the teaching of the New Philosophy be forbidden. The chancellor of the university, however, was Magnus Gabriel De la Gardie, who happened also to be chancellor of the realm and the leading personage in the regency; and De la Gardie – cultured, learned, very much the man of the world – declined to be stampeded into strong action. Hoffwenius did indeed pretermit his lectures, but he did not cease to disseminate his ideas; and his *Synopsis physica* (1678) speedily established itself as the university's textbook of physics. By the 1680s Cartesianism had firmly entrenched itself in Uppsala, at least in regard to medicine and the natural sciences. In 1686, however, there came a reaction. Encouraged perhaps by the death of De la Gardie in April of that year, the Uppsala theologians, led by the quarrelsome Professor Schütz, induced the Estate of Clergy to send a memorial to the king requesting the transferring of the natural sciences from the faculty of medicine to that of theology, the censorship of Cartesian books and disputations, the prohibition of 'hurtful novelties', and the imposition of a test of competence in Aristotelian philosophy upon all candidates for examination.[33] Charles XI, though impeccably orthodox himself, was not prepared to accept these demands without investigation, and accordingly referred the petition to the university. As might have been expected, the university split on the issue: on the one hand the faculties of medicine and philosophy, on the other the faculty of theology. The king had therefore to resolve the matter himself. In 1689 he made his decision: henceforward neither Aristotelianism nor Cartesianism was to be either forbidden or enjoined. But to this solomonic judgement was added an important rider: the Cartesians were to forbear from any 'philosophical criticism' of the Bible. This in fact gave the church what it really wanted; and though Cartesianism retained its hold upon medicine and the sciences, and may have been a factor in the scientific efflorescence of Sweden in the eighteenth century, the 1690s saw a strong Aristotelian revival in other fields of study.

The victory of orthodoxy was less clear cut in regard to Pietism. Pietism was indeed a healthy reaction against the increasing aridity of orthodoxy; it was an attempt to recapture the vernal enthusiasm of the Reformers, which seemed to have withered under the fierce heat of theological polemic. It stood for a greater concentration on the practice of piety, preached a religion mystical and emotional, and tended to a Christocentrism which at times luxuriated in the morbid imagery of Christ the Bridegroom and dwelt overmuch on the Blood and Wounds of the Passion. These excesses laid it open to the reprobation of the austere, but its fervid piety was nevertheless both salutary and necessary. In its dynamism, its intense preoccupation with the problem of personal salvation, its abhorrence of luxury and philistine attitude to the arts, it bore some resemblance to certain types of Puritanism. Such an approach to religion must always be present or latent in any Christian society: even Axel Oxenstierna thought favourably of Lewis Bayly's *Practise of Piety* (which was later to inspire Bunyan), and Karl Karlsson Gyllenhielm found sufficient edification in Johann Arndt's *Vier Bücher vom wahren Christenthum* to sponsor its translation into Swedish (1647). But it first became explicit in Johannes Matthiae, who seems to have been influenced not only by Bayly, but by Lancelot Andrewes and Willem Teellinck. The eclipse of Matthiae after 1660, however, effaced his influence, and the Pietist movement proper did not really take root until the 1680s, with Olof Ekman and Christian Scriver, who was a personal friend of Spener and chaplain to Queen Ulrica Eleonora, the pious widow of Charles X.

At first it aroused no great opposition: in the 1690s Uppsala permitted its students to frequent Spener's university of Halle; and it even seems to have gained a foothold in the faculty of theology. But the more aggressive type of Pietism propounded by Spener's successor August Hermann Francke was a different matter. The church soon came to realise that the Pietist movement, with its individualist approach to religion, its impatience with the regular routines of parochial piety, its anarchical tendency to a loose congregationalism, was irreconcilable with the established church order. Swedish Lutheranism was strong because it was based on the parish; it was a collective faith suited to a collective village society of which the church formed the natural centre, and of which the parson was the natural leader and arbiter. The cement that held it together was compounded in part of pagan customs in Christian guise, popish practices whose significance had been conveniently forgotten, and respect for clerical authority. The Pietist conventicle, overriding and breaking down parochial associations, replacing the old local community by a community of the 'saved', was a danger which must either be resisted or somehow absorbed. The church on the whole opted for resistance. The authorities began to thunder against conventicles; Charles XII, disliking Halle as a Prus-

sian university, forbade his subjects to study there; and in 1706, from
the depths of the Polish bogs, he found time amid the labours of his
campaign to launch against the Pietists the Edict of Lusuć. Before
Pultava, however, the Pietist movement had only limited success; the
defences of orthodoxy, reinforced by the crown, held fast. A dozen
years later they were showing signs of crumbling. The tragic and disastrous years after 1709, marked by pestilence, defeat and despair, provided exactly the kind of moral climate in which Pietism could flourish,
and it is hardly surprising that the Swedish prisoners of war in Siberia
should have turned to it for consolation in their forlorn condition. Its
message was so clear, it so obviously provided a much-needed infusion
of spirituality into official religion, that it was no wonder that a man
such as Jesper Swedberg (deeply committed to his pastoral functions,
but no Pietist himself) should have welcomed the positive elements of
its teaching. Swedberg insisted that theological studies were futile if
they did not lead to Christian conduct; he castigated the church's
excessive preoccupation with faith at the expense of morals; he demanded (as Durie also had done) not a *theologia verbalis* but a
theologia realis; and he was not afraid to endorse what seemed to him
to be good in Arndt, Bayly, Spener and even Molinos. When the Age
of Greatness ended, though the great days of Pietism were still to come,
it had administered much the same kind of jolt to the church of Sweden
as John Wesley was later to administer to the church of England.

But no more than a jolt. By and large Swedish Lutheranism, in 1718
as in 1611, retained its impressively monolithic character, at least as
regards doctrine. As to ceremonies, the story was very different. The
Church Ordinance of 1571 had been neither sufficiently precise nor
sufficiently comprehensive to ensure uniformity; and already at
Uppsala in 1593 it had been recognised that some clearer definition was
needed. The *Handbok* of 1614 attempted a more general regulation of
services; the *Psalmbok* of 1645 won a wider acceptance than its com-
petitors; and an official collection of prayers was published in the same
year. But the *Handbok* was not universally followed, and there was
nothing to hinder private individuals from producing hymn-books and
collections of prayers of their own. Ecclesiastical arrangements varied
from diocese to diocese, according to the taste and fancy of the bishop.
No uniformity in the ordination oath; no agreement on church fees
(vagabond priests often stole business from incumbents by performing
funerals at cut-price rates); protracted debates as to whether exorcism
and the sign of the cross should or should not be used in baptism. In the

absence of firm direction, it was inevitable that bishops should make
their own regulations; and Oxenstierna complained in 1636 that they
issued ordinances about christenings, marriages and funerals which had
no basis in law. The bishops on their side were impenitent; their object
was to secure uniformity of usage within their own dioceses, and they
had no great enthusiasm for general regulations which would set bounds
to their 'evangelical liberty': Rudbeckius told the council in 1636 that
diversity in liturgical use was preferable to disturbance. In vain did the
Form of Government prescribe uniformity; in vain did Christina's
Accession Charter promise to secure it. The privileges granted to the
Clergy in 1650 surrendered the point by expressly giving to bishops the
right to make their own diocesan regulations, in so far as they were
necessary to good order. Nothing, it seemed, short of a full revision of
the Church Ordinance could provide a national solution to the problem; and for that the church had to wait until 1686.

II. CHURCH AND STATE 1611–1680

Among the main preoccupations of the church in the seventeenth
century was the central issue of its relation to the state. After 1527,
when Gustavus Vasa forced some sort of Reformation upon clergy
and people, the church might indeed seem delivered over into the
sovereign's hands; and certainly the king's actions in the years that
followed amounted in fact, if not in theory, to the assertion of an almost
untrammelled royal supremacy. Yet the appearance was to some extent
illusory; for even Gustavus Vasa would have conceded that he intervened in church affairs only when the bishops seemed to him to be
failing in their duty. If on the one hand ecclesiastics were henceforward
debarred from meddling in temporals, on the other the lay power
interfered in spirituals only when it must: church and state were regarded as separate spheres. As long as Gustavus Vasa lived this was not
fully apparent; but in the Church Ordinance of 1571 it was clearly
spelled out: the king's only concern with the church was to be to confirm (not appoint) bishops, to see that the Word of God was rightly
preached, and to ensure that a sufficient supply of godly ministers was
forthcoming. The idiosyncratic liturgical initiatives of John III, however, and the fears provoked by his search for a reconciliation with
Rome, made some clearer definition of state–church relationships necessary, and produced a demand for a general council of the church which
led to the meeting at Uppsala in 1593. But though the Uppsala meeting,

and the Charter which Sigismund had to accept as a condition of his coronation, guaranteed the church against the danger from Rome, it did little to safeguard it against royal attempts to impose a type of Protestantism of which it might not approve. Under Charles IX the monarchy once again tried to exercise a royal supremacy in much the same way as Gustavus Vasa had exercised it. The lay power encroached once more on the church's preserves, as well in matters spiritual as in questions of order, usage and discipline. The separateness of the two spheres seemed directly challenged, and to that challenge the clerical Estate responded with determined resistance.

In taking this line, the church could appeal to the respectable authority of the Reformers themselves. Article 28 of the Confession of Augsburg had laid it down that *'non commiscendae sunt potestates ecclesiastica et civilis'*: the king's *jus reformandi* was to be the extreme remedy of the church's constitution, not its daily bread. Melanchthon had written that it was the duty of a king to be *minister et executor ecclesiae*; and if he had also said the prince was *praecipuum membrum* of the congregation, he never forgot that he was still *membrum* and not *caput*. As the sixteenth century drew to its close, however, German Lutheranism – perhaps as a measure of security against the Counter-Reformation – acquiesced, at first tacitly, then explicit, in a shift in this balance of forces, a commingling of the two spheres. More and more princes came to exercise a real supremacy in church affairs, and Lutheran Germany saw everywhere the emergence of a *landesherrliche Kirchenregiment*, based *inter alia* on the contention that the princes had by the terms of the peace of Passau fallen heirs to the sovereignty which previously had inhered in the Emperor. Political theorists were not slow to provide a justification for the change. The church, it was now argued, was compounded of three estates: *status politicus*, to whom the care of the church in all external things was entrusted; *status ecclesiasticus*, which was concerned with matters of faith and the discharge of priestly functions; *status oeconomicus*, the mass of the congregation, which participated in church affairs in virtue of its rights in regard to the appointment of ministers. The lay power was thus accepted as an integral part of the church, rather than as an authority set over against it; whether it should also be a preponderant part was still an open question. The balance was tipped more firmly in the prince's favour by Erastus, who laid it down that, as far as the church was concerned, *'internae guberator est deus: externae moderator est magistratus unicus'*.[34] From this it was a short step to the contention that *respublica non est in ecclesia, sed ecclesia in republica*. If this was indeed so, there could be no doubt that the sovereign was *praecipua pars* in the three estates of which the church was composed, and that he must be considered as *custos utriusque tabulae*. If, however, Erastus's conclusion were rejected, it was still possible to accept the concept of the three estates while denying to *status politicus* any pre-eminence over the other two. And this in fact was the position taken up by most Swedish churchmen in the first half of the seventeenth century, as a sort of second line of defence once the older theory of separation had so fallen out of fashion as to be defensible only with difficulty. It was an attitude which was based not only on religious but on political considerations; for under John III and Charles IX the church had been opposing absolutist tendencies as well as objectionable doctrines; and the revolution which evicted King Sigismund in 1600 had been as much a political as a religious movement. Against Charles's *jus reformandi* they opposed *jus subditorum* – a principle which had constitutional no less than religious applications.

In 1611, at a moment when the accession of Gustavus Adolphus as a minor presented an opportunity to hold the monarchy to ransom, the Clergy had extorted what they believed were satisfactory guarantees of the church's rights – as indeed in many respects they proved to be. But though Gustavus might be personally pious, doctrinally unexceptionable, and by the close of his reign invested with unique moral authority, the 1620s saw the beginning of a long struggle between church and state which did not end until 1686. Reduced to its elements, the quarrel turned on whether the state was within the church, or the church within the state. Gustavus, like his father, had no doubt about it: he referred on one occasion to 'our sovereign fatherland, and God's church *that dwells therein*'.[35] His clergy, on the other hand, believed that kings were no more than '*defensores, directores, patroni*, or something of that sort, since they are there only for an outward convenience and usefulness, and society even without them can have its complete form and *esse*'.[36] Mixed up with this fundamental disagreement were other issues: the clash between diocesan autonomy and centralised administration; the struggle of the Clergy to secure and defend its privileges as an Estate of the realm. Laurentius Paulinus Gothus told the council in 1636: 'We ask to be maintained in that dignity which God has given us. *Nam nos sumus legati Dei*.'[37] In one aspect, moreover, it was a question not only of church versus king, but also of cleric versus layman, since the church, in the effort to defend what it believed to be its rights and privileges, came into collision with the nobility's claim to a specially favoured status; while the nobility, in the exercise of their privileges, frequently rode roughshod over the rights of congregations, flouted the church's disciplinary authority and abridged those tithes upon which the clergy relied for their support. Under a monarch such as Charles IX, church and nobility had been able to form a common front against the extension of the prerogative and the menace of a 'rule of secretaries'; but against noble privileges which threatened their own order, the clergy found natural allies in a peasantry which felt itself in danger of enserfment. And however hard they fought against the crown's authority in church affairs, they rallied to its side in support of its efforts to curb an over-mighty aristocracy, and consistently advocated a *reduktion*. Thus the Clergy's attitude was determined, not only by their claims as *status ecclesiasticus* within the Christian polity, but also by their claims as one of the four Estates of the Realm within the Swedish state. The debate on the respective rights and authority of church and king was at all times liable to be affected by social and political side-winds, and became a sort of ring-dance in which every participant was liable to change partners: material and class interests were always modifying the stances of the theologians. And finally, divisions within the church itself – of higher clergy against lower, of modernists against conservatives – wove a new thread into an already confusing pattern.

The argument tended to focus itself on certain specially tender areas in church–state relations: on appointments to livings, and the crown's right of *régale*; on the election of bishops; on the church's right to make such regulations as might be requisite for good order; on disputes about jurisdiction and the enforcement of church discipline; on the nature of the body to be entrusted with the revision of the Church Ordinance. But the first and for some time the most obvious battleground was provided by Gustavus Adolphus's proposal to set up a *consistorium generale*.

The plan was first put forward in 1623. It aimed at creating a central administrative and supervisory council for church affairs, composed both of lay and clerical members. This body was to function as a supreme appellate court in ecclesiastical and 'mixed' causes, thus disburdening the council of state of a good deal of troublesome business; it was to assume responsibility for schools, hospitals and poor-law administration; it was to secure uniformity in liturgical usage; and it was to act as a forum for hearing cases between bishops and their clergy.

The proposal did not otherwise trench on the authority of the bishop within his diocese, and it carefully excluded matrimonial causes and disputes about presentations to benefices. In these respects it was no doubt more moderate than the corresponding arrangements usual in Lutheran Germany; but it is none the less clear that it was inspired by the example of German consistories, and that it was, as its opponents complained, a foreign importation. The king was delegating his right of inspection, and his duty to be *defensor et nutricius ecclesiae*, to a standing administrative board on which the lay power would be strongly represented.* Thus the church would have been subjected to the same process of administrative centralisation as was already being applied to other aspects of government; the *consistorium generale* would have been in fact a *collegium* for ecclesiastical affairs. And by its creation the church would have been placed firmly inside the state, and a long step forward taken in the direction of giving Sweden a *landesherrliche Kirchenregiment* on the German model.

It was no wonder that the bishops reacted strongly against these proposals. The leader of the opposition was Johannes Rudbeckius, bishop of Västerås. To Rudbeckius the plan was a violation of the Church Ordinance, and was besides in conflict with the teaching of the Reformers. He particularly disliked the prospect of interference in church affairs by three members of the council: that the same persons should sit one day in the *hovrätt* and the next in the chapter was, he considered, an arrangement only fit for papists, who 'appropriate both swords to themselves, and have one foot in the pulpit and another in the town hall'. 'Once we let the politicians in', he warned his colleagues, 'they will have it all their own way.' [38] A mixed consistory would be a *monstrum*; lay assessors would be exercising the authority of bishops. This, we may be sure, was really where the shoe pinched: 'No one', exclaimed Rudbeckius indignantly, 'ever heard of any bishop having to stand examination and render an account of his administration.' [39] It was not that the episcopate was insensible of the need for some body to exercise a general supervision over church affairs; they were indeed quite prepared to contemplate the institution of a consistory – provided it was firmly under their own control. But they were not in the least impressed by the example of Lutheran Germany: on the contrary, they

* The lay representatives would have been the high steward and two members of the council who were members of the *hovrätt*. Misgivings were not confined to the clergy: Per Brahe, for instance, feared the setting up of a *consistorium inappellabile*, in which a plea of noble privilege might not avail.

thought it an example to be avoided. As to the difficulty of 'mixed' causes, they considered it exaggerated, and contended that existing diocesan machinery was well able to deal with the problem.

The intransigent opposition of Rudbeckius and his colleagues eventually produced a stalemate: in the face of their compact opposition Gustavus Adolphus was forced in the end to a compromise which promptly became a dead letter. With the coming of the regency and the domination of the state by the high aristocracy the church was even less ready to acquiesce in an arrangement which might well have reinforced that domination; and when the idea was revived by Christina in 1649 in the hope of strengthening her control of the church, they opposed it for the same reasons which had moved them in the time of Gustavus Adolphus. After 1649, the scheme for a *consistorium generale* was as good as dead: the church had defeated both monarchy and nobility.

Yet there were by this time some at least among the bishops – Matthiae, Emporagrius, Stigzelius – who would have been glad to save it, if only because they were convinced that there could be no really effective church discipline if the aid and sympathy of the laity were not enlisted in the enforcing of it. These were the men who had envisaged some sort of presbyterian form of parochial government with the same end in view; and they would have been very ready to run the risk of the politicians' getting a foothold in the central administration of the church for the sake of the reinforcement of spiritual authority which their collaboration might be expected to bring with it. But since such an arrangement now seemed out of the question, the church was driven to develop an alternative central authority of its own. The Estate of Clergy, assembled at each *riksdag*, seemed the best available body for the job: it was, after all, the *status ecclesiasticus* incorporate. By the mid-century it had established a prescriptive right to act as a kind of appellate court for ecclesiastical problems; and to it were referred many of the difficulties with which the *consistorium generale* had been designed to deal. It became something like a real consistory; and when transacting such business it did in fact call itself *consistorium regni*. The reported debates of the Estate of Clergy amply reveal with what energy (and at what inordinate length) it applied itself to matrimonial tangles, educational matters and clerical squabbles, until at length it was consigned to oblivion by Charles XI.

Until that happened, the church could feel that it had beaten off the challenge of the state, and was effectively master in its own house. And that meant in fact that it was effectively under the control of the bishops. In no Protestant country did the episcopate achieve such a concentration of admitted authority and real power as in Sweden. Each diocese was to a great extent an isolated unit, with its own customs and procedures, possessed of a strong diocesan self-consciousness, hostile to clerical intruders. Parishes were as far as possible reserved to clergy of the diocese – hence much trouble with members of the nobility who came back from the German wars and installed former field chaplains in livings to which they had the presentation; and no member of the clergy might travel outside the diocese without his bishop's permission. The bishops indeed ruled their dioceses like so many popes, with an authority which varied only with the personality of the holder of the see.[40] And for the most part they were eminently fitted to rule. The Swedish episcopate in the seventeenth century could show a long line of commanding figures: men of piety and learning, vigorous administrators, undaunted champions of the church's rights. Johannes Rudbeckius, Petrus Jonae, Laurentius Paulinus Gothus, Isak Rothovius, Samuel Enander, Canutus Hahn, were men whose personal qualities would probably have made them illustrious in any age of the church's history, and certainly did so in this. They were both judges and lawgivers, businessmen and educators. They accomplished prodigies of labour, were constant in visitation, diligent in the training of priests, active in the care of the poor. They presided over the *gymnasia*, which were indeed usually of their creation. They preached with evangelical zeal, catechised incessantly, fostered learning, literature and the arts, and made of their cathedral towns real outposts of civilisation in a backward country.

This benevolent autocracy was only partly mitigated by the existence of chapters; for the chapters were of a kind peculiar to the Swedish church. They did indeed still include the Swedish equivalents of dean, archdeacon and (sometimes) treasurer; but since Charles IX's time these diocesan dignitaries had been swamped by the *lektors* in theology of the local *gymnasia* or, in the case of Uppsala, by the professors of the university. The church's monopoly of education, and the fact that the main purpose of education was the production of priests, made the change intelligible; but it sometimes had the effect of divorcing the clergy of the diocese from its central administrative organ – though Rudbeckius, for one, created what he called a *consistorium majus* composed of *capitulares rurales*, which gave the average parson some chance of making his voice heard. And it meant too that if the bishop, as frequently happened, made appointments to the *gymnasium* on his own authority, he could to some extent hand-pick a chapter to suit himself. Relations between a bishop and his chapter naturally varied with the personalities concerned. Laurentius Paulinus Gothus met with compact resistance on his translation to Uppsala – perhaps because his predecessor had been too old and too easy-going; but on the whole the impression clearly emerges that the bishops had the upper hand. Rudbeckius was sufficiently confident of his own authority to permit the institution of a system of weighted voting in the chapter of Västerås (with four votes to himself); but it seems to have been applied only occasionally, and we are scarcely surprised to hear that the bishop was never voted down.

Nevertheless there were not wanting challenges to the power of the episcopate. Axel Oxenstierna held that decisions by chapters ought to be on a democratic basis; and he spoke for many laymen when he told the bishops in 1640: 'You make sumptuary laws, prohibiting *luxum* in marriages, and this no doubt is laudable enough . . . but it is not your place to do it: you may indeed rebuke scandal; but not make laws about it.'[41] '*Ferre leges*', as he had remarked on a previous occasion, '*est magistratus.*'[42] But it was not only laymen who were disturbed by the bishops' proceedings. In 1629 Johannes Baazius, the vicar of Jönköping, made a frontal attack on them, accusing them of arrogating unwarranted authority to themselves, overriding the views of their clerical inferiors, packing the Estate of Clergy with their own nominees, and behaving as though they alone were the church. Baazius's broadside was so intemperate in tone that it defeated its own ends: the clergy of the dioceses of Strängnäs and Västerås, for instance, felt impelled to rally to their bishops' support. But it did reflect a growing feeling of resentment, based at least in part on the widening social gulf between the episcopate and the country parson. That feeling, as we shall see in a moment, erupted with startling violence at the *riksdag* of 1650.

Yet it was difficult to see how a measure of diocesan autonomy (and hence, almost inevitably, of episcopal legislation) was to be avoided, as long as Church Ordinance of 1571 remained the church's only guide; and nearly three generations of intermittent debate failed to reach agreement on any revision of it. There was no question of producing something wholly new: Laurentius Petri himself had foreseen that his ordinance might require to be elaborated and completed, and it was generally agreed that it must remain the basis for any future regulation; all that was needed was that the lacunae in it should be filled. But as

soon as an attempt was made to do this, they stuck fast either on points
of doctrine (e.g. the adoption of the Formula of Concord), or of ceremonies (e.g. exorcism), or upon the delicate question whether laymen
should be permitted to have a share in the work. The clergy produced
drafts of their own in 1619 and 1626, but they were not such as Gustavus
Adolphus could approve. The regency toyed with the idea of setting
the chancery to tackle the job, and Christina actually instructed Johan
Adler Salvius to do it. A mixed commission sat for some months in
1650, and again from 1655 to 1659, but it did not get very far. Rival
versions were drawn up by Matthiae, Laurelius and Emporagrius;
but all for one reason or another proved unacceptable. It was only in
1682 that the Estate of Clergy agreed upon the full text of a new
ordinance; and this was promptly wrecked by an unlikely combination of king, Nobility and Peasantry. The Peasantry complained of the
clergy's greed for fees, of the excessive rigour of some forms of church
discipline, of the clergy's 'popish' pretensions; the Nobility attacked
humiliating public penances, and the fact that a man might be punished
twice for the same offence, once by a civil, once by an ecclesiastical
court; and behind the agitation were the royal secretaries, who perhaps
already looked forward to the day when the church should receive its
law at the king's hands.

Meanwhile church discipline had to go on as best it might. And
indeed it went on with astonishing vigour and success. Religious duties
were enforced, morals were supervised, fines, penance or excommunication were imposed, with a rigour which extended (even if somewhat
tempered) to the nobility. (Matthiae, characteristically enough, advocated discrimination in the nobility's favour.) The drunkard, the
swearer, the gossip, the caller of names, the brawler in church, the
caster of spells, even the privileged undergraduate, were firmly called
to account; marital disharmony was rebuked, and ill-assorted couples
constrained to live together in a semblance of amity; divorce was
granted in appropriate cases; while those who were backward in paying
their tithe received a pungent reminder of their obligations. There
was indeed no rigorous enforcement of the Sabbath as a day of rest,
once morning service was over: Swedberg was wistfully envious of
English standards in this respect. But not even Puritan New England,
much less the old England of the major-generals, could show so far-
reaching an interference with the privacy of the individual. Of course
there were abuses, and even psychological cruelty, as for instance in
regard to the penance of standing naked at the church door, or sitting

in the 'whore-bench'. But the low level of morality, and the extreme violence of ordinary life, made some such correctives necessary.[43] And the system was effective because it was recognised as being necessary, and so was not on the whole unpopular. The parson carried the same prestige, and exercised over his parish the same sort of authority and leadership, as the bishop in his diocese; though that authority was supported, far more than the bishop's was, by the active aid and collaboration of his flock. For the parish, like the diocese, was a world in itself – a tightly integrated community which differed in customs and dress from its neighbours across the parish boundary: when it was proposed to cut off a slice of one Värmland parish and transfer it to an adjacent parish in Närke, the change was resisted on the ground that parishioners would be subjected to 'foreign' customs.[44] And this sense of community was the life-blood of an essentially democratic form of parochial self-government, which was to have far-reaching effects upon Swedish society. The vicar was assisted, not only by his church-wardens, but by a committee of six or twelve parishioners who helped with church finance and administration, and above all with church discipline; and all were accountable to the vestry, which comprised all parishioners (including women and nobles) and met once a year to receive a report of their stewardship. Vigorous lay participation made the parish a vital force in the life of the church, made church member-ship a real concern to the individual, and probably helped to lay the foundations for the political education of the nation.[45]

This normally satisfactory relationship was made possible because the average country parson, in origin, outlook, standard of living and way of life, was so close to those in his spiritual care. Competition for livings was fierce, for throughout the whole century there seems to have been a slight over-production of priests. This meant that there was no problem of non-residence; and pluralism was confined to an extremely small section of the clergy comprising bishops, university teachers and regimental chaplains. It meant too that a man might remain for most of his days in the parish to which he was first appointed. His family might indeed stay much longer; for clerical dynasties were common, and a parish might easily descend from father to son through three or four generations.[46] This identification with the locality was reinforced by the practice known as 'conserving the house', whereby parishes were given to those who would undertake to marry the widow of the previous incumbent. It was an arrangement convenient to all parties: to the parish above all, since the parson's wife was frequently a benevolent matriarch whom parishioners would not wish to lose, and because the practice relieved them from responsibility for making other provision for her; to the new incumbent, because otherwise she would have been entitled to receive the tithe and inhabit the vicarage for the first year of his incumbency; for the widow, because once that year of grace was over she might find herself condemned to a life of the bitterest poverty and social degradation. But it could on all too many occasions lead to unsatisfactory appointments, and to a grotesque and unseemly discrepancy in the ages of the spouses.

Perhaps 30 per cent of the clergy were born in peasant homes; and of the 40 per cent or so who were sons of the manse, many curates and assistants must have lived on very much the same level as the poor cottagers of the parish.[47] They saw at close quarters the effect of the alienation of crown lands, and the threat of enserfment which it seemed to imply; and they had a direct interest in the peasants' demand for a *reduktion*, since the heavier the burden upon him, the harder it was for him to pay his tithe. Very different were the circumstances of some of the great bishops. Matthiae, favoured by Queen Christina, had been given lands in noble tenure, was a shareholder in a copper works and a paper mill, and was in a position to lend money to the government and to private persons. Enander was allowed to buy noble lands for himself, his wife and his male heirs, and was himself ennobled. Georg Gezelius was sufficiently well off not to bother to take a receipt for a loan of 300 copper *daler*. Svebilius worried about finding suitable investments for his wealth, and put some of it into land. Swedbergs's two wives (both of whom were daughters of the clergy) each brought him a sizeable fortune, part of which he devoted to financing the publication of his numerous books; though he took pride in the prudent economy of his second wife, who wore her mother's wedding-dress (then sixty years old) when she married him. Such persons were clearly moving into a different social stratum from that of the ordinary parson (and still more that of the wretched unbeneficed clergy), and often enough they had laid the foundation of their fortunes by securing a position as tutor to a noble family. (Mobility upwards was, however, offset by mobility downwards: clerical dynasties could in a few generations degenerate, under the influence of isolation in a backward environment, from the episcopal level to that of sexton, gravedigger and finally peasant.)[48] The upper clergy, and the episcopate particularly, were a tightly-knit family group, linked together by a bewildering network of intermarriages: it was rare in the second half of the century to find a bishop who was not related by marriage to at least one of his colleagues on the bench. It is true that this advance in social standing was not peculiar to the upper clergy, but tended to apply (though in much inferior degree) to them all. Certainly the clerical Estate provided one of the most clearly defined patterns of social mobility which the age could show: the progression peasant–priest–official–nobleman, in the space of three or four generations, is a classic stereotype of Swedish social history; and it became still more marked after the mid-century, when an increasing number of parsons' sons began to seek careers, not in the church, but in the civil service. (However, Swedberg complained to Charles XI that the *reduktion* had practically blocked this avenue to preferment.)

Yet the feeling of alienation between upper and lower clergy was undoubtedly there, and it was exacerbated by the beginning of the practice of ennobling the sons of bishops. The lower clergy suspected the bishops of sympathising with the nobility, and looked with jealous eyes on men like Matthiae and Enander. The suspicion was less than fair; for probably only Matthiae was a committed supporter of noble privilege and an opponent of the *reduktion*, and Archbishop Lenaeus was certainly a warm defender of the interests of the peasantry. But unfair or not, in 1650 these feelings led to very sharp clashes in the Estate of Clergy. At the *riksdag* of that year the lower clergy, led by Terserus (not yet a bishop), broke out into formal rebellion against their episcopal superiors, held private conclaves from which the bishops were shut out, told them that if they would not support the peasants' demands they had no business to be present, and howled them down in debate; and it was only with difficulty that the tact and sympathy of Lenaeus was able to restore a decent semblance of unity to the Estate.

Nevertheless, despite these divisions, the Clergy, as an Estate of the Realm, had well-defined interests common to them all, and as an Estate they played a part of considerable importance at the *riksdag*. Often their actions were essentially defensive – the product of their fear of the nobility: hence their dislike of the regency in 1633, and their reluctance to accept the Form of Government as 'eternal'; on this occasion they went so far as to threaten to refuse supply until their grievances were redressed. Hence too their pressing for the acceptance of Charles Gustavus as hereditary prince in 1650; hence their obstinate rearguard action to prevent the annulment of his testament in 1661; hence, finally, their willing support for the absolutism of Charles XI. Their political activities did not endear them to the aristocracy: if the church resented the meddling of politicians in its affairs, the politicians equally resented the church's meddling in theirs. In 1650 one indignant nobleman was heard to say that it was time to 'root out these vermin'; and Magnus Gabriel De la Gardie later remarked acidly that they 'took needless care of the country's secret and important affairs'.[49]

If so, it did not cause them to lose sight of their own sectional interests. Above all they struggled to obtain a grant of privileges which should define and safeguard their individual and corporate rights in the same way as those of the Nobility were defined by the privileges of 1612. The demand for privileges had been put forward as early as 1593, and it was renewed in 1617; but when Gustavus Adolphus died in 1632 it was still unsatisfied. The rights and authority of the clergy were still in great measure a matter of custom and common consent, rather than of specific enactment. There was always the danger that the state might on occasion try to take their servants for the army, or commandeer their farmhands for a *corvée*, or impose upon them its own candidates for livings, or attempt to collect taxes from which they claimed to be exempt; there was need for their right to impose *levem coercitionem* upon sinners and recalcitrant clergy to be recognised more formally; and there were signs in the early thirties that some members of the nobility were ready to take advantage of the lack of any precise definition of the extent of clerical privilege. In 1636, therefore, Bishop Rudbeckius was moved to draw up a very forcible statement of the clergy's case. His *Privilegia quaedam doctorum* was an attempt to justify their claims upon historical and comparative grounds, and it provoked extreme indignation in the government, first by reason of its provocative citation of pre-Reformation precedents, and secondly by the acerbity of its style, and its thinly disguised attacks on the nobility. To Johan Skytte it seemed that 'a more dangerous book had not appeared in Sweden these hundred years';[50] and the situation was not much improved by the fact that Rudbeckius seems to have modelled his demand for privileges on the *Postulata Nobilium* of 1594. Axel Oxenstierna, scenting in Rudbeckius's performance a challenge to his own authority, took trenchant action: having summoned him to appear before the council and explain himself, he charged him with 'laying the foundations of a popish authority', administered a magisterial rebuke, and forced him to apologise.

Yet though Rudbeckius had been guilty of a tactical error, his colleagues were right to intercede for him. For the clergy had real ground for disquiet; they really needed privileges for their protection: as

Rudbeckius himself had said, without them 'we become peasants'.[51] And it was not a matter which concerned the Estate of Clergy only; it involved the balance of forces in the state. As the Bishop of Växjö put it in 1650: 'Soon there will be no more than two Estates, the king and the Nobility; and then if the nobles should set themselves against the king there will be none to help him.' [52]

This no doubt was a consideration which was not lost upon Queen Christina. At all events, in 1650 the Clergy at last got what they wanted. The privileges given to them in that year mark the high tide of the church's influence within the state. They secured the bishops' right to be consulted about presentation to livings in the crown's gift, and gave them power to restrict the number of chaplains that might be employed by the nobility; they placed clerical revenues on a firm and definite basis of law; reaffirmed *privilegium fori* for the clergy, and *de facto* accepted the *consistorium regni* as the supervisory body for the church; guaranteed a proper provision for education, and recognised the clergy's control of it; endorsed the bishops' right to make regulations for the government of their dioceses; and for the first time gave legal status to the machinery of parochial self-government. Had it been possible to reach agreement on a revised Church Ordinance, much of this might have been unnecessary; as it was, the grant of the privileges amounted to a recognition by the crown that it must come to terms with reality and make the best of the situation as it existed. It had also one other important feature, this time of a constitutional kind; for it was an outstanding example of *de facto* legislation under the guise of a privilege to particular persons. And since it was already common ground that no Estate would concur in passing laws which infringed the privileges given to another, the grant of 1650 seemed to entrench the church's rights and liberties so firmly that it would be difficult in future to abridge them.

III. THE CHURCH AND THE ABSOLUTISM 1680–1718

So indeed it might have proved, if the Swedish constitution had remained as it was in 1650. But the coming of absolutism in the years after 1680 brought changes to the church which matched those which were taking place in the state. In little more than a decade the problems and controversies which had engaged the church's attention for more than three-quarters of a century were almost all resolved; and resolved not by agreement but by royal fiat. Charles XI reduced the church to a condition of subjection such as it had not known since the time of Gustavus Vasa. A stream of royal edicts imposed a new pattern upon ecclesiastical affairs; dogma, ceremonies, the relationship of church and state, ecclesiastical organisation, church discipline, were all firmly taken in hand, with results which were to set their mark on the church for many years to come.

Most of these changes were effected by the great Church Law of 1686, which at last provided the revision of the Church Ordinance for which men had contended for so long. It was the work mainly of a layman, Erik Lindschöld, and it was communicated to the Estate of Clergy only after it had received royal approval. They found it expedient to accept it 'with particular satisfaction', and it did indeed define and clarify much that had hitherto been doubtful or obscure. But the definition, in very many respects, was in a sense to which such a man as Rudbeckius would never willingly have assented. Some provisions, it is true, were not unduly disturbing. There was not much about dogma, and what there was suited the church well enough: a long controversy was ended by the statement that henceforward the *Liber Concordiae* was to be accepted as a symbolic book. In regard to ceremonies, the Church Law announced flatly that uniformity was now the law: there was to be no more variation according to the whim of this or that bishop. A new catechism (1688), a new *Handbok* (1693) – which incidentally enjoined the sign of the cross in baptism – and a new *Psalmbok* (1698) ensured that there should be no doubt as to what was intended. A new School Ordinance (1693), though educationally reactionary, imposed uniformity of practice in this field also. The king's concern for a godly preaching ministry was made manifest in the elaborate directions about the matter and manner of sermons – including the salutary injunction to use plain Swedish and eschew overmuch Latin. The competence of the clergy was to be ensured by regular ordination examinations and by a prohibition on the ordination of anyone under the age of twenty-five. Catechising was now to be compulsory, and fines were to be imposed upon parents whose offspring played truant from catechism classes.

So far there was little with which even the most prickly churchman could quarrel, but there followed provisions which marked a radical shift in the balance of power. So, for instance, in regard to crown livings. The *reduktion* had swept into the king's hand the presentation to very numerous livings which had previously been in the gift of noble patrons; and the Church Law gave clear warning that the process would continue. It continued to such effect that by the end of the century it was only in the poorest livings that the presentation still remained in the hands of the bishop and the congregation; and even for these the king now reserved his right to install his own candidate. By 1693 no fewer than 178 of Finland's 199 parishes had been declared to be livings in the gift of the crown. The effects of the change were unfortunate: ambitious seekers after rich preferments thronged the corridors of power; appointments were made by favour, or simony, or to the first-comer; and not seldom were granted in reversion. So too in regard to the appointment to bishoprics: as before, the chapter drew up its list of candidates and presented them to the king; but now he assumed the right to ignore their recommendations entirely, and to force upon them a man of his own choice. But the most decisive change came in regard to jurisdiction. The clergy now lost their *privilegium fori*, and were in future to be tried in the ordinary courts; and though deprivation was recognised as being the business of the bishop and chapter, it was henceforward only the corollary of a verdict in which they had had no share. Most of the apparatus of church discipline was at a stroke transferred from the ecclesiastical to the lay power. Henceforward penance was to be essentially a *punishment*, and a punishment inflicted only by a lay court: the duty of the ecclesiastical authorities was simply to see that it was performed; they became the mere agents of the state in a matter of public policy. And very soon the practice grew up of sentencing men to penance, not only for habitual drunkenness or sexual delinquencies, but for an essentially civil crime such as theft. The chapters were indeed for the first time given a recognised legal status; but in so far as they retained jurisdiction they were now subordinate to the Supreme Court, to which an appeal would lie in all cases save those which concerned doctrine or the failure of a cleric to discharge his priestly functions. Parochial self-government, *e silentio*, was suffered to remain; and at that level the old machinery of moral discipline continued to function without interference; but the judicial powers of bishops and chapters were whittled away almost to nothing. (The Church Law left them with the right of excommunication, on the ground that it had a long tradition behind it; but drily remarked that the king's laws were so effective that it was not envisaged that the right should come into play very often.) With the clerical judicial powers went the authority of the *consistorium regni*; Charles XI peremptorily forbade the use of the term in future. The reports of the debates in the Estate of Clergy dramatically illustrate the change: before 1686 the Estate devoted a major part of its time to matrimonial causes, clerical irregularities and private feuds between one member of the Estate and another; after 1686 practically all this business falls away, and they were free to concentrate on financial grievances, attempts to escape the allotment system, and the menace of Cartesianism.

They could not complain that the new custodian of the manners and morals of the nation neglected his duty: in 1687 came a statute against breaches of the Sabbath; orthodoxy was buttressed by the establishment of a censorship, first by the chancery (1684), and afterwards by the creation of the post of *censor librorum*. And in 1688 the king introduced the punishment of the stocks for young delinquents, smokers in church-yards and those who disturbed the piety of worshippers by audible con-versation or other unseemly behaviour. But the implications of the Church Law were spelled out most clearly in the Instruction for Provin-cial Governors of 1687. For among the duties which that instruction laid upon them was the duty to 'maintain religion and the proper forms of worship, so that the Word of God be taught and preached with truth, purity and zeal, and no delusive heretical doctrines be disseminated, openly or secretly, among our subjects'.[53] It is true that the governor who came upon traces of heresy was directed to alert the bishop and see to it that he did something about it; but it was a new thing in Sweden for a lay official to be charged with the safeguarding of doctrine and ceremonies. Moreover he was to see to the care of churches, schools and hospitals – a charge which had hitherto been exclusively clerical; and he was even to keep an eye on parsonages to ensure that there were no dilapidations, and if necessary to call vicar or congregation to account. Clearly, the old dispute about whether the state were in the church, or the church in the state, had now been decisively resolved. Where Charles IX, Gustavus Adolphus and Axel Oxenstierna had all retired baffled, Charles XI had succeeded: succeeded without a struggle, and almost without a protest.

And indeed it was not altogether surprising if the Estate of Clergy accepted these revolutionary changes almost as a matter of course. The *riksdag* had in 1682 virtually surrendered its legislative rights into the king's hands; and if he might legislate by royal edict for the state, it was not illogical that he should do the same for the church. In the ecclesiastical as in the lay sphere, the objective was now a centralisation of authority and a uniformity of practice, in the interests of efficiency; and we may well believe that only the sovereignty of the crown could have cut the Gordian knots of ecclesiastical controversy. Charles XI had no wish to function as *summus episcopus*, and was careful to steer clear of questions of doctrine; but he did not therefore intend to tolerate a situation in which his sovereign authority could be stopped short at the churchyard wall or the chapter-house door. Two limits set bounds to his absolutism: one was his respect for law; the other was his deep personal piety and real humility of spirit: he would never have suffered his courtiers (as Louis XIV did) to turn their backs on God in order to adore God's vice-gerent. He was indeed devoted to the church's interests (among other things he was a great builder of churches), and the clergy understood this very well: he was almost as much the Swedish church's king as Queen Anne was the English church's queen. It was not mere flattery that prompted Haqvin Spegel to say of him that 'by his great and many virtues he was as like Almighty God as any mortal man can be';[54] and if Jesper Swedberg never went quite as far as this, his admiration and affection illuminate many a page of his autobiography. The combination of this devotion to the person of the sovereign, with the acceptance (for very intelligible social and political reasons) of a *de facto* absolutism for which it would be reassuring to find a theoretical justification, produced a native theory of divine right, propounded with greater or less moderation in *riksdag* debates, episcopal charges and academic dissertations. Though in some aspects – as for instance the doctrine of passive obedience and non-resistance – it bore obvious resemblances to similar theories in contemporary England and may even have been influenced by them, it contrived to flourish without any Filmerian reliance upon the paternal authority of Adam. It preferred to pin its faith on the Epistle to the Romans;[55] or (in its more extreme manifestations) on the horrific schedule of royal prerogatives deployed by Samuel *in terrorem* when the perverse Israelites clamoured for a king;[56] and though it asserted that the monarch's authority over his people was given to him by God, it would not have admitted that he was *solutus legibus divinis*.

Only one voice was raised (at least, above a whisper) to challenge this new royal absolutism in church affairs, and to denounce the divine-right theory which supported it; and that voice was speedily silenced. The eccentric Jakob Boëthius, vicar of Mora, was moved to protest against those who encouraged the king to think that 'in those things which pertain to Christ and the rule of His congregation, he is to legislate and ordain according to his will and pleasure': for this seditious utterance he was condemned to life imprisonment, and actually served a sentence of thirteen years. There was no place for Fénélons in Caroline Sweden.

And though many sympathised with Boëthius's sufferings, there were few to echo his opinions, at least for as long as Charles XI was alive. The absolutism did no doubt bind the church pretty tightly; but on the whole it bound it comfortably too. Only the years of disaster after Pultava could reawaken the desire for autonomy which had been so strong in the first half of the century. Then indeed Boëthius was seen as the champion of a constitutional cause. Yet though the revolution of 1719–20 swept the absolutism away, clergy and peasants were sufficiently mindful of what Charles XI had done for them to renew the old alliance against the threat of aristocratic domination. And though in 1720 it might seem that for the church, as for the state, the absolutism had been no more than an episode, a temporary aberration, a good deal of its ecclesiastical work remained. The laicisation of church discipline had come to stay, and the religious legislation of the reign of Charles XI provided the norm for the eighteenth century.

But after 1720 the clergy found themselves for the first time confronted with an omnicompetent parliament which saw no reason why it should be precluded from regulating church affairs. In matters ecclesiastical, as in so many other ways, the *riksdag* of the Age of Liberty was the inheritor of the prerogatives and political attitudes of the crown: it was symbolic that in 1727 the non-clerical Estates revived for a moment Gustavus Adolphus's plan for a *consistorium generale*. The Clergy were still strong enough to block that project. They were still strong enough to secure the outlawing of conventicles by the act of 1726. But henceforward they would always be torn between the doctrine of popular sovereignty on which the new constitution rested, and the older theory of politics which gave them special rights as *status ecclesiasticus*. The great days of Rudbeckius and Paulinus had gone beyond recall, and the new leaders of the clerical Estate must of necessity be politicians – and indeed party politicians – quite as much as churchmen. A Hat such as Browallius, a Cap such as Serenius, would play a great part in the life of the state; but it was not a part which would have seemed very fitting to the great bishops of an earlier day.

Nevertheless the seventeenth-century church had stamped Sweden with an imprint slow to fade. Until the middle of the nineteenth century the Swedish church – and hence, in no small measure, Swedish society – retained the shape into which it had been cast in the first half-century after 1600. It was the seventeenth century, far more than the sixteenth, which established the traditions, the moral authority, the durable orthodoxies, of the Swedish Lutheran church. In an age when Lutheranism

elsewhere appeared to be sunk in torpor or given over to arid disputa-
tion, Swedish Lutheranism developed a vigorous inner life, an effective
organisation, a social authority and a self-assurance in its relations
with the state which set it apart from all other Lutheran churches. It
did no doubt inhibit or stifle much that might have been fruitful and
good. It was narrow, authoritarian and intolerant. But its organisation,
its practice, its social attitudes, were excellently well adapted to the
very special kind of society to which it had to minister. And by its
laborious hours of catechising, by its patient battle with illiteracy, by
its civilising influence upon a rude and violent people – in short, by
its unique contribution to education at all levels – it laid the foundations
of the modern Swedish state.

5. Charles X and the Constitution

STELLAN DAHLGREN

CHARLES X GUSTAVUS is one of the rulers whom Swedes have traditionally considered as their hero kings. No doubt two others in the same category – Gustavus Adolphus and Charles XII – are somewhat better known abroad, for each more immediately evoked the old concept of romantic heroism: the one, long considered as a champion of the faith and a martyr; the other, ennobled by the tragic grandeur with which nationalist historiography has invested the collapse of the Swedish empire. What put Charles X among the hero kings was first of all his quality as successful warrior and commander. He participated personally in his battles, won great victories in the field, and conquered fresh territories for Sweden. His untimely death, even though it was on a sick-bed, no doubt contributed to the halo crowning his historical personality. Anecdotes of heroism sprang up and clustered round his name. Most of them lack proof, and the king himself is now no longer admired for his heroic qualities. Historians today are more interested by other qualities in Charles X than his talents as a commander and his personal valour. The myth of the hero king is now in course of replacement by a many-sided picture of an able, and in many cases ruthless, politician.

Charles X's reign of six years (1654–60) has in fact been the subject of a good deal of recent research. And the reason for this attention may well be that the problems with which his government was faced present in concentrated form many of the great questions of politics which confronted Sweden as a great power. The solutions to them reached by Charles and his advisers proved in some essential respects untenable; but it can scarcely be denied that they had a grasp of what those problems were, and that they expended much effort in an attempt to find some kind of permanent answer to them.

I

Before passing to the main theme of this essay, therefore, we may take a look at some of the more important of these questions. One of them was the simple question of Sweden's continued existence as a great power; others concern the state's finances, and the distribution of political power. This latter relates directly to our main theme.

It is clear now, as we look back on it, that the Swedish empire in the seventeenth century could continue to exist only as long as it continued to expand. The provinces which Sweden had conquered on the continent, from Estonia to Bremen–Verden, were lands which were coveted by the states that bordered upon them, and were therefore in constant danger of being lost. They could be preserved only by means of an active foreign policy, which in certain situations crossed the borderline into war. For contemporary Swedish statesmen it was a matter of course that their country must remain a great power. Charles X, whose training had been to a great extent military, saw the solution in expansion by force of arms. The problem of maintaining the empire intact was already acute when he came to the throne, for the Russians had just launched an attack on Poland, and war was raging in the immediate neighbourhood of Sweden's Baltic possessions. A strengthening of the Russian position in this region could be seen, and was seen by Charles and his advisers, as a danger to Sweden's lands on the other side of the sea. But at the same time both the king and certain of his counsellors strongly desired to add new areas to the Swedish realm; above all Prussia and Courland. Their acquisition would bring important economic and commercial advantages, and this probably counted for much in Charles's calculations.

For these reasons Charles X in 1655 began a war with Poland. It was a war directed against Poland rather than Russia, because the provinces Charles wished to acquire were Polish possessions. The war thus begun continued throughout his reign, and in due course led to a war with Russia, and also with Austria and Brandenburg. Despite Charles's great victories over the Poles it produced no results; and the peace settlements concluded after his death did no more than restore the *status quo* on these frontiers.

Greater successes, however, were won against another enemy. Denmark, who by the peace of Brömsebro in 1645 had been compelled to cede some of her provinces to Sweden, attacked Charles in 1657 in an attempt to recover what she had lost: the recurrent wars between Denmark and Sweden in the seventeenth century can be regarded, at least in part, as a struggle for the position of primacy in the north. Charles soon imposed peace on Denmark, and at Roskilde in 1658 secured the definitive acquisition for Sweden of Skåne, Halland, Blekinge and Bohuslän. But in a few months he began a new war, this time to conquer Denmark itself, and so put an end for ever to the constant threat to Sweden's security which was posed by Denmark's very existence. His attack may be seen also as an attempt to ensure Sweden's position as a great power, independently of her possessions on the continent. But he died before he was able to bring this war to a successful conclusion, and the peace which followed his death left the problem unresolved.

Thus it may be said that Charles X had a clear idea of the dangers which threatened the empire's existence, and made efforts, on the grand scale, to remove them. The problems he confronted were indeed the same problems which were one day to vanquish Charles XII; and Charles XII tackled them, by and large, on the same lines as those which had been followed by his grandfather.

Another of the great questions which troubled seventeenth-century Sweden, as it troubled so many other countries, was that of the finances of the state. The foreign policy and administrative apparatus necessary to great-power status entailed very large expenditures. Sweden was a poor country, and such resources as she possessed were besides very unevenly distributed. The main source of wealth was the possession of land; and land, and the revenues from land, were mainly in aristocratic hands. But the land which the nobility owned or exploited was to a large extent exempt from the burden of taxation. If the finances of the state were to be strengthened, one of the few ways which were open was to exact more taxes from the nobility personally, or to impose taxes on its land. Another possibility was to transfer land from the nobility to the crown, so that the state might be free to impose full taxation upon the farms that lay upon it. It is this latter line of action which is known in Swedish historiography under the name of *reduktion*.

The circumstance that the nobility were in possession of such large holdings of land, and of the revenues which flowed from it, arose partly from the fact that during the earlier part of the seventeenth century they had acquired large numbers of farms and revenues from the crown, either by purchase or as donations. At one *riksdag* after another the non-noble Estates demanded that the crown should resume these alienations. Their arguments were political – alienations increased the power of the nobility – but also financial. They held that the crown ought to live on incomes which were as far as possible certain and not susceptible of variation; revenues from land seemed to them to fulfil this condition. The aristocracy on the contrary contended that land in noble hands was better cultivated than would otherwise be the case, and hence was an advantage for the country as a whole; while the crown should be supported by the cash revenues from tolls, excises and contributions. And they took this line above all because it was the leading families among them who had received most from the crown and would consequently stand to lose most by a *reduktion*.

Thus the problem of the finances was viewed from two opposing standpoints. Charles X came down on the side of the non-noble Estates. At the *riksdag* in 1655 he forced through a limited *reduktion*, which affected those lands, land revenues and rights which the nobility had acquired from the crown since 1632. (For the *reduktion*, see below, Chapter 7.) In this connection, however, one particular aspect of the financial problem is to be noted. During the seventeenth century (as indeed later) men took on the whole a static view of the activities of the state in peacetime. War entailed special arrangements, which were considered as extraordinary. When the country was at peace, the expenses and revenues of the state were on the whole constant from one year to another: the finances could run on a 'normal budget'. This view is strikingly manifest in the eighteenth century, when it was even laid down in the constitution that the finances of the state should conform to the budget of the year 1696; and before that the budget of 1662 was often cited as the norm to which the state ought to conform. Those revenues and expenditures which continued unchanged from year to year were termed 'ordinary'. War expenditure, on the other hand, was accounted 'extraordinary', and special provision had to be made for it, distinct from the ordinary budget. It must, however, be emphasised that this was a set of principles which those who drew up the budget often found it impossible to stick to in practice, in part because the ordinary revenues might prove deficient. Hence it not seldom happened that such income as there was had to be applied to the most urgent needs, irrespective of whether it fell under the category of ordinary or extraordinary revenue.

It is against this background that we must see Charles X's *reduktion*. This is indeed a question upon which the opinion of historians is divided. It has been contended that Charles X, in conflict with the views of some of his council, overrode the distinction between an ordinary and an extraordinary budget; and in support of this theory it has been pointed out that in the spring of 1655, at the very moment when he was negotiating about a *reduktion*, he was making great efforts to collect money for his war with Poland: the *reduktion* and the financing of the war were in fact closely connected. The preparations for war, it is argued, made it possible for the king to force through his demand for a *reduktion*, since the budget deficiency which the gains from the *reduktion* were partly designed to cover arose from the vast expenditures on mobilisation. The theory is not implausible, but in my view it rests upon a misunderstanding of the financial arguments which were being exchanged in the spring of 1655. It derives its main support from the perfectly correct observation that the two main 'ordinary' revenues (customs dues, and the *régale* on copper) were in 1655 diverted from the ordinary budget in order to finance the war. But this had no effect on the plans for a *reduktion*. When the king and his advisers were reckoning what they needed from a *reduktion*, they based their calculations, as far as we can judge, on the supposition of an ordinary budget of which the customs and the copper *régale* formed a constituent part at the normal figure, and in which war expenditures were not included. The concept of a normal budget was very much in their minds in 1655.

Charles X had in fact planned a *reduktion* even before his accession. It appears quite clear, from his recorded utterances and the measures which he undertook, that he considered the *reduktion* a necessary measure quite irrespective of whether Sweden were at war or not. In his view, the crown's ordinary budget ought to rest as far as possible upon revenues from land. And indeed the revenues resulting from the *reduktion* were assigned to 'ordinary' income. His preoccupation with fighting a war during the remainder of his reign must not be allowed to obscure the fact that he wanted a reform of the finances of lasting significance for domestic policy. His son, Charles XI, took up these ideas, and succeeded also in realising them to an extent which his father probably never envisaged but would scarcely have disapproved.

The third main problem which occupied Sweden during her Age of Greatness presents aspects of particular interest during the reign of Charles X. It is the problem of the distribution of political power within the state, and the struggle for ascendancy to which it gave rise. To this question the remainder of this essay will mainly be devoted. And we shall consider it from two closely related aspects: the constitutional, and the political.

II

The constitutional problem in seventeenth-century Sweden has been the subject of many historical studies. They furnish us with a description and analysis of the rights and functions of those organs of society which were mainly responsible for political decisions, as also of the conflicts between them. Those organs were of course the crown, the council, and the four Estates assembled at the *riksdag*; to which may be added one other factor worth remembering, at least at certain periods: the chancellor of the realm, and his office, the chancery. The history of relationships between these various bodies can be interpreted in various ways. The emphasis may be placed upon the struggle between them, and a dramatic picture presented of their undeniably obvious antagonisms. But it is also possible to lay stress upon their collaboration, a collaboration without which society would have lapsed into anarchy. For indubitably there were certain political objectives which were common to practically all politically conscious persons in contemporary Swedish society: the continued existence of the state, of the Lutheran religion, of the monarchy and of the constitution. But as to what the crown and the other political organs were really entitled to do, within the framework of the constitution – on that there was no agreement. Disputes on such points tended to crystallise on certain critical occasions, especially the accession of a new sovereign; and then a delimitation of powers would be laid down in writing, partly in the so-called Accession Charters, sometimes also in major constitutional enactments such as the Form of Government promulgated after the death of Gustavus Adolphus in 1634. Nevertheless such documents could give a very wide latitude for the uncontrolled exercise of power, and even a violation of the letter of them could take place without incurring retribution. Much, it is clear, depended on the political situation of the moment.

At the time of Charles X's accession the relation between these various political forces was approximately the following. The great majority of the Swedish people stood outside politics altogether. The political institution which represented the largest social group was the Estate of Peasants, but at meetings of the *riksdag* it played a relatively subordinate part: it considered it to be its main business to try to prevent the taxes on the peasantry becoming too heavy, but otherwise it largely conformed to the actions of the other Estates and of the crown. It functioned also as a channel for local interests up and down the country, since its members presented to the Diet the grievances – especially the economic and judicial grievances – of the various localities they represented. Thus the *riksdag* was on the whole dominated by the three upper Estates. The Estate of Clergy and the Estate of Burghers had now begun to play a larger part than in earlier years, but the leading Estate was still that of the Nobility. This Estate's method of repre-

sentation was peculiar to itself, in that every noble family had the right
to be represented by one of its members. But what above all ensured
the political ascendancy of the Nobility was perhaps not so much their
predominance in the *riksdag* as the circumstance that only Swedish
noblemen might become members of the council of state. And the
council, which acted not merely as adviser to the crown, but also
directed the work of the departments of the central government (the
collegia), was as a rule recruited only from the uppermost ranks of the
aristocracy. Naturally, therefore, they tended to take the part of the
higher nobility against the lower. Often enough, however, the interests
of higher and lower nobility coincided, and in such a case the council
acted for the Estate as a whole.

The real basis of the Swedish constitution was that portion of the
medieval Land Law (c. 1350) which dealt with the rights of the crown,
and the king's relations with his councillors. Its provisions were
summed up in the coronation oath which was sworn by every monarch
– and therefore also by Charles X – upon his accession. According to
its antique provisions the king's governing power was limited principally
in the following ways:

1. He was bound by the law of the land, and might not punish any
   man, nor take his property away from him, except according to
   the law.
2. He must govern with the advice of the council, which must be
   composed only of Swedish men.
3. He might not tax his people except under the following circumstances: if the country was attacked by enemies; upon the occasion of his coronation; on the marriage of his children; and in
   order to build his castles. In these cases, representatives of the
   people were to be summoned in every province, to determine the
   amount of aid to be granted.
4. He might not establish new law without the people's consent.

Since the time of the Land Law, the *riksdag* had succeeded in establishing a customary right to represent the people in matters of taxation
and legislation. New taxes could indeed be imposed at any time, but
the *riksdag* must give its consent to them. And this consent was required
also for the levying of troops, since this was considered to be among
the heavier burdens imposed upon the country. And as we have seen, it
was also established that the council should consist of noblemen, and

none other. What was disputed was how far the king had the right summarily to resume lands which he or previous rulers had alienated from the crown: on this point, the phrasing of the Land Law was obscure.

Such, in very broad outline, was the constitutional situation at the moment of Charles X's accession. He was at that time a man of thirty-two; but hitherto he had not played any very active part in domestic politics. His mother was Gustavus Adolphus's half-sister Katarina; his father, Johan Casimir of the Palatinate; he was thus Queen Christina's cousin. Johan Casimir settled in Sweden for good in 1622; but after the death of Gustavus Adolphus neither the aristocratic government of the regency, nor Christina herself, gave him any leading position in the state: obviously they feared that the prestige he derived from his close relationship to the royal family might make him a threat to political stability.

Charles, however, was the next heir to the throne if Christina should die without issue, and the idea of a marriage between them was from time to time a real possibility. In 1646–7 he was angling for it, on his own account and through his confidants; but Christina gave him a flat refusal, despite the fact that she had earlier been attracted to him. Nevertheless his nearness to the throne made it necessary that his education take account of the possibility that he might one day succeed her. The most important duty of a king, according to contemporary ideas, was that he should be capable of leading the country's armies; and Charles was accordingly trained as an officer, and as such distinguished himself in the Thirty Years War. As generalissimo he had charge of the liquidation of Sweden's German commitments after the peace of Westphalia. It was an operation which covered political and financial no less than military matters, and he seems to have carried it out with conspicuous ability, though he took a tougher line with the other parties to the peace than Christina desired, and this produced some coolness between them.

By this time, however – at the end of the 1640s – Christina was already working to secure Charles's eventual succession to the throne. The personal motives which impelled her to these efforts have not been wholly satisfactorily cleared up, and may indeed be partly inaccessible to historical investigation. At all events, at the *riksdag* of 1649 she succeeded in obtaining his acceptance as successor in the event of her dying without heirs of her body. The following year she forced through his recognition as hereditary prince, after declaring that she would never marry: the *riksdag* then resolved – under strong pressure from the queen – that Charles should inherit the throne upon her death, and that after him it should pass to his heirs male. At the same time Charles put his name to a document in which he bound himself, as king, to rule the country with the advice of his council according to the law of Sweden and the privileges of the Estates. Christina had now made it possible for her to step down from the throne without endangering the existence of the monarchy; and after having prepared the way through negotiations with the council and with Charles, she obtained the *riksdag*'s assent to her abdication, and in 1654 Charles was proclaimed king.

Charles's accession entailed upon him the obligation not only to swear a coronation oath but also – in common with Gustavus Adolphus, Christina and other previous monarchs – to subscribe to an Accession Charter; and the negotiations about what this should contain took place in connection with the *riksdag* which met in the spring of 1654. His objective in these negotiations was to secure for himself the greatest possible liberty of action. Such a tactic was no doubt natural enough in any ruler, but it was especially typical of Charles X: as we shall see from some later examples, it characterised his policy on a wide variety of occasions. The fact that he had already been recognised as hereditary prince in 1650 put him in a relatively strong position when the time came for him to ascend the throne. He had no need to fear that the council or the *riksdag* would prescribe a long series of conditions as the price of accepting him as sovereign. Moreover, when it was a question of maintaining the prerogatives of the crown he may well have had the support of the queen, either manifested by direct action on her part, or by indirect influence in the background: the part she played in the affair is not clear, but it is likely that she helped to secure the rejection of the demand that her successor should be bound by the tenor of the Form of Government of 1634, with all its aristocratic overtones. But what appears most plainly from the sources for these negotiations is the support which Charles received from the old chancellor, Axel Oxenstierna. It was he who led the discussions about the terms of the Charter in the committee which the *riksdag* elected to deal with the matter. In that committee, Oxenstierna took the line that the provisions of the Land Law provided, on the whole, a sufficient security. The Accession Charter must indeed be framed to include a promise that Charles would observe the oath which the Land Law prescribed for kings; but further than that, in Oxenstierna's view, all that was required was that he should promise to protect the privileges of the Estates and consult 'the leading personages' among his subjects if he should wish to be begin an offensive war.

The chancellor's argument incorporated an implicit polemic against the proposal, originally put forward by the Estates, that Charles should give the same Charter as Gustavus Adolphus had given: a Charter which in many respects limited the power of the crown. When Oxenstierna rejected, with particular explicitness and decision, those provisions in Gustavus Adolphus's Charter which forbade the conclusion of peace, truce or alliance without the consent of council and *riksdag*, he was in great measure acting as the new king's advocate; as he also was when he maintained that the sovereign must be free to begin a defensive war without needing to obtain the consent of anyone.

And in fact the final text of the Charter gave Charles very great freedom in the matter of foreign policy. Oxenstierna's first draft, indeed, had said nothing about it at all; and the obligation which was in the end incorporated was formulated without precision. If strictly interpreted it implied simply a general promise that the king would do his best to keep the country out of war. According to another interpretation, the provision meant that Charles promised not to begin a war without the consent of council and *riksdag*. It is possible, and perhaps also probable, that the clause was interpreted in this latter sense by certain contemporary politicians, though we have no specific proof of it. We are ignorant also of what significance Charles himself attached to this particular undertaking. But inasmuch as the provision is unclearly formulated it cannot be said to have bound the king to seek the consent of council and *riksdag*, if he should wish to begin an offensive war. It was rather the political situation in each context as it arose that would decide whether the king could risk a decision without consultation of council and Estates.

It can indeed be said that it was the political situation which would determine whether the king considered himself able to act in contravention of his Charter or not. It is very rarely that the Charter is explicitly cited as a guideline for royal actions. Yet the importance which was attached to these Charters on the accession of each new sovereign does suggest that the promises they contained were kept in mind as having a bearing upon political behaviour, even though they might not be explicitly alluded to. It was clearly only rarely that it was in the king's interest to refer to the promises he had given, and the members of the council, or other politicians, probably did not venture to spell them out to the king in so many words: that might have been considered as an infringement of the king's sovereignty. It must at all events have been to a ruler's advantage if the Charter could be couched in vague and ambiguous terms, since thereby it became the less binding; and this certainly applied to the provisions concerning foreign policy in the Charter of Charles X.

In regard to domestic affairs too, that Charter turned out to be little more restrictive than the constitutional provisions of the Land Law. The right of the *riksdag* to represent the Swedish people, for instance, was not laid down in it; which meant that the crown could turn to, or devise, other more tractable organs for collaboration with the nation, as for instance local meetings of Estates, or negotiations with each Estate in isolation. The most important addition to the terms of the king's oath, from a constitutional point of view, was a provision that all changes which were necessary to the security and welfare of the realm must be undertaken with the consent of council and *riksdag*. But this promise offered but a feeble guarantee, since it did not clearly indicate for what precise type of measure a common resolution of king, council and *riksdag* was required.

From all this it is clear that Charles X could be well content with his Charter. In the light of his later actions as king we are entitled to see his Charter as an expression of his dexterity in securing himself a large liberty of action by the use of vague formularies in important documents. And this skill in negotiation appears still more clearly if we look more closely at the clause in his Charter which we have just considered. Before his accession he had discussed with Christina and the council the carrying-out of that *reduktion* which he had earlier planned, and to which we have already alluded. The privileges of the nobility, however, which had been given them by Gustavus Adolphus, laid it down that the crown might not infringe their property rights; and thereby opposed a bar to any *reduktion*. A promise to maintain privileges had been contained in the king's oath, and it was also included in Charles X's Charter. Charles, however, succeeded in extorting from Christina (who did not share his opinion on the necessity for a *reduktion*) permission for him to annul the rights she had given to the nobility, provided he obtained the consent of council and *riksdag*. And he did in fact try to get such a concession introduced into his Charter, and with that end in view drafted a paragraph which included such a reservation. It was this paragraph which was in the end diluted to become the provision that all alterations in the interests of the welfare and security of the realm were to be undertaken with the council's and *riksdag*'s consent. Thus this obscurely worded clause was primarily intended to cover a *reduktion*, and made it possible for Charles to carry it through without a breach of his promise to uphold existing privileges. So that here too we can see an example of Charles's efforts to leave the way open for the future realisation of his political objectives by methods which left his hands free.

III

The liberty of action which Charles thus secured at his accession was duly exploited during his reign. In what follows we shall in the first place direct our attention to the period down to July 1655, when the political situation underwent alteration as a consequence of the king's departure for his continental campaigns.

In regard to foreign policy, the most important event in this period was the attack upon Poland. This meant that the peace which Sweden had enjoyed since the Westphalian settlement of 1648 was broken by a typical war of aggression. If our argument is correct, it is clear that Charles was legally fully entitled to begin this war without the *consent* of the *riksdag*, even if it were conceded that the Charter bore the interpretation that the *approval* of the *riksdag* was required. The same reasoning applied to the necessity for asking the consent of the council. Nevertheless before the war broke out the king did discuss his plans both in the council (December 1654) and in the *riksdag* (April 1655); and he did in fact obtain the consent of both to the war. How is this line of action to be explained?

The truth is that the bare recital of these facts gives a somewhat misleading impression of the process by which the decision was arrived at. Docent Hans Landberg has recently shed light on the political and financial measures involved in Charles's war preparations; and it is clear that in both respects he had no easy time of it. The decisive period in the preparations for the Polish war can be fixed at about the New Year of 1655. It was then that the hiring of mercenaries, and other financial and military measures, really began in earnest. A very considerable time was needed to arrange for the financing of mobilisation and for the expansion of the army to fit it for offensive military action. The process of reorientation could not be carried through without the support of the bureaucracy, the army and the taxpayers. And with these measures the council and the *riksdag* had no option but to concur. It was not so much a constitutional question: it was a question of practical politics. The part the *riksdag* had to play was clear enough: it must grant a number of taxes, in particular extraordinary war aids; and it must grant levies of troops with which to fight the war. In terms of the constitution Charles could indeed have by-passed the *riksdag* and sought the financial co-operation of the people in other ways; but this was scarcely practical politics in a situation in which he was still in the country and had no special excuse for not summoning a *riksdag*. Moreover there was other business which made it appropriate that a *riksdag* should be held; and one piece of business in particular, of singular importance, in which the king needed both the consent and aid of the *riksdag* if it were to be effected: namely, the *reduktion*.

It is with these considerations in view that we must appraise Charles's proceedings of 1654-5. If he were to begin his policy of territorial expansion at all, he needed the support of those sections of the population who would assist him either by service in war or by giving him financial backing. And this was a plain necessity, irrespective of what the Charter might say. Not less essential was the support of the council. In December 1654 the king's spokesman in the council pushed the members into agreeing to give their backing to a war in Poland. Fortified by this, he continued his war preparations, which included not only the raising and equipping of troops but also diplomatic and military measures of far-reaching effect. When the *riksdag* met, in March 1655, it found itself confronted with what was virtually a *fait accompli*. To thwart Charles's plans at this juncture would have entailed heavy financial loss for the country with nothing to show for it in return, and at the same time would have gravely weakened the prestige of the country, the king and the council.

From Charles's proceedings it is plain that he did not consider the real participation of the *riksdag* in the decision to make war with Poland either necessary or desirable. His object was to extort their approval for a war which was to all intents and purposes already begun. Formally, he complied with what the Charter required (even if it were interpreted in a sense disadvantageous to him); actually, the Estates were out of the game before it started.

The second great piece of business at the *riksdag* of 1655 concerned the *reduktion*. As we have seen, this was a question which also had important constitutional aspects. In the final paragraph of his Charter, Charles had contrived to reserve his right to carry through a *reduktion*, though he had been forced to acquiesce in the necessity to seek the consent of council and *riksdag* as a condition for doing so. As far as the *riksdag* was concerned, we may note that the desire of the three lower Estates for such a measure made its support, rather than its opposition, probable.

The king raised the question in the council in the months before the *riksdag* of 1655 assembled; and he had to fight a hard battle before the members consented to a *reduktion* on the scale that he demanded. Among other things the council suggested a number of alternative measures which would have borne less hardly upon them and upon the high nobility in general. Charles countered this by threatening to turn for support to the non-noble Estates. He threatened also to curtail some of the nobility's privileges. The council thereupon agreed to a modest *reduktion*. But with this the king was not satisfied; and bit by bit, with the help of support from the *riksdag*, he manoeuvred them into a resolution of much wider scope. The course of events presents a characteristic pattern which appears also in the great political decisions of 1650 and 1680: the crown is able to enforce its will by playing upon the split between the council and the Estates, and on the divisions within the Estates themselves.

Recent historians have rightly laid stress upon the constitutional significance implicit in seventeenth-century attitudes to the state's revenues. The crown, for its part, was anxious to obtain revenues which were independent of parliamentary grant – revenues which from a constitutional point of view could be considered as 'ordinary income', and were thus immune from interference by other elements in the state. But it was a matter of dispute as to what was really included in the category of revenues dependent on a grant by the *riksdag*: whether the need for such a grant applied to all direct taxes (even those which had only relatively recently been levied annually); and also whether it applied to customs and excise. The king wished to treat as many imposts as possible as ordinary revenues; the council and the *riksdag* took the opposite line, since it was to their advantage to be able to control as large a proportion as possible of the state's finances. On the other hand, as the situation was in 1655, it might well seem from the council's point of view that to refuse to extend the king's ordinary revenues was the greater of two evils, since if they did so he would be able to use this refusal as an argument for widening the scope of the *reduktion*, and that would of course hit the council and the high nobility. However, the council adopted the tactic of trying to persuade the king to accept, at any rate for the moment, grants of limited duration – which meant that from a constitutional point of view they would fall into the category of extraordinary rather than ordinary revenue – in place of the income which would accrue if the *reduktion* were carried out. This, however, he refused to do. He had more to gain constitutionally from the resumption of alienated estates, since the greater part of the income which would arise from them would in the future be independent of conciliar and parliamentary approval.

Nevertheless from a financial point of view the *riksdag* of 1655 was by no means an unqualified success for the king. At its close he complained that certain revenues had not been accepted as ordinary, but had been granted only for a limited period; and he did not relinquish the idea of the possibility of extending the *reduktion* in the future: he had, after all, the support of the lower Estates, and the option still remained open. He refused, moreover, to confirm certain privileges which had entailed a loss of ordinary revenue to the crown, and so ensured that he should be free to withdraw them at some future date.

As to the money for war preparations, he tried as far as possible to tap resources which lay outside the sphere of interest both of council and *riksdag*. It may be said in fact that the very free hand which he secured in regard to finance was an essential precondition of his expansive foreign policy. There was no body in the state to exercise control over how he employed the resources at his disposal: in order to finance his military measures he could use whatever sources of income he chose, within the limits imposed by other important claims upon them. Nor was there any other constitutional check upon his freedom either to seek new sources of income, or to raise the rates for the old, than the vague obligation not to impose new taxes without the consent of the elected representatives of the nation. The fact that Charles's Charter gave him a free hand in regard to foreign policy enabled him to use his financial powers to forward his warlike designs.

Customs dues and similar impositions had long been reckoned as among the revenues which were freely at the crown's disposal, even if the Estates from time to time put forward claims to participate in fixing what they should be. And many of the most important sources of income which the king (to some extent in collaboration with the council) applied to the expenses of mobilisation did in fact consist of customs and commercial dues. In part they were old impositions at enhanced rates; in part they were quite new. There was no possibility for the Estates to exercise any influence in the matter. And the king in fact concluded a great contract by which important revenues of this kind were farmed out to two financiers, without the *riksdag*'s being consulted at all. In addition he borrowed a great deal of money to defray the levy of troops and other preparations, by pledging the revenues of the state; and did so, incidentally, against very widely differing guarantees of repayment: in this matter, the king, his advisers and his creditors displayed considerable inventive ingenuity – and indeed no little hardihood. For it was an open question how these huge state debts could ever be repaid. One possibility, of course, was that the war would prove so profitable that it would pay for itself; and it seems reasonable to assume that it was the hope of this that lay at the bottom of Charles's proceedings. But the king had also to envisage the possibility that sooner or later he would be forced to turn to the Estates to help him to liquidate the state's indebtedness, and this might well lead to intensified demands on their side for some control over expenditure. A third possibility was to contrive that some particular group paid the piper: either the financiers (but that would probably destroy the state's credit, which was a valuable asset) or those noblemen who had earlier been given estates and revenues by the crown, and could easily be attacked with the help of other elements in society. So that from this angle too it paid Charles to keep open the possibility of an extended *reduktion*.

IV

Charles X's proceedings during the first year of his reign had been marked by resolute action directed to certain clearly defined political objects: an expansive foreign policy, and a long-term financial reform at the aristocracy's expense. In pursuing these aims he had exploited with great ability the possibilities for independent action which the constitution gave him. It is not too much to say that his mobilisation measures strained the constitutional framework almost to breaking-point. The same traits characterise his policy during the following years of war, until his death in 1660. For the whole of this period he was out of the country, excepting only the three months he spent in Göteborg in the spring of 1658 preparing for fresh campaigns, and the last months of his life when (also in Göteborg) he opened a new *riksdag*.

After the meeting of the Estates in 1655 Charles conducted his foreign policy with increasing disregard for all opinions but his own. In part this was a consequence of the fact that he was no longer in Sweden, and so was not accessible to the influence of a united council, still less to that of the *riksdag*. The council as a body remained at home. Individual members of it accompanied the king to Poland, not to act as the representatives of their colleagues, but to perform administrative or military services. The king gave the council in Sweden the task of functioning as a home government; but with foreign policy it was not allowed to concern itself. The instruction which he issued for them forbade them, for instance, to enter into commitments to foreign ambassadors: all questions of foreign policy were to be referred to the king. The effect of all this was that the king not only conducted the campaigns but also had the entire direction of diplomacy in his hands. On the treaties and alliances which he concluded the council in Sweden had no influence to speak of. Certain members of the council, particularly the chancellor, Erik Oxenstierna (son of Axel, who had died in the autumn of 1654), might indeed be listened to; but this was rather in virtue of his office and his personal capacity than as a council member. After Erik Oxenstierna died in the autumn of 1656 there remained no adviser capable of exercising any strong and continuous influence on foreign affairs. Indeed it was only when the king lay on his deathbed in 1660 that he proceeded to fill Oxenstierna's office; and the man he appointed, Magnus Gabriel De la Gardie, had played no part of any importance in foreign affairs during the king's lifetime.

It is nevertheless true that the king not infrequently wrote to the council in Sweden to ask their opinion on matters of foreign policy. But the council usually treated these enquiries with extreme caution: its members did their best to guess what it was that the king really wanted and which line of action he was inclined to favour, and shaped their answers accordingly. Counsel which had been framed on these lines could hardly carry much weight, especially since it was not based on the full information which was at the king's disposal, and anyway often came too late, after the decision had already been taken. That the king took the trouble to write to the council at all was probably because he wished to give them suitably filtered information and to spur them, and other government officials in Stockholm, to an active support of his policy.

As time went on, however, Charles began to hold meetings of those members of the council who were near his person; and these meetings he obviously wished to treat as equivalent to ordinary council sessions. Just when he began to adopt this procedure is not clear. The minutes of these gatherings begin in the autumn of 1656, but are scanty for that and the following year. During 1658 and 1659 they became more numerous. It is worth nothing that the king permitted men who were not council members to attend them, particularly in the last two years of his life. This method of doing business constituted in practice an attack upon the special status and authority to which the council, as the recognised advisory body to the sovereign, was entitled by the constitution. It is possible that one reason for these meetings of councillors was that Charles felt himself in need of the opinions and suggestions of others as to how his policy was to be conducted; but for this purpose he had no need to summon meetings of this sort. It seems more likely that his action was determined by the fact that in his coronation oath he had sworn to rule his kingdom 'with the council's counsel': hence he was safeguarding himself against the accusation of having violated his promise. And it was also an advantage, especially when a major political decision was to be taken, to be able to point to the fact that he had the support of those members of the council who were with him in the field. This was an argument which he used on at least one important occasion. It is worth while to examine it a little more closely, since it had important constitutional implications.

It concerns the antecedents to the outbreak of the second war against Denmark in the summer of 1658. In February the peace of Roskilde had brought Charles's first war with Denmark to an end: as we have seen, with large gains for Sweden. It may be noted incidentally that the council had only to a small extent been a party to the discussion of the peace terms, and the *riksdag*, of course, not at all. The minutes exist of a meeting of the council at the king's headquarters in Denmark which can be dated to one of the days during which negotiations were in progress. There is no note of who took part in it, but the only persons besides the king who are recorded as having spoken are Admiral Wrangel and the two negotiators Ulfeld and Bielke, of whom only the latter was a council member. The minute gives no support to the idea that the council had any appreciable influence on the drafting of this important treaty. And the council in Sweden was put in the picture only after the peace had been concluded.

After the peace of Roskilde, Charles returned to Sweden with an authority which was enormous: after all, he had just inflicted a crushing defeat upon the arch-enemy Denmark. Nevertheless great problems remained still to be solved. Sweden was still at war with three states: Poland, Russia and Austria. A fourth, Brandenburg, could be expected to declare war at any moment.

At Göteborg Charles gathered the whole council around him, and in a series of meetings discussed the various military possibilities. His plan was now to transfer hostilities to Germany in order to force

Brandenberg and Austria to acquiesce in Sweden's acquisition of Prussia. There is no sign that he encountered any serious difficulty from the council in the course of these discussions, even though an individual here and there came forward with an expression of his wish for peace. One reason for the council's complaisance must have been the great accession of authority which the king had derived from his conclusion of peace with Denmark. As long as he continued to be successful it was difficult to demand a peace which would certainly have entailed Sweden's relinquishing those areas of Poland already occupied by the Swedish armies, and among them Prussia. And to retain those areas Sweden had no option but to take the offensive in Germany.

To Göteborg the king also summoned a committee of representatives tives of the three upper Estates to discuss questions of foreign policy. One motive for summoning only selected representatives, rather than a full *riksdag*, may well have been that it was considered expedient to confine information on foreign affairs to a relatively narrow circle in order to obviate the risk that secret information should leak out to ill-disposed foreign powers.

It is important to emphasise that this 'committee of the Estates' was by no means representative of the *riksdag* as a whole, and indeed scarcely deserved its name. That the Estate of Peasants was entirely unrepresented is in itself no matter for surprise, since it often happened that it was excluded when foreign affairs were under discussion, the peasants being considered incapable of understanding them. From Charles's point of view their absence was an advantage, since as a general rule they were in favour of peace because they feared the heavy burdens which war brought with it. But the Estate of Burghers had only eight representatives present, and these came from only four towns (Stockholm, Göteborg, Norrköping and Kalmar): compare this with the *riksdag* of 1655, when seventy-five towns were represented. The Nobility were represented mainly by the governors of the various Swedish provinces and by higher civil servants who had come to Göteborg in the course of their official duties; though since the council participated in the discussions and signed the committee's resolution, they may be reckoned as representing the Nobility too. Of all the Estates, that of the Clergy was best represented, since its members on the committee were drawn from every diocese in Sweden. No clergy or burghers from Finland were present.

It is clear that in calling this committee meeting Charles took advantage of the fact that neither his Charter nor its predecessors defined what form meetings of the Estates should take. It is also obvious that the king arbitrarily decided who should be summoned, and that he tried to ensure that they were persons who could be expected to back him. This is particularly true of the representatives of the Nobility, who consisted almost exclusively of higher civil servants from whom he could demand loyal support. The summonses to the clergy, moreover, were directed mainly to the bishops. That the handful of Burghers who were present considered that they represented only themselves emerges from the fact that they affixed their own seals to the committee's resolution, and not, as was usual, the seals of their towns.

The committee of Estates proceeded to give the king a free hand to transfer his armies to Germany for an attack on Austria and Brandenburg. And here too there was no sign of any serious opposition. But it was typical of Charles that he took care to insert into the resolution of the committee a form of words which gave him extremely wide discretion, and in reality covered even attacks on other continental powers other than those which were his immediate objective. For the committee handed over to the king the whole direction of the war and foreign policy, and among other things declared that he must be free to attack any and every enemy who stood between him and the welfare of the state. It is indeed clear from the context that they were thinking primarily of war against Austria, Brandenburg and Poland; but the phrasing was quite general, and it gave Charles complete liberty. The council was not even mentioned. Apparently the resolution was drafted in the king's chancery. The minutes make no mention of any discussion of it: it was read on 21 May and immediately signed by the representatives of the Estates. With that the committee was dismissed, and Charles went off to his army in Holstein to prepare for his German war. Only a month later he took the decision to renew the attack on Denmark, and on 7 August he and his troops landed on Sjaelland. The goal now was the incorporation of Denmark into Sweden.

As we have seen, Charles was in a position to utilise the terms of the committee's resolution to justify this decision to attack a country with which Sweden had only recently concluded peace. But he also collected together those members of the council who happened to be with him, and a formal vote was taken on the question of the new war. They gave him their unanimous support. Yet it must be noted that it was only a minority of the council that was in attendance. We have minutes of three meetings at which the question was discussed. In these meetings a total of nine of the council's thirty-eight members were present; and no more than six of them were present at any one meeting. Thus the king talked to the council members in relays; and this must have given him even better opportunities to put pressure upon them. Moreover six of the nine were professional soldiers who might be expected on military grounds to opt for a war with Denmark as a promising alternative. The civilians, on the other hand – who formed a majority of the whole council – were much under-represented.

It was thus a weak and distorted representation of the Estates that in 1658 threw the reins on Charles's back, to conduct foreign policy as he pleased; and a weak and distorted representation of the council that concurred in advocating an attack on Denmark. But this did not stop Charles, in the great letter which he wrote to the council in Sweden on 4 August 1658 reporting his decision to attack Denmark, from adducing both these meetings as giving support to his policy. He writes, for instance, that 'the Estates' at Göteborg gave him a free hand to invade those countries which had inflicted damage on Sweden.[1] He does not, indeed, assert that the committee really included Denmark among them; but it is obvious that he exploits that generality in the wording of the committee's resolution to which allusion has been made above. He further lays very strong emphasis on the circumstances that all the members of the council with whom he had discussed the question in Denmark had advocated the war; and he mentions one meeting of council members in addition to the three of which we have minutes, and one councillor, in addition to the nine already known to us (a soldier, of course!), and one diplomat who was not a member of the council at all, as being in favour of war. When at Göteborg in 1660 Charles drew up his proposition to the *riksdag*, he included in it the statement that the committee of Estates in 1658 had laid stress on the danger of war from Denmark, and asserted that the council members at his headquarters had judged the war to be necessary.

From all this it is clear that Charles was anxious to show that he did not take the decision to attack Denmark arbitrarily. No doubt it is true that he was not explicitly bound by his Charter to consult council and Estates. But it strengthened his position if he could make it appear that they had supported him; the fact that both were most unsatisfactorily represented on this occasion was a circumstance which he found it convenient not to notice. He was anxious to give the appearance of being a constitutional king, despite the fact that his skilful tactics had deprived the organs of the constitution of all real say in one of the most important decisions of his reign. His manoeuvres in 1658 are typical of his consistent effort to keep the real power in his hands as far as possible: as we have already seen, during the war years he practically conducted his foreign policy in person. The fragment of the council which he collected round him in Poland or in Denmark was too weak, and also too divided, to be able to act as any sort of counterpoise.

The same effort to keep the effective power in his own hands can be discerned also in internal affairs after 1655; though here the picture is complicated by the fact that it was not possible to control domestic policy in the same way as he dealt with foreign affairs and military matters. This is true, for instance, in regard to finance. Certainly Charles's armies abroad lived mainly on the resources of the lands in which they operated. But the war also demanded continued financial support from home. As we have seen already, the needs of the state could not be supplied when it came to direct taxation and the raising of troops without some sort of consultation with the Estates. But there was nothing to say that this consent must necessarily be obtained at meetings of the *riksdag*. And Charles and his council used this circumstance so that such war taxes and militia levies as were required, over and above what had been granted at the *riksdag* of 1655, were obtained from a number of meetings of representatives of the Estates in various parts of the country. The provincial governor, or other commissioners sent out by the king or the council, accordingly negotiated with representatives of the people in the various provinces of Sweden and Finland. Naturally it was possible to justify such a proceeding on the ground of the practical difficulties, both for king and Estates, which would be entailed by the summoning of a *riksdag* at a time when war was raging. But we cannot avoid the conclusion that the king must have felt it to be in his interest to keep the Estates divided. It must have been easier to enforce assent to demands for men and money in this way than by holding a *riksdag* at which the leaders of the Estates could concert a common resistance. The tactic was essentially the same as that which Charles employed when he summoned the committee meeting at Göteborg, and when he gathered together those members of the council who were with the army to give him their advice.

There were, however, some burdens which were imposed upon the people during the reign which were never negotiated with them at all. Such were some of those which resulted from the movement of troops through the country. Quartering and maintenance, for instance, fell to a large extent upon the shoulders of the population in the towns and

in the countryside. The obligation to provide transport facilities became heavier in wartime also. In those areas which were exposed to
the danger of war (Finland, the frontier provinces on the side of Denmark and Norway) the population was itself forced to take a share in
defence, in addition to quartering and maintaining such of the king's
troops as might be in the neighbourhood. Sometimes there were in-
formal negotiations about this, sometimes not. Thus the war, which
was to so large an extent the king's personal policy, came to entail
burdens whose magnitude neither the *riksdag*, nor any other form of
popular representation, had had a hand in determining.

In regard to the general financing of the war, Charles continued the
methods which he had employed to provide for the preparations in
1655. One group of persons who found themselves (without being
consulted) 'lending' money for the war was the civil service, which in
Charles's time was forced to accept the fact that large portions of its
salaries were permanently in arrear. The king also arranged for the
pawning of certain estates and revenues, some of which had already
been resumed to the crown at the *reduktion*. Constitutionally there could
be no formal objection to such a proceeding, since there was nothing
explicit to forbid it. But since the result by all reasonable calculation
must in the end be (and actually was) that the Estates would be called
upon to pay at least a portion of the debt, it may be said that they were
put in a position in which they were forced to grant supplies to defray
expenses which had already been incurred.

Nor is it irrelevant to notice that Charles's large-scale hiring of
troops – and most of his army consisted of mercenaries – was one way
of avoiding recourse to the assistance of the Estates in providing manpower for the war. Money for mercenaries, on the other hand, could be
obtained by the methods we have described, without going to the
Estates at all. However, Charles had certain long-range plans for
creating a standing army which should be independent of the Estates'
goodwill. The *reduktion* was conceived as an instrument for such a
development. A portion of the resumed estates or revenues was to be
assigned to officers and soldiers, who would thereby be provided with
means of support over which the *riksdag* would cease to have any control. Another possibility which Charles had in mind was that the Estates
should undertake to provide, for an unlimited period, a certain number
of soldiers for every province. The military situation did not permit
the realisation of these plans, but here too Charles XI was to put into
effect some of the ideas of his father.

It is at all events clear that the influence of the *riksdag* upon taxation, and upon the raising of troops, was in many ways nullified during Charles's reign. And this demonstrates what opportunities were presented for arbitrary personal rule by the lack of precision in the constitution.

The other counterpoise to the prerogative which the constitution provided was the council; and in one respect the council was able to establish a strong influence upon domestic policy. Those of its members who remained in Sweden to carry on the central administration functioned during the king's absence as a home government ruling in the name of the council as a whole. The king provided them with an instruction before he departed; it was formulated in provisional terms, since he declared that he would soon be home again. The promise of a speedy return was repeated on several occasions, and actual preparations for it were made at least once, though nothing came of it. But the prospect of his early reappearance must have contributed to the home government's sense of insecurity and made them disinclined to risk any very far-reaching initiatives. Moreover the king manifested particular anxiety to receive frequent reports from the council and the *collegia* about the situation at home, and not infrequently complained when he felt that they had neglected to provide them. In fact a very large number of letters were exchanged between the king and members of the home government – not only official letters, but private correspondence between Charles and his confidential informants. The king seems to have been very well supplied with information about what was going on in the council and the government offices; and this impression is confirmed by the private memoranda which were kept by his secretary of state, Edward Ehrensteen. This constant reporting – and not least the private letters, which the council must certainly have been aware of – must have acted as a check on its activities. The same was true of the minutes of its meetings, which had always to be kept.

The council's liberty of action was moreover limited in another way. According to the king's instruction (which was renewed at Göteborg in 1658) it was its job to deal with current business. Its main task may be said to have been to keep the home defences up to strength, prevent revolts within the country, and rally the forces at its disposal against any attack from without, with particular reference to Denmark. Council members were to supervise the administration, but none of them was to meddle in matters which were officially the concern of any of the others. The appointment to offices was retained by the king in his own hands.

The council did indeed make provisional appointments, but often enough the king revoked them. He also retained supreme judicial power: the council was permitted to deal with certain carefully defined matters, but for the rest Charles forbade it to play any part in the judicature. On one occasion the governor-general of Finland wrote to the council complaining about the judgement of the Supreme Court in the case of an officer in Finland. The council did not venture to express an opinion on the case, but recommended him to apply to the king. Charles sent the governor-general a swingeing rebuke, and declared that the Supreme Court was responsible only to himself, 'being placed by God as the supreme judge over all worldly judgements'.[2]

Nor was the council permitted to have any say in the execution of the *reduktion* which had been agreed upon in 1655. This was carried out by a government department specially created for the purpose, the College of the *Reduktion*, which was responsible directly to the king. Persons who complained to the council about the resumption of their estates were always (as we can see from the minutes) referred to the College of the *Reduktion*. During the first year of its existence the College pursued its work with very little interference even from the king. Soon, however, its members began to disagree on how the provisions of the *reduktion* statute were to be interpreted; and many senior civil servants, inside and outside the council, were dissatisfied with its activities and considered that its standards were unduly rigorous. These complaints were conveyed to the king – among others, by Erik Oxenstierna. The king then directed the College to refer all important cases to himself, his intention being to supervise the resumptions personally, since he wished to be in a position to consider whether in particular cases there were or were not circumstances which made a resumption desirable. But it was hardly possible for Charles to fight a war in Poland and Denmark and supervise the *reduktion* at the same time; and this was probably the reason why the College's operation gradually came to a standstill. Nevertheless when the king was at Göteborg in 1658 he did decide a number of important questions concerned with the *reduktion*. Neither the council not the committee of Estates took any part in these decisions, despite the fact that what was at issue was the interpretation of the resolution which they had taken in common in 1655.

The council's control of domestic policy was obviously largely dependent upon what financial resources it had at its disposal, and these did not give it much room for manoeuvre. The Exchequer College dealt with the administration of the crown's revenues, and the only concern the council had with it, according to its instruction, was to offer it help and advice when asked to do so. The Exchequer College itself had little room for manoeuvre either, since Charles himself decided the pattern of the budget each year, and forbade the College (and the council) to make any alteration in his arrangements. The consequence was that whenever the council asked for money for this or that purpose, the senior officials in the Exchequer College, and especially its president, Herman Fleming (who was also a member of the council), referred it to the king's arrangements, and declared that they were not at liberty to override them. This frequently caused great annoyance, as may be seen from the correspondence between senior officials, and particularly from letters to the most senior member of the council, the high steward Per Brahe. Brahe was one of the few members of the council who were prepared to stand up to Charles X. He was absent from Stockholm for lengthy periods, engaged in directing the defence of the southern provinces against the Danes; and several senior officials wrote to him asking him to return in order to exert his authority to see that necessary measures were taken, and to act as a counterpoise to Herman Fleming, who was considered to be putting obstacles in the way of raising money, and hence of the prosecution of the war.[3] Behind this episode we can clearly perceive a conflict which in the last resort relates to the opposition between crown and council. Herman Fleming acted as the king's confidential agent at home, inasmuch as he saw to it that the king's wishes were respected, and that the council did not take too many liberties with them. He was also the head of the College of *Reduktion*, a position which strengthened his hand, since the *reduktion*, as we have seen, was outside the council's control. He was further appointed by the king to the headship of the admiralty. Fleming was a convinced believer in a strong monarchy, and urged on Charles measures against the aristocracy which were more provocative than Charles was prepared to acquiesce in. In 1660, after the king's death, Fleming himself narrated that one of the king's favourite expressions – and it is reasonable to suppose that he used it in conversation with Fleming by way of explaining why he did not pursue more radical policies – was 'Can't be helped: I must tack.'[4] The fact that Fleming occupied such important posts in the home government is one main explanation of why the council as a body did not have a more effective influence during Charles X's reign.

For the last year of his life the king was away in Denmark, and during this period he weakened the position of the government in Stockholm still further by summoning to him some of the most senior officials both inside and outside the council: to all appearances he was taking over more and more of the direction of home affairs as the reign drew to a close. Immediately before his death Charles signed a will in which he nominated a regency for his young son. Its composition reveals his desire to ensure that it should maintain the interests of the monarchy. Of those interests, the leading champions among the regents were the queen, the king's brother Adolf Johan, and Herman Fleming; and between them they were to have a majority of votes in the regency. The council of state and the nobility, however, took action in common to prevent the acceptance of this testament; and the regency government was given a different constitution which enabled it, with the council's support, to pursue a policy in the interests of the aristocracy. The conflict between crown and council which underlay the whole of Charles's reign thus came into the open in the struggle over his will.

It should now to some extent be clear why it was that the council was not better able to maintain its position in the 1650s. But there was one other factor which perhaps had more general application than those which we have so far examined, and of it a word must be said. This was the dependence of those of the high aristocracy who were members of the council upon the crown (at least, when the king was not a minor) for a large number of advantages. Members of the council were seldom councillors pure and simple: they either occupied, or sought to occupy, other offices to be held simultaneously with their council membership. But it was the king who controlled appointments and had offices in his gift; and that meant that those who opposed him exposed themselves to the risk of losing the influence and emoluments which were the accompaniments of high office. The sovereign also had control of a number of economic privileges which he could bestow on the council and the nobility: he could, for instance, give away or sell crown-farms and the income that arose from them. Previous monarchs had done this on a large scale. In this respect Charles X's reign brought a great alteration, since he refrained entirely from selling farms and rents, and was extremely sparing in the giving of donations in Sweden and Finland. In the conquered territories he was more open-handed; but the vast majority of the donations he gave there became valueless, since these areas were lost to Sweden at the peace settlements which followed his death.

But the king also used the *reduktion* itself as a means of binding the nobility to him; for he made exceptions, and gave exemption from its operation, showing particular favour to the council and the high aristocracy – no doubt because it was from these elements that those senior civil servants and soldiers were recruited upon whose services he was most dependent. But it is typical of him that as a rule he granted these exemptions only for a limited time, which meant that those who were so favoured were always in danger of having the privilege withdrawn if they should incur the king's displeasure.

v

Charles X's methods of ruling thus reveal him as in many ways a very typical representative of sixteenth- and seventeenth-century Swedish monarchy, as it existed before the coming of absolutism in 1680. Within the limits of a fairly flexible and partly vague constitution, successive sovereigns made it their object to maintain the prerogatives of the crown. With this end in view they employed methods and policies which were closely interrelated. They secured huge monetary resources to finance their wars by exploiting financial devices over which the *riksdag* had no control. They attempted to win over influential elements in society by distributing offices and revenues. They sought for their own advantage to confine the influence of *riksdag* and council within certain limits.

But Charles X's policies are of course also the reflection of the special problems which he had to confront, as well as of his own political personality. In comparison with earlier rulers he took a tougher line with the nobility, among other things by threatening them with cancellation of their privileges, but above all through the *reduktion*. This brought immediate loss to the nobility and threatened them with further blows in the future. Yet at the same time he was able to use the *reduktion* to bind to himself men of whom he stood in need, by exempting their lands from resumption. But for the individual nobleman there was a world of difference between the old days, when he could obtain a donation as the reward for service, and the new state of affairs in which he was to consider himself rewarded if he were to retain his property at all.

This policy was also partly responsible for the fact that the council found such difficulty in asserting itself against Charles X. Another reason which could be adduced was his habit of keeping its proceedings under meticulous scrutiny. Equally notable was the extent to which he circumscribed its activities on the home front. And it was a distinctive feature of his methods that he split up the council into different sections, and used the handful of members he took with him on his campaigns to secure political and constitutional support for his decisions.

A major element in Charles's handling of affairs seems to have been his skill as a political tactician, which revealed itself in his ability, when confronted with major decisions, to impose (or settle for) ambiguous forms of words which from his point of view left him in the advantageous position of having his hands free. Sometimes, as in the matter of the *reduktion*, this entailed the consequence that a conflict arose about the interpretation to be placed upon the terms of an agreement which delayed its being carried out. But Charles clearly thought it preferable to keep open the possibility of forcing through a resolution more favourable to himself at some time in the future, rather than to tie his hands for the sake of a short-term success.

To a certain extent Charles also curtailed the influence of the Estates, by his practice of turning to other forms of representative gatherings than the *riksdag*. But he also needed the support of the *riksdag* if his military designs were to be pursued with any vigour, and this was probably the main reason why he summoned, in 1660, the *riksdag* which was in session when he died. In a longer view, moreover, it is clear that he needed the non-noble Estates as a counterpoise to the council and the nobility: after all, it was with the support of the *riksdag*, and in particular of the non-noble Estates, that Charles XI was to establish absolutism.

The reign of Charles X constitutes in many respects an important phase in Swedish seventeenth-century history. He tackled the central problems – problems of foreign policy and of finance – which underlay Swedish existence as a great power. Some of his plans neither he nor any later ruler succeeded in realising. Yet his policies achieved, by the acquisition of Skåne and the southern provinces, and by the resolution on the *reduktion* in 1655, results of enduring importance. And many of his projects and initiatives were to be carried out, or developed further, by his son and his grandson, Charles XI and Charles XII. How far this is also true of his constitutional objectives must remain an open question. As far as we can see, he accepted the constitution to which he pledged himself at his coronation, though he did indeed give it an elastic interpretation. In virtue of his political achievements he stands out as a powerful representative of the ideal of strong monarchy.

6. Magnus Gabriel De la Gardie

GÖRAN RYSTAD

In the long line of statesmen who played a part in Sweden's Age of Greatness, not the least conspicuous figure is that of chancellor Magnus Gabriel De la Gardie. No doubt his achievements as a politician and statesman have often been severely critcised, and that not without good reason; but still it is true that his career and his life's work are perhaps more intimately bound up with Sweden's short-lived spell of greatness than those of any other statesman of his age. His passionate interest in the arts, moreover, gave him an additional dimension which was wanting in most of them. Yet at the same time the contradictions in his personality, his weaknesses of character, and his failures, have something in them which not only gives us a better understanding of the problems which Swedish statesmanship had to wrestle with, but also makes him a less impersonal and more humanly intelligible figure than the majority of his contemporaries.

I

The family of De la Gardie was of French origin. It came to Sweden in the 1560s in the person of Pontus De la Gardie, who carved out for himself a distinguished military career in the Swedish service, and particularly in John III's wars against Russia. Pontus married one of John's natural daughters, and their son Jakob was a soldier whose reputation as a commander eclipsed even that of his father. Jakob taught Gustavus Adolphus the art of war; was by him created a count; and as marshal of the realm filled the highest military office in Sweden. At the beginning of the 1620s he was entrusted in the king's absence with the supreme command of the Swedish forces in Livonia in the war against Poland; and it was in Livonia, in 1622, that Magnus Gabriel De la Gardie – destined to be the most brilliant representative of his family – was born.

Through his mother Ebba Brahe, Magnus Gabriel was related to most of the ancient noble families of Sweden, but in the view of many contemporary observers the De la Gardies were never wholeheartedly accepted by the old nobility as their social equals. They viewed the family's rapid advancement with distaste; they looked with jealous eyes at the many testimonies of royal favour which were showered upon it; and it may well be that these feelings contributed to the difficulties which Magnus Gabriel was to encounter when he became chancellor. He received a very careful education. In Matthias Mylonius, later ennobled under the name of Biörnklou, and finally a member of the council of state, he had a teacher of unusual competence and ability; and it was with Mylonius as tutor that he went to the University of Uppsala in 1635. In 1639–40 Magnus Gabriel was chosen as Uppsala's *rector illustris*: the office was purely formal and honorific, but he seems to have taken it more seriously than was usual – a presage perhaps of what he was later to do when he became the university's chancellor.

By 1640 it was time for him to undertake his peregrination, that extended tour of Europe which then formed part of every young nobleman's education. He went first to Germany; but most of his time abroad was spent in the Netherlands, and especially in Leyden, where among other things he studied classical eloquence, law, political theory, philosophy and mathematics. From the Netherlands he went on to France; and his stay in that country was to exert a lasting influence upon him. It made him throughout his life a devoted admirer of French culture; and it led him in matters of foreign policy to be a consistent advocate of a close association with France. In the intervals of his academic pursuits, moreover, he frequented the French court and took an active part in French society. The experience endowed him with social graces and elegant manners which were not without their influence on his future. In 1644 the outbreak of war between Sweden and Denmark brought him back to Sweden. His original intention was to join the army with a view to embarking upon a military career; but in the event he remained in Stockholm at Christina's court, and soon became her declared favourite. In January 1645 he was made a colonel in the Lifeguard, and a few months later he was betrothed to Maria Eufrosyne, the queen's cousin and the sister of the future Charles X. In the following years he became a leading figure in court life, and Christina showered favours on him with a lavish hand. His French manners, elegant sophistication and imposing presence no doubt made a great impression on the young queen; but there was also a political motive behind the almost provocative profusion with which she bestowed distinctions upon him: it was her method of making a demonstration against the dominance which Axel Oxenstierna and his associates had acquired during the period of the regency, and which

Christina was finding increasingly irksome. In the spring of 1646 – in defiance of Axel Oxenstierna's advice – De la Gardie was sent on an extraordinary embassy to France which can probably be reckoned not only as the most splendid, but also as the most extravagant, in Swedish history: in the end it cost nine times as much as the original estimate. These excesses did not pass without criticism. The rise of the De la Gardie family already provoked irritation among many of the older nobility, and the queen's unexampled munificence to Magnus Gabriel was gall and wormwood to many of them. As regards the embassy, however, Christina shielded him from any possible attack by discharging him from all responsibility for its organisation, or for the costs it had entailed. Politically its results had been small.

The years that followed showed no slackening of the tide of favours and promotions. In May 1647 the queen forced through his acceptance as a member of the council of state, though he was at that time still under the age of twenty-five; in April 1648 he was made general in the Swedish forces in Germany, where he was to be second-in-command to Field-Marshal Karl Gustav Wrangel. The war was now in its final stages, and the only military activity of any consequence in which De la Gardie took part was the siege of Prague. When peace was concluded, rich rewards were paid out to the Swedish commanders from the indemnities which had been secured by the treaty; and in this matter too the queen's intervention led to his being singled out in a manner which bore no rational relation to his real service, and which inevitably aroused bad blood. In 1649 he was created field-marshal and at the same time given the lucrative appointment of governor-general of Livonia. He did not stay there long. The air of the court was the breath of life to him, and he returned from his governorship to play a leading part in the brilliant festivities which took place in connection with the coronation in 1650. In 1651 he was made lord chamberlain; and next year his unprecedentedly rapid ascent was crowned by his appointment as treasurer. Thus at the age of thirty he had risen to be one of the five great officers of state.

Apart from these constant preferments to ever more exalted offices, the queen showed her favour by the grant of enormous economic benefits in the form of donations and revenue assignments. In Sweden he possessed, all told, several hundred farms in Uppland, Västmanland, Ostergötland and Västergötland. In Germany he was given the whole island of Wollin, and in the Baltic provinces the counties of Osel and Pernau. But even at this stage he was expending the greater part of his huge income in building or rebuilding at his many castles and manors, and in laying out gardens around them: it was a passion which was to hold him throughout his life.

There was in De la Gardie's character a strain of irresolution, an underlying feeling of insecurity. It manifested itself in the fact that in the full tide of his incomparably rapid ascent he was haunted by the fear that he might after all be a failure, might lose his great position and be thrust aside. In itself, no doubt, it was not a very surprising reaction. He must have known well enough that his success was not commensurate with the services he had rendered. And certainly he had some ground for anxiety; for he knew that the old chancellor Axel Oxenstierna and his circle of relations looked upon him with mistrust. Even his own brother-in-law Charles Gustavus could not always view with equanimity the stream of distinctions which Christina showered upon him; a certain feeling of rivalry was unavoidable. And finally Christina herself, unstable and capricious as she was, was an uncertain factor. Her conspicuously strong interest in him induced in some quarters a belief that it proceeded from a deep attachment on her side. It is clear that there was never really any question of there being anything in the nature of an intrigue between them, and it certainly does not appear that De la Gardie was at any time in love with her. But it seems not unreasonable to assume that Christina was in reality much more strongly drawn to the handsome young count than she would perhaps have been prepared to admit to herself. If so, it would at least provide an intelligible psychological explanation for the cold ruthlessness which she displayed when De la Gardie was disgraced.

In 1652 Count Magnus fell ill of a fever which kept him in bed for six months. On his recovery he perceived that the queen was now surrounded by a new group of favourites, some of them Swedes, some foreigners. He became uneasy, felt himself unjustly eclipsed and neglected, and tried by various means to recover his former ascendancy. When on one occasion the queen extolled to him the loyalty and fidelity of some of the new men, his habitual touchiness led him to complain of the indifference with which the queen now treated him; and from this he proceeded to assert that he was the victim of calumny, and even to allege that there were persons who accused him of treason. Christina at once demanded to know who these persons were. De la Gardie named the queen's master of the horse, the German Baron von Steinberg. Steinberg, on being summoned, denied the accusation; and the situation became increasingly unpleasant for De la Gardie, who was forced to admit that he had his information only at second hand, and named as his informant another of Christina's favourites, the Livonian Schlippenbach. Confronted with De la Gardie, Schlippenbach indignantly repudiated the allegation. In the course of the painful scene which followed, De la Gardie lost his head completely; he called Schlippenbach a rogue and a villian; and Schlippenbach retorted in kind. The matter had now become an affair of honour, and the queen contemptuously forbade De la Gardie the court until he had avenged the insult. His reaction was to attempt to justify and excuse himself by sending her an elaborately written petition, full of fawning apologies and displaying a somewhat naïve belief that she would once more take him into favour. Her reply (which she took care should be made public) has become famous: ice-cold, pitiless, annihilating. It tells us a good deal about De la Gardie, but even more perhaps about Christina. It includes the following passages:

It is no business of mine to provide remedies for your misfortunes. The recovery of your honour lies in your own hands. What indeed have you to hope from me? What could I do for you except to deplore and censure your behaviour? The friendship I once felt for you compels me both to the one and to the other; and however disposed I might be to overlook your offence, I cannot without being untrue to myself pardon the damage you have done to your own character. . . . Henceforward I can feel for you only compassion; but that too cannot avail you, since you have yourself destroyed the value of the kindness which once I showed you. On your own admission you are unworthy of it; you have out of your own mouth, and in the presence of many persons of distinction, condemned yourself to banishment. . . . How can you venture to appear before me, after what you have done, and the insults you have swallowed? I am filled with shame when I think of the depth to which you have degraded yourself, and of how many times you have grovelled to those whom you have so gravely injured. At that unhappy encounter your behaviour was neither magnanimous, gentlemanly nor generous. Do not imagine that tears and humility will ever induce me to feel the least sympathy for you. To remember you as little as possible, to speak of you still less – this is the limit of what I can bring myself to do in your case, . . . I must make you realise that you are unworthy of my respect after the fault you have committed; and this is the last service that I can render you.[1]

One can only speculate on what lay behind Christina's shattering treatment of De la Gardie. Certainly her reaction bears no reasonable
relation to the events which provoked it; and the explanation is probably to be found in the fact that she had become profoundly disillusioned
with him. She had been strongly attached to him; she was a somewhat
unattractive and unfeminine woman; and perhaps at the root of the
matter lay the disappointment produced by an unreciprocated passion.

De la Gardie sought assistance in various quarters. His mother Ebba
Brahe tried in vain to intervene. The queen's cousin Charles Gustavus
refused to meddle in the matter, and confined himself to advising De la
Gardie to 'comport himself like a Christian in his disagreeable situation,
for in this world a prudent man will seek always to command himself
and subdue his passions, confronting the vanities of this life with *con-
stantia animi*, which is pleasing to God as well in good as in evil fortune'.[2] This was not advice which De la Gardie was capable of following.
In a succession of lachrymose epistles he appealed to Christina once
again; her only answer was to remove him, without investigation or
sentence, from his office of treasurer and to put the exchequer under
the direction of Herman Fleming, with the title of president. She also
deprived him of a number of his estates; and when she abdicated in
1654 she contrived that among the lands assigned to her for her support
were De la Gardie's island of Osel and a part of the fiefs he held in
Germany.

The queen's abdication meant, from De la Gardie's point of view,
that there was once more a chance to recover his political influence,
and that his banishment from court and exclusion from high office came
to an end. By virtue of his near relationship to the new king he might
hope once again to occupy the exalted station which his previous career
had secured for him. And in fact Charles X did employ him in various
responsible positions. But their relations seem never to have been particularly cordial: they were men of very different types; and in any
case Charles had a shrewd eye for Magnus Gabriel's weaknesses. In
1655 he was indeed appointed chancellor of the University of Uppsala,
and in the same year was restored to his office of treasurer; but he never
took a very active part in discharging the duties of this office, and it is
doubtful whether Charles ever intended that he should. He had no part
in shaping the terms of the *reduktion* of 1655, and its execution demanded a man of a very different temper – such a man, for instance, as
Herman Fleming. The king preferred to use him on missions in connection with those wars against Poland and Russia which filled almost the

entire reign. On 1 June 1655 he was appointed governor-general of Livonia, and was at the same time put in charge of the military forces in the area between Lake Ladoga and the Dvina. It was a task which had the strongest attraction for him; for in fact he dreamed of a military career in the style of his father and grandfather. It soon became apparent, however, that he lacked the qualities required for the profession of arms. He showed no ability as a commander, and on repeated occasions his lack of resolution and his ineffectiveness as a strategist led to military reverses which drew upon him Charles's sharply expressed displeasure. Nor was the situation mended by De la Gardie's propensity for lengthy jeremiads and complaints about his bad luck.

When hostilities against the Russians came to a halt in the spring of 1658 De la Gardie was given the task of leading the embassy which was to negotiate peace with the Poles; and for a diplomatic commission of this sort he showed considerably more aptitude. But the death of Charles X at the beginning of 1660 put the Swedish negotiators in a difficult position; and the definitive peace of Oliva, which finally conceded Sweden's right to Livonia in return for a surrender of her other claims, was perhaps as favourable as could be expected in the existing circumstances.

II

When De la Gardie returned to Stockholm in June 1660 Charles X had been dead for some months; and the great question now concerned the arrangements for the regency, which must necessarily be a long one. Charles X had left a will, according to which the regency was to consist of the queen-mother (who was to preside and have two votes); Charles's brother, Duke Adolf Johan (who was to take over the office of marshal, which happened to be vacant); Per Brahe, as high steward; Magnus Gabriel De la Gardie, now advanced from the office of treasurer to that of chancellor. Herman Fleming was to replace him as treasurer, and Karl Gustav Wrangel was to be high admiral. The general feeling in the council of state was that they were not in any circumstances prepared to have Adolf Johan as a member of the regency. He was a difficult man to deal with, obstinate and extremely touchy about his own dignity; but apart from this the presence of two members of the royal family on the council, as envisaged by the will, would much diminish the ability of the high aristocracy to look after its own interests. In the event it proved easy to enlist the support of the Estate of Nobility in excluding the duke from the regency; and the three inferior Estates, though with some hesitation, concurred in this step. But when the council proceeded to fill the other high offices of state according to the provisions of the will, they met with fierce opposition in the House of Nobility. The Nobility demanded that, since they had been recognised as having *jus improbandi* (i.e. the right to reject Adolf Johan's candidature), they ought also to have the *jus approbandi*, by which they meant that, though the council might be entitled to put forward proposals for appointments to offices, the Estates should be entirely free to approve or reject the candidates they suggested. Faced by this attitude the council was compelled to beat a retreat, with the result that the regency was constituted differently from what had at first been intended. Lars Kagg, whom the council had proposed for marshal, was accepted; and so too was Magnus Gabriel De la Gardie, who was their candidate for the chancellorship. But the Estate of Nobility refused, by a large majority, to have Herman Fleming as treasurer. They demanded that the council put forward another name, and as a result the office was given to Gustav Bonde.

Behind the Nobility's intransigence there no doubt lay a general desire to assert a right to have a voice in the composition of the regency and in appointments to the high offices of state. But this was not the whole explanation: there were reasons of a more material nature. As we have seen, Charles X's will would have given the post of treasurer to Herman Fleming. But Fleming had made himself heartily detested by his colleagues in the Estate of Nobility. They regarded him as one of the most zealous advocates of the hated *reduktion* which had been forced through in 1655; and in no circumstances were they now prepared to accept him as director of the nation's finances.

The Addition to the Form of Government, which was accepted by the Diet of 1660, involved the consequence that the power of the council was enhanced in relation to the regency, while that of the *riksdag* was strengthened in relation to both. This change was in itself sufficient to ensure that the opportunities for the chancellor to dominate policy, as Axel Oxenstierna had dominated it during the regency for Christina, were now curtailed. But De la Gardie in any case lacked the personal qualities which could have enabled him to fill Oxenstierna's place. He could not command the firmness, the strength and the consistency of purpose which had characterised his predecessor; he easily lost heart when things went badly, and he often wearied of the demanding and laborious work in council and chancery. He was in the habit of spending long periods away from Stockholm, on his estates in the country; and at such times his adversaries would get the upper hand in the government and divert policy to new lines. On his return after such absences the chancellor did indeed often show energy and resolution, and by the weight of his authority and his skill in dialectic was able time and again to resume effective control of affairs and reverse decisions which had been taken while he was away. But his adversaries soon rallied; and these recurrent struggles set a stamp of weakness and inconstancy upon the whole regency. The adversaries were moreover formidable: the treasurer Gustav Bonde; Sten Bielke, who was later to succeed him in that office; Clas Rålamb, one of the country's leading legal experts, who before his election to the council had been something of a leader of the lesser nobility; Matthias Biörnklou, who once had been De la Gardie's tutor; Johan Gyllenstierna, who was to become the chancellor's leading opponent; and several others. The clashes between the chancellor and his adversaries were in the main to come either over finance or over foreign policy; and the event was to show that those who opposed him on financial questions were as a rule also opposed to his conduct of foreign affairs.

The financial situation which confronted the regency was certainly not an enviable one. Christina's reckless extravagance had led to a catastrophic diminution in taxes and crown rents, since the landed possessions of the nobility had been enormously increased by donations and revenue assignments. The *reduktion* which had been agreed upon under Charles X had been put into effect only to a very inconsiderable extent, and his incessant wars had still further worsened the already precarious financial position. The new treasurer, Gustav Bonde, stood for a consistent policy of economy. At all costs the crown's expenditures were to be kept down, so that it might be possible to proceed with an annual repayment of its debts, in the hope of liquidating them entirely by the time Charles XI reached his majority. The difficulties in the way of any such programme were obvious, not least because the country's position as a great power made it necessary to maintain a strong army at a time when the absence of any major war deprived it of the prospect of obtaining the subsidies, or of levying the contributions, which had formerly covered the major share of the cost of the army's maintenance. The budget which Gustav Bonde presented in 1662 was of extreme austerity and was marked by a conservative estimate of income, and the cutting down of every conceivable item of expenditure. The advocates of economy looked upon it as a kind of model budget, which should fix the pattern of financial policy for the whole of the duration of the regency.

Bonde's programme was undeniably sound in essence, but it was not without a certain narrowness and inflexibility. It did not show much imagination when it came to estimating the chance of increased yields in the crown's revenues, and it was too exclusively directed to the reduction of expenditure, not always with a proper consideration of how necessary the expenditure might be. From the beginning De la Gardie emerged as a harsh critic of Bonde's policies; and this clash over finance was to last, with increasing bitterness, throughout the whole decade. Now as later he saw the solution to Sweden's difficulties in a more flexible financial policy, and he brought forward a series of proposals whereby the crown's revenues might be made more productive. His suggestions bore witness both to his energy and his ingenuity, and some of them did in fact prove to be fruitful; but they were all alike characterised by a tendency towards too sanguine a view of the possibilities: too often his estimates of income were quite unrealistic, while in other instances his proposals were impracticable, if only because the crown's credit had already been severely shaken.

It is significant moreover that De la Gardie, in contrast to Bonde, was at best only tepidly interested in the *reduktion* of alienated estates. Like many of his noble colleagues he considered that the land was best exploited when it was in noble hands. And apart from this he considered that the key to an improved financial situation lay not in increasing the yield of the old imposts upon the land, but rather in the expansion of trade, manufactures and mining, which would provide the crown with a revenue in cash rather than in kind.

On the whole it may be said that Bonde and those who thought like him had the greater share in shaping financial policy during the earlier years of the regency. But in 1666 Bonde died, and in the years that followed the budgets increasingly reflected the chancellor's opinions: that of 1668 was wholly his work. It looked well on paper; but in February 1668, while he was still (as usual) in the country after the Christmas holidays, his opponents mustered for the attack. They set up a commission of enquiry; and the result of that commission was the so-called *Blue Book*, which subjected the chancellor's budget, and his financial policies in general, to caustic criticism. Objection was taken to a multitude of new – and, it was suggested, unnecessary – items of expenditure, and at the same time a large part of the items on the revenue side were shown to be dubious, since they could scarcely be counted on to yield as much as was estimated, if indeed they produced any revenue at all. The chancellor's return to Stockholm was naturally followed by a bitter struggle, from which De la Gardie did in fact emerge victorious, among other reasons because he was able to point to a number of obvious errors in the *Blue Book*'s statistics. Until 1670, therefore, he continued to direct the finances; but in that year, taking advantage of another of his prolonged absences and egged on by his enemies, the Exchequer College once more took them under its own control. And since it now became obvious that the chancellor's sanguine calculations had in only too many instances been proved ill-founded, he was not this time able to upset his co-regents' resolutions, despite the fact that he went so far as to threaten to ask leave to resign his office.

The second main problem of the regency concerned foreign policy. For the first few years after 1660 Swedish statesmanship was decidedly pacific. This was in part an absolute necessity, in view of the fragile basis of Sweden's position as a great power, since the main object must naturally be to take care of the country's security by pursuing a balancing policy amid the shifting pattern of European alliances. How best to do this in the various situations which arose proved, however, to be a constantly recurring source of controversy. De la Gardie consistently advocated an alignment with France, while his opponents on various occasions pressed for a rapprochement with the enemies of Louis XIV. This is not the place to examine in detail the intricate pattern of foreign relations during this period. But a particular interest attaches to the conflicts between the chancellor and his adversaries in connection with the formation of the Triple Alliance between England, Sweden and the Dutch in 1668.

After the peace of Breda in 1667 Louis XIV directed his efforts towards isolating Spain and the Dutch as a preliminary to the next round of French aggression. In 1668 this policy provoked an alliance between Holland and England. For Sweden the choice now was whether to attach herself to France – which would afford guarantees against Danish plans for revenge, avert political isolation, and at the same time possibly diminish the pressure of Dutch commercial predominance – or whether to move over to the Maritime Powers. The chancellor, of course, advocated the former policy; but there was a strong party in the council against him which included Sten Bielke, Clas Rålamb, Johan Gyllenstierna and Matthias Biörnklou (who was considered to be their leading expert on German affairs). This group also included the chancellor's leading opponents on finance; and this was no accident.

For an alignment with the Maritime Powers was considered to involve distinctly less risk of Sweden's being dragged into hostilities; and it would thus diminish the burden of defence expenditure, which was an absolute precondition for the realisation of a policy of strict economy. Despite De la Gardie's resistance – which was based not only on his general pro-French attitude, but also upon a deep mistrust of England – his opponents forced through Sweden's adhesion to the Triple Alliance. But the decision had not been reached without a violent quarrel, which only the personal intervention of the queen-mother more or less succeeded in patching up.

In April 1672, after an intense struggle within the council of state, Sweden concluded an alliance with France which was ultimately to involve her in a devastating war. It was a step which had its origins in the fact that the Triple Alliance had been shattered by England's adhesion to France in 1670, while at the same time a number of German princes had moved over to the French side, either by committing themselves to military aid, or to the extent of promises of benevolent neutrality in the event of an armed conflict between France and the Dutch. On the other hand Brandenburg, which for many years had been no friend to Sweden, drew closer to Holland. These events threatened Sweden with political isolation; and the situation became especially serious when it became clear that France, failing an alliance with Sweden, might seek the friendship of Denmark. The threat of a major European conflict made Swedish military preparedness indispensably ncessary; but the country's economic situation rendered this extraordinarily difficult, unless some subsidy could be obtained. In the course of the protracted discussions in the council, De la Gardie, predictably enough, urged an alliance with France. But it must be emphasised that he had no more intention of paving the way for Swedish participation in the war than his opponents had: his objective, like theirs, was a policy of holding the balance. The object of both was to break out of the political isolation which seemed to threaten the country; and it was hoped that the mere presence of a strong Swedish army in Pomerania would be an effective means of keeping the peace in Germany. De la Gardie aimed moreover at combining adhesion to France with the assumption by Sweden of the role of a mediating power; this would on the one hand make it possible to avoid direct participation in the war, and on the other could be expected to lead to a relaxation of international tension.

Little by little De la Gardie rallied support for his diplomatic plan of campaign. Even previously avowed enemies – the most notable example being Clas Rålamb – were at last convinced that association with France on the lines which he suggested was the best means of solving the problem of security; and on 16 April 1672 the French alliance was at last concluded. Among those who declined to be convinced by De la Gardie's arguments was Johan Gyllenstierna. Subsequent historians have long condemned the treaty in unmeasured terms. They have accused De la Gardie, as its main architect, of irresponsibility, of having been guided only by the hope of French subsidies, and indeed almost of having acted as the paid agent of France. It is only in comparatively recent years that the advances of historical scholarship have finally made a clean sweep of all such notions.

When the great war broke out, and England and France attacked Holland, Sweden took the initiative in an attempt at mediation which at first seemed not without some prospect of success, but which soon ran into insurmountable difficulties. In the years 1673–4 the war took a decided turn for the worse, from the French point of view, and a comprehensive anti-French coalition was formed under the leadership of Austria and Spain. Among the states that joined that coalition were Brandenburg, and also (which for Sweden was even more menacing) Denmark. France increased pressure upon Sweden to comply with her obligations under the alliance. Sweden's ally possessed a powerful means of persuasion in the shape of the promised subsidies, which she now threatened to refuse to pay until the Swedish army had actually attacked Brandenburg. De la Gardie made great efforts to finance the necessary military preparations elsewhere, by means of short-term loans and anticipations of revenue; but when it came to the point it was in fact difficulties of supply which precipitated the outbreak of war at the end of 1674: the Swedish commander in Germany found himself forced to invade Brandenburg territory because he could no longer support his troops in Swedish Pomerania. It was an act which marked the bankruptcy of Swedish policy. When in the autumn of 1675 the *riksdag* met for Charles XI's coronation, the country was at war, not only with Brandenburg but also with Austria, Holland and Denmark. And these events dealt a shattering blow to Magnus De la Gardie's political position.

Despite the fact that the Addition to the Form of Government (1660) implied a certain increase of authority for the *riksdag* in relation to the council and the regency, the period of Charles XI's minority had been marked by the virtually unlimited predominance of the high

aristocracy in the government of the country. In the event, the functions
of the regents had been exercised by the council *in corpore*; and the
council was a body which was very largely recruited from the titled
aristocracy. Ever since 1611, and indeed for many years before that,
Swedish domestic politics had been characterised by a struggle for
power between this council aristocracy, which aimed at entrenching
its political influence, and the monarchy, which sought to set limits to
that influence with the aid of the lesser nobility and the three non-noble
Estates. At the *riksdag* of 1672, when the minority came to an end, it
naturally became a burning question whether Charles XI's assumption
of authority would mean that the council would be more or less eclipsed
and would be deprived of that central position in the life of the state
which it had latterly occupied. From the council's point of view it was
disturbing that Charles XI was surrounded by a group of young noblemen of royalist tendencies who were openly antagonistic to it, and that
an increasing opposition to it could be discerned in the non-noble
Estates – opposition provoked not least by the council's slackness in
carrying through the *reduktion* which had been agreed upon in 1655.

It is against this background that the production of a draft Accession
Charter must be seen which would have entailed, in a number of important points, the satisfaction of the interests of the council aristocracy,
and the provision of safeguards for the continuance of the council's
political influence. The draft had indeed been worked out by a committee of the House of Nobility, but it was very much in the spirit of the
council aristocracy, and there can be little doubt that it emanated from
them. It might seem reasonable to assume that among those who
promoted it was the council's leading figure Magnus Gabriel De la
Gardie. His position within the council had been decidedly strengthened
during the closing years of the regency; the bitter struggles with his
colleagues which had marked the preceding period seem by this time
to have been damped down; and he had been able, as we have seen, to
carry the acceptance of his line on foreign policy. Nevertheless there
are convincing reasons for concluding that the chancellor not only
had no share in drawing up the draft Charter, but was in fact directly
opposed to it.

De la Gardie had been the especial favourite of Queen Christina.
By his marriage with the sister of Charles X he was intimately linked
with the new Palatine dynasty; and his appointment by that king to the
office of chancellor was considered (and certainly with justice) to have
been motivated by the consideration that his relationship to the royal

family made him the most likely person to take care of its interests. No doubt it is true that he disappointed these expectations in the matter of Charles X's testament; but even so he can hardly be accounted one of the typical council constitutionalists. If we may trust contemporary opinion, moreover, there still subsisted a strong and long-standing antagonism between the upstart family of the De la Gardies, whom successive sovereigns had so lavishly favoured, and the old high-aristocratic families such as Oxenstierna, Brahe, Stenbock, Banér, Sparre and others. Charles XI was young, shy, intellectually un-developed, and his interest in the business of government was at this time limited. For the chancellor, as his near relation, he had always shown the greatest regard, and there was every reason to suppose that once the regency came to an end De la Gardie would enjoy a position of great influence: he himself confidently expected it. He had conse-quently no motive for supporting a manoeuvre which would limit the king's freedom of action – and therefore, in fact, his own – to the advantage of the council. And in fact during the first years of Charles XI's personal rule it was De la Gardie who was the real director of Swedish policy. This meant, among other things, that the importance of the council tended to diminish, and that government business tended to pass into the hands of a kind of inner cabinet dominated by the chancellor. His position was further strengthened by the fact that the council acquired a number of new members, close political associates of the chancellor, and foremost among them his son Gustav Adolf De la Gardie, who was also, of course, the king's cousin.

It is from this period, when the chancellor stood at the pinnacle of his political career, that we have a character sketch of him written by a shrewd observer, the Italian diplomat Magalotti. Magalotti described him as

certainly the handsomest man one could wish to meet, of a lively genius and a natural eloquence. He speaks Latin, Italian, French, German and Dutch. He has a knowledge of history which is more than respectable, has made some study of philosophy, understands political questions excellently well, and is deeply versed in the politics of Europe. Men say that he is inconstant and quick to take offence, and when he is moved to anger allows himself to be carried away beyond what he really intends; and this has on more than one occa-sion done him a hurt in negotiations he was engaged in. He is the worst economist and the greatest spendthrift in the world, main-

tains a numerous army of servants, an expensive table, and squanders
vast sums to furnish his establishments, lay out his gardens, and
carry on his building plans: it is said that he is engaged at one and
the same time upon building works in forty or fifty different places.
He is of a generous temper, and possesses more distinguished manners than others of his countrymen. He loves his children, loves his
wife, and enjoys her love in return. He has a considerable weakness
for women; but favourites he has none. To the clergy he is courteous,
and is in consequence much liked by them.[3]

Nevertheless signs soon began to appear that the chancellor's position
was beginning to be undermined – and this for various reasons. The
decisive factor, as will appear, was that he lacked some of the qualities
which were absolutely indispensable to any man who aspired to be
a Swedish Mazarin. He had no staying power, and his indolence induced him to spend long periods in the country on one or other of his
estates, while the threads of government slipped through his fingers,
and important questions might be decided without him. His opponents
in the council were given increased room for manoeuvre; and the want
of any unifying force in the government became glaringly obvious. He
lacked also the strength of will which is necessary to a real statesman,
and which alone makes it possible to impose a policy against tough
resistance, or maintain the authority to carry through a necessary
change of course. And already the storm-clouds were gathering.

De la Gardie had been the most eager promoter of the French
alliance of 1672; and the line in foreign policy which was the basis
upon which that alliance was grounded was peculiarly his own. It was
essentially a policy of peace. But the turn of events proved that in
this matter his predictions had been wrong, while those of his leading
adversary, Johan Gyllenstierna, had been right. Sweden had been
dragged into a war which she was totally unequipped to wage. Its outbreak revealed not only that De la Gardie's foreign policy was a failure,
but also that the country's finances were in a condition which seemed
to threaten complete collapse, and which crippled the war effort. In
the summer and autumn of 1675 the domestic crisis came to a head at
the *riksdag* which opened at Uppsala towards the end of August.

By that time Swedish arms had sustained the sharp reverse of
Fehrbellin; and the very day after the king delivered his message to the
Estates came the news of Denmark's declaration of war. These events
provided the immediate occasion for the attacks which the Estates now

launched against the former regents. What they demanded, in the first place, was an explanation of the foreign policy that had been pursued and of the way in which the country's resources had been applied. The upshot was the appointment, with the king's consent, of a commission of investigation drawn from the Estates themselves. It was the labours of this commission which were to provide the basis for those rigorous proceedings against the regents which – even more perhaps than the *reduktion* – were to break the economic power of the council aristocracy.

III

The action of the Estates, and their demand that the regents should be called to account, gave the death-blow to De la Gardie's authority; but from a purely personal point of view he seems to have been more deeply affected by a quite different matter, namely the accusation, levelled against him during the sessions of the *riksdag*, of having uttered treasonable words about the king. The affair provides an excellent example of those devious manoeuvres, obscure intrigues and bizarre whispering campaigns for which this decade was notorious. And among those concerned in it, as in so many of such incidents, was that curious character Count Gustav Adam Banér, a notorious intriguer and a litigant of unsavoury reputation. He was the son of the famous field-marshal of the Thirty Years War, Johan Banér; but his own claim to remembrance depends entirely upon the many scandals in which he was involved.

It happened that, after a meeting of the Estate of Nobility, Banér was standing talking to another nobleman. As though by accident, he picked up a closely written slip of paper which was lying on a window-sill. Its contents proved to be of the most serious nature. They amounted to an accusation that a man in one of the highest offices of state had said to two members of the council that the country would never be right until 'that lout' (i.e. the king) had been cleared out of it. A committee of the Nobility handed over this paper to Charles XI, with a report of how it had been discovered. Charles XI appears to have been in some doubt whether the discovery called for any special action. He assured the members of the council that despite the contents of the paper he did not entertain the least distrust of any of them. But when the council came to discuss the matter, De la Gardie delivered a strongly worded attack, first against the author of the libel, and secondly (on the assumption that the statements in it were true) against the person who might have made the alleged remark, and against the two council members who, by listening to it without denouncing him, were in his view no better than traitors and villains.

On the following day Clas Rålamb and Knut Kurck (both members of the council) presented themselves to the king and offered evidence to which they said they were prepared to swear. According to their depositions, the chancellor had, about a year before, taken them on one side and, speaking of the king, had said: 'We must get that lout away; he does no good, God damn it, here at home.' The evidence of two members of the council – one of them, Clas Rålamb, being one of the country's leading legal experts, and the other a man of high reputation, who incidentally was to fill the office of president of a Supreme Court a year or two later – was undeniably of great weight, especially as they were prepared to affirm it upon oath. Nevertheless it must be said that it is probable, indeed almost certain, that this was a particularly heinous example of false accusation. De la Gardie was of course to a very large extent dependent upon the favour and confidence of his royal relative. It was mainly in virtue of it that he had been able to thrust his opponents aside, and to keep the reins of government in his hand for so long, despite a certain lack of personal energy and capacity for hard work. That he should have made the kind of remark which was attributed to him simply does not make sense. Clas Rålamb and Knut Kurck had long been his bitter enemies; and it is inconceivable that he should have said anything to them which they could later use against him.

De la Gardie, naturally enough, was furiously angry at the accusations and indignantly protested his innocence. The king accepted his statements and took the line that the affair should be reduced to the level of a private quarrel between accusers and accused. The chancellor initiated an action for slander against Rålamb and Kurck in the Supreme Court; they declined to enter an appearance, and instead attempted to bring a charge of high treason against him in which they would appear as witnesses for the prosecution. At this point the king, weary of the venomous accusations and counter-accusations, and disturbed by these domestic brawls at a moment when the country was in grave difficulties, forbade both parties to pursue the matter any further. The affair was to be definitively closed. But an intense hostility remained.

It is pretty clear that neither Clas Rålamb, nor Knut Kurck, nor Gustav Adam Banér, can be acquitted of having a hand in the production of the libel; and there is strong presumptive evidence that the Speaker of the Estate of Burghers, Olof Thegner, was also involved.

But in the chancellor's view it was none of these who really pulled the strings, but a man more dreaded, and an enemy a thousand times more detested, than any of them – Johan Gyllenstierna.

What part then did Johan Gyllenstierna really play at the *riksdag* of 1675? It is clear that he took the same line as the opposition in the matter of the attacks upon the financial and foreign policy of the regency, and from our knowledge of his relations with the chancellor we may assume that he viewed with satisfaction any action which might tend to undermine De la Gardie's position. But was it he who hatched the charge of high treason? Or was he at least involved in the business? Among the reasons for thinking so is perhaps the fact that he was related to Gustav Adam Banér, the discoverer of the paper, and had at least to some extent been involved in some of his previous political intrigues. There were reports, moreover, both from this and the preceding *riksdag*, that he had contacts with the leader of the opposition in the Estate of Burghers, burgomaster Olof Thegner, who, as we have seen, was probably involved in the plot. It can also be established that Gyllenstierna was one of those members of the council who resisted taking measures calculated to hush up the affair at an early stage. On the other hand, the main argument against his having played any leading part in the affair is the complete absence of real proof. If Gyllenstierna was indeed mixed up in it, he contrived to cover his tracks completely.

It is at all events clear that the plot against the chancellor which was concocted during the course of this *riksdag* was co-ordinated with the violent attack by the Estates upon the regency's foreign policy and administrative record, for both of which De la Gardie appeared to be principally responsible. Its object was to overthrow him, and to deprive him of political influence. This chimed in well with Johan Gyllenstierna's political objectives; though in the absence of proof we are not entitled to assume that he was at the bottom of the intrigue, or was even implicated in it. But at all events it is plain that as a result of the attitude of the *riksdag* the struggle to control the government ended in a decisive defeat for De la Gardie. And the chancellor, who had never been a good fighter when things went against him, threw in his hand; for a considerable time to come his energies seem to have been virtually paralysed.

But the Estates' proceedings, which led among other things to the appointment of a commission of investigation whose first concern was the administration of the finances during the minority, produced effects which in fact dealt a heavy blow not only to De la Gardie, but to the whole council. Immediately after the end of the *riksdag* Charles XI quitted Stockholm; and his stubborn refusal during the following months to have any personal contact with the council was undoubtedly a reflection of the catastrophic loss of prestige and power which that body had suffered as a result of the Diet. At his headquarters in Skåne, from which he led the defence against the Danish invasion, Charles XI was surrounded entirely by secretaries drawn from the lesser nobility. And it was to his headquarters that he summoned, in the summer of 1676, Johan Gyllenstierna: a member of the council, no doubt, but also the man who was soon to obtain a position of personal dominance, and to organise what might be called a sort of military dictatorship – the germ from which royal absolutism was soon to develop. The mortal danger to the position of the council which was implicit in Gyllenstierna's growing power produced a not unexpected result: in the spring of 1677 a reconciliation came about between De la Gardie and the Kurck–Rålamb faction who had hitherto been his bitterest foes. As Johan Gyllenstierna's brother Göran put it, in a letter to him: 'Herod has shaken hands with Pilate.'[4]

There were two conceivable counterpoises to the tendency of the king and his powerful minister to move towards an absolutist régime: one was the *riksdag*, the other was the council. After the reconciliation in the council the newly consolidated party of resistance attempted to mobilise both possibilities. On the one hand they hoped to obtain the summoning of a Diet; on the other they tried to establish a permanent delegation at the king's headquarters. The former method had this to be said for it, that it would be impossible for the king and Gyllenstierna to take no notice of the Diet's wishes, least of all in the existing catastrophic financial situation. But on the other hand it was a very questionable expedient, and indeed might prove a dangerous one, since the council could by no means be sure that feelings in the *riksdag* would be favourable to them. It was therefore upon the second method that they concentrated their efforts.

In the following weeks a bitter struggle developed between headquarters, where Johan Gyllenstierna now occupied a dominant position, and the council in the capital. Here De la Gardie now had the support of the governor of Stockholm, Clas Rålamb, the president of the Supreme Court, Knut Kurck, and the treasurer, Sten Bielke. All had once been his sworn enemies, but they now stood shoulder to shoulder with him in the contest with Gyllenstierna. They could feel that they

had won an initial success when in the autumn of 1677 Charles XI at
last felt obliged to permit the council to send a delegation to his headquarters in Skåne. But if they were to have much chance of carrying
their point, it was of great importance that De la Gardie should be one
of the members of that delegation. In the event it arrived without him.
For on 28 August the chancellor, who had resumed command of the
operations in Västergötland, met with a severe defeat at Uddevalla. It
was a defeat which was to have grave consequences not only for himself but for the whole council. The military effects of the battle of
Uddevalla were perhaps not particularly serious; but the event made
a most unfavourable impression at headquarters, and in Charles XI's
mind De la Gardie was now written off as a military failure. A striking
incapacity for fighting on the defensive had always been one of his
weaknesses as a statesman. He now abandoned the struggle altogether,
and for the rest of the year directed his efforts to securing permission
to relinquish his command. One other consequence of the reverse was
that he excused himself from accompanying the delegation of the
council to headquarters.

The attacks which at the *riksdag* of 1675 had been directed against
the regency, and in particular against the chancellor, had led him to
prepare a written apologia in which he repudiated the allegations
against him and defended the motives for his policies. The accusations
which he was most concerned to rebut were that he bore the main
responsibility for the alliance with France and Sweden's consequent
involvement in the war; that he had taken foreign bribes; and that it
was mainly by his fault that the finances had been mismanaged during
the minority. His memorial is dated February 1676, and is entitled
A Short and Plain Remonstrance.[5] It was written at a time when he had
broken off relations with the council, that body being then dominated
by men who were his enemies; and by his own account it was intended
only for the eyes of the king, to whom it was in fact sent in three instal-
ments.

In *A Short and Plain Remonstrance* the chancellor met the attacks
upon him by arguing that the responsibility for the French alliance was
shared by a great majority of his colleagues, and in any case could not
be considered to have been the cause of the war: it had lasted for two
and a half years before war broke out, and at that time had only another
six months to run. The sending of troops to Germany was a measure
intended for the defence of the country, and had been decided on only
after mature debate in the council. Their dispatch was by no means

tantamount to a determination to enter the war, nor were hostilities made unavoidable by lack of supplies, since it would have been possible to find quarters for the troops elsewhere. As to the third main charge – that the attack upon the elector of Brandenburg was a blunder – he was prepared to concede that as events had turned out it had some substance, though he disavowed all responsibility for the decision. He repudiated with indignation the accusation that he had taken French money for himself, and retorted by insinuating that there were others who had received considerable amounts of ready cash; a large sum, he alleged, had been paid out to France's enemies in Stockholm by the Spanish ambassador, de Nuñez. He then proceeded to indicate the real causes of Sweden's disasters. They included the vacillation and squabbling which marked the council proceedings, the military errors of the marshal, the many mistakes in the field of foreign policy – for instance, that 'no attempt had been made to concert measures with France in good time', that 'all action was taken too late, and almost none at the right time, despite the repeated representations of the government',[6] and so forth. Finally the chancellor sharply rejected the charge that he was mainly responsible for the ruinous administration of the finances during the regency; on the contrary he had on numerous occasions used every effort to restore the finances, and had laboured disinterestedly – at the cost of making many enemies – to do away with abuses.

Charles XI gave De la Gardie's memorial a most unfavourable reception. He feared that its effect would simply be to widen the rift in the council and cripple the united effort which was necessary in order to master the extremely critical position resulting from the successful Danish invasion of Skåne and Halland. He therefore imposed a categorical veto upon its dissemination.

But the chancellor was deeply imbued with the desire to justify himself, not least in the face of new attacks which were being made on him as a result of the fact that his memorial, despite the king's prohibition, had leaked out. And apart from this, the political situation had now been modified by the reunion of De la Gardie with his former opponents in the face of the increasing trend towards absolutism. It is against this background that we must see the appearance of a new, more detailed defence from the chancellor's pen, the famous *Vindiciae Veritatis*.[7] This new memorial, which appeared at the time of the Halmstad *riksdag* of 1678, bears a superficial resemblance to the *Short and Plain Remonstrance*, but an analysis of its contents reveals significant differences. As we have seen, *A Short and Plain Remonstrance* had made serious reflections on the conduct of the council, and had attempted to shift the whole blame to their shoulders. There is still some trace of this in *Vindiciae Veritatis*, but the whole course of events is now presented in a new light. The chancellor now associates himself with the council's actions; he asserts a common responsibility for their decisions and enters vigorously into a detailed defence of them. The French alliance was not only justifiable, it was the best step that could have been taken in the existing situation. The rupture with Brandenburg was in the last resort justified, and was in conformity with the plain interests of the country, having been caused by 'the elector's own actions and his precipitate proceedings against Sweden'.[8] When war broke out, the position as regards manpower, ammunition and finance was as good as when Charles X began hostilities in 1655. In strong contrast to his previous attitude, the chancellor now asserts the identity of his own policy with that of the council, and energetically defends it, insisting that 'their counsels had been directed with the greatest prudence'.[9] But he still refused to acknowledge that he bore any particular responsibility beyond that which attached to the council as a whole.

Nevertheless *Vindiciae Veritatis* was by no means devoid of violent personal attacks. Those who contended that the chancellor – either in person or (when he wished to keep in the background) through his agents and tools – had had a decisive influence on the domestic and foreign policy of the government, and who therefore blamed him for all the mistakes that had been committed, should be punished for their malice: 'I esteem such presumptuous fledgeling statesmen for talebearers and libellers, and to them and all their arguments I answer simply that they are shameless liars. I am content to leave the defence of what has passed to those who are bound, when called upon to do so, to appear before their king and country; but I am not prepared to be judged by any and every malicious, incompetent and shamelessly prejudiced critic who may come forward.' [10]

There can be no doubt for whom this was intended. The fundamental difference between *A Short and Plain Remonstrance* and *Vindiciae Veritatis* lies in the fact that in the latter the object of his frenzied invective is not the council but Johan Gyllenstierna. The explanation for the country's misfortunes is now seen to lie in the 'double-dealing and artful, abominable intrigues, such as never were known in the loyal and sober Sweden of an earlier day'.[11] And De la Gardie concludes his pamphlet with a comprehensive commination of his malevolent enemies, who are indeed also in his view the enemies of their country: 'Such slanderers are worse than murderers; and God, who shuts the gates of His eternal kingdom against all men of blood, will remember and judge such men after their deserts.' [12]

But Gyllenstierna's influence with the king was strong; and the chancellor was well aware of the risks he was taking. He did not doubt that his enemies 'would never be quiet, until God in His justice thrusts them into the pit which they dig for others; and that day will surely come'. The subsequent course of events was to show that the chancellor was very ready to do his best to ensure that that day was not too distant.

By the autumn of 1678 De la Gardie was ready to pass from defence to attack. Together with his previous opponents he concerted an action which in fact represents the last united effort of the council to preserve its political position and to stand fast against a current which was setting strongly towards the establishment of absolutism and its own degradation. This attack took the form of a desperate attempt to overthrow Johan Gyllenstierna, and also his brother Göran who, as Johan's trusted agent and as the mouthpiece for the views of headquarters, had built up for himself a strong position in Stockholm in opposition to the council.

On 30 September 1678 the marshal, Johan Gabriel Stenbock, was dispatched by the council from Stockholm on a mission to the king's headquarters in Skåne. Stenbock was one of the most influential members of the council, well esteemed by Charles XI, and a bitter adversary of the Gyllenstiernas. He took with him on his journey to the king a memorial and a letter which bore the signatures (besides that of De la Gardie) of the high steward Per Brahe, Knut Kurck, Clas Rålamb and Stenbock himself. Its purport was to represent to the king the need to institute a thorough investigation of certain pieces of information which had come into De la Gardie's possession, and which were of the utmost importance to the security of the king's person and the safety of the state. The source of this information was stated to be Count Gustav Adam Banér. Beyond this the letter contained no particulars; but the affair was set out more at length in a letter from the chancellor to Charles XI which Stenbock seems also to have taken with him; and no doubt Stenbock was also expected to give a verbal report upon the case. With the aid of these two letters, of the minutes of the discussions in the council, and of a couple of narratives later drawn up by De la Gardie, we can form some idea of the material upon which the council based their request for an enquiry. They amounted to nothing less than an accusation against Johan Gyllenstierna of treasonable conspiracy.

Some years earlier – not later, at all events, than the summer of 1676, and possibly even before that – Count Gustav Adam Banér had called upon De la Gardie with a story of secret intrigues and traitorous designs against the security of king and kingdom, which Johan Gyllenstierna was alleged to be preparing. Some time later, at the Halmstad *riksdag* of 1678, Banér had again approached the chancellor with stories of plottings by the Gyllenstierna brothers which menaced the safety of the king's person and the security of the realm. Among the witnesses whom Banér had cited were the vice-president of the Supreme Court, Arvid Ivarsson Natt och Dag, and Lieutenant-Colonel Per Lillie. And the charges which Banér made against Johan Gyllenstierna, if we may believe the chancellor's statement, were as follows. He was said to be contemplating playing the part of a Swedish Cromwell – the reference being of course to the leading share which Cromwell had taken in bringing about the fall of the monarchy, and to his subsequent dictatorial régime. Banér reported also that Johan Gyllenstierna had invited him to undertake the role of Ireton. However, Gyllenstierna's interest in English history was not confined to the Cromwellian period. He had also taken it upon himself to drink a health to the memory of Essex, the favourite of Queen Elizabeth, who had allowed himself to be involved in conspiracy and had ended his life on the block. This was obviously intended to suggest that Gyllenstierna and Essex were men of the same kidney: chosen favourites who had devoted themselves to treasonable plotting. As early as 1660, according to Banér's account, Johan Gyllenstierna had been thinking of a republic, and after Charles XI's majority he had directed all his efforts to preparing a revolution in the constitution. His brother Göran was said to have been privy to his designs, and had among other things shown to various people a copy of a chronicle of Eric XIV, in which those passages which related to the king's deposition had been specially marked. The insinuation here, of course, was that the Gyllenstiernas wished to demonstrate that there was a precedent for deposing a monarch. Johan Gyllenstierna had also taken steps to prepare the ground in other ways. He was said to have desired to prevent the king's coronation at the Uppsala *riksdag* of 1675. This put an entirely fresh aspect upon the sensational attack on De la Gardie on that occasion – an attack in which Gustav Adam Banér himself had been involved. The objective, it appeared, had by no means been simply to overthrow the chancellor: what Gyllenstierna intended was a provocation which would discredit the king, whether he protected De la Gardie or not. Afterwards, when the war broke out, the Gyllenstiernas had persuaded Charles XI to keep away from Stockholm, in order that he might be entirely under their influence. And after inducing the king to take measures of one sort or another at their instigation, they constituted themselves the severest critics of those measures, and 'reprehended them with impudent and shameless words'. But though the plots of Johan Gyllenstierna had been directed primarily against the king, they had also aimed at his old enemy De la Gardie. He had told Banér that he would surrender whole provinces to the Danes rather than conclude a peace which might enable the chancellor to rehabilitate himself. The chancellor was to be made the scapegoat for Sweden's involvement in a war which she lacked the resources to wage with success; for if in spite of everything the war had a successful outcome, that would be considered as implying a vindication of his policies. In this situation, then, Johan Gyllenstierna, by Banér's account, was ready recklessly to sacrifice the interests of his country in order to satisfy his personal vendetta against the chancellor. But the most serious of Banér's accusations was that Johan Gyllenstierna and his tools had deliberately exposed the king to the greatest dangers in the hope that he might be killed in action. In short the object of all the plots which Banér now discovered had been 'the wicked and evil intent' to deprive Charles XI of the affection of his subjects, expose his person to danger in the hope that he might fall in battle, and finally to turn the country into a republic. Realising the hazards of the game he was playing, Johan Gyllenstierna had sold or mortgaged practically the whole of his property, against the possibility that he might be detected and forced to leave the country in a hurry.[13]

Such was the material upon which De la Gardie and the council grounded their request for permission to initiate an investigation. And it is clear that Banér, as the council's witness for the prosecution, occupied a key position. On many occasions De la Gardie emphatically asserted that he had raised the matter in the council only upon Gustav Adam Banér's urgent representations. But it is by no means certain that this was so. From surviving correspondence it appears that Banér refused to comply with the chancellor's demand that he should put his depositions in writing. According to information from vice-president Arvid Ivarsson Natt och Dag, Banér was in fact furious when the chancellor broached the question in council. And finally Banér made all speed to depart for Ingria (of which province he was governor-general), despite the efforts of the chancellor and the council to persuade him to stay.

The attempt to overthrow Johan Gyllenstierna by a charge of treasonable conspiracy was in fact a desperate gamble. The result was devastating – but not for Gyllenstierna: he was already far too well dug in for that. Charles XI ordered the council to desist from its examination of witnesses; and instead of the brothers Gyllenstierna being tried for treason, they brought actions for false accusation against various council members. The total defeat of the council was manifested in other ways also. Clas Rålamb, one of its most influential members and one of the strongest champions of its interests, was deprived of his post as governor of Stockholm and packed off to Jönköping to be president of the Supreme Court there. His successor in Stockholm was none other than Göran Gyllenstierna. Nor was his fall an isolated case. A similar fate overtook De la Gardie. Crushed by the failure of the attack on the Gyllenstiernas, he asked leave to go into the country for a time for the sake of his health. Undoubtedly he envisaged only a relatively short absence; but Charles XI seized the opportunity to get rid of him for good and all. Johan Gyllenstierna was by this time on good terms with another member of the council, the treasurer Sten Bielke, who for years had been a notorious enemy of the chancellor; and it was to Bielke that the leadership of the chancery and the council was now entrusted. In contrast to what had happened on previous occasions when De la Gardie had been temporarily away from Stockholm, an Instruction was now issued to his deputy. And at the same time there were other indications that henceforward the council was to be subjected to stricter control.

The tenor of Bielke's Instruction strengthens the assumption that the intention was to bring about a permanent change in the leadership of the chancery and the council. It began with an expression of Charles XI's displeasure at the slowness and negligence which had marked the council's proceedings, attributing them to the fact that there had been nobody who had 'manifested a constant concern, or a sense of responsibility, for getting its business done'. This scarcely veiled censure of De la Gardie's way of discharging his official duties was underlined by a special injunction to Bielke to strive to improve relations between the government and the people, and to secure harmony at the council board. This last was obviously an allusion to the struggles between factions in the autumn of 1678, whose backwash was still perceptible in the litigation now in progress between the Gyllenstiernas and the council witnesses. The Instruction also made it clear that Sten Bielke was to retain his post until the king himself should be pleased to relieve him of it — a provision which was intended to provide a safeguard against the possibility that the chancellor might return to Stockholm and resume his duties. That this was a real anxiety appears from the fact that even after De la Gardie left Stockholm in July 1679, with the assurance that he would be prepared to return as soon as the king might require his services, he showed that he was not willing entirely to relax his influence on the course of affairs. Sten Bielke complained to Charles XI that the chancellor, despite his absence, was trying to meddle with chancery appointments, though Bielke had refused to acquiesce in his interference. He also enquired what he was to do if De la Gardie should return to Stockholm and attempt to resume control of the office.

By the end of September the chancellor had still received no command to return to the capital, and he accordingly wrote to Charles XI expressing his gratitude at being allowed some months' leave to recover his health, and enquiring whether it was the king's wish that he should forthwith resume his official responsibilities, or whether he should take a further period of recuperation. He was much concerned to emphasise that he had no intention of abusing the king's good nature, nor of neglecting his duties, but was ready to return to work. In reply he was directed to remain in the country until Charles XI should himself have returned to Stockholm. In December 1679 the king quitted Skåne, and in January 1680, when he was at Kungsör, De la Gardie made yet another effort. He wrote to the king; and he also waited on him in person, professing his readiness to move back to Stockholm and resume his office. Once again the king declined the suggestion, declaring that any alteration in Bielke's instructions would only cause confusion. De la Gardie was ordered to remain in the country until after Charles XI's wedding, when the king would himself assume the direction of public business.

Thus all the chancellor's attempts to recover the leadership of the council and the chancery had been repulsed. Six months later Sten Bielke too was relieved of his office, which was given not to De la Gardie but to Bengt Oxenstierna. The change was made necessary by the death of Johan Gyllenstierna in June 1680; for though in recent years Bielke had indeed been concerned with foreign as well as with domestic policy, he had acted only in a subordinate capacity. In this field he was clearly inferior to Bengt Oxenstierna, who had been employed on various diplomatic missions during the war and had earlier acquired a thorough first-hand knowledge of foreign affairs. When Per Brahe died in the autumn of 1680, the king appointed De la Gardie to be his successor as high steward: formally it was a promotion; in reality it set the seal on the political degradation which was implicit in his removal from the exercise of his function as chancellor in the spring of 1679.

IV

As we have seen, Magnus Gabriel De la Gardie had been appointed to the chancellorship of the University of Uppsala by Charles X, and in that office he rendered the university very important services. This was true in particular during the 1660s, when for a considerable period he worked hand in glove with the celebrated Olof Rudbeck, who was for some years the university's rector. With De la Gardie's active support there was an expansion in the teaching of hitherto neglected scientific subjects, and new departments were founded. This is true not least of Rudbeck's famous Botanic Gardens, which De la Gardie subsidised liberally from his own pocket. He also collaborated with Rudbeck in that comprehensive modernisation of the university's teaching accommodation which was carried through in the years after 1660: it was these years which saw the building of the Gustavianum, an anatomy theatre unequalled anywhere in the world at that period.

For many years, therefore, De la Gardie's tenure of the chancellorship of Uppsala was marked by vigorous activity and fertile initiatives. He also played a leading part in regard to the country's second university, which was instituted in 1668 at Lund, as a centre for the conquered southern provinces. The fact that it was instituted at all, in the face of the opposition against the scheme (not least on financial grounds), is to a considerable extent due to his exertions. Yet even his work as university chancellor revealed his characteristic weaknesses. Economic calculations which erred on the side of optimism, landed Uppsala in crises in which professors were not paid their salaries and building activities had to come to a stop; and there were occasions too when he was not able to keep his temper when dealing with the academic staff. Nevertheless his services to Uppsala were very great. Among them was the magnificent donation, in 1669, of a priceless collection of manuscripts, including an extremely valuable series of Icelandic documents. But the greatest treasure of all was the Silver Bible, *Codex argenteus*, a Gothic translation dating from the sixth century, written on purple-coloured parchment in gold and silver letters. The Swedes had taken it as booty when they captured Prague in 1648, and when Queen Christina left Sweden after her abdication she took the manuscript with her. Thereafter it found its way to Holland. De la Gardie purchased it, caused it to be encased in that binding of beaten silver which has given it its name, and presented it to the University of Uppsala. It still remains the most splendid bibliographical treasure in Swedish possession.

The gift to Uppsala was not an isolated incident. As a statesman De la Gardie has been harshly, and often justly, criticised; but as a patron of the arts it is universally agreed that no Swede of that age is to be compared with him. Among his many other interests it is perhaps worth while to point out his extraordinarily important services to archaeological and antiquarian studies. He made money available for the purchase of manuscripts and books, he financed archaeological expeditions, catalogues of runestones and other antiquities, and himself took an active share in the work. He also showed a rare appreciation of the problems involved in the preservation of antiquities, and induced the government to issue mandates for the protection of ruins, chambered cairns, runestones, tumuli, stone-circles and so forth. Instructions were issued to both lay and ecclesiastical authorities for the listing, protection and care of ancient monuments. It was De la Gardie also who induced the government to agree to the creation of a College of Antiquities, which was in fact not so much a college as a kind of learned academy, and may be considered as one of the predecessors of the existing Academy of Letters, History and Antiquities. Indeed it has been said that any account of De la Gardie's patronage of the arts in fact embraces the whole cultural history of Sweden in his time. The poet George Stiernhielm, the brilliant jurist Johan Stiernhöök, the scientist Olof Rudbeck, the philologist Lars Norrman, painters such as David Klöcker Ehrenstrahl, architects such as Nicodemus Tessin the elder and Jean De la Vallée – these are only some of a long line of distinguished personalities in many fields who were given commissions by De la Gardie, or enjoyed his support in one form or another. His interest in education was not confined to the universities. In a series of memorials dating mainly from the 1650s and 1660s he proposed schemes for the reform of the schools. His attitude to school curricula was throughout marked by an attempt to diminish the privileged position hitherto enjoyed by theology in the educational system, and to provide a more varied and practical type of schooling. Another notable characteristic is his reiterated demand for selection strictly according to ability, which he saw as a means of limiting the size of educational establishments, and which derived from his fear that more students would obtain degrees than the country really required, and thus lead to the emergence of a proletariat of the learned. But behind these anxieties also lay a consideration which was to him at least equally important: the preservation of the privileged interests of the aristocracy. By the middle of the seventeenth century the trend towards entering the civil service was threatening to make it an overcrowded profession. The nobility by long tradition claimed a pre-emptive right to all such civilian appointments. The competition for these jobs from able and well-educated commoners thus became an increasing matter for concern to them; and this was especially true when the ending of the Thirty Years War, and the reduction of the army to a peace footing after the death of Charles X, sharply curtailed the prospects of appointments and promotion in the armed forces. De la Gardie was strongly imbued with a feeling for his order, and he was anxious to do everything possible to improve the educational opportunities for the children of the nobility. The possibility of increased social mobility as a result of the influx of gifted non-noble students into the country's educational establishments was not a prospect which he viewed with approval.

De la Gardie's record as a statesman has undoubtedly suffered from the dispersion of effort which marks his career. For long periods – and they often happened to be critical periods from a political point of view – he would quit the capital and drop his work in the government to devote himself entirely to his estates. What mainly absorbed his interest was building; but he also gave much time to the laying-out of splendid gardens, with orangeries, pavilions, fountains, basins and sculptures of one sort or another. In this matter he was something of a pioneer as far as Sweden was concerned. In a number of instances he himself made the sketches for the work to be undertaken. Most of his enormous income was devoted to satisfying his insatiable appetite for architecture. Even if Magalotti's statement that in the mid-seventies he was simultaneously engaged in building activities at forty or fifty different places all round the country is something of an exaggeration, it is still true that the erection of new buildings or the drastic reconstruction of old ones was going forward at many of his castles at the same time.

He owned estates in practically every portion of the Swedish empire. Outside Sweden proper he had large possessions in Finland, in

Pomerania, and not least in Livonia. It has been estimated that his revenues from the county of Arensburg, on the island of Osel – one of Queen Christina's many benefactions – were alone sufficient to give him a yearly income twenty times as large as the official salary of a member of the Swedish council. This particular estate, as we have seen, was lost as a result of Queen Christina's abdication; but he later managed to obtain the county of Pernau in compensation, and that too was extremely lucrative. In Sweden itself he had numerous estates in the centre of the country; but most of his territorial empire, which at its maximum embraced more than a thousand farms, lay in Västergötland. It was here that was situated the county of Läckö; and Läckö castle, on Lake Väner, became the most costly and ambitious of all the chancellor's many building enterprises. It numbered 248 rooms, many of them furnished with extraordinary splendour; and the domestic staff at times ran to something over two hundred persons.

De la Gardie had a cultivated taste which was unusual in the Sweden of his day, and his own contributions bear witness to a connoisseurship and judgement which were no doubt partly acquired in the course of his early visits abroad. In his building activities he sought in the main to realise the ideals of French and Italian baroque, and he spared no expense in recruiting qualified persons to assist him. As his architects he relied mostly on Jean De la Vallée and Nicodemus Tessin the elder; but to a very considerable degree he himself took an active share in planning and projecting. Great quantities of drafts and sketches in his hand have been preserved; and often the architects were given detailed instructions to guide them in their work.

He was a keen art collector; and in the notes of the inventories of his various castles – and not least of his magnificent palace in Stockholm, which bore the name of Makalös ['Nonesuch'] appear paintings by many famous hands: Titian, Tintoretto, Lukas Cranach, Hans Holbein the younger, and many others.

Despite his wealth and his enormous income the chancellor had at times considerable difficulty in raising cash to pay for his costly building projects. On occasion he was forced to sell some of his property, and above all to mortgage it; and this applied not only to land but also to jewels and other personal ornaments. Lack of money could also mean that his designs for buildings had to be carried out on a more modest scale than appears in the original grandiose plans.

Charles XI's *reduktion* hit the De la Gardies harder than any other family among the nobility. In part this was because they were of comparatively recent origin, so that their estates included a smaller proportion of hereditary family lands and allodial possessions than was the case with the old aristocracy, and therefore were more exposed to the operation of the *reduktion*. But what definitively broke De la Gardie was the fact that he was at the same time more harshly dealt with than any of his colleagues by the commission of enquiry into the conduct of the regents. By the judgements of the so-called Great Commission he was condemned to make restitution to the crown to an amount of no less than 350,000 silver *daler*. When one remembers that even in his palmiest days the former chancellor, despite his vast revenues, had found difficulty in putting his hand upon liquid assets, it is easy to understand that these sentences must have been ruinous for him. At the same time as he was losing masses of land and farms by the operation of the *reduktion* he was expected to produce the means to pay the sums demanded by the judgements of the Great Commission. This could be done only by selling and pawning his landed property, which was indeed often taken in execution and sold by auction. But at this moment the greater part of the Swedish aristocracy found itself in similar financial difficulties, so that the land often fetched only a small fraction of its real value.

What is interesting, however, is the fact that although the De la Gardie family really was impoverished by the *reduktion* and the commission, it was not very long before they were flourishing once more and in possession of a long string of extensive estates. The forced sales of property under Charles XI had depressed prices and given a brilliant opportunity for enterprising speculators with money at their command. Fabian Wrede, a member of the king's council and a bitter opponent of De la Gardie, was among those who now succeeded in acquiring extensive landed estates. They passed by inheritance to a granddaughter who eventually married into the De la Gardie family, bringing with her no fewer than eighteen manors as dowry. Another collection of estates which had been the property of another of the *reduktion*'s large-scale dealers in land, the marshal Johan Gabriel Stenbock, came once again into the ownership of the De la Gardies in the same way.

But for Magnus De la Gardie, now broken in health and spirits, the the last years of life were a period of constant humiliation. One by one his estates passed from him, even the proud county of Läckö. He had hoped after his fall from power to be able to retire into private life and devote himself to what was perhaps his first love – the management of his property; but this was not to be vouchsafed to him. One single estate remained to him; and at Vänngarn he lived out his last years. Even this was made possible only by the king's grace, for in reality it too was liable to be resumed to the crown. In the same way his wife Maria Eufrosyne was permitted by her royal nephew to retain her property at Höjentorp, together with a small pension. There was now not the least possibility of leading the kind of aristocratic life which they had in earlier years accepted as natural. Their chattels and their personal possessions were pawned or sold one after the other; their servants left because there was no money to pay their wages. From an existence which had now lost all its charms, and seemed to promise only further humiliations and adversities, Magnus Gabriel De la Gardie turned to seek consolation in religion. He had already shown an aptitude for versification, but in the hymns which he wrote in his last years there was a personal note and a depth of feeling which were new, and which are exemplified in a stanza which has become classic, and still holds its place in the hymnology of the Swedish church:

> I from life's stormy ocean come
> Home to a friendly strand.
> What though my flesh lie in the tomb?
> My soul is in God's hand.
> From darkness into light I move,
> From poverty to wealth of love,
> From strife to rest eternal.

7. The *reduktion*

KURT ÅGREN

WHEN we in Sweden speak of the *reduktion*, we mean as a rule – unless we are speaking to absolute specialists – those resumptions of alienated crown lands which were the consequence of the resolution of the Diet of 1680, and of the Diets which immediately followed it. But the resumptions which occurred in the two last decades of the seventeenth century were not a unique event in Swedish history. The crown had scarcely begun to give away estates to private persons or institutions before the need and the demand for the revocation of its gifts made itself felt. Already in the Middle Ages, therefore, decisions were taken on more than one occasion, approving the recovery by the crown of lands which it had earlier alienated. The most successful of these older *reduktions*, however, was that which occurred at the beginning of the country's modern history, when Gustavus Vasa at a stroke deprived the institutions and representatives of the Roman Catholic church of the greater part of their landed wealth. The resolution authorising this *reduktion* was taken at the Diet of 1527, and represents as it were the economic side of the religious changes which were taking place in Sweden and in Europe at that time: the parallel with what happened in the England of Henry VIII is sufficiently obvious.

During the sixteenth century, and especially during the first half of the seventeenth, the transference of lands from the crown to the nobility proceeded at an ever-accelerating rate. The *reduktion* of 1680 which Charles XI and his coadjutors carried through put a stop to this process. But already in 1655 Charles XI's father, Charles X, had forced through a resolution in favour of a *reduktion*. Charles X's *reduktion*, however, was neither as far-reaching as his son's, nor as ruthlessly logical in its application. For this the explanation no doubt lies in his early death, and in his preoccupation during his short reign with other and more pressing affairs of state (see also above, Chap. 5). But certainly he and his son had the same objective in view.

In what follows it is with Charles XI's *reduktion* that we shall mainly be concerned. My object is to attempt to shed light on this *reduktion* primarily in its economic, social and political aspects, and to avoid as

far as possible discussion of the purely technical problems. But in order
to do this we shall need a certain amount of preliminary information
which may itself seem to be of a somewhat specialised and technical
nature. And this because the circumstances of Swedish fiscal administration were themselves of a rather special kind. For this reason too we
shall have to sacrifice precise terminology in favour of more general
description, which offers a better chance of being understood. If there
should be any English reader who aspires to a full and adequate knowledge of Swedish cameralism, the only consolation which I can offer to
him is that it is a knowledge which few professional Swedish historians
possess.

When in the thirteenth century the Swedish state adapted itself to
the new military techniques of the age, and began to build strong
places and castles for purposes of defence instead of fitting out offensive
fleets on the old Viking lines, one consequence was that the peasantry's
obligation to furnish and man such fleets was transformed into an
obligation to assist in the building and provisioning of the new castles.
The peasants' duty to do military service, which had become more or
less pointless in an age of heavy-armed cavalry, was converted into
standing taxes upon their farms. These taxes, which were paid in kind,
became in time the most important revenues of the Swedish state,
despite the fact that the political leaders of the seventeenth century, in
their search for a basis for Sweden's great-power aspirations, made
earnest efforts to change the position so as to obtain an income in cash
rather than in commodities. For a great power the policy of cash income was no doubt a necessity. But it took no account of the realities
of the Swedish situation; and by clinging to it the Swedish state was
eventually put in a position in which it was dependent upon foreign
subsidies. The *reduktion* may be said to be a recognition of the fact
that the policy was impracticable in a society with the economic structure of seventeenth-century Sweden. The crown's alienation of land
to the nobility was another consequence of this shortage of cash resources. This brings us to a consideration of what the crown was in a
position to do, in the way of selling or giving away land, and of the
conditions under which such alienations could take place.

In general, cultivated land in Sweden was divisible into three
categories, depending upon who was its owner. (Practically all the land
that was cultivated, irrespective of ownership, was cultivated by
peasants; before the *reduktion* there is good reason to think that
demesne farming was of very small importance.) The first category of

farm was owned by the man who worked it, that is, by the peasant.
Such farms were called 'tax-farms'. The second category was owned by
the crown, and the cultivator paid the king a rent which was in many
respects comparable with the tax paid by the owner of a tax-farm: these
were the so-called 'crown farms'. The third category comprised farms
owned by a nobleman, the so-called *frälse*-farms (see above, p. 106 n.).
These farms were exempt from a proportion of the taxes due to the
state: just how large the proportion might be was laid down in the
privileges of the nobility, and depended on how far the farm lay from
the nobleman's manor. The peasant on a *frälse*-farm paid a rent to the
noble owner, just as the crown-peasant did to the crown. How this rent,
and the other burdens on the land, compared with the corresponding
obligations upon crown- and tax-peasants will be a question for our
consideration when we come to discuss the social consequences of the
reduktion.

The land which a nobleman owned might have come into his possession in a variety of ways, and might consequently be held upon
different terms; and this was to have significance for the effect of the
reduktion on different persons and families. If the land was alloidal –
that is, if the nobleman occupied it with full rights of ownership – it
was obviously better protected against a *reduktion* than property which
had been acquired on quasi-feudal terms – that is, with some limitations
upon the right of ownership. The old family estates which had formed
part of the family inheritance from time out of mind were obviously
allodial. But side by side with these were lands which had come to a
family as the result of the crown's violation of that clause in the Land
Law [1] which forbade kings to diminish the assets of the crown by giving
lands away; and these too were held by allodial right. Such gifts were
especially common in the sixteenth century. Towards the end of that
century, however, a new form of royal gift began to emerge. Donations
of land were now accompanied by 'feudal' restrictions, the most important of which was the recipient's obligation to seek confirmation of
the gift at every change of sovereign. The model for these 'feudal'
donations was the counties and baronies, which started their short life
in the middle of the sixteenth century; and these in turn took as their
pattern the great duchies which had been created in order to provide
for Gustavus Vasa's sons. This new form of donation gave the crown
a tighter hold over alienated land, and also the possibility for some
future ruler to recover it for the crown by refusing to confirm the donation of his predecessor. In 1604, at the Diet of Norrköping, the Estates

resolved that in future no donations should be made except on 'feudal' conditions; and this, as may be seen, entailed not only an obligation to seek confirmation from each succeeding ruler, but also a limitation upon testamentary rights. Properties given away upon these new terms were termed, clumsily enough, 'Norrköping-resolution estates'. This did not mean, however, that after 1604 the nobility had no more opportunity to acquired lands from the crown as allodial holdings. For on the one hand the central government sometimes violated the terms of the Norrköping resolution; and on the other hand the crown, from the time of Gustavus Adolphus onward, was forced to sell estates in order to raise ready money to pay for its wars. And land purchased from the crown in this way was regarded as allodial, just as was the land which James I was selling off in England at about the same time.

I. THE LEGISLATION

An appropriate place to begin our survey is the *reduktion* which was voted in 1655, and which may be considered as the predecessor of the much more comprehensive legislation of the 1680s. The resolution of 1655 was taken at a moment when the imminence of war created a demand for a stock of capital in cash, and against a background of social unrest: the demand for a *reduktion* was the translation of that unrest into political terms. It affected different classes of land in different ways; here we shall consider only its more important provisions. In the first place all former crown lands, irrespective of how they had come into the possession of their present owners (whether as gifts, pledges or by purchase), were to be restored to the crown if they happened to lie within the so-called 'inalienable areas'. By this was meant places or regions where the revenues from farms were considered to be indispensable to the crown, and where alienations had in consequence been forbidden. No fewer than eighteen categories of 'inalienable areas' were listed in the resolution, the most important being those designed for the maintenance of the army and the metallurgical industry. In the second place it was provided that one-quarter of all estates donated after 1632 (the year of Gustavus Adolphus's death) were to be handed back to the crown – though the nobility was given the option, for the next three years, of paying a tax (the so-called 'contribution') equivalent to the tax revenue from the estates which were to be reduced. In the third place all lands which had been given away in allodial tenure in defiance of the Diet's resolution of 1604 were to be converted into

Norrköping-resolution estates – that is, they were to be held on 'feudal' terms.

It can hardly be said that during the remainder of Charles X's reign this *reduktion* was carried through as energetically as it might have been, for these were years when the king was for the most part engaged in war outside the country. The impetus sagged still more after his death, when the country was ruled by a high-aristocratic regency; and this despite the fact that the regents' actions were narrowly scrutinised by a Diet whose powers were now greater than ever before. But in 1672 Charles XI came of age; Sweden concluded an alliance with France in order to obtain French subsidies; and Louis XIV invaded Holland. As a result of the subsidy treaty Sweden was drawn into the war and given the task of containing the forces of Brandenburg. And in 1675 the Swedish army in Pomerania was defeated by the Great Elector at Fehrbellin. It was a clear indication that the Swedish war machine was not as formidable as was generally supposed; and the first sign of a change of opinion on this point was a declaration of war by Denmark. The Swedish fleet was swiftly put out of action, and it was only with the utmost difficulty that the Swedish armies were able to defend the southern provinces against the Danish attempt at reconquest. (At the peace of Copenhagen in 1660 Sweden had gained her present frontiers on the side of Denmark and Norway as a result of the cession by Denmark of Skåne, Halland, Blekinge and Bohuslän.) As to the German provinces, Sweden proved incapable of holding them by her own exertions, and recovered them only through the intervention of her powerful ally, France.

Such then was the situation which faced the Diet in 1680. The country was indeed at peace; but it was a peace secured only by heavy sacrifices, and after it had become evident that Sweden's resources were inadequate to maintain a military strength commensurate with her pretensions as a great power. The king had increased his prestige by his leadership during the war against Denmark; and his campaigns had given him opportunities, in discussions with his intimates and in the absence of his council (who stayed in Stockholm and were forbidden to visit him at headquarters), to make plans for the future government of the country.

In the Proposition which he now laid before the Diet, Charles XI laid bare the critical economic situation in which the country found itself; and in particular he pointed out the necessity of refurbishing the nation's defences by sea and land. The Proposition offered no suggestion as to where the means for this programme were to be found, but there were men in the House of Nobility who were ready to supply that omission. In the Estate of Nobility there was a tradition of hostility to the ruling aristocrats of the council and the great landed proprietors; and the bearers of that tradition were now reinforced by persons who in the existing situation could buttress principle with hopes of personal gain.

One first result of the activities of the royalist party in the House was that the investigation into the conduct of the regents became a question of intense topical importance; and its work was pushed on with the idea of thereby providing the crown with financial resources. This commission of enquiry, designed to settle accounts with Charles XI's guardians, had been appointed at the Diet of 1675 with members drawn from each of the three highest Estates, and had been charged with the duty of scrutinising the council's administration of the country during the king's minority. In 1678, at the Diet of Halmstad, members had called for information about the progress of the commission's work. On that occasion they had called in vain, but in 1680 their thirst for information was amply satisfied. The collaboration between the king and the royalists in all four Estates, and possibly the idea that the most crying needs of the exchequer might be met by the sums to be exacted in restitution from councillors who had failed in their duty, prepared the way for the setting-up of an extraordinary tribunal drawn from the Estates, which was to adjudge the degree of criminality which attached to the regents, and determine what restitution was to be exacted from them. The commission of enquiry makes, indeed, no part of the *reduktion*; but it is intimately linked with the need to cover the deficit in the budget, and with the movement towards absolute monarchy.

While Charles X had as far as possible kept the three non-noble Estates outside the negotiations which led up to the *reduktion* of 1655, the resolutions for a *reduktion* in 1680 took shape in debates in which the lower Estates took a vigorous part, even though the most dramatic and most decisive moments occurred in the Estate of the Nobility. It was the Estate of Peasants, true to tradition, who first raised the question of a *reduktion*; and they followed it with the equally traditional gambit of seeking the collaboration of the Clergy and the Burghers. All three then forwarded to the king a joint memorial demanding the revocation of alienated lands, and this memorial the king referred to the Estate of Nobility. In the course of a debate upon a matter of principle – the question as to how far the non-noble Estates had rights against the

Nobility – the leader of the royalist group in the House, Admiral Hans Wachtmeister, put forward a concrete proposal which was destined to provide the basis for the resolution for a *reduktion*. Wachtmeister moved that the lands which the crown must resume should comprise the estates in the overseas provinces, the counties and baronies, and the Norrköping-resolution estates; with the proviso that the very poorest nobles should be exempt from the obligation to make restitution. And by irregular procedures, which violated the rules of order of the House, the assent of the Nobility to a *reduktion* on these lines was obtained.

The resolution of the Diet did in fact include those categories which Hans Wachtmeister had suggested. But besides this, of course, the *reduktion* which had been decided on in 1655 was now really to be enforced: this applied especially to lands within the 'inalienable areas'. In all other cases the *reduktion* of 1680 was so much more stringent than its predecessor that its implementation automatically involved the prosecution of that of 1655. As to the safeguarding of the interests of the lesser nobility, which Wachtmeister had promised, the Diet's resolution was so formulated as to exclude from the operation of the *reduktion* all persons whose total income from Norrköping-resolution estates did not exceed 600 silver *daler*. It is easy to see that this promise must have tempted that portion of the nobility which was not well provided with land to vote for the measure.

By the *reduktion* resolution of 1680 most lands which were held on 'feudal' terms would revert to the crown; there would remain only smaller properties whose annual value did not exceed the stipulated 600 *daler*. In contrast to this, the resolution of 1655 had not touched the counties or baronies, nor the Norrköping-resolution estates donated before 1632. But this was not all. At the next Diet, in 1682, the king propounded the now familier question as to how the state's debts were to be paid. The non-noble Estates were ready with the answer: an extended *reduktion*. This new revocation was to fall upon the poorer members of the nobility also; so that all sections of the first Estate could now rally to the view that a further *reduktion* was not the right way to tackle the problem. But the king cut the ground from under their feet, and put a stop to all discussion, by forcing the Diet to admit that the medieval Land Law did in fact give him the right to revoke fiefs as well as to bestow them. And by admitting as much, the Diet put the whole business of the *reduktion* into the king's hands: he was now free to recover crown lands irrespective of when and upon what conditions they had been given away.

In some respects distinct from the *reduktion* proper, but dealt with by the same governmental machinery, was the problem of estates which had been bought of the crown, or received from it as security for a loan. It was clear that these could not be construed as falling under the provisions of the Land Law regarding the king's rights over donations, since they had been acquired in return for some sort of consideration. The zealots for the *reduktion*, however, were quite equal to this difficulty. By arguments which to the layman appear as a better testimony to their ingenuity than to their impartiality, they were able to disallow, wholly or in part, former purchases and pledges, and to demand compensation from the present owners of such lands. Thus the only lands which a nobleman could now hold with a full security of tenure were those estates which could be proved to have been noble land from the beginning: at all events, this was the position in principle, though in actual fact the principle was never pressed to its logical conclusion.

II. THE CONSEQUENCES FOR THE CROWN

Behind the king's skilful and persistent efforts to carry the *reduktion* of 1680 it is possible to conceive at least three motives, corresponding to the three objectives to which a *reduktion* might be supposed to have been directed. One of those objectives could have been economic; another political; a third social. Or to put it in more concrete terms, the king may have wanted either to balance his budget, or to vanquish the powerful council aristocracy and so make the way plain for absolutism, or to rescue the peasantry from noble oppression by bringing back the administration of their lands once more under the crown's control. Among ninteenth-century historians there was a strong tendency to see this last objective as one of the king's prime interests. It was an interpretation which was based upon the idea that the history of Sweden had been made by a union of the king with a free and independent commonalty, and that in the national harmony the nobility had been a dissonant element. But though it might have been supposed that the liberation of the peasantry would have provided the champions of the *reduktion* with admirable propaganda material, they nowhere adduced this as one of their aims. And the future course of events, at least in the short run, makes it open to question whether any significant improvement in the condition of the peasantry in fact occurred.

No: the principal purpose of the *reduktion*, without any doubt, was to reduce the finances of the country to order. It would therefore clearly

be of the greatest interest if we could ascertain the economic results of
the *reduktion,* and set the crown's gains against its expenses and its
debts. We should then be in a position to discuss what the *reduktion*
meant to the crown in concrete terms. But it unfortunately happens
that there is no reliable investigation which gives an exhaustive survey
of the great *reduktion* in terms of the areas and the cash involved. The
explanation of this state of affairs lies in the size, the difficulty and the
contradictoriness of the source-material available to the researcher. It
would seem to be an impossibility for a single scholar to work his way
through this mass of material and arrive at a valid picture of the *reduktion*'s economic results. At the University of Uppsala a group of historians is at present engaged in investigating and clarifying some parts
of the operation. When their researches are complete there is no doubt
that much that is now hidden will be revealed, and we shall be able to
say that we have come to the beginning of the end of this gigantic
enterprise; but up to the present the team has not published any of its
findings, though we do have a modern investigation of the *reduktion*
of 1655 and its progress down to 1660.[2] The only existing monograph
on the *reduktion* as a whole was published as long ago as 1849.[3] Three
years later, in 1852, there appeared the seventeenth volume of a general
history of Sweden, in which the *reduktion* was given extensive treatment.[4] Both these accounts are packed with exact figures for the number
of estates resumed, and the gains made by the crown. But anyone who
takes the trouble to look more closely at them – and they are somewhat
sparingly provided with references to the sources – will find that the
figures are not derived from any thorough investigation and collation
of the source-material; they are based on isolated extracts, and extracts
whose reliability is at least open to question until it has been tested. It
is in every way understandable that these two scholars, pioneering their
way through material which was not at that time arranged with their
purpose in view, should not have been able to undertake the precise
analysis which the task required. But though we may understand how
their results were arrived at, that does not oblige us to put any great
faith in them. And in fact it can be shown that suspicion of Fryxell's
and Svedelius's figures is not unjustified. In particular cases and details
we are able to compare their work with modern studies. For instance:
in a table showing the revenue which accrued to the crown from resumed estates, Svedelius gave a figure for the island of Osel of 858
silver *daler*; a modern investigation gives a figure of 14,700 silver *daler*.[5]
As to Fryxell, his statements about the *reduktion* of 1655 can now be

compared with the results given in Stellan Dahlgren's dissertation of 1964. This is most easily done in regard to resumption of estates in the 'inalienable areas'; and the difference appears most strikingly for those estates which were resumed in order to provide resources for financing the navy. Fryxell gave their revenues as 20,738 silver *daler*; Dahlgren gives it as 13,393. Other individual items show similar discrepancies, and not always in the same direction – Fryxell's figures are not always larger than Dahlgren's. These errors, as will be seen, are not concerned with major items in the *reduktion*, but they are cited here in order to show that since individual figures do not stand up to criticism, the sum totals are bound to be misleading.

It was nearly a hundred years before Eli Heckscher made the next attempt to illustrate the *reduktion* by statistics based on research into the primary sources.[6] And though his account was obviously superior to those which had preceded it, its author had likewise had neither the time nor the facilities for the careful sifting and evaluation of the material which is necessary if statistics are to be used as a secure basis for a judgement upon the *reduktion*'s effects. It may be remarked, moreover, that Heckscher expressed himself with much greater caution than his predecessors when it came to giving figures, and that though exact statistics are indeed to be found in the tables appended to his book, he refrained from making use of them.

The situation then is that at present we have no statistics which can be used, with any reasonable degree of safety, to make possible a verdict on the concrete results of the *reduktion*. And however much one may hope that such a pessimistic prognostication may prove wrong, one is forced to express the foreboding that we never shall. The best hope seems to be that eventually we may be provided with so many special studies devoted to a particular topic or a particular geographical area that plausible generalisations for the whole may become possible.

The reliability of the few figures which are given here, though they make no pretence at absolute precision, is thus to be accepted only with reservations. But at least it can be contended that they give a more or less fair picture of the orders of magnitude involved. It has been calculated that three-quarters of the farms which had been alienated to the nobility, in one way or another, now returned to the ownership of the crown. This would imply that within the limits of Sweden proper (that is, excluding Finland, the overseas provinces and those recently acquired from Denmark – all of which were hard hit by the *reduktion*) the nobility's share of the cultivated land of the country dropped from two-thirds to one-third. The national debt, which in 1681 was estimated at between 40 and 50 million silver *daler*, had by 1697 fallen to about 10 million. The diminution was accounted for, to a large extent, by the fact that estates which had been pawned or sold by the crown had been reckoned as part of the debt: many of them had now reverted to the crown without any compensation.

But if the result of the *reduktion* cannot yet be expressed in exact figures, it is possible to give an indication of its effects in other ways. At the Diet of 1693, when the resumption of lands must be considered to have been more or less at an end, the king informed the Estates that the country's finances were now in such good order that he had no need to impose any extra taxes, over and above the standing revenues. Now this was something exceptional. The consequences of great-power status – and in particular the wars, and the need to safeguard the conquered provinces – had during the whole period entailed expenses which the crown had been unable to meet without having recourse to extraordinary taxation. But now, as the century drew to its close, the old medieval idea that 'the king should live of his own' was really for a moment attained. It was an ideal which the non-noble Estates, and especially the Estate of Peasants, had contrived to keep alive throughout the whole of the seventeenth century. But it was ironical that a programme first put forward in the Middle Ages by the aristocratic opposition which was grouped round the council should now be carried through by an absolute king, who took care to provide himself with pledges that increased taxes would be forthcoming should any extraordinary occasion arise.

For a country such as Sweden, committed to the role of a great power but conscious that in the two preceding decades her position had begun to weaken, the essential objective, now and in the future, was the maintenance of an effective army. It was indeed the lamentable condition of the defences which provides the clue to the successful imposition of the *reduktion* at the Diet of 1680. It was imperative that the government should be able to dispose of the new financial resources which it had acquired in such a way as to increase the stability of the armed forces. And with this end in view it fell back upon an organisation which did indeed already exist, but which was now developed in such a manner that it is scarcely an exaggeration to speak of an innovation. In earlier years the army had been provided with soldiers, in the main either by the conscription of the peasants or by the recruiting of professional mercenaries. Conscription involved the drafting of, e.g., every tenth man of military age, and it had in the past been an all-too-frequently recurring affliction. It was now replaced by the so-called allotment system (*indelningsverket*). As far as the cavalry was concerned, this meant that the tax revenues from certain farms were assigned to the maintenance of each regiment. Officers, both in the cavalry and the infantry, were provided with housing on crown-farms. In regard to the infantry, the government made contracts with the peasants in each province, by which they engaged to furnish a certain number of foot-soldiers, and to provide each one with a cottage for his maintenance. In return, the peasantry were freed for the future from conscription.* The whole reorganisation was made possible by the increasing revenues, in the form of taxes from farms, which the *reduktion* brought to the crown. And broadly speaking it may be said that the success of the *reduktion*, from the crown's point of view, was demonstrated by the fact that Sweden's military prestige – thanks, at least in part, to the performance of the new-style army – experienced its last great revival in the first decade of the reign of Charles XII.

The *indelningsverk* brought an order to the country's finances which their previous administrators could scarcely have dreamed of. But on the other hand the system presupposed normal conditions; and it inhibited any flexibility in the utilisation of the revenues upon which it was based. The system did no doubt last for centuries; but its weakness was strikingly revealed when Charles XII's wars entailed financial conditions which were no longer normal. For those conditions the system was not suited, and it broke under the strain. It is no doubt true that everyone suffered during the emergency of the war years, but officers in the military and civil services suffered more than most, for their wages dried up, and were diverted to fill the deficits in the exchequer. The outcome of this development can be seen in that political revolt of the serving classes which in 1719 broke the Caroline absolutism, and replaced it by the rule of the Estates under the leadership of the Nobility, and so inaugurated the so-called 'Age of Liberty'.

It remains to mention one wider aspect of the results of the *reduktion*, which sprang from the thinking that lay at the root of it. This was the breach with those principles of finance which had been held by the

---

* Strictly speaking, the use of the term *indelningsverk* to describe a purely military organization is too narrow; in a wider sense it implied that every item of expenditure was linked to a definite source of revenue, so that the organization came to apply not only to military but also to civil expenditures. For further discussion of the military *indelningsverk*, see below, Chapter 8.

architects of Sweden's greatness. For them, the provision of financial resources had always been an intractable problem. The Swedish economy was not constituted so as to provide what was mainly needed for the recruiting of troops and their maintenance in the field – namely, money. The revenues consisted for the most part in the commodities which the peasants paid as tax. It was in many cases this lack of cash resources which had led to the alienation of crown lands: the king was forced to provide for his servants, and pay their wages, by means of commodities rather than money – that is, by means of the taxes paid in kind from the farms which he gave them; the parallels with medieval feudal methods of financing armies and administration need no emphasis.

But the financial problem also led to other consequences. We can perceive, in the men of Axel Oxenstierna's generation, a deliberate attempt to arrange the Swedish economy in such a way that the country should yield revenues in cash rather than in kind. They staked the country's future on the metallurgical industries and on trade: this is the period when towns were founded, and monopolies created for the trade in copper, iron and tar. And the sale of royal lands is another manifestation of these attempts to convert the natural produce of the country into monetary capital. In connection with this policy there emerged a theory that the crown ought not to live on butter, sheep and geese which the peasants paid in tax, but upon the duties and excises arising from a flourishing trade. Considered from this point of view, the sovereigns who alienated land from the crown to the nobility were perfectly right. By doing so, the crown would free itself from the task of administering revenues with which it had really no business to be concerned. The nobility would see to it that the land was more efficiently farmed; their purchasing power would consequently increase; and this in turn would help to increase the crown's revenues in cash. It is of course not always certain that all those who championed these views did so because they were convinced that they were valid, and without regard to their personal interest. But however that may be, experience in the end showed that the theory did not hold water. The transformation was not a success. The debts of the state increased, and Sweden became dependent upon foreign subsidies if the budget were to be more or less balanced.

It is easy to see that Charles XI's *reduktion*, and the *indelningsverk*, involved a sharp break with the older theory. Expenditures were now linked directly to the land and its yield. It was not perhaps a step in the direction of progress, but in the existing situation it was perhaps a necessity.

In the introduction to this section it was pointed out that the monarchy might also have had political objectives in forcing through the *reduktion*. And it can scarcely be denied that side by side with the resolutions in favour of a *reduktion* was a movement towards royal absolutism, marked successively by the degradation of the council, the subjection of the Estate of Nobility, and the liberation of the king from the Diet's control of taxation. And considered very broadly it does appear probable that in prosecuting the *reduktion* Charles XI discerned the prospect of a monarchy whose hands should no longer be tied, when it came to deciding on the disposition of the country's revenues, by the need to consider opposing forces able to appeal, in the Diet and council, to their constitutional rights. Yet it does not seem very likely that the intention was to break the economic power of the nobility and its leaders in the council in order the more easily to introduce an absolutist form of government. This is not to deny, however, that the powers of resistance of the aristocracy must certainly have been weakened, once they had been forced to acquiesce in the *reduktion*, just as those of the council were similarly weakened by the results of the commission of enquiry.

It is in fact somewhat pointless (as it tends to be in such cases) to speculate about what it was that Charles XI in his inmost heart really sought. It is more profitable to indicate the concrete results of the *reduktion* as far as they affected the crown. They may be summarised as follows. The king was able, after a time, to balance the state's finances without having recourse to the Diet's tax-granting powers. He obtained resources which enabled him to carry through a reorganisation of the defences, and also of the civil administration, which brought efficiency and stability. That reorganisation involved a clear departure from the principles which had earlier provided the basis for the financing of Sweden's great-power aspirations. Parallel with this process, the constitution evolved towards absolutism; a development which took place principally at the expense of the Diet's leading Estate, the Nobility, and of the aristocracy's topmost social layer, the council – that council which for practically the whole century had played so great a part in the government of the country.

Finally, a word about the *reduktion* in the conquered provinces. Here the resistance was stronger than in Sweden. The local nobility contended, not without justice, that their lands were entitled to special treatment, and that the *reduktion* was being carried through in a way

which was not in accordance with the laws which had been guaranteed
to them at the time of the conquest. In the Baltic provinces in particular,
where the *reduktion* brought in large sums, the alarm and indignation
were especially great and led to direct clashes with the crown (see
above, pp. 44–5).

III. THE REDUKTION AND THE NOBILITY

In this section I shall try to do two things: firstly, to explain those
divisions of opinion within the Estate of Nobility which we noted earlier,
and show how they developed; and secondly, to discuss the social and
economic consequences of the *reduktion* as far as the nobility was
concerned.

Whenever the Swedish Diet came to discuss how the country's financial problems were to be solved, opinion tended to fall into one or other
of the two schools of thought to which we have already referred: on the
one hand was the view that the treasury should draw its revenues from
the land; on the other the view that the income of the state ought mainly
to come from tolls, excises and other revenues arising from commerce
and industry. Neither side was much concerned to support its position
on a basis of economic theory: in each case the arguments were purely
practical.[7]

It was entirely natural that the proposal for a resumption of alienated
crown lands should first have been put forward by the non-noble Estates.
The Clergy and the Peasants had started the idea as early as 1612. At
the Diets of 1649 and 1650, what had formerly been a proposal had
become a demand: the non-noble Estates launched their attack upon a
broad front, sought the support of the sovereign, Queen Christina, and
undoubtedly made a dent in the aristocracy's defences. In the 1630s
and 1640s what may be termed another and milder form of *reduktion*
had been tried, in the shape of demands for the curtailment of those
aristocratic privileges which provided for the total or partial exemption
of the peasants of the nobility from the duty of paying tax to the crown.
These demands had had some success, for by the middle of the century
this particular form of noble privilege had been in many essential respects eroded. But since the increase in the crown's revenues as a result
of such curtailments still fell far short of what was needed, another way
was tried. The nobility undertook for their own persons to make grants
to the crown – the so-called 'contributions' – despite the fact that this
was an infringement of the cardinal point in their privileges, their per-

sonal exemption from taxation. It was a solution which had been tried before, at the end of the sixteenth century; but after 1650 it became the rule.

Thus the nobility reached a position in which they were confronted with the stark choice between a *reduktion* or 'contributions'. In 1655, as we saw, they chose a *reduktion*; but by that time it was clear that whichever they chose there was no avoiding a *reduktion* within the 'inalienable areas'. And besides, the *reduktion* which was then agreed to was of limited scope; and it offered the option of paying a contribution for some time to come, since the *reduktion* of one-quarter of the Norrköping-resolution estates could be at least postponed by paying a sum of money equivalent to the revenues which would otherwise have accrued to the crown from the lands to be resumed; so that the *reduktion* could in fact be turned into a contribution at the option of the individual.

But at the Diet of 1664 the question of a *reduktion* was raised again; and thereafter it was constantly on the agenda of successive Diets until the final decision of 1680. And it is in the debates of the House of Nobility at the Diets of the 1660s and 1670s that the clash of opinion within the Estate on the question of '*reduktion* or contribution?' is most sharply defined. At the Diet of 1680 the Nobility, deeply divided and under heavy pressure from the king and the other Estates, finally opted for *reduktion*, only to find themselves immediately confronted with a demand for a contribution as well. The sense of shock which they then experienced appears from the official minutes of the Estate: 'Thereupon', the clerk recorded, 'there fell as it were a silence in the Chamber.'[8] The contribution, moreover, was no once-for-all payment: at every Diet down to 1693 (when the king declared that he could manage without any extra grants) the Nobility were compelled to renew it.

The interesting problem in this case is to define the considerations which produced this split in the Nobility, and so facilitated the carrying of Charles XI's *reduktion*. The notion that the crown could get along without the incomes which flowed from the land in the form of taxes and dues had proved, when it came to hard facts, to be altogether too remote from reality: hence the fact that the Nobility were forced to choose between *reduktion* and contribution. The standpoint of each side on this question is vividly reflected in two quotations. That of the opponents of a *reduktion* is expressed in Gustav Oxenstierna's remark in the course of a debate in 1672 that 'It is a hard thing, Herr Stålarm, to lose what is one's own';[9] while that of the advocates of a *reduktion* is represented by Christopher Gyllenstierna in 1680, when he said: 'It is a heavy burden to have to pay the contribution every year, simply because a handful of persons are sitting on most of the land in the country.'[10] Here then we have a classic, perennial division of opinion: one group hanging on to its property, another group seeking to deprive them of it; and historians have tended to base their accounts upon a simple dualistic pattern of this sort. The distinctive marks of those persons who constituted the first group, it is considered, were high birth, a title and landed property. The second group is supposed to be associated with recent ennoblement, lower social standing within the Estate, and dependence for their income on emoluments rather than land.

Unfortunately, however, reality cannot in general be made to conform to simple and easy patterns. In theory, no doubt, we ought to be able in this question to isolate three groups within the nobility:

1. A group whose landed possessions were of such a nature that it would be hard hit by a *reduktion*.
2. A group whose lands were exclusively, or almost exclusively, such as could reasonably be expected to escape *reduktion* – that is, lands of indisputable allodial nature. In contrast to the former group, this group ought to have preferred a *reduktion* to a contribution.
3. A group with no land at all, or very little, and which depended for their maintenance on their income from state service. This group need not take into account the possibility of financial loss. It ought to have chosen the alternative which would give most advantage to the crown, and hence would provide the best guarantee that the crown would be in a position to pay the wages of its servants. Nor ought this group to have felt any repugnance to voting a contribution as well as a *reduktion*.

But of course there cannot have been any grouping of interests as clear-cut as this. There must have been a spread of borderline cases from one end of the spectrum to the other. Indeed, borderline cases may well have been normal. But most noblemen, confronted with the bitter necessity to provide the crown with supplies, must have been forced to weigh which alternative was going to injure them least.

As in so many other cases in regard to the *reduktion*, we lack the research which might form a solid basis for a discussion of the attitude of different groups to the measure. An investigation of this kind would provide us with a picture of the distribution, among various categories of the nobility, of old allodial estates, land purchased from the crown and land acquired by donation. In the absence of this information, all we can do is to adduce arguments to suggest some modification of the traditional pattern of a high aristocrary of landed property on the one hand, and a petty nobility hungry for the *reduktion* on the other. And the first objection to this categorisation concerns the tendency to assume that the serving nobility and the high aristocracy were opposing groups. In seventeenth-century Sweden the serving nobility may be said without much exaggeration to have comprised the entire Estate. Moreover it was the high aristocrary who occupied the highest posts, and consequently who drew the biggest incomes from service. Among such people there must consequently have been a strong motive to ensure that the state had sufficient means to pay its servants' wages. Even from the point of view of strict class interest, therefore, it was by no means clear that the high aristocracy would give a predictable and almost automatic negative to the question of resuming crown lands. An investigation by the present writer gives a measure of support to this way of looking at the problem.[11] The investigation dealt with a single person, the lord treasurer Sten Bielke: a baron, a man of ancient lineage, the owner of many estates; a man, therefore, who fits all the criteria for one of our groups, since he was a member of the high aristocracy, one of the hereditary nobility and a landed magnate. Yet though he was certainly not among the smaller landowners in the Estate, the income he drew from state service can be reckoned at as much as two-thirds of that which he drew from his property. But at the time the Diet met in 1680 the crown had been in arrears with his wages since the year 1675, and was in addition his debtor in other respects. If we look at the accounts for his estates, moreover, we shall find that he could not reasonably have expected that any very large proportion of them would be affected by a *reduktion*.

The case of Sten Bielke admittedly provides no general proof of anything; but it can at least be used to support the contention that we must not take it for granted that a representative of the old high aristocracy must necessarily have been an opponent of the *reduktion*, even though his landed property was extensive. To this may be added the fact that, as Stellan Dahlgren demonstrated in his dissertation, it was precisely the members of the council and men like them who escaped most lightly from the *reduktion* of 1655, thanks to the king's intervention in their favour. The hope of similar treatment in 1680 may well have existed in nobles who might consider that their position gave them some prospect of bringing influence to bear upon Charles XI.

We may therefore sum up the argument about the reactions of the nobility to the resolution of 1680 as follows. The problem of groupings within the Estate can be considered to be only partly solved. It is, however, a clear gain that we have got away from the old idea of distinguishing them according to moral criteria – as, for example, 'patriots', or 'tools of the monarchy'. Economic and social considerations offer a safer basis of classification; but even this can afford no certainty without proper investigation of the social and economic factors in each case.

When it came to analysing the effects of the *reduktion* upon the nobility, the older textbooks contrasted an impoverished first Estate (with the royal favourites forming an exception) with a peasantry happily liberated from oppression. More modern textbooks, utilising Heckscher's work, have modified that picture. The view now is that the commission of enquiry, by its proceedings against the ministers of the minority period, was probably more damaging than the *reduktion* as far as the leaders of the old aristocracy were concerned. One of the most brilliant of them, Magnus Gabriel De la Gardie, whose personal income is said to have been equal to one-twentieth of the total revenues of the country, was especially hard hit by the enquiry, and it happened also that the greater part of his lands consisted of donations on 'feudal' conditions. De la Gardie himself stated that he was reduced to destitution, and looked forward to death as an escape from misery. Yet on the other hand the fortunes of the De la Gardie family are also adduced as an example of how the high aristocracy recovered from the crash: already in the next generation their lands began to expand again, by inheritance or by marriage. And in fact, it is argued, the great noble estates were not entirely disrupted. In the effort to raise money to meet the demands of the commission of enquiry, and of the *reduktion*, large amounts of land were thrown on to the market. The price of land fell; and persons with capital and inside information about available bargains could build up new estates of their own. Thus land passed into new ownership; and this brought with it a social and economic restructuring of the noble Estate. The purchasers might quite well belong to the old high aristocracy; but they were also drawn from the new nobility which Charles XI created. In particular, men who were employed in the administration of the *reduktion* are considered to have had opportunities to buy land on favourable terms.

To arguments on these lines there can in general be no great objection, though it must be observed that they are built on inadequate research into the surviving sources. The examples which are adduced are not sufficient to support the generalisations which are based on them. And in particular it must be pointed out that the assertion that there was a fall in land prices – a point fundamental to the whole line of argument – is no more than an assumption, and has not been proved. On the other hand there does seem to be rather more solid evidence for the conclusion that the nobility did for the most part succeed in salvaging their family seats (*säterier*). The crown was concerned only with the revenues from the land; it was not particularly interested in whether those revenues came from one kind of farm or another. This gave the nobility the chance to make arrangements with the crown whereby a farm which was due to be reduced could be exchanged against another which was exempt; and so the visible signs of noble landownership – the manor-houses with their dependent farms – could in great measure remain in noble hands. But it still remains to be proved that this meant that the old method of allowing the land to be worked almost exclusively by peasants was replaced by demesne farming of the continental type.

In the present state of research, therefore, it is not possible to say much with any certainty about how the effects of the *reduktion* were distributed between various levels of the Estate of Nobility. Their monopoly of the right to own *frälse*-land, at all events, was not affected: it was to continue more or less untouched for another century. But before we proceed to the next section some attempt must be made to summarise our conclusions about the nobility. We have seen that the demands for a *reduktion*, first put forward in the non-noble Estates, came gradually to find an echo in the first Estate also. Attempts to avert a *reduktion* by the waiving of their privileges on minor issues proved insufficient to silence these demands, and eventually they were presented with the choice between *reduktion* and contribution. For several successive Diets the Nobility acquiesced in contributions, despite the fact that by so doing they infringed that freedom from personal taxation which was the kernel of their privileges. But in 1680 they were forced to accept the *ultima ratio* of a *reduktion*; only to find that contributions were still to be required of them. The success of the crown was due partly to divisions within the Nobility which had already become apparent before 1680. It is indisputable that these divisions were for the most part rooted in economic and social causes; but it is no easy matter, in view of our lack of any large-scale investigation into the disposition and structure of landowning, to feel sure that we can construct the right categories, or place individuals in the right pigeonhole. The same lack of basic research makes it impossible to generalise about how the nobility was affected, socially and economically, by the experience of the *reduktion*. Historians have quite rightly abandoned the old idea of a first Estate despoiled to the point of absolute impoverishment. Instead they think now in terms of a transference of land within the Estate. But this modification of the older picture should not allow us to forget that the crown emerged from the *reduktion* much richer than before. And the crown's gains were the nobility's loss.

IV. THE REDUKTION AND THE PEASANTRY

In terms of any broad survey of Swedish society as a whole, it can hardly be denied that the changes which affected the nobility – an infinitesimally small proportion of the population – are strictly speaking of little interest compared with what happened to the peasantry; for in the seventeenth century the peasantry formed a majority so large that virtually every Swede was included in it.

The older view of the *reduktion*, as we have seen, held that it was designed to rescue the historic freedom of the Swedish peasant from the threats of the first Estate. Today we think so no longer; but we do think that in the long run the consequences were much the same as if it had been true.

Before we can decide this question, we must first of all be clear about the position of the peasants before the *reduktion* took place. As we have seen, there were three categories of peasants: peasants of the nobility (*frälse*-peasants), peasants of the crown, and tax-peasants, distinguished on the basis of who owned the land they worked. The land of *frälse*-peasants was owned by the nobility, that of crown-peasants by the crown; and both these categories paid dues (either rent, or taxes) to the owner, in return for the right to cultivate the land. Tax-peasants were freeholders, and they paid tax to the crown. It goes without saying that the right to undisturbed possession was more secure for them than for the two former categories.

The increasingly extensive acquisition of land by the nobility, especially during the seventeenth century, meant that more and more crown- and tax-farms came into noble possession. When this happened, crown-peasants were put in the same position as the old *frälse*-peasants; but former tax-peasants presented a more difficult problem. The crown had no right to alienate their farms, since the peasants held them in freehold. All that it could do was to transfer to the nobleman its right to collect the tax which the farm was due to pay. The tax-peasant thus transferred came therefore to occupy an intermediate position: like other tax-peasants he still owned his farm; but like *frälse*-peasants he paid his dues not to the crown but to the nobleman. This intermediate group of peasants came to be called, in later cameralist terminology, 'tax-*frälse*-peasants' (*skattefrälsebönder*).

It should in this connection be pointed out once again that no peasant was wholly exempt from paying taxes to the crown; even *frälse*-peasants paid some fraction of the normal rate of tax levied upon farms which had not passed into noble hands – how large a fraction being decided by the tenor of the privileges of the nobility, and in special cases by resolution of the Diet.

The impression that the nobility oppressed their peasants is derived mainly from the complaints which the Estate of Peasants brought forward at each Diet, and which were grouped together under the rubric 'the grievances of the commonalty'. In the main they resolved themselves in allegations that noblemen increased the burden of taxes, treated the peasants arbitrarily, and tried to force them from their farms. Now if we look more closely at these grievances it becomes clear that at least the first and third points must have referred only to the *skattefrälsebönder*. The other *frälse*-peasants can scarcely have had any legal right to demand that no alteration should be made in the dues exacted from each farm. The owner was clearly entitled to fix the yearly rent; and the peasant could then take his choice between accepting the terms that were offered, or looking for a farm elsewhere. Moreover, since it was only *skattefrälsebönder* who actually owned their farms, it was only they who were exposed to pressure to dispose of them.

As to how far the grievances of the commonalty reflected the real situation, it ought not to be necessary to point out how dangerous it is to try to get at the truth by the use of material which was in fact propaganda designed to influence the political situation. It may be remarked in passing that we find complaints against a nobleman which are identical with those which had been directed against the crown's bailiff in the years before the farm had passed into noble hands. Moreover the readiness of the crown to investigate how far complaints were justified, and to bring them before the courts, shows that it was not prepared to tolerate arbitrary proceedings on the part of the nobility. It is in fact

quite clear that the propaganda of the seventeenth century is not sufficient to prove that the liberties of the peasantry were in danger. We
must go to the nobility's own account-books if we are to obtain an
answer to this undoubtedly crucial question. And when we do so, there
are two questions which it is profitable to ask: (1) Was the increase in
tax burdens greater for those peasants who were under the nobility
than for those who were under the crown? (2) Did peasants under the
nobility, to any considerable extent, have to cede the right of ownership
to their farms, in order that the nobility could do as they liked with
them? In any investigation of this kind, it is the *skattefrälsebönder* who
must provide the main centre of interest.

I shall now give the results of one such investigation. It was an enquiry which was indeed restricted to a relatively limited area and a
small number of farms; but it provides evidence which can be used to
offset generalisations based on the 'grievances of the commonalty'.[12]

The taxes and burdens imposed upon the Swedish peasant were of
very many kinds. For the sake of simplicity we may here distinguish between three different types: (i) dues payable in commodities or in money; (ii) labour services, such as day-work or the
obligation to provide transport (*skjutsfärder*); (iii) conscription, i.e. the
obligation to provide the armed forces with recruits. Now from a comparison, category by category, between royal and noble accounts, it
appears that in this particular area no changes (with one exception)
were made in the burdens comprised in (i); and this is true for all the
peasants (whether they had formerly been tax-peasants or crown-
peasants) who had passed under noble control as a result of the crown's
alienations of land. There can be no question here of any relative
worsening of the peasant's position. The exception in question really
falls under (ii). For it appears that in a number of cases noblemen who
were short of hands on their estate substituted day-work for a part of
the payments due to them in money or goods. It is of course very difficult to evaluate such services against the dues which they replaced; but
the important thing in this connection is the fact that this substitution
of day-work for payments did not apply to *skattefrälsebönder*: in their
case the norms for day-work laid down by the Diet were inflexibly
adhered to. There are even cases in which a steward complains to his
master that he is having difficulty in getting the work of the estate done,
since so many of the peasants are *skattefrälsebönder*, and they refuse to
do more services, or other services, than those fixed by law. So we see
that in regard to the first two points the *skattefrälsebönder*, and prob-

ably the alienated crown-peasants also, did not find their position getting worse. Everything then turns on the third point, the incidence of conscription.

The method adopted for carrying out the conscription was to form, in each recruiting area, a number of so-called 'files', each consisting of a definite number of peasants or farms; and from every file one foot-soldier was taken as a conscript. In general the files which were made up of peasants of the nobility contained more men than the files which were made up of crown-peasants: sometimes the relation between them favoured the peasants of the nobility by as large a proportion as one to two, which meant that they ran half as much risk as other peasants of being taken for a soldier. This was an advantage which the *skattefrälsebönder* also enjoyed. It is true that in general (though not always) they had to pay the nobleman for it; but the sum demanded was not large, either in itself, or in relation to the advantage which an easing of the burden of conscription was considered to entail. And that the risk of conscription was really felt to be a heavy burden, is attested by unanimous contemporary evidence. It has been contended that the fact that the nobleman had the possibility of himself selecting which man in the file should be taken for a soldier was a threat to the peasant's liberty: troublesome peasants might in this way find themselves being blackmailed into submission. It is indeed very probable that such things did occur; but before we decide how hardly this bore on the peasant, there are some other considerations which must be taken into account. In the first place, the noble landlord would always have to bear in mind that a farm provided him with an income. He could not simply deprive it of its labour force at his own caprice: if he did, he would destroy one of his sources of revenue. In the second place, the peasants of the nobility can only be considered to have been prejudiced if it can be shown that selection from files of crown-peasants proceeded on a more objective basis. And this there is good reason to doubt. It can be demonstrated, moreover, in the case of specific, limited areas, that the number of *skattefrälsebönder* among the conscripts was not greater than their share in the total number of peasants under the nobility might lead one to expect. It does not appear, therefore, that *skattefrälsebönder* were especially badly treated in this respect.

The upshot of all this, then, is to show that *skattefrälsebönder* lived in conditions which tended to be better, and which in no circumstances were worse, than those of their fellows whose lands the crown had not alienated. But once more it must be emphasised that the investigation on which this result is based was of limited scope, and restricted to a limited geographical area.

There remains the other question, as to how far *skattefrälsebönder* were forced to cede the right of ownership to their farms. At the root of this problem lay the attempts of the nobility to found manors, which carried with them various advantages, especially of a fiscal nature. In order to create a manor, the nobleman had first to evict the peasants on the spot – or so at least it is supposed. And for *skattefrälsebönder* this implied that they had first to be deprived of their right of freehold. As it happens, nobody has shown that in actual fact peasants were evicted when manors were formed; but leaving that point on one side, it is possible to calculate for certain parts of the country how large a proportion of freehold land was turned into noble manorial demesne. In the central provinces of Uppland and Södermanland, the demesne lands seem to form about 10 per cent of the area of peasant freehold. This percentage is certainly too high, since the study which provides the basis for the calculation gives too high a figure for the number of manor farms.[13] Moreover my investigation into the condition of the peasantry in Uppland, as it is revealed in the private estate papers of the nobility, shows no example of a case in which the acquisition of the right of ownership to *skattefrälse* land was accompanied by the creation of a new manor. It is perfectly clear that noblemen did indeed *purchase* the title to *skattefrälse* farms; but in the present state of our information it cannot be maintained that they made intensive efforts to acquire titles to land with the idea of establishing their family seats upon it.

It appears then that the picture which emerges from my investigation conflicts at all points with that which is created by the 'grievances of the commonalty'. And it may well be asked: if this new picture is the true one (though in view of the limited area of research it cannot be considered as fully confirmed), why did the Estate of Peasants come forward with a demand for a *reduktion*? If they were doing reasonably well, they would have had no real motive for wanting any change. But though it might be the case that the noble did not oppress his peasants, that did not in itself necessarily imply that they were well off. The war of 1675–80 had without doubt increased the demands upon the peasantry. Although we lack knowledge of how far they had possibilities of simultaneously increasing their incomes, it may be presumed that in general the war had resulted in a worsening of their condition. For those peasants who were under the nobility there was an obvious temptation to blame the deterioration upon their landlords. And those peasants whose farms had not been alienated by the crown were affected too, in that the alienations meant that there were fewer peasants left to meet the main burden of the crown's demands: a situation which became especially obvious when it came to the conscription. Add to this the fact that the advantages which the peasants of the nobility enjoyed were severely cut down during periods of war. The difference between crown files and noble files was diminished, and new imposts were levied to which the privileges enjoyed by peasants of the nobility did not apply. This general deterioration of conditions was particularly noticeable, and applied with special force to the peasants of the nobility, during the war which immediately preceded the Diet of 1680. And the discontent which this produced was duly exploited by the king when the Diet came to consider the *reduktion*.

How then did the changes which the *reduktion* brought with it affect the peasantry? The *reduktion* was not carried through for their sake; but its effects may for all that have been to their advantage. Many peasants, with their farms, were now taken away from the nobility and once more put under the crown. But for a great part of these peasants the alteration was more apparent than real. The *indelningsverk* meant that it was still the nobility (as servants of the state) who collected the tax due from the farm: the difference was that since the noble now looked upon the tax as his pay, he was no longer as concerned with the farm's welfare as he had been when it formed a part of his own estates. On the other hand, one immediate advantage of the *reduktion* was that conscription came to an end, and was replaced by a system whereby soldiers were supplied and maintained by the peasants themselves.

In the long run the *reduktion* meant that the number of peasant freeholders increased. In the course of the eighteenth century crown-peasants acquired the possibility of buying the freehold to their land from the crown; and this certainly contributed to give increased stability and weight to the Estate of Peasants in the centuries that lay ahead. But this was not a consequence which can be said to have been foreseen when the *reduktion* was carried through.

Thus as far as the peasantry was concerned the conclusion to be drawn from this account is that the demands for a *reduktion* need not have been produced by the oppression and misery arising from the tyranny of the nobility. But on the other hand Sweden's bellicose foreign policy must have led to a general increase in their burdens, and the advantages enjoyed by the peasants of the nobility must have been sensibly diminished, whenever war produced an acute crisis. The only immediate major gain which the *reduktion* brought to the peasantry was the change in the system of recruiting. And in the long run, as an indirect consequence of the *reduktion*, there was an increase in the proportion of peasants who owned their land.

V. CONCLUSION

It may perhaps seem that this essay is made up of complaints about the paucity of systematic studies, and the unreliability of most of those which are available. But it has seemed to me only right to indicate clearly how uncertain the position is, and particularly how tentative are all the statistics which I have given. Yet despite this obvious lack of solid underpinning, it is possible to make certain assertions about the *reduktion* and its consequences. The crown's gains by the *reduktion* are obvious. The king secured the possibility of creating a civil and military administration which – at least in peacetime – functioned better than ever before; its weakness lay in the fact that it lacked sufficient flexibility to make it easily adaptable to the period of warfare which lay immediately ahead. The reorganisation of the administration also implied a departure from the theory, dominant in the first half of the century, that the crown ought to subsist on the revenues arising from mining and from trade; instead, fiscal administration was once more linked, as a matter of principle, to the revenues from the land. Side by side with the *reduktion* went the movement towards absolute monarchy: the basis of royal power was strengthened by the fact that the king became independent of grants by the Diet.

The gains of the crown were paid for by the losses of the Nobility, or at least of a part of them. The *reduktion* by no means destroyed the position of the Nobility as the leading Estate of the realm; but it seems likely that it effected a transfer of assets within the Estate itself. It was indeed the differences in the amount of land held by some members of the Estate, as against that held by others, which had produced that split within the Nobility which had facilitated the carrying of the *reduktion* in the Diet.

As far as can be seen from investigation into trustworthy sources, those peasants who were under the Nobility were not in such a comparatively intolerable position as to motivate a demand for a *reduktion* from their side; it was the wars of the seventeenth century that increased their burdens, and it was because they saw a chance of alleviating them that the Estate of Peasants turned to a *reduktion*. The advantages they derived from it were neither many nor great. It did indeed prepare the way for an expansion of peasant freeholding. That expansion, as far as we can judge from the general course of events, must probably have come about in any case. But without the *reduktion* it might well have taken more violent forms.

8. The Swedish Army, from Lützen to Narva

ALF ÅBERG

WHEN in the year 1632 Gustavus Adolphus met his death upon the battlefield of Lützen, the Swedish army had already received in broad outline the organisation which it was to retain for the remainder of the century. Two years later the strength of the permanent forces was laid down by the Form of Government of 1634. Henceforward the army of the Swedish–Finnish realm was to consist of eight regiments of cavalry and twenty-three of infantry, Sweden proper providing five of the one and thirteen of the other. The regiments were assigned definite recruiting areas, often coinciding with provincial divisions, and they were named after the province from which they drew their men: almost all of those which took shape in the years after 1634 continued in existence until the great reduction of the armed forces in 1925.

I. RECRUITMENT AND ORGANISATION

The military organisation which Gustavus Adolphus left behind him was based, as was that of no other country in Europe, upon long-standing and well-tried national traditions.

During the later Middle Ages there had been a clear-cut distinction between the method of recruiting infantry and that for raising cavalry. The infantry was furnished by the peasants of the various provinces: in each parish the men of military age were divided into 'files' of ten or twenty men, each file providing one man for the forces; so that there was something like a system of conscription, resting on free agreement between the provinces and the king. The cavalry, on the other hand, was drawn not from the mass of the population but from the nobility, as a result of personal agreement between the nobleman and his sovereign. Any man who was prepared to do military service on horseback enjoyed exemption from taxation for his estates. Nobility was not at first hereditary and the number of horse to be provided by any individual was determined by the size of his estates. Nor was service in person required, for the nobleman was entitled to send a substitute, paid by himself (the so-called *sventjänare*), to serve in his place.

The organisation of the army in the seventeenth century corresponds very closely with these medieval methods of recruitment: Gustavus Adolphus, while seeking to create a modern and flexible military structure, recurred deliberately to traditional procedures. And the way in which he solved the difficult problems which confronted him became the standard pattern for his successors on the throne.

In the native armies of Gustavus Adolphus (as distinct from the foreign mercenary troops) the infantry was supplied by yearly conscriptions in each of the provinces, and it was in his time that the method of conscription was finally systematised. Each year the parson would draw up a list of those in his parish capable of bearing arms, and these lists would subsequently be used by the conscription commissioners (who included both military and civilian representatives) as a basis for dividing up the conscriptable material into files. The size of the files – they might be of ten, fifteen or twenty men – was determined each year by the *riksdag*; but all males between the ages of eighteen and forty were liable to be taken to serve. Persons with no visible means of support were automatically drafted, but the recruiting of criminals was not permitted. In 1642 the basis of conscription was modified: the files were now organised not as groups of so many men but rather as groups of so many farms. It was a change which was to the advantage of the authorities, since they were now able to calculate in advance exactly what resources of manpower would be available, and take their measures accordingly. Infantrymen were paid a small yearly wage by the state; but Gustavus Adolphus decided that in addition the peasants in each file were to make over a small allotment of land to the conscript: this would provide subsistence for his family when he was away at the wars, and give him a place to live in when not on active service. It was a device as brilliant as it was simple: the state would get a standing army on the cheapest possible terms; and when peace came the soldiery would beat their swords into ploughshares. In practice, however, the scheme ran into some difficulties. The peasants showed no great desire to hand over portions of their land; and the fact that more and more farms passed by royal donation into noble hands entailed the consequence that they could no longer be included in the files. Nevertheless it was an idea which would one day come into its own.

As with the infantry, so with the cavalry; which in the time of Gustavus Adolphus was likewise raised in accordance with long-standing principles. The nobleman continued as before to do his knight-service (*rusttjänst*). But the number of horse which the nobility provided by this method was far too few to furnish the army with the cavalry arm which was essential to victory in the field; and it was therefore decided that any person who was willing to provide a trooper, and equip him with arms and accoutrements, should be granted exemption from taxation for his farm. Such a person might himself choose to serve; or he might send a *sventjänare* to serve in his place. Like the foot-soldier, he would receive a yearly wage.

On the basis laid down in 1634 the Swedish–Finnish army was designed to number some 30,000 foot and 8,000 horse. But side by side with these troops there were of course large numbers of hired mercenaries in the Swedish forces; indeed in the latter years of the Thirty Years war the main burden of the fighting fell upon troops of this sort, for the most part Germans and Scots: on occasion there might be as many as 50,000 of them under the Swedish colours.

It was in the reign of Gustavus Adolphus also that a permanent organisation was for the first time provided for the artillery. The government was able to induce a number of armaments manufacturers and weaponsmiths to migrate to Sweden; private entrepreneurs established gun foundries; and a vigorous armaments industry came into being. Guns became lighter and more easily manoeuvrable, their number was increased, their manufacture standardised; especially important were the light 'regiment pieces', which could be moved by a couple of men. It was Gustavus Adolphus too who formed the first unit of fortification officers, responsible for building and besieging fortresses, and also for certain other services. Their chief, the quartermaster-general, was a member of the general staff, and he and his officers undertook such typical staff duties as reconnoitring roads and rivers, arranging encampments and quarters, drawing maps and so forth. In the Archives of the War Ministry there is preserved a large collection of maps and plans of fortresses, as a memorial to their activity at head-quarters.

Simultaneously with the organisation of the regiments in 1634, the army was provided with a central administrative authority, the College of War: its continued existence until 1865 is a testimony to the modernity and adapability of Gustavus Adolphus's work. To the College of War every regiment was required to make a return of its strength, equipment and stores; and whenever any major change in strength occurred, it was the practice to send in also the regimental rolls, with their lists of the names of officers and men: the Archives of the War Ministry contain a comprehensive series of such rolls, extending back to as early as 1620.

At the close of the seventeenth century, Gustavus Adolphus's organisation of the army was modified into its final form. For the last twenty years of the century Sweden enjoyed an interval of peace; and during the whole of that time Charles XI (who was an absolute monarch) laboured to solve the problem of how to maintain a standing army in peace as well as in war. He found the resources he needed by resuming the estates which the crown had alienated to the nobility. The resumption was resolved on at the *riksdag* of 1680, and at once royal commissioners began the work of recovery. For not until a solid basis for the army's support had been provided would it be possible to carry through the great plan for national defence which Charles XI had in mind.

The military organisation created by Charles XI goes under the name of *indelningsverket* (lit. 'allotment system'). In fiscal terms the word signifies simply an arrangement whereby the crown allotted certain farms or revenues by way of wages to its servants; and it is clear that civil servants – e.g. bailiffs and clergy – could be, and were, paid in this way. But the *indelningsverk* for the army was nevertheless much the most important aspect of the system; and for more than two hundred years to come it would set its mark upon the countryside. In Charles XI's time that system took its final shape, but in almost every respect he did no more than build upon precedents from the past, and it is therefore more accurate to call his military arrangements 'the later *indelningsverk*', and to use the expression 'the earlier *indelningsverk*' to describe the methods of Gustavus Adolphus.

The basic principles governing pay and recruitment in the armies of Charles XI and Charles XII were almost all developments of earlier procedures; under these monarchs they became more uniform and standardised, but that was all. As before, infantry and cavalry were recruited and maintained by different methods. Hitherto, as we have seen, the infantry had been furnished by conscription; and there had frequently been complaints in military quarters that the force conscripted varied in number from year to year. In the time of the regency and of Queen Christina, many 'army farms' had been handed over to the nobility by the crown, so that officers did not know from one year to the next how many farms were at their disposal, and consequently how many soldiers they could raise. With the peasants too the old method of conscription was unpopular, since it put them to great expense, and exposed them to sharp practice by officials. Both crown and commonalty were therefore anxious to replace it with something better. From the point of view of the king and the army command, what was wanted was an arrangement which would ensure that every regiment should be at a constant strength both in peace and war. In the province of Dalarna and in some other parts of northern Sweden this condition had indeed already been met, for these provinces had for years been exempted from annual conscriptions in return for an undertaking to provide and maintain a stipulated number of men. The arrangement had been tested in war and had functioned relatively well.

At the Diet of 1682 the king proposed that it should now be extended to cover the whole country. Every regiment was to be kept at a constant strength by the province from which it came, and was to be maintained by that province in all circumstances. The Estate of Peasants gave their support to this proposal, which constituted in effect a free agreement between crown and commonalty; and in confirmation of that agreement the king concluded separate contracts with the provinces which defined the obligations of each of them. By the terms of these agreements each regiment was to be kept at a fixed strength of 1,200 foot. Farms were to be grouped in pairs, each pair now constituting a 'file', and maintaining its own soldier. Commissioners were set up in every province to see that the burden of obligation was evenly spread over the whole area. Only a very few farms were exempt from the new arrangements: they included certain of the farms of the nobility, and also farms belonging to postmasters and innkeepers.[1] Every 'file' of two farms had now to find the soldier which was required of it; and the number of potential candidates naturally varied from province to province: it often happened that a 'file' might be driven to look for a recruit from far afield – for instance, from the impoverished and populous provinces of Dalarna and Småland. This was possible because the terms which could be offered to candidates were attractive. When a man joined the army he received a sum of money, and he was entitled to a yearly wage, food, clothing and quarters, if possible in the form of a cottage with a small plot for tillage and grazing. In the northern parts of the country, where cultivated land was in short supply, the soldier as a rule was given house-room on the farm of one of the local peasants; and everywhere he was bound in peacetime to work as a labourer for one of the peasants in the 'file'. And when he went off to the wars, his wife was left to work his holding with the assistance of the neighbours.

In comparison with the old conscription the new system had several major advantages. The soldier was always at hand if the call should come to active service. If he died at home on his holding or fell in battle, the 'file' would automatically provide a replacement for him – an obligation which became a heavy burden during the long wars of Charles XII's time. In order that any one 'file' should not be called upon to bear an unduly heavy burden, company commanders in such circumstances drew up a rota of the 'files' which supplied them with recruits, and called for replacements from each of them in turn. For it was essential that the peasant-owner should not himself be forced to quit his farm; when the soldiers went off to the wars, it was the peasant's business to stay at home and ensure the continuation of agricultural production.[2]

In regard to the cavalry, as in regard to the infantry, the arrangements established by Charles XI brought no revolutionary innovations; for here too the king proceeded on the lines of earlier practice. The basis of the system was the conclusion of freely negotiated agreements with private persons who were willing to undertake to provide a horseman; and for this it was essential that they should be in possession of a flourishing farm and be in a sound financial position. In most cases such agreements were concluded with yeoman farmers, though many 'persons of standing' (*ståndspersoner*) were also prepared to enter into them. The terms offered were in fact very attractive. Anyone who provided a cavalryman and equipped him with horse and arms, secured exemption from taxation for his farm and was in addition excused from participation in the 'file' system. His farm was termed a *rusthåll*, and he himself *rusthållare*.

Already in Gustavus Adolphus's time, as we have seen, it had been not unusual for the *rusthållare* to stay at home and let a substitute *sventjänare* serve in his place. Under Charles XI this became the general practice. The *rusthållare* was bound to give his *sventjänare* a fixed yearly wage, and to provide him with house-room; in most cases he would be given a cottage to live in. From the cavalryman's point of view, however, the new arrangements implied a lowered social status: his horse and his equipment were no longer his own property, and he was now the servant and farmhand of his *rusthållare*, and entirely dependent upon him. Those who benefited from the new system were the *rusthållare*, who in general belonged to the class of wealthier peasants. Such persons now formed a superior class within the Estate of Peasants, bound together by common interests and the fact that they now stood in a position of owing, for their own persons, direct military obedience to the sovereign.[3]

So much for the men in the ranks. The same principles applied also to the officers, both commissioned and non-commissioned: they too drew their pay from farms specially allotted to their support, and situated within the area upon which their regiments were based. A farm was assigned to each of them for quarters; and it was the king's will that they should live on it, so that they might be in a better position to keep an eye on the way it was worked, and also on the behaviour of the men under their command, who would of course also be located in the same district. If no suitable house for them happened to be available, the king had one built to standard specifications which varied with the rank of the officer concerned: a captain was entitled to a farmhouse containing four rooms and a kitchen. With their low roofs and wooden walls they were hardly distinguishable from the usual peasant farmhouse. Once the officer's house was ready for him, he was bound to see that it was maintained in good order: before any officer went to a new post, his farm was inspected by a board of assessors composed of civil and military representatives, who drew up a full report upon its condition. There were something like three thousand officers' farms in Sweden, and five hundred in Finland; and the reports upon them which are preserved in the Archives of the War Ministry afford a unique possibility of tracing the architectural history of these buildings for a century or more.[4]

Once the new organisation of the infantry and cavalry was completed, every regiment proceeded to draw up a full statement of the arrangements upon which it now depended for pay and recruits: every 'file', every *rusthåll*, was carefully noted, together with the company or regimental number which had been assigned to it. It was the king's will that his work should endure; and for that reason he personally signed every one of these schedules, with a declaration that they were to be unalterable for all time.

The total strength of the army based on the new system (including newly raised regiments from the provinces of western and southern Sweden which had been acquired from Denmark–Norway in the course of the century) amounted to eleven cavalry regiments and twenty-three infantry regiments; that is, 11,000 horse and about 30,000 foot. But in addition to these, of course, the army included large numbers of hired mercenaries. The *indelningsverk* was never applied to the Baltic provinces or to Swedish Pomerania; and it was here that the mercenary regiments were stationed, dispersed in towns and fortresses, and maintained and paid by the state. In addition, there were mercenaries in the Lifeguards, the Regiment of Artillery and the Fortification Corps. In all, the mercenary troops amounted to about 25,000 men in peacetime.

In one specific respect there is a clear difference between the army of Gustavus Adolphus and that of Charles XI, and this is in regard to the types of men composing it. In the Swedish regiments of Gustavus Adolphus's army the majority of the troops had consisted of peasants and peasants' sons, either serving as troopers in respect of their own farms, or carrying the musket and trailing the pike in the foot regiments. The army of Charles XI and Charles XII, however, drew its manpower from other ranks of society: it recruited men from the landless proletariat of the countryside. The core of the army, the buckler of the realm, was now provided by farmhands, cottars' sons and servants. They were a hardy folk, accustomed from childhood to obey their temporal and spiritual superiors. They had no property of their own: the uniform they wore, the arms they carried, belonged not to them but to the company in which they were enrolled. In the army they lived together as a community; their comrades in the ranks came from the same village, and old acquaintance provided a natural bond of union between them before ever they were called upon to take the field. It was not difficult for them to reconcile themselves to the strict discipline which prevailed while they were in training, or in the field, for most of them had certainly a more secure existence in their military cottages than they could have enjoyed as civilian day-workers for peasants and landowners. They could therefore accept Charles XI's stern insistence upon the duty of obedience: 'Commands will be carried out soberly and silently without any observation on the part of those whose business it is to obey.' When they were in the field it was the custom for one of the regimental chaplains to hold a service in camp every morning and evening, and the doctrine he expounded was clear and to the point: as long they feared God and honoured the king, no more was expected of them. Thus by its method of recruitment, and as a result of its training, the army of Charles XI and Charles XII was welded into a coherent entity, and that entity was dominated by a uniform Lutheran creed (see above, Chapter 4).

The composition of the corps of officers too was no longer the same as in former days. They were now paid servants of the crown, with no other profession than the army; and they had learned to obey the commands of their superiors without argument or reflection. In theory every soldier could now rise to the highest commands; and in a number of cases this actually happened. Erik Dahlberg, the able director of the Swedish fortifications system, had begun as an N.C.O.; and Rutger von Ascheberg, who became field-marshal, and was responsible for the integration of the provinces acquired from Denmark, had risen from being a simple trooper. Most officers, of course, lived out their lives in the lower ranks of the service. They were decidedly more at home with the sword than with the pen; though it is worth noting that the spread of literacy within the army was remarkably wide.

In order to maintain a check upon the state of the arms and equipment of officers and soldiers, Charles XI initiated a system of regular musters of the regiments. For the native regiments these general musters occurred every third year. Before they took place a great roll was prepared, and on this roll it was the king's custom to note such mistakes and deficiencies as he discovered. All these rolls are still preserved in the Archives of the War Ministry, and they constitute a source of great value for genealogical research.[5]

Soldiers tended to try to remain in the army to the last possible moment, for the pay it afforded, if exiguous, was at least certain. Men were in fact permitted to remain up to the age of forty: when they reached it, they were obliged to quit the service – and the cottage that went with it. A man who had served long and well might be assigned a small yearly pension, but the transition from soldier to labourer would mean, both socially and economically, a step downwards. If, however, he was able to get one of his sons accepted as his successor, it was possible for him to stay on undisturbed in his cottage until the day of his death. The rolls afford many instances of 'files' and *rusthåll* where the uniform descended from one generation to another. Officers too were assured of a small pension; but for them too retirement from the army in most cases meant a lower standard of life. When an officer died, or fell in battle, his family would be compelled the leave his official house; and the minutes of the housing commissioners from the period of the Great Northern War tell of many officers' widows who 'live in the parish in great poverty', or who have 'vanished, no one knows where'.

Charles XI's *indelningsverk* was an organisation created in peacetime, but so constructed that it should also be able to function in time of war. The *rusthållare* was expected to be a man of solid property, who would be able to maintain his trooper without the crown's aid; the provinces had pledged themselves to furnish a definite number of footsoldiers, as well in war as in peace. Yet the new system has been sharply criticised, both on military and economic grounds. The military historians have urged against it that it was fatally lacking in adaptability; the economic historians have complained that in thus tying the maintenance of the army to a revenue paid in kind rather than in cash, and so perpetuating a state of affairs which other sectors of society had already left behind them, it was economically reactionary.[6] As to the military criticism, it must be conceded that it is in some instances justified, though we may well ask ourselves whether any conceivable military organisation could have coped perfectly during the disastrous closing years of the Great Northern War. It is certainly a fact that after the catastrophes at Pultava in 1709 and Tönningen in 1713 whole armies were somehow raised by the new methods. And when additional regiments were formed in excess of the establishment, the *rusthåll* and 'files' of the new system played their part. It is not difficult to show that the *indelningsverk* gave evidence of its elasticity and its ability to produce the necessary reserves in wartime; on the whole it continued to be the recruiting organisation, both for old and new units, throughout the entire war. Much more serious is the objection that it contributed to perpetuating a medieval type of economic organisation in Sweden. Yet in this matter Charles XI's thinking was absolutely logical. By tying a portion of the country's assured revenues to the army he left himself free to dispose of other revenues in cash for unforeseen expenditures. In times of peace the army was self-supporting, and was no longer dependent for its existence on the accident of parliamentary supply.

II. STRATEGIC FACTORS

Sweden was a peasant country, and in the seventeenth century more than 90 per cent of the population lived on the land. It was therefore the country areas which provided the essential basis for the organisation of the army; and in peacetime the troops were quartered out in the villages from one end of the country to the other. This extreme dispersion presented very difficult problems in regard to strategic preparedness. It took much time before an army could be collected; and during the whole of that time an invader was left with a relatively free hand in the frontier provinces. One solution to this difficulty was naturally to effect a mobilisation in good time, and concentrate the army in the threatened area before the enemy had completed his preparations; but any such concentration of troops in a particular region always entailed severe problems of maintenance. The magazines which had been assembled in advance did not last very long, and the local population became exasperated by military requisitioning of supplies. It was not possible to keep the army for any length of time on a war footing in Sweden; either the troops must be sent home again, or they must be transferred to enemy country and find their subsistence there.

Gustavus Adolphus had shown how it could be done, by his territorial strategy during the Thirty Years War. The initial narrow bridgehead in Germany, between the Oder and the Peene, had been expanded by systematically overrunning wider and wider areas between the river lines. These areas became his supply bases, and from them he collected food and fodder, men and money. It was a strategy which aimed at ensuring that the army should be capable of supporting itself from the territories it occupied. After his death, the generals who succeeded to the command of the Swedish armies in Germany succeeded also to the strategy which he had initiated. It became their object to protect the base areas on the Baltic coast, and simultaneously to attempt, by recurrent offensives, to cut off the Imperialist troops from their supply areas, and so bring about their exhaustion. The same strategy was employed by Charles X during his wars in Poland and Denmark. The attack which he launched upon Poland in the summer of 1655 was planned on the grand scale, and its objectives were far from being limited: but behind the planning lay the sober realities of economics. Many officers had come home from Germany after the wars, and were now without employment; the situation in which they found themselves, and their hopes for the future, are illustrated in a letter written in 1651 from Arvid Forbus (a member of the College of War) to one of his relations: 'Money is here so scarce, now the wars are at an end, that it is hardly to be got; and there be many now who wish to God that a new war might begin.'[7] Sweden was now, no doubt, a great power, but she could neither maintain a great army in peacetime, nor take the risk of disbanding it. By his attack on Poland, Charles X solved the problem of its maintenance: Sweden herself was freed from the burden of supporting it: war should sustain itself on enemy soil.

It was not until Charles XI's time that the problem of how to keep up a standing army in peacetime was really solved; but he too was confronted with the same strategic problems as his predecessors. By what means were the troops, scattered as they now were over their new 'allotments', to be concentrated in the shortest possible time and transferred to whichever front might be threatened? For nearly twenty years

Charles hammered away at this problem. It was under his personal direction that Erik Dahlberg and Rutger von Ascheberg reconnoitred the road systems of southern and western Sweden. New roads were built throughout the country, especially in the recently acquired provinces of the south. Their function was that of the old Roman roads: to enable troops to be moved rapidly to and fro, and to facilitate the swift reduction to order of any disturbed districts. The king himself carried through surveys of the frontier regions on the side of Norway. The concentrations against Denmark which took place in 1683 and 1689 provided a test of the army's ability to bring together large masses of troops within a short space of time, and the experience then gained was put to good use in preparing a definitive mobilisation plan. It is apparent from the king's papers that he himself took an active part in drawing it up.[8] Whenever a regiment assembled for its triennial muster it was his habit to make a note on the regimental roll of how long it took every company to collect its men and march them to the place appointed for the regiment's manoeuvres. These notes are always quite precise. For the company commanded by the major of the Uppland regiment he wrote: 'In fair weather the company can muster within 24 hours. The maximum distance to be covered by any soldier in order to reach the muster place is 23 km; and from there they can march to Stockholm in three days.' Provincial governors sent in reports on the main roads in their provinces, and suggested suitable night-halts for the troops; and on the basis of these reports the king and his collaborators drew up for every regiment a register of roads and halts between their recruiting areas and the great harbours of southern, western and eastern Sweden. Every scheme was scrutinised by the king personally, and his papers contain sketches of some of the main roads, with details of how many kilometres a day the troops could be expected to cover. In connection with these plans for mobilisation, the king caused maps to be made of every province. That for Skåne is particularly notable; being based on methods, and executed in a style, which was not to be excelled until the nineteenth century. All along these roads the state established a system of inns, which were to serve as overnight quarters and bivouacs for troops on the march; while some inns which were already in existence were pulled down, or transferred to fresh locations, in order that they might better meet military needs. By 1697, the year when Charles XI died, the master plan for mobilisation was at last complete. It was preserved in the College of War in Stockholm; but every colonel of a regiment, every commander of a company, had been sent maps and orders detailing how his unit was to be moved, and the route by which it was to travel, when the word came for the army to be alerted.[9]

In the course of the seventeenth century the Swedish–Finnish realm was expanded by the acquisition of extensive new territories. Skåne, Halland and Blekinge were wrested from Denmark; the Sound became the frontier between the two countries. From Norway, Sweden gained Bohuslän, together with the two provinces – Jämtland and Härjedalen – which lie to the east of the mountain chain running from north to south throughout the Scandinavian peninsula. On the other side of the sea, the Baltic provinces and large areas in north Germany became part of the Swedish realm, and served as bastions and outworks of the empire. Thus Sweden found herself with long frontiers which were difficult to defend either by sea or land, and this entailed difficult problems of strategy. Charles XI sought to solve them by strengthening existing fortresses, and at the same time building new ones according to the most modern principles. The man responsible for these new defence works was Erik Dahlberg, who personally drew the plans of the fortifications. The building work was carried out by able engineer officers, who in many cases had received their training in France and Holland. At the close of the century there were more than fifty fortresses and some forty redoubts guarding the country's frontiers.

Charles XI's strategy was based upon a foreign policy which was essentially pacific, and the military system he created was clearly defensive in character. Protected by a chain of fortresses to the west, south and east, Sweden was to remain armed and alert, her dominions linked together by a Baltic which had become a Swedish lake. An enemy trying to break through the country's defences at any point would be checked by the garrisons of the fortresses until the main army had been assembled, and would then, by deployment of the fleet, be ejected from the areas he had occupied.

Charles XI placed great reliance upon Erik Dahlberg; but their appraisals of the strategic situation were based on differing approaches to the problem. The wars in Poland, Germany and Denmark had given Sweden a somewhat one-sided concern with dangers which lay to the south. In the years 1675–9 Charles XI had been forced to fight a bloody war against Denmark, whose king, Christian V, sought in vain to recover the lost provinces east of the Sound; and even after peace was made Denmark was regarded by Charles XI as the arch-enemy. He wished therefore to concentrate the defences of the country in the southern provinces, and the great coastal fortresses of Göteborg, Karlskrona and Wismar became the objects of his especial care. Dahlberg, for his part, was not opposed to strengthening the defences of these places, but he would have wished to see a larger share of the resources available for fortification spent on defensive works in the Baltic provinces and in the archipelago to the east of Stockholm. Again and again, in his memoranda to the king, he recurred to this question. The fortresses along the eastern frontiers of the empire, he wrote, were neglected and falling into ruin; and the Russians had their eye on them. It was of special importance to strengthen the redoubt at Nyen, on the Neva, which barred a Russian advance to the Gulf of Finland; yet it was now so decayed that it could not hold out for twenty-four hours against the superior forces which the Russians could bring against it. It was to be on the site of this redoubt that Tsar Peter was later to build St Petersburg.[10] Yet Charles XI's reaction to Dahlberg's remonstrances was always to defer the question of the eastern fortresses to some future time: the most essential work, he insisted, must receive priority; and for him Denmark seemed to be a more imminent threat than Sweden's eastern neighbour. This proved to be a military and political miscalculation; yet here too Charles was building on the traditions of the Thirty Years War and of Charles X's time. Many of the younger men among his advisers also pressed for the strengthening of the eastern frontier, but to them too the king turned a deaf ear. Recollections of his early years, memories of the Danish attack on Skåne, may well have given a permanent twist to his strategic thinking.

III. TACTICS

In matters of tactics, no less than of strategy, Charles XI linked up with the traditions from the period of the Thirty Years War. Gustavus Adolphus had in his time been a pioneer in the art of war. No commander before him had achieved the same plastic collaboration between the different arms of the service: detachments of musketeers had been planted among his cavalry, to pave the way by the effects of fire-power for the attack by the mounted arm; the infantry units had had light field-pieces asssigned to them in order to achieve greater intensity of fire. Cavalry became once again an offensive arm, and the sword its characteristic weapon; and battles were often decided by cavalry attacks à l'arme blanche. His campaigns were campaigns of movement, his strategy markedly offensive; and this style of fighting continued to dominate Swedish thinking for the whole of the later seventeenth century.

Gustavus Adolphus's tactical traditions were carried on by his generals, who had all learned their trade from him. But not by them only; for the new methods which the king had introduced were generally adopted throughout Europe. His enemies learned from his example; and the old mass-formations, of which the Spanish *tercio* had been the best example, began to be replaced by Swedish linear tactics, which permitted a more effective development of fire-power. In order to establish a superiority over the enemy, therefore, Swedish commanders of the next generation were forced to develop and refine upon the king's tactical heritage.

Johan Banér did not merely inherit the king's offensive spirit; he pushed it a stage further. Like his master, he saw a decision by battle as the ultimate objective of operations. In 1634 he was given supreme command of the Swedish armies in Germany; and until his death seven years later he remained at the centre of military operations. He was a master of the art of improvisation; and he had the gift of extracting the utmost advantage from the qualitative superiority of his troops. And never were his boldness and his offensive spirit more in evidence than in his great victory at Wittstock on 24 September 1636. On this occasion the Imperialists, superior in numbers to their adversaries, had established themselves strongly on a number of heights; and Banér thus found himself at the start of the battle in a difficult position. He took the audacious step of dividing his army. While his centre and right attacked the enemy, the left wing, led by the Scottish General James King, was to execute a wide enveloping movement and fall upon the enemy's rear. A desperately hard-fought battle ensued, and it took King much longer than had been expected to work himself round into position. As evening fell, the Swedish ranks were beginning to break. But at the last moment came the distant sound of the prearranged signal: King had reached his objective. The Imperialist cavalry succeeded in breaking out of the ring which now encircled them, but all their guns and baggage fell into the hands of the Swedes, and in the relentless pursuit that followed their infantry suffered disastrous losses. It is difficult to decide whether Banér, when he made his plans, had consciously aimed at a victory of annihilation. He certainly expected that the enemy would at least capitulate on the battlefield; and it is clear that only defective reconnaissance by the Swedes permitted the Imperialist cavalry to escape. In any event, Banér's tactics at Wittstock exhibited new features – especially perhaps his division of his army into two independently operating groups – and those features make the battle unique in the military history of the period.

The Swedish commander in Germany from 1641 to 1645 was Lennart Torstensson. He too placed particular emphasis on mobility: every superfluous element in the baggage-train was pruned away; and his rapid marches became proverbial. Of especial importance was his contribution to the development of the artillery. He created a field artillery which became an independent arm, with precise functions of its own. He was able to put this new weapon to the test at the battle of Jankow, on 24 February 1645. At Jankow the Swedes and Imperialists were in approximately equal strength – about 15,000 men apiece. The Swedes made their way forward through woody terrain to attack the enemy's left wing. They succeeded in occupying certain heights, and moved their guns up on to them. When the Imperialist cavalry rode in to the attack they were met with a murderous fire and were either scattered or mown down. This was the moment for the Swedish cavalry to launch its counter-attack. The Imperialist cavalry was surrounded and forced to capitulate on the battlefield. The battle of Jankow was a triumph for Torstensson's military genius. For the first time in Swedish history the issue of a battle was decided by the gunners; and throughout the whole engagement the collaboration between the artillery and the other arms was exemplary.

The methods of one commander were assimilated and applied by his successor. Charles X had served under Lennart Torstensson before succeeding to the chief command himself, and in strategy and tactics he followed his tutor's footsteps. His distinctive characteristic as a commander was his reliance upon *Blitzkrieg*, achieved by swift and unexpected troop movements; but he was responsible also for other innovations which are worth noting. The war in Poland was a war of movement, and as it progressed the king was led to diminish the strength of the infantry and correspondingly increase that of the cavalry. The dragoons, who were a species of mounted infantry, were now equipped in such a way as to be able to fight either on horseback or on foot. The armour of the cavalry was lightened. Cavalry squadrons were now stationed among the infantry units, in order to give them greater hitting-power.

Under Charles XI, systematic researches were carried out into the tactical methods of his predecessors. Erik Dahlberg caused battle plans to be made of Charles X's battles, using a schematic method to mark the course of the attack and the critical moments of the engagement; and these plans were used for the purposes of study. But Charles XI did not content himself with the lessons he could draw from Sweden's own wars; he tried also to keep track of tactical developments on the continent. One of the few occasions on which he was really open-handed to his officers was when it was a question of granting them permission to go abroad. At least two-thirds of the officers of the Lifeguard saw service in the French, Dutch and German armies during the years of peace. They came home full of ideas and presented the king with suggestions on a wide variety of topics. He was always ready to listen to them, and in the majority of his regulations there are traces of foreign influences.

This brings us to the art of war as it was practised by Charles XII, an art which he made famous over the whole of Europe. What then were the tactics which he employed? In what respects did they differ from contemporary practice on the continent? Some fifty years ago the Swedish General Staff published a massive volume entitled *Charles XII on the Battlefield*, in which it was contended that his way of fighting was something quite new, pioneering later developments and vastly superior to the 'linear tactics' which were used by commanders in western Europe. A later generation of military historians has declined to accept this thesis. They have pointed out that linear tactics were normal in *all* countries by the end of the seventeenth century, and that the army of Charles XII was not, either in armaments or in tactics, very different from contemporary armies in western Europe.[11] Except at the battles of Narva and Holofzin, which were special cases, Charles XII did in fact use linear tactics. The difference between Caroline and western methods did not lie in the order of battle; it lay in the way tactics were applied and in Charles XII's skill in exploiting the possibilities of the offensive. And this is true both for infantry and for cavalry.

Gustavus Adolphus had experimented with a style of fighting which was based on effective collaboration between musketeers and pikemen. In the course of the seventeenth century developments on the continent tended to place increasingly strong emphasis on fire-power at the expense of impact. By the end of the century muskets and pikes had generally been replaced by flintlocks, and this further intensified fire-power. The infantry became in general the defensive arm, protecting itself against cavalry – now once more the battle-winner – by means of bayonets inserted into the muzzle of the firearm and by grenadier units equipped with hand-grenades. But if continental armies abolished the pike, the Swedish armies of Charles XI and Charles XII retained it. One-third of the foot trailed the pike, while the remainder carried firearms or were grenadiers. The tactical unit was the battalion, consisting of four full companies totalling 600 men. And in contrast to the situation on the continent the Swedish regulations were based on the supposition that the infantry was to be used offensively: in attack the men would be four deep, with the pikemen in the centre and the musketeers and grenadiers on either wing. The two rear ranks fired when they were within 40 metres' distance of the enemy; the two front ranks gave a salvo when they saw the whites of their enemies' eyes. Then at the command 'fall on' the battalion attacked with pikes and swords, under cover of the powder smoke. It often happened that the impact of an infantry attack produced a quick decision, as at Narva on 20 November 1700. On this occasion the Swedish foot was drawn up in columns, and in that formation advanced to attack the long, thin Russian lines; within a short time it had broken through them, and it was then able to roll them up without much further trouble.

It has been contended that this attack in column was the really new and revolutionary feature of Caroline warfare. But the fact is that Charles XII used column tactics only in special circumstances, for the storming of fortified positions, as at Narva and Holofzin. The real novelty in his infantry tactics was that the Swedish army was able to emancipate itself from formalism and to use formations in depth to give extra weight at critical points, as required. It was at all events one of the preconditions for this style of fighting that the troops should be so trained and disciplined that they should be capable of advancing head-on into enemy fire without replying to it. These methods often achieved great success; but they could on occasion lead to heavy reverses, as for instance with the unsuccessful attempt to storm the Russian fortifications at Veprik in January 1709, when 1,200 officers and men were killed or wounded in a purposeless demonstration of the 'fall on' principle.

The tactical unit for the cavalry was the squadron, consisting of either 250 or 150 men. For the attack, they were drawn up in three ranks: the *ryttmästare*, who commanded the squadron, rode ahead of his men, while the lieutenant took his place behind them, and the cornet, who carried the standard, rode in the middle of the front rank. Already in the time of Gustavus Adolphus it had been usual to attack with sword or sabre, after the horsemen had discharged their pistols. The method of attack employed by Charles XII's cavalry is precisely described in the king's regulations for 1685. When riding forward to the attack, the troopers were to be in the closest possible order, flank to flank and knee behind knee. At a distance of from 100 to 150 metres from the enemy they were to put their horses to the gallop. And they were not to discharge their pistols until they saw the whites of the enemy's eyes – that is, a distance of some 25 to 40 metres. This attack at a full gallop, as enjoined in Charles XI's regulations, was a novelty for Sweden: hitherto cavalry had attacked at the trot. The new style also had a powerful psychological effect, by spreading terror in the ranks of the enemy. At the battle of Fraustadt on 3 February 1706 it was the new-style Swedish cavalry which carried off the victory by their violent assault from both wings. The time was clearly ripe for the new tactic: soon after Charles XI issued his regulation for cavalry, Prince Eugene of Savoy introduced similar procedures into the Austrian army.

In any essay on the Swedish armies of the seventeenth century, the artillery really deserves a chapter to itself.[12] It was Gustavus Adolphus who was the great reformer of the artillery, by his standardisation of types, calibres and equipment, and by his solution of the problem of devising a transportable field artillery. Charles X continued his work and gave to this branch of the forces the solid organisation which it had previously lacked: all the artillerymen in the country were now combined into one large regiment. Charles XI followed in his father's footsteps and gave particular attention to the types and quality of the guns provided: the field artillery was equipped with modern and easily-manoeuvrable pieces. In peacetime the artillery was dispersed in fortresses scattered all over the empire, the largest concentrations being in Stockholm, Göteborg and Riga; but on mobilisation, detachments were drawn from the fortresses to form a field regiment, which accompanied the army in the field. No rules were laid down for the positioning of the guns in battle; the artillery was designed to be an auxiliary arm, and it was assumed that its deployment would on each particular occasion conform to the dispositions of the horse and foot. Charles XII has been criticised for basing his tactics mainly on *l'arme blanche*, and for his failure during his Polish and Russian campaigns to make full use of the artillery which his father had created. But his extended lines of communication made it very difficult for him to maintain the supply of ammunition for his heavy guns, and this may well have been one reason why the artillery played such a minor part in his army. Another reason, however, may have been a failure of tactical judgement. Carl Cronstedt, who commanded the artillery in Charles XII's time, said of his king: 'At the beginning of the war His Majesty had a sort of contempt for the artillery; but later bitter experience taught him how valuable a weapon it could be.' The reference here is to the battle of Pultava, on 28 June 1709, when Charles XII allowed his guns to remain idle in the baggage-train, while horse and foot were sent to attack 200 Russian cannon with swords and bayonets. The result was catastrophic for the Swedish army.[13]

Charles XI had aimed at the intimate collaboration of all arms, but he had well understood that this was not to be effected without years of constant training. At least once a month his companies were mustered for exercise, and once a year the whole regiment was collected for manoeuvres. These were to take place, as the king wrote in his regulations, 'on suitable open ground near some wood or hill, where the regiment can encamp for at least a fortnight'; and during that time the colonel and his officers were to instruct and drill the troops in everything which they would need to know 'in the field and against the foe'. And in between these periodical training sessions, officers would be called together for courses of instruction in the new regulations. At these annual musters it was the king's habit to supervise the proceedings himself. The soldiers would be put through a course of musketry, and the king would distribute prizes to the best shots. He was constantly concerned to maintain a high morale in his troops: at the end of each period of manoeuvres he collected them around him and asked them if they had any complaints against their officers, assuring them that they might rely upon their being investigated. It sometimes happened that the soldiers complained that the officers used them as unpaid labourers on their farms; if a complaint of this sort was found to be substantiated, the offending officer was immediately dismissed the service.

Charles XI's *Journal* has much to say of the unceasing work of training the army. Thus on 24 April 1689 he wrote: 'I was out with Field-Marshal Ascheberg on Djurgården, and had four companies of the Guard practising how to deal with caltrops.' In addition to the periodical exercising of companies and regiments it was also his practice to organise manoeuvres on a larger scale. In the summer of 1686 he collected about 4,000 men for battle training, in the course of which they were to simulate the storming of a redoubt and repel an imaginary enemy landing. (Such sham fights were not always free from danger: on the last day of this one the king, riding at a full gallop, collided heavily with a lieutenant-colonel; both were thrown to the ground; and the king was sufficiently badly hurt to keep his bed for the next ten days.[14] On another occasion he met with an accident while testing a baggage-waggon: the waggon overturned and the king hurt his knee so badly that he was unable to move for several weeks.) The artillery too received similar training under the king's supervision, and was set to target practice on Ladugårdsgärde, on the outskirts of Stockholm.

The regiment which the king preferred to use when he was trying out new tactical ideas was that of the Lifeguards. This was an élite corps. In peacetime the men were quartered on the citizens of Stockholm; and were responsible for doing guard duty at the royal palace. Every summer the Lifeguards pitched their square white tents on Ladugårdsgärde, and here the king mustered them in person. Here in April 1694 the king tried out for the first time the new style of fighting which his son Charles XII was to employ with such success against the Poles and the Russians. Charles XI intended the Lifeguards to be a wholly Swedish unit; the many German-speaking officers from the Baltic provinces who served in it were gradually got rid of, and in their place the king appointed almost exclusively young men from the lesser nobility, often the sons of his closest collaborators. Future officers had to begin in the ranks, so that they could get to know the men and be better equipped to command them. They were trained both in fortification and gunnery. The Lifeguards in this way served the purpose of a cadet school, and their officers were often sent out to the regiments stationed in the country in order to train them in 'the new drill'. Almost 40 per cent of the officers who served in the Lifeguards under Charles XI rose to the rank of colonel or beyond, or came to fill high positions in the civil service.[15]

In the course of the 1690s the Swedish army was completely re-equipped. Small articles of equipment were ordered from craftsmen in the area in which each unit was stationed; swords were procured from large-scale suppliers. The king himself was accustomed to check the army's boots and to test its saddlery. If he judged a piece of leather to be below standard it was his habit to cut it to pieces himself, so that nobody should be able to make use of it. It was also his habit to test the sharpness of the swords by making his soldiers try if they could cut a feather floating in the air.

When Charles XI died in 1697 his work of military reorganisation was almost complete. The schedules for the 'allotment system', signed by the king's hand, lay in the College of War; the plans for mobilisation were there too; and the regimental commanders on their farms had their own copies of those plans and were ready to put them into action. The regiments were fully equipped; the training of troops was still in full swing on the principles which Charles XI had drawn up. The art of war, as he envisaged it, was laid down by regulations, and tested at manoeuvres. The Swedish army was a highly finished instrument when the young Charles XII took it into his hands.

In the spring of 1698 Charles XII was presented by the aged Erik Dahlberg with a memorandum on the defence of the empire, which embodied plans to protect the eastern frontier and the east coast of Sweden against a Russian attack. It included a detailed report on all the decaying fortreses in the Baltic area, and painted an alarming picture of a future in which the Russians would be masters of the Baltic, and Russian fleets would ravage the Swedish skerries.[16] But Dahlberg's representations fell on deaf ears. He returned to his command in Riga, and when in 1700 war broke out with a sudden attack on that fortress he was ready to meet it. If the eastern frontier held firm during this opening phase of the Great Northern War, it was to Dahlberg that it owed its salvation.

Charles XI's 'allotment system' was now put to the test. Already in August 1699 there had been a partial mobilisation of certain units, and in December of the same year all regimental commanders received orders by express to have their troops ready to march. In March 1700, upon the arrival of the news of the attack on Riga, came the general order for troops to proceed to their places of concentration. The cavalrymen collected their mounts and harness from their *rusthållare*. The foot received their equipment, every tentful of men being responsible for its own implements; and they assembled at their corporal's cottage, with fourteen days' provisions in their knapsacks. Here they received their arms and ammunition, and then set out upon the march to their destination. The platoons grew to companies, the companies to regiments, as they followed the routes which had been laid down for them. Thirty-two kilometres was a day's march; and at night they pitched their tents in bivouacs already appointed and prepared for them. Moving according to a predetermined timetable, they concentrated on their ports of embarkation. The entire operation went off without a single hitch. The march schedules were adhered to. As Sweden plunged into the long war that lay ahead, she mobilised with an absence of fuss and a certainty of effect which even today are impressive.[17]

And so they sailed across the sea to Narva, which was already threatened by the Russian invaders. The young king who led them had at his command an army which was certainly the best-trained and best-equipped force ever to be sent to defend the frontiers; and on the battlefield of Narva it was to apply the lessons it had learned during the long period of training at home.

Bibliography

I. THE EXPERIENCE OF EMPIRE: SWEDEN AS A GREAT POWER

General

J. Rosén, *Svensk historia*, i (Stockholm 1962).

E. F. Heckscher, *Sveriges ekonomiska historia från Gustav Vasa*, i.2 (Stockholm 1936).

S. Grauers, 'Till belysning av Nystadfredens verkningar', in *Historiska studier tillägnade Sven Tunberg* (Stockholm 1942).

Finance

S. A. Nilsson, 'Reduktion eller kontribution. Alternativ inom 1600-talets svenska finanspolitik', *Scandia* (1958).

S. Lundkvist, 'Svensk krigsfinansiering 1630–1635', *Historisk tidskrift* (1966).

K.-R. Böhme, 'Geld für die schwedischen Armeen nach 1640', *Scandia* (1967).

H. Landberg, *Statsfinans och kungamakt. Karl X Gustaf inför polska kriget* (Kristianstad 1969).

Military developments

Kungl. Svea livgardes historia, iii–iv (Stockholm 1954–66).

Generalstaben, *Karl XII på slagfältet*, i–iv (Stockholm 1918).

Foreign policy

Den svenska utrikespolitikens historia, i.2–3; ii.1 (Stockholm 1952–60).

The provinces

J. Rosén, 'Statsledning och provinspolitik under Sveriges stormaktstid. En författningshistorisk skiss', *Scandia* (1946).

R. Liljedahl, *Svensk förvaltning i Livland 1617–1634* (Uppsala 1933).

A. Perandi, *Die Aufgaben und Funktionen der Estländischen General-Gouvernementsregierung während der schwedischen Zeit* (Dorpat 1935).

O. Liiv, *Suur näljaaeg Eestis 1695–1697 – Die grosse Hungersnot in Estland 1695–1697* (Dorpat 1938).

R. Wittram, *Baltische Geschichte* (Munich 1954).

E. Öpik, *Eesti talurahva 'Rootsi-truudsest' Pöhjasöja ajal. Eesti ühendamisest Venemaaga ja selle ajoloosisest tähtsusest* (Tallinn 1960).

—— *Talurahva mõisavastane võitlus Eestis Pöjhasöja esimesel 1700–1710* (Tallinn 1964).

H. Palli, *Mezdu dvumya voyami za Narvu. Estoniya v pervye gody Severnoi voiny 1701–1704* (Tallinn 1966).

A. C. Meurling, *Svensk domstolsförvaltning i Livland 1634–1700* (Lund 1967).

P.-E. Back, *Herzog und Landschaft. Politische Ideen und Verfassungs-programme in Schwedisch-Pommern um die Mitte des 17. Jahrhunderts* (Lund 1955).

—— 'Striden om Nebenmodus. En studie i Karl XI : s pommerska finanspolitik', *Karolinska förbundets årsbok* (1958).

J. Peters, 'Unter der schwedischen Krone', *Zeitschrift für Geschichtswissenschaft* (1966).

K.-R. Böhme, *Bremisch-verdische Staatsfinanzen 1645–1676. Die schwedische Krone als deutsche Landesherrin* (Uppsala 1967).

E. Dunsdorf, 'Der Aussenhandel Rigas im 17. Jahrhundert', *Conventus primus historicorum Balticorum Rigae . . . 1937* (Riga 1938).

A. Attman, *Den ryska marknaden i 1500-talets baltiska politik 1558–1595* (Lund 1944).

K.-G. Hildebrand, 'Ekonomiska syften i svensk expansionpolitik 1700–1709', *Karolinska förbundets årsbok* (1949).

2. THE SWEDISH ECONOMY AND SWEDEN'S ROLE AS A GREAT POWER

Books and articles mentioned in the references to this chapter are, with the exception of Heckscher, excluded from the bibliography.

General study of the economy

E. F. Heckscher, *Sveriges ekonomiska historia från Gustav Vasa*, i.1–2 (Stockholm 1935–6).

The 'home countries', the provinces and the satellites

A. Luukko, *Suomen historia 1617–1721* (Suomen historia, viii, Helsinki, 1967).

E. Kuujo, *Taka-Karjalan verotus v:een 1710* (Helsinki 1959).

A. Åberg, *När Skåne blev svenskt* (Stockholm 1958).

H. Kellenbenz, *Holstein-Gottorp, eine Domäne Schwedens* (Leipzig 1940).

Population estimates

S. Sundquist, *Finlands folkmängd och bebyggelse i början av 1600-talet* (Stockholm 1931).

—— *Sveriges folkmängd på Gustaf II Adolfs tid* (Lund 1938).

E. Jutikkala, 'Can the Population of Finland in the 17th Century be Calculated?', *Scandinavian Economic History Review*, v (1957).

G. Lext, *Mantalsskrivningen i Sverige före 1860* (Göteborg 1968).

J. Vasar, *Die grosse livländische Güterreduktion*, i-ii (Tartu 1931).

The metals in the economy

B. Boëthius, *Gruvornas, hyttornas och hamrarnas folk* (Stockholm 1951).

E. F. Heckscher, 'Un grand chapître de l'historie du fer. Le monopole suédois', *Annales d'histoire économique et sociale*, iv (1932).

K.-G. Hildebrand, *Fagerstabrukens historia*, i (Stockholm 1957).

J. Wolontis, *Kopparmyntningen i Sverige 1624–1714* (Helsingfors 1936).

A. Olsen, 'Kobberpolitik i den svenske Stormagtstid', *Scandia*, x (1937).

E. F. Heckscher, 'Den europeiska kopparmarknaden under 1600-talet', *Scandia*, xi (1938).

—— 'Europas kopparmarknad och den svenska kopparen', *Historieuppfattning – materialistisk och annan* (Stockholm 1944).

Farming, trade and shipping

T. Lagerstedt, 'Sädesodling och boskapsstock under 1600-talet', *Ymer* (1968).

G. Enequist, *Nedre Luledalens byar* (Uppsala, 1937).

D. Torbrand, *Johannishus fideikomiss intill 1735* (Uppsala 1963).

E. Dunsdorfs, *Der grosse schwedische Kataster in Livland 1681–1710* (Stockholm 1950).

K. R. Melander, 'Poimintoja taloudellisesta tilasta Pommerissa 30-vuotissodan aikoina', *Historiallinen aikakauskirja* (1923).

B. Boëthius and E. F. Heckscher, *Svensk handelsstatistik 1637–1779* (Stockholm 1938).

S. Gerentz, *Kommerskollegium och näringslivet* (Stockholm 1951).

E. Dunsdorfs, *Der grosse schwedische Kataster in Livland 1681–1710* (Stockhistoricorum Balticorum Rigae . . . *1937* (Riga 1938).

G. Jensch, 'Der Handel Rigas im 17. Jahrhundert', *Mitteilungen aus der livländischen Geschichte*, xxiv.2 (Riga 1930).

A. Loit, 'Sverige och Ostersjöhandeln under 1600-talet', *Historisk tidskrift* (1964).

H. Piirimäe, *Kaubanduse küsimused Vene-Rootsi suhetes 1661–1700 A.* (Tartu 1961).

A. Soom, 'Varutransporterna mellan Sverige och de svenskägda baltiska gårdarna under 1600-talet', *Svio–Estonica*, xviii (1967).

O. Bjurling, 'Stockholms förbindelser med utlandet under 1670-talets växlingar', *Forum navale*, x (1951).

—— *Skånes utrikessjöfart* (Lund 1945).

E. Dunsdorfs, *Merchant shipping in the Baltic during the 17th Century* (Pinneberg 1947).

Financial problems

P. V. A. Hanner, *Rikshuvudboken av år 1623* (Stockholm 1952).

V. Kerkkonen, 'Ruotsi–Suomen finansseista 16–luvun alkupuoliskolla', *Historiallinen arkisto*, lii (1947).

H. Landberg, *Statsfinans och kungamakt. Karl X Gustav inför polska kriget* (Kristianstad 1969).

G. Wittrock, *Karl XI:s förmyndares finanspolitik* (Uppsala 1914).

—— *Karl XI:s förmyndares finanspolitik från blå boken till franska förbundet 1668–1672* (Uppsala 1917).

R. Blomdahl, *Förmyndarräfstens huvudskede* (Stockholm 1963).

—— 'Karl XI, förmyndarräfsten och enväldet', *Historisk tidskrift* (1965).

—— *Förmyndarräfstens slutskede* (Stockholm 1968).

A. Munthe, 'Likvidationskommissionen', *Meddelanden från Svenska Riksarkivet för år 1931* (Stockholm) 1932.

E. Blumfeldt, 'Reduktionen på Osel 1681–1694', *Svio-Estonica*, xiv (1958).

A. Isberg, *Karl XI och den livländska adeln 1684–1695* (Lund 1953).

The nobility as a ruling élite, and social mobility.

P. E. Fahlbeck, *Sveriges adel*, i (Göteborg 1898).

R. Swedlund, *Grev– och friherreskapen i Sverige och Finland. Donationerna och reduktionerna före 1680* (Uppsala 1936).

M. Jokipii, *Suomen kreivi– ja vapaaherrakunnat*, i–ii (Helsinki 1956–60).

C. von Bonsdorff, *Om donationerna och förläningarna samt frälseköpen i Finland under drottning Kristinas regering* (Helsingfors 1886).

'Ofversigtlig framställning af kronoabalienationerna i Finland vid drottning Kristinas tronafsägelse', *Historiallinen arkisto*, x (1889).

T. Söderberg, *Den namnlösa medelklassen* (Stockholm 1956).

The economic armament

K.-R. Böhme, 'Geld für die schwedischen Armeen nach 1640', *Scandia*, xxxiii (1967).

R. Torstendahl, *Svensk krigsförsörjning och underhållstjänst i Danmark 1657–1660* (Carl X Gustaf – studier, i, Kristianstad 1965).

H. Landberg, *Krig på kredit, Svensk rustningsfinansiering våren 1655* (Carl X Gustaf – studier, iv, Kristianstad 1969).

E. Wendt, *Amiralitetskollegiets historia*, i (Stockholm 1950).

A. Korhonen, 'Utskrivningen av krigsfolk i Finland under trettioåriga kriget', in *Det förgyllda stamträdet*, ed. Pentti Renvall (Falun 1964).

A. Viljanti, *Vakinaisen sotamiehenpidon sovelluttaminen Suomessa*, i–ii (Turku, 1935–40).

—— 'Finnish Soldiers on the Baltic Ramparts', *Revue internationale d'histoire militaire*, no. 23 (1961).

N. K. Grotenfelt, *Anteckningar om indelta dragoner i östra Finland 1644–1721* (Helsingfors 1940).

In the Swedish and Finnish Public Record Offices (*Sveriges Riksarkiv, Finlands Riksarkiv*), the Swedish Army Archives (*Krigsarkivet*) and the Central Archives of the Soviet Republics in the Baltic area there is a large amount of source material, which it has been impossible to deal with in this context. Only central financial questions – like the poll-tax lists in the Finnish Public Record Office (for Finland, the provinces of Kexholm and Ingria), the French subsidies, the hoarding of silver, the 'satisfaction' money of the Westphalian peace – have been systematically treated, mostly on the basis of these unpublished sources.

3. ESTATES AND CLASSES

General surveys of seventeenth-century social history are: Eli F. Heckscher, *Sveriges ekonomiska historia från Gustav Vasa*, i.2 (Stockholm 1936); Tom Söderberg, *Den namnlösa medelklassen* (Stockholm 1956); Sten Carlsson, *Bonde – präst – ämbetsman* (Stockholm 1962), and for the position at the end of the period the same author's *Ståndssamhälle och ståndspersoner 1700–1865* (Lund 1949). For the Estates in their political relationships, see Birger Lövgren, *Ståndsstridens uppkomst* (Stockholm 1915); the volumes by Nils Ahnlund and Sven Grauers in the collective work *Sveriges riksdag* (Stockholm 1932–3); Nils Runeby, *Monarchia mixta. Maktfördelningsdebatt i Sverige under den tidigare stormaktstiden* (Uppsala 1962).

The impact of noble privileges on the peasantry may be collected from: Hakon Swenne, *Den svenska adelns ekonomiska privilegier 1612–1651 med särskild hänsyn till Alvsborgs län* (Göteborg 1933); Erik Brännman, *Frälse-köpen under Gustav II Adolfs regering* (Lund 1950); Sven A. Nilsson, *På väg mot reduktionen* (Stockholm 1964); Kurt Agren, *Adelns bönder och Kronans. Skatter och besvär i Uppland 1650–1680* (Uppsala 1964).

For the Burghers in general, besides the works of Heckscher and Söderberg listed above, reference should be made to the numerous town histories which have appeared in the last thirty years or so; to C. F. Corin, *Självstyre och kunglig maktpolitik inom Stockholms stadsförvaltning 1668–1697* (Stockholm 1958); and (for the crafts) to Ernst Söderlund, *Hantverkarna*, ii, forming vol. viii of the series *Den svenska arbetarklassens historia* (Stockholm 1949).

For the clergy, see Gunnar Suolahti, *Finlands prästerskap på 1600- och 1700-talen* (Stockholm 1927); Carl-E. Normann, *Prästerkapet och det karolinska enväldet* (Stockholm 1948).

For the civil service, see Birger Steckzén, *Krigskollegiets historia*, i (Stockholm 1930); and the collective works *Kungl. Maj:ts kanslis historia*, i (Uppsala 1935) and *Kammarkollegiets historia* (Stockholm 1941).

4. THE SWEDISH CHURCH

The standard modern history of the church is *Svenska kyrkans historia*, of which vol. iv.1 (Stockholm 1938), by H. Holmquist, covers 1611–32, and vol. v (Stockholm 1935), by H. Pleijel, covers 1680–1772. Vol. iv.2 remains unpublished, but the gap is filled by the outline in H. Holmquist, *Från Reformationen till romantiken* (Stockholm 1940). The history of the Reformation is treated in English in M. Roberts, *The Early Vasas* (Cambridge 1968), and that of the church under Gustavus Adolphus in the same author's *Gustavus Adolphus*, i (1953).

Most of the great bishops have been the subject of important studies: among them are H. Lundström, *Laurentius Paulinus Gothus*, i–iii (Uppsala 1893); H. Cnattingius, *Johannes Rudbeckius och hans europeiska bakgrund* (Uppsala 1946); R. Holm, *Joannes Elai Terserus* (Lund 1906); H. Holmquist, *D. Johannes Matthiae Gothus och hans plats i Sveriges kyrkliga utveckling* Uppsala 1903), and Bror Jansson, *Johannes Matthiae Gothus och hans plats i gudstjänstlivets historia* (Lund 1954); O. Hassler, *Linköpings stift under Samuel Enander*, i (Lund 1935); F. Petersson, *Olaus Svebilius intill ärkebiskopstiden* (Stockholm 1940); G. Göransson, *Canutus Hahn* (Stockholm 1950). *Jesper Swedbergs lefwernes beskrifning*, ed. G. Wetterberg (Lund 1941), is a vast rambling autobiography, packed with fascinating and informative detail.

For Durie's ecumenical activity, see G. Westin, *John Durie in Sweden* (Uppsala 1936); for the syncretist controversy, S. Göransson, *Ortodoxi och synkretism i Sverige 1647–1660* (Uppsala 1950) and *Den synkretistiska striden i Sverige 1660–1664* (Uppsala 1952). Student peregrination is dealt with in the same author's *De svenska studieresorna och den religiösa kontrollen från reformationstiden till frihetstiden* (Uppsala 1951).

For Pietism, see Emmanuel Linderhielm, *Pietismen och dess första tid i Sverige* (Stockholm 1962).

For the problems of church–state relations, see the luminous survey in O. S. Holmdahl, *Studier öfver prästeståndets kyrkopolitik under den tidigare frihetstiden*, i (Lund 1912); and H. Cnattingius, *Den centrala kyrkostyrelsen i Sverige 1611–1636* (Stockholm 1939); H. Lundin, *Joannes Baazius' kyrkliga reformprogram* (Lund 1944); S. Kjöllerström, *Kyrkolagsproblemet i Sverige 1571–1682* (Stockholm 1944); Carl-E. Normann, *Prästerskapet och det karolinska enväldet* (Stockholm 1948). For *consistorium regni*, see Sven Lindegård, *Consistorium regni och frågan om kyrklig överstyrelse* (Lund 1957).

For the catechism and the Bible, see Hilding Pleijel, *Katekesen som svensk folkbok* (Lund 1942), *Bibeln i svenskt fromhetsliv* (Lund 1941) and *Hustävlans värld* (Stockholm 1970). The problems of church discipline appear vividly illustrated in *Johannes Rudbeckius dagbok*, ed. B. R. Hall (Stockholm 1938), and there is a good survey of parochial self-government in R. Gullstrand, *Bidrag till den svenska sockensjälvstyrelsens historia under 1600-talet* (Stockholm 1932), and its sequel, K. H. Johansson, *Svensk sockensjälvstyrelse 1686–1862* (Lund 1937).

Gunnar Suolahti's *Finlands prästerskap på 1600- och 1700-talen* (Stockholm 1927) is in a class by itself as a sociological study in depth, but as its title implies it is valid only for Finland.

The Church Ordinance of 1571, and the various drafts of its amendment, are printed in *Kyrko-ordningar och förslag dertill före 1686*, i–iii (Stockholm 1872–87), while Charles XI's Church Law is available in J. Schmedemann, *Kongl. Stadgar . . . [etc.] . . . angående Justitiae och Executions-Ahrender* (Stockholm 1706). The debates of the Estate of Clergy for the period 1642–1714 are printed in *Prästeståndets riksdagsprotokoll*, i–iv (Uppsala 1949–62).

5. CHARLES X AND THE CONSTITUTION

K. Agren, *Adelns bönder och kronans. Skatter och besvär i Uppland 1650–1680* (Uppsala 1964).

F. F. Carlson, *Sveriges historia under konungarne av Pfalziska huset*, i (Stockholm 1855).

S. Dahlgren, 'Kansler och kungamakt vid tronskiftet 1654', *Scandia* (1960).

—— 'Herman Fleming', *Svenskt Biografiskt Lexikon*, lxxvi (Stockholm 1964).

—— *Karl X Gustav och reduktionen* (Uppsala 1964).

K. E. F. Ignatius, *Finlands historia under Carl X Gustafs regering* (Helsingfors 1865).

B. Kentrschynskyj, 'Karl X Gustav inför krisen i öster 1654–1655', *Karolinska förbundets årsbok* (1956).

H. Landberg 'Decemberrådslagen 1654', *Karolinska förbundets årsbok* (1968).

—— 'Kungamaktens emancipation', *Scandia* (1969).

—— *Krig på kredit. Svensk rustningsfinansiering våren 1655* (Carl X Gustaf-studier, iv, Kristianstad 1969).

——*Statsfinans och kungamakt. Karl X Gustav inför polska kriget* (Uppsala 1969).

S. A. Nilsson, *På vag mot reduktionen* (Stockholm 1964).

B. Odén, 'Karl X Gustav och det andra danska kriget', Scandia (1961).

S. I. Olofsson, *Carl X Gustaf. Hertigen – tronföljaren* (Stockholm 1961).

N. Runeby, *Monarchia mixta. Maktfördelningsdebatt i Sverige under den tidigare stormaktstiden* (Uppsala 1962).

G. Rystad, 'Med råds råde eller efter konungens godtycke? Makten över ämbetstillsättningarna som politisk stridsfråga under 1600-talet', *Scandia* (1963).

R. Torstendahl, review of H. Landberg's works (above), *Historisk tidskrift* (1969).

G. Wittrock, *Carl X Gustafs testamente* (Uppsala 1908).

6. MAGNUS GABRIEL DE LA GARDIE

The leading part played by Magnus Gabriel De la Gardie in both the political and cultural life of Sweden's Age of Greatness results in his cropping up in various contexts in historical literature dealing with the period. Biographical treatments of his career are, however, somewhat sparse. The main work is still Rudolf Fåhraeus's *Magnus Gabriel De la Gardie* (Stockholm 1933), though there is also an article by G. Wittrock in *Svenskt Biografiskt Lexicon*, x (Stockholm 1931).

For his career as a statesman and politician, see, among others: F. F. Carlson, *Sveriges historia under konungarne av Pfalziska huset*, i–ii (Stockholm 1855–74); O. Varenius, *Råfsten med Karl XI:s förmyndarstyrelse*, i–ii (Uppsala 1901–3) and 'Högförräderimålet mot Magnus Gabriel de la Gardie', in *Festskrift tillägnad C. G. Malmström* (Stockholm 1897). Also G. Wittrock, *Karl XI:s förmyndares finanspolitik*, i–ii (Uppsala 1914–17); and G. Rystad, *Johan Gyllenstierna, rådet och kungamakten* (Lund 1955). There is a large literature on De la Gardie and foreign policy. The principal authority is Birger Fahlborg, with his massive work *Sveriges yttre politik 1660–1672* (Stockholm 1932–61), and his important essay 'Sveriges förbund med Frankrike 1672', *Historisk tidskrift* (1935). See too Georg Landberg, *Den svenska utrikespolitiken historia*, i.3, *1648–1697* (Stockholm 1952).

De la Gardie's relations with Queen Christina are treated in the numerous biographies of the queen: see especially Sven Stolpe, *Queen Christina* (abridged English trans., 1966), and Curt Weilbull, *Christina of Sweden* (English trans., Stockholm 1966).

For De la Gardie as a landed magnate, see *inter alia* B. Planting, *De jordrika stormännen* (Stockholm 1952); J. A. Almquist, *Frälsegodsen i Sverige under storhetstiden* (Stockholm 1931); and Eli Heckscher, *Stormaktstidens sociala omvälvningar* (Stockholm 1943).

The chancellor's work for education is treated in C. Annerstedt, *Uppsala universitets historia*, ii (Uppsala 1910); J. Rosén, *Lunds universitets historia* (Lund 1968); and S. Edlund, *Magnus Gabriel De la Gardies inrikespolitiska program 1655* (Lund 1954).

His work as a builder is treated in, e.g., S. Karling, 'Jakob och Magnus De la Gardie som byggherrar i Estland', *Svio–Estonica* (1938); and G. Lindahl, *Magnus Gabriel De la Gardie, hans gods och hans folk* (Stockholm 1968). His importance for the artistic and cultural life of Sweden is illustrated in a diversity of contexts: besides the works already listed, see, e.g., K. E. Steneberg, *Kristinatidens måleri* (Stockholm 1955); Kajsa Rootzen, *Den svenska baletten* (Stockholm 1945); S. Karling, *Trädgårdskonstens historia i Sverige* (Stockholm

1931); A. Hahr, *Konst och konstnärer vid Magnus Gabriel De la Gardies hov* (Stockholm 1905).

7. THE REDUKTION

In addition to the works cited in the notes, use has been made of Jerker Rosén, *Det karolinska skedet. Karl XI:s och Karl XII:s tid* (Lund 1963), which provides a survey of the background, execution and consequences of the *reduktion*, and is based on the results of previous research, which it treats with appropriate caution. The following is a list of works previously cited, in chronological order:

V. E. Svedelius, *Om reduktionen af krono– och adeliga gods under k. Carl XI:s regering* (Stockholm 1849).

A. Fryxell, *Berättelser ur svenska historien*, xvii (Stockholm 1852).

E. Heckscher, *Sveriges ekonomiska historia från Gustav Vasa*, i.2 (Stockholm 1936).

E. Blumfeldt, 'Reduktionen på Osel 1681–1694', *Svio-Estonica* (1958).

S. A. Nilsson, 'Reduktion eller kontribution. Alternativ inom 1600-talets svenska finanspolitik', *Scandia*, xxiv (1958).

S. Dahlgren, *Karl X Gustaf och reduktionen* (Studia Historica Upsaliensia, xiv) (Uppsala 1964).

K. Agren, *Adelus bönder och kronans. Skatter och besvär i Uppland 1650–1680* (Studia Historica Uppsaliensia, xi), Uppsala 1964).

—— 'Gods och ämbete. Sten Bielkes inkomster inför riksdagen 1680', *Scandia*, xxxi (1965).

8. THE SWEDISH ARMY, FROM LÜTZEN TO NARVA

Alf Aberg, *Indelningen av rytteriet i Skåne 1658–1700* (Lund 1947).

Sven Agren, *Karl XI:s indelningsverk för armén* (Uppsala 1922).

Claes Grill, *Statistiskt sammandrag av svenska indelningsverket* (Stockholm 1855–6).

Torsten Holm, *Från allmogeuppbådet till folkhär* (Stockholm (1943).

Evald Kumm, *Indelt soldat och rotebonde* (Stockholm 1949).

Gustaf Petri, *Kungl. Första Livgrenadjärregementets historia*, i–iv (Stockholm 1926–62).

Michael Roberts, *Gustavus Adolphus: A History of Sweden 1611–1632*, i–ii (1953–8).

—— 'Charles XI', in *Essays in Swedish History* (1967).

John E. Roos, *Uppkomsten av Finlands militieboställen* (Helsinki 1933).

Folke Wernstedt, *Kungl. Svea livgardes historia*, iv (Stockholm 1954).

Theodor Wijkander, *Oversikt av svenska krigsförfattningens historiska utveckling* (Stockholm 1866).

Notes and References

1. THE EXPERIENCE OF EMPIRE   *Sven Lundkvist* (pages 20–57)

1. Statistics taken from G. E. Axelsson, *Bidrag till kännedomen om Sveriges tillstånd, på Karl XII:s tid* (Visby 1888), p. 113.

2. *Ibid.*, pp. 107 ff.; F. Arwidsson, *Försvaret av östersjöprovinserna 1708–1709* (Gävle 1936), pp. 17 ff.

3. Quoted in Folke Wernstedt, *Kungl. Svea Livgardes historia*, iv (Stockholm 1954), 7.

4. Cf. S. Lundkvist, 'Svensk krigsfinansiering 1630–35', *Historisk tidskrift* (1966).

5. *Svenska riksrådets protokoll 1654–1656* (Stockholm 1923), pp. 30 ff. See also H. Landberg, 'Decemberrådslagen 1654. Kark X Gustav, rådet och rustningsfrågan', *Karolinska förbundets årsbok* (1968), pp. 43–68.

6. For the campaigns, see Lars Tersmeden, *Kungl. Svea livgardes historia*, iii.2 (Stockholm 1966), and for the financing of the armies, H. Landberg, *Statsfinans och kungamakt. Karl X Gustav inför polska kriget* (Uppsala 1969), which summarised the results of his researches; in this connection his *Krig på kredit. Svensk rustningsfinansiering våren 1655* (Carl X Gustaf-studier, iv, Kristianstad 1969), is of importance, esp. pp 125 ff.

7. Intensive negotiations with Cromwell for naval support had led to no result.

8. *Svenska riksrådets protokoll*, viii (Stockholm 1898), 180.

9. *Ibid.*, x (Stockholm 1905), 182 ff. (Oxenstierna was quoting Gustavus Adolphus, and it seems likely that the 'thwarting' to which he was referring was the thwarting, not of his own authority, but of the king's) [*ed.*].

10. I have had the advantage of discussing these problems with Fil. Lic. Alexsander Loit, who is engaged in investigating the course of the *reduktion* in Estonia.

11. A survey of the Swedish period in Pomerania from the Marxist point of view is to be found in J. Peters, 'Unter der schwedischen Krone', *Zeitschrift für Geschichtswissenschaft* (1966), pp. 33 ff., which also touches on certain aspects omitted here, e.g. the links between the Pomeranian and Swedish nobilities.

12. Sten Carlsson, 'Finlands ämbetsmän och Sveriges rike under 1700-talet. Grupper och gestalter', *Studier om individ och kollektiv i nordisk och europeisk historia* (Lund 1964), pp. 60–75.

13. Statistics from Table in *ibid.*, p. 71. The criterion for place of origin is not always a man's birthplace, but sometimes the place where he grew up: in doubtful cases, the place he lived in during his teens.

14. Statistics from Table in *ibid.*, pp. 73–4.

2. THE SWEDISH ECONOMY AND SWEDEN'S ROLE AS A GREAT POWER 1632–1697   *Sven-Erik Aström* (pages 58–101)

1. E. F. Heckscher, *Sveriges ekonomiska historia från Gustav Vasa*, i.2 (Stockholm 1936), 367.

2. P. A. Forsström (Hainari), *Kuvaus Inkerinmaan oloist Ruotsinvallan aikana*, i (Sortavala 1890), 30–68.

3. In addition to the Osterbotten regiment, Riga also had a battalion from the Nyland-Tavastehus regiment, and at times also companies from those of Abo and Björneborg.

4. Source for Table 4: S.-E. Aström, *From Cloth to Iron: The Anglo-Baltic Trade in the Late Seventeenth Century*, i (Helsingfors 1963), 37.

5. Based on Heckscher, *Sveriges ekonomiska historia*, i.1 (Stockholm 1935), appendix v.2, p. 20. Heckscher does not make it clear that the customs area in 1685 was much more extensive than in 1637.

6. A. Soom, *Der baltische Getreidehandel im 17. Jahrhundert* (Lund 1961).

7. By Gustavus Adolphus's *riddarhusordning* of 1626 the Estate of Nobility was divided into three classes: the counts and barons; the descendants of members of the council of state; and those who did not fall into either of these categories.

8. Sources for Table 6: A. A. von Stiernman, *Matrikel öfwer Swea Rikes Ridderskap och Adel uppå des begäran wid 1751 års Riks-Dag utgifwen med Historiska och Genealogiska Anmärkningar*, i-ii (Stockholm 1754–5); P. E. Fahlbeck, *Sveriges adel*, i (Göteborg 1898).

9. L. M. Bååth and A. Munthe, *Kungl. Statskontoret 1680–1930* (Stockholm 1930), p. 32.

10. F. Lagerroth, *Statsreglering och finqnsförvaltning i Sverige till och med Frihetstidens början* (Skrifter utg. av Fahlbeckska stiftelsen, xi, Malmö 1928), pp. 129–30.

11. Riksarkivet, Stockholm: Statskontorets arkiv. Kungl. reglemente, etc., 1695.

12. Sources to Table 7: (a) Riksarkivet, Stockholm: Kammarkollegiets arkiv. Rikshuvudboken 1633 ('Rijckzsens Kortta Generalräkning pro Anno 1633') and Rikshuvudboken 1677. Amounts reckoned in silver *daler* in the accounts have been converted to *riksdaler* on the basis of (1633) 1 rd = 1·5 silver *daler*; (1677) 1 rd = 2 silver *daler*. (b) E. Falk, *Sverige och Frankrike* (Uppsala 1911), p. 129. (c) E. Wendt, *Det svenska licentväsendet i Preussen 1627–1635* (Uppsala 1933), p. 205.

13. Klaus Zernack, *Studien zu den schwedisch-russischen Beziehungen in der 2. Hälfte des 17. Jahrhunderts*, i (Giessen 1958).

14. Försvarsstaben, *Från Femern och Jankow till Westfaliska freden* (Stockholm 1948), pp. 90 ff.

15. He was ennobled under the name Trana. He had worked his way up during the Polish war, and had managed to levy the taxes on the recently acquired province of Kexholm. His biography is extremely illuminating both from an economic and a social point of view: it contradicts the idea that the Thirty Years War was simply the great opportunity for the old Swedish and Finnish nobility, and reveals the possibilities (and the risks) which the permanent war economy presented to the rising men: A. Korhonen, *Erkki Antinpoika* (Helsinki 1953).

16. K.-R. Böhme, *Bremisch-Verdische Staatsfinanzen 1645–1676* (Studia Historica Upsaliensia, xxvi, Uppsala 1967), pp. 34, 205, 444 ff., 539.

17. F. Redlich, 'The German Military Enterpriser and his Work Force: A Study in European Economic and Social History', I–II, *Vierteljahrschrift für Sozial- und Wirtschaftsgeschichte*, Beihefte 47–8 (Wiesbaden 1964–5).

18. The extent of counties and baronies appears from Eino Jutikkala's historical atlas, *Suomen Historian Kartasto – Atlas of Finnish History* (2nd edn, Porvoo 1959), which has an introduction and captions in English.

19. Cf. the discussion in Syen A. Nilsson, *På väg mot reduktionen* (Stockholm 1964).

20. Heckscher, *Sveriges ekonomiska historia*, i.2, p. 315.

21. F. F. Carlson, *Sveriges historia under konungarne av Pfalziska huset*, v (Stockholm 1879), 245.

22. Cf. R. Carr, 'Two Swedish Financiers: Louis de Geer and Joel Gripenhielm', in *Historical Essays 1600–1750 presented to David Ogg*, ed. H. E. Bell and R. L. Ollard (1963), pp. 26–34.

23. Riksarkivet, Stockholm: Statskontorets arkiv. Diverse statsförslag 1687–1700.

24. C. von Bonsdorf, *Abo stads historia under sjuttonde seklet*, i (Helsingfors 1894), 437.

25. Wendt, *Det svenska licentväsendet i Preussen*, pp. 257–8.

26. Sources for Table 8: (a) Riksarkivet, Stockholm: Subsidieräkenskaper. The *riksdaler* is taken as 1·5 silver *daler*. (b) Falk, *Sverige och Frankrike*, p. 129. (c) A. Munthe, *Joel Gripenstierna* (Stockholm 1941), pp. 69 ff.

27. Riksarkivet, Stockholm: Satisfaktionspenningar.

28. Cf. Th. Lorentzen, *Die schwedische Armee im dreissigjährigen Kriege und ihre Abdankung* (Leipzig 1894), p. 176.

29. Bååth and Munthe, *Kungl. Statskontoret*, 97.

30. Karl Marx, *The Secret Diplomatic History of the Eighteenth Century*, ed. Lester Hutchison (1969). Marx's work was published in article form in the *Sheffield Free Press* in 1856, and in an expanded form in the *Free Press* in 1856–7; in book form it was published in a somewhat mutilated version by his daughter Eleanor Marx (1899). The new edition (which exists only in English) is therefore most welcome. Marx's analysis is based on pamphlets of the early eighteenth century, and on material in the British Museum; it is a pity that he did not have access to State Papers, Russia, and State Papers, Sweden, in the Public Record Office.

3. ESTATES AND CLASSES   Stallen Dahlgren (pages 102–31)

1. Sten Carlsson, *Bonde – präst – ämbetsman* (Stockholm 1962), pp. 16 ff.

2. *Svenska riksrådets protokoll*, xiv (Stockholm 1916), 272.

3. 'Jonas Petris dagbok från riksdagen 1650', *Handlingar till Skandinaviens historia*, xxii (Stockholm 1837), 162.

4. Quoted in Hakon Swenne, *Den svenska adelns ekonomiska privilegier 1612–1651 med särskild hänsyn till Alvsborgs län* (Göteborg 1933), p. 314.

5. Edvard Philipsson Ehrensten, *Oförgripliga Bewis emot Adelens Rättighet öfwer Skatte-Gods* [1649] (Stockholm 1769), p. 4.

6. Quoted in Sven Grauers, *Sveriges riksdag*, i.4, *Riksdagen under den karolinska tiden* (Stockholm 1932), p. 87. The diarist was Erik Duraeus.

7. Quoted in Helge Almquist, *Göteborgs historia. Grundläggningen och de*

första hundra åaren, i,*Från grundläggningen till enväldet (1619–1680)* (Göteborg 1929), p. 599.

8. 'Jonas Petris dagbok från riksdagen 1650', p. 147.

9. Quoted in J. A. Westerlund and J. A. Setterdahl, *Linköpings stifts herdaminne* (Linköping 1919), pp. 63 ff.

10. *Rikskansleren Axel Oxenstiernas skrifter och brevväxling*, II.xii(1) (Stockholm 1930), 658–9.

11. Samuel Enander in fact was, in 1658; but he did not use his new noble name of Gyllendadler, and never took his seat in the House of Nobility. [*ed.*]

12. *Svenska riksrådets protokoll*, xiv, 390.

13. Quoted in Sven Edlund, *Magnus Gabriel De la Gardies inrikespolitiska program 1655. Ett bidrag till den ståndspolitiska och pedagogiska debatten under 1600-talen* (Lund 1654), pp. 270, 271.

14. Heckscher, *Sveriges ekonomiska historia*, i.2, p. 345.

15. *Svenska ridderskaps och adels riksdagsprotokoll från och med år 1719*, i (Stockholm 1875), 119.

16. *Svenska ridderskaps och adels riksdagsprotokoll . . . från sjutfondi århundradet*, v (Stockholm 1873), 317.

4. THE SWEDISH CHURCH Michael Roberts (pages 132–73)

1. A. A. von Stiernman, *Samling utaf . . . kongliga stadgar, bref och förardningar angående religion* (Stockholm 1744), pp. 93–4.

2. *Svenska riksrådets protokoll*, vi (Stockholm 1891), 774.

3. Quoted in Carl-E. Normann, *Prästerskapet och det karolinska enväldet* (Stockholm 1948), p. 68.

4. *Jesper Swedbergs lefwernes beskrifning*, ed. G. Wetterberg (Lund 1941), i, 136.

5. *Prästeståndets riksdagsprotokoll*, i (Uppsala 1949), 317.

6. K. G. Leinberg, *Finska prästerskapets besvär och Kongl. Majestäts därpå gifna resolutioner* (Helsingfors 1892), p. 4.

7. C. G. Styffe, *Konung Gustaf II Adolfs skrifter* (Stockholm 1861), p. 632.

8. Quoted in R. Holm, *Joannes Elai Terserus* (Lund 1906), p. 160.

9. Matthias Heffenreffer, German theologian (1561–1619).

10. Stiernman, *Samling*, p. 157.

11. Quoted in E. G. Léonard, *A History of Protestantism* (1965), ii, 200.

12. B. Whitelock, *A Journal of Swedish Ambassy* (1855), i, 187–8.

13. i.e. the extreme right wing of Lutheranism: see E. A. Léonard, *A History of Protestantism* (1967), ii, 18.

14. Bror Jansson, *Johannes Matthiae Gothus och hans plats i gudstjänstlivets historia* (Lund 1954), pp. 99–100.

15. Quoted in Hilding Pleijel, *Katekesen som svensk folkbok* (Lund–Malmö 1942), p. 30.

16. Emmanuel Linderhielm, *Pietismen och dess första tid i Sverige* (Stockholm 1962), p. 17.

17. For a suggestive parallel (and contrast) in Catholic countries, see John Bossy, 'The Counter-Reformation and the People of Catholic Europe', *Past and Present* (1970), pp. 65 ff.

18. *Prästeståndets riksdagsprotokoll*, i, 103.

19. Whitelock, *Journal of Swedish Ambassy*, i, 412.

20. Quoted in Holm, *Terserus*, p. 144.

21. *Kyrko-ordningar och förslag dertill före 1686* (Stockholm 1881), ii, 57; and *ibid.*, 52–8, 79–90, for the debates.

22. Linderhielm, *Pietismen*, p. 65.

23. *Diarium Gyllenianum eller Petri Magni Gyllenii Dagbok 1622–1667* (Karlstad 1962), p. 208.

24. *Kyrko-ordningar och förslag dertill*, i, 145.

25. Quoted in R. Gullstrand, *Bidrag till den svenska sockensjälvstyrelsens historia under 1600-talet* (Stockholm 1923), p. 62.

26. Quoted in H. Pleijel, *Hustavlans värld* (Stockholm 1970), p. 19.

27. H. Pleijel, *Karolinsk kyrkofromhet, pietism och herrnhutism 1680–1772* (*Svenska kyrkans historia*, v) (Stockholm 1935), p. 194.

28. *Svenska riksdagsakter*, i.2 (Stockholm 1932), 71.

29. Stiernman, *Samling*, p. 122.

30. *Johan Ekeblads brev till brodern Claes Ekeblad 1639–1655*, ed. Sture Allén (Göteborg 1965), ii, 7.

31. *Prästeståndets riksdagsprotokoll*, i, 293.

32. Hence too the temporary setback of 1664, when the *riksdag* resolved that persons frequenting suspect universities, or who were found on returning to be doctrinally unsound, were on conviction to be dealt with as *turbatores patriae*: Stiernman, *Samling*, p. 113.

33. *Prästeståndets riksdagsprotokoll*, iv, 303–4.

34. Quoted in Hans Cnattingius, *Johannes Rudbeckius och hans europeiska bakgrund. En kyrkorättshistorisk studie* (Uppsala 1946), p. 49.

35. *Rikskansleren Axel Oxenstiernas skrifter och brefvexling* (Stockholm 1888), I, i, 458; my italics.

36. Quoted in O. Holmdahl, *Studier öfver prästeståndets kyrkopolitik under den tidigare frihetstiden* (Lund 1912), i, 156.

37. *Svenska riksrådets protokoll*, vi, 336.

38. *Ibid.*, p. 341.

39. *Ibid.*, p. 338.

40. It was said of Isak Rothovius that he took his creed from Luther but his ecclesiastical law from the pope: Holm, *Terserus*, p. 135.

41. *Svenska riksrådets protokoll*, viii, 27.

42. *Ibid.*, vi, 425.

43. Laurentius Paulinus Gothus, on his translation to Uppsala, recorded that he found in the diocese 'an incredible barbarism and *inscitiam*'.

44. *Diarium Gyllenianum*, p. 249.

45. Contrast the failure of the Counter-Reformation's attempt to revivify parochial organization as a means to an intenser spiritual life; Bossy, in *Past and Present* (1970), pp. 63–5, 60.

46. At Hakarp in Småland one such dynasty of parsons lasted from 1597 to 1793: Sten Carlsson, *Mellan Bolmen och Holaveden* (Jönköping 1951), p. 62.

47. Statistics borrowed from Sten Carlsson, *Svensk ståndscirkulation 1680–1950* (Uppsala 1950), pp. 27–8.

48. See Gunnar Suolahti, *Finlands prästerkap på 1600- och 1700-talen* (Stockholm 1927), pp. 30–1.

49. Quoted in Sven Edlund, *Magnus Gabriel De la Gardies inrikespolitiska program 1655* (Lund 1954), p. 271.

50. *Svenska riksrådets protokoll*, vi, 247.

51. *Ibid.*, p. 308. Though perhaps it was stretching privilege pretty far to demand that a student be privileged to evict a fellow lodger who disturbed him in his studies: Cnattingius, *Johannes Rudbeckius och hans europeiska bakgrund*, p. 203.

52. *Prästeståndets riksdagsprotokoll*, i, 173.

53. *Samling af instructioner för högre och lägre tjenstemän vid Landt-Regeringen* (Stockholm 1852), p. 303.

54. Quoted in Normann, *Prästerskapet och det karolinska enväldet*, p. 169.

55. Romans xiii: 1–3: 'Let every soul be subject unto the higher powers. For there is no power but of God: the powers that be are ordained of God. Whosoever therefore resisteth the power, resisteth the ordinance of God: and they that resist shall receive to themselves damnation. For rulers are not a terror to good works, but to the evil.'

56. 1 Samuel viii: 11–17.

5. CHARLES X AND THE CONSTITUTION *Stellan Dahlgren*
(pages 174–202)

1. Riksarkivet, Stockholm: Riksregistraturet (Misplaced under 1656).

2. K. E. F. Ignatius, *Finlands historia under Carl X Gustafs regering* (Helsingfors 1865), p. 127.

3. See, e.g., letters from Schering Rosenhane in Per Brahe's correspondence in Skoklostersamlingen, Riksarkivet, Stockholm.

4. G. Wittrock, *Carl X Gustafs testamente* (Uppsala 1908), p. 137, n. 1.

6. MAGNUS GABRIEL DE LA GARDIE *Göran Rystad* (pages 203–36)

1. Sven Stolpe, *Drottning Kristina: den svenska tiden* (Stockholm 1960), pp. 99–100.

2. *Ibid.*, p. 99.

3. Lorenzo Magalotti, *Sverige under år 1674*, ed. C. M. Stenbock (Stockholm 1912), pp. 101–2.

4. Göran Rystad, *Johan Gyllenstierna* (Stockholm 1959), p. 106.

5. Printed in *Dela Gardiska Archivet*, ed. P. Wieselgren, vii (Lund 1836), 1–23.

6. *Ibid.*, p. 17.

7. *Ibid.*, pp. 36–118.

8. *Ibid.*, p. 84.

9. *Ibid.*, p. 93.

10. *Ibid.*, p. 109.

11. *Ibid.*, pp. 93–4.

12. *Ibid.*, p. 118.

13. Göran Rystad, *Johan Gyllenstierna, rådet och kungamakten* (Lund 1955), pp. 187–97.

7. THE REDUKTION   *Kurt Agren*   (pages 237-64)

1. Magnus Eriksson's Land Law (*c.* 1350) among other things regulated the relation of king to council, and came to be regarded as a fundamental constitutional law for nearly four centuries thereafter.

2. Stellan Dahlgren, *Karl X Gustaf och reduktionen* (Studia Historica Upsaliensia, xiv, Uppsala, 1964).

3. V. E. Svedelius, *Om reduktionen af krono- och adeliga gods under k. Carl XI:s regering* (Stockholm 1849).

4. A. Fryxell, *Berättelser ur svenska historien*, xvii (Stockholm 1852).

5. E. Blumfeldt, 'Reduktionen på Osel 1681-1694', *Svio-Estonica* (1958).

6. Heckscher, *Sveriges ekonomiska historia*, i.2.

7. For a full discussion of this question, see Sven A. Nilsson, 'Reduktion eller kontribution. Alternativ inom 1600-talets svenska finanspolitik', *Scandia*, xxiv (1958).

8. *Svenska ridderskaps och adels riksdagsprotokoll*, xii (Stockholm 1896), 126.

9. *Ibid.*, xi (Stockholm 1894), 283.

10. *Ibid.*, xiii (Stockholm 1896), 71.

11. Kurt Agren, 'Gods och ämbete. Sten Bielkes inkomster inför riksdagen 1680', *Scandia*, xxxi (1965).

12. Kurt Agren, *Adelns bönder och kronans. Skatter och besvär i Uppland 1650–1680* (Studia Historica Upsaliensia, xi, Uppsala 1964).

13. *Ibid.*, pp. 2 ff.

8. THE SWEDISH ARMY, FROM LÜTZEN TO NARVA   *Alf Aberg*
(pages 265-87)

1. Sven Agren, *Karl XI:s indelningsverk för armén* (Uppsala 1922), p. 111 ff.

2. Gustaf Petri, *Kungl. Första livgrenadjärregementets historia*, iii (Stockholm 1958), 59 ff.

3. Alf Aberg, *Indelningen av rytteriet i Skåne 1658–1700* (Lund 1947), p. 190.

4. John E. Roos, *Uppkomsten av Finlands militieboställen* (Helsinki 1933), p. 64.

5. Alf Aberg, 'Indelningsverket', in *Historiska bilder*, ii (Stockholm 1950), 376 ff.

6. See, *inter alia*, T. Wijkander, *Oversikt av svenska krigsförfattnings historiska utveckling* (Stockholm 1866), pp. 180 ff., and Eli Heckscher, 'Naturahushållning', in *Ekonomi och historia* (Stockholm 1922).

7. Elof Tegnér, *Svenska bilder från 1600-talet* (Stockholm 1896), p. 108.

8. Alf Aberg, 'Karl XI:s militära arbetspapper', in *Festskrift till Gottfried Carlsson* (Lund 1952), pp. 212 ff.

9. 'Karl XI:s uppmarschplaner för de ständiga truppförbanden i det Egentliga Sverige', *Meddelanden från Kungl. Krigsarkivet*, iv (Stockholm 1926).

10. Alf Aberg, *Karl XI* (Stockholm 1958), p. 188.

11. Folke Wernstedt, 'Lineartaktik och karolinsk taktik', *Karolinska förbundets årsbok* (1957), pp. 153 ff.

12. See Theodor Jakobsson, *Artilleriet under Karl XII:s striden* (Stockholm 1943).

13. For the battle of Pultava, see Gustaf Petri, *Karolinska förbundets årsbok* (1958). For the part played by artillery in the battle, see the articles by Jonas Hedberg, Georg Medwedjev and Waldemar Granberg in *ibid*. (1961). There is a description of the battlefield today in Alf Aberg, *I karolinernas spår* (Stockholm 1959).

14. *Karl XI:s almanacksanteckningar*, ed. Sune Hildebrand (Stockholm 1918), pp. 119, 157.

15. Folke Wernstedt, *Kungl. Svea livgardets historia*, iv (Stockholm 1954), 187 ff.

16. Ludvig Munthe, *Kungl. Fortifikationens historia*, iii.2 (Stockholm 1911).

17. Folke Wernstedt, 'Några detaljer från arméns mobilisering och uppmarsch vid Store Nordiska Krigets utbrott', *Karolinska förbundets årsbok* (1926), pp. 87 ff., and Alf Aberg, 'Rutger von Ascheberg och tillkomsten av den karolinska armén', *ibid*. (1951), pp. 170 ff.

Notes on Contributors

MICHAEL ROBERTS, D.Phil., Fil. Dr (*honoris causa*, Stockholm), F.B.A., M.R.I.A., is Professor of Modern History in The Queen's University, Belfast. His publications include *Gustavus Adolphus: A History of Sweden 1611–1632* (2 vols, 1953, 1958), *Essays in Swedish History* (1967), *The Early Vasas: A History of Sweden 1523–1611* (1968), and *Sweden as a Great Power: Government, Society, Foreign Policy* (1968). He is an Honorary Fellow of Worcester College, Oxford.

ALF ÅBERG is on the staff of Krigsakrivet, Stockholm. His publications include *Indelningen av rytteriet i Skåne 1658–1700* (Lund 1947); *Karl XI* (Stockholm 1958).

KURT ÅGREN is Lektor in History in the University of Uppsala. His publications include *Adelns bönder och kronans. Skatter och besvär i Uppland 1650–1680* (Studia Historica Upsaliensia, xi), x Uppsala 1964).

SVEN-ERIK ÅSTRÖM is Professor of Economic History in the University of Helsinki. His publications in English include *From Stockholm to St Petersburg: Commercial Factors in the Political Relations between England and Sweden 1675–1700* (Helsinki 1962), and *From Cloth to Iron: The Anglo-Baltic Trade in the Late Seventeenth Century*, vols i and ii (Helsinki 1963–65).

STELLAN DAHLGREN is Lektor in History in the University of Uppsala. His publications include *Karl X Gustav och reduktionen* (Studia Historica Upsaliensia, xiv) (Uppsala 1964).

SVEN LUNDKVIST is Docent in History in the University of Uppsala. His publications include *Gustav Vasa och Europe, Svensk handels- och utrikespolitik 1634–1657* (Studia Historica Upsaliensia, ii) (Uppsala 1960).

GÖRAN RYSTAD is Docent in History in the University of Lund. His publications include *Johan Gyllenstierna, rådet och kungamakten* (Bibliotheca historica Lundensis, ii) (Lund 1955); *John Gyllenstierna* (Stockholm 1957); *Kriegsnachrichten und Propaganda während des dreissigjährigen Krieges* (Lund 1960).

Index

Absolutism, 15, 42, 44, 50, 51, 54, 76, 105, 119, 120, 122, 171, 195, 244; *see also* Church and, 167 *et seq.*; *see also* Charles XI

Accession Charter, 128, 179

Adolf Johan (Duke), 209

Africa Company, 124

Agricultural developments, 46

Agriculture, by aristocracy, 62, 123; by peasants, 62, 105, 131; in Finland, 62; in Kexholm, 69; supporting armies, 61, 269 *et seq.*; *see also* Barley, Grain, Land tax Peasants

Alienation of Crown Lands, 87, 107, 238; opposition to, 88, 107, 117, 176, 239, 251; see also *Reduktion(s)*

Allodial tenure, see *Reduktion(s)*

'Allotment system', see *Indelningsverk*

Altmark truce, 92

Altranstädt, 58

Andersson, Erik, 85

Antichrist, 119

Archangel, 30

Aristocracy, see House of Nobility

Armies (foreign), 25, 29

Army (Swedish), 9, 18, 22 *et seq.*, 265–7; artillery, 267; chaplains, 136; Charles X as generalissimo, 85, Charles XI tactics, 278; Charles XII tactics, 281; College of War, 267; conscription, 247, 260, 265; devotion manuals, 136; engagements (1630–2), 64; entrepreneurs, 86, 267; 'file'

recruiting, 269; finances, 22, 23, 52, 84, 93, 96, 185, 196, 265–87; Finnish dragoons, 64; Finnish light cavalry, 63; foreign officers, 55; fortifications, 27, 267; garrisons in provinces, 28, 64, 75, 93; *indelningsverk*, 14, 15, 18, 25, 98, 248, 268 *et seq.*; literacy, 273; Magnus De La Gardie in, 205; maintenance in peacetime, 275; manpower losses, 85; mercenaries, 22, 24, 25, 99, 185, 196; noble officers, 126; numbers, 24, 27, 74, 99; of the Rhine, 94; provincial agreements, 26, 63; recruiting cavalry, 265; recruiting infantry, 265; regimental musters, 273; reserves, 27; strategy, 20–39, 64, 274 *et seq.*; substitutes, 266, 270; uniform standardisation, 67

Assimilation policy, 45

Baltic ports, 1, 30, 31, 87, 92; exclusion of foreign ships, 71

Baltic provinces, 8, 20, 23, 30, 40 *et seq.*; contribution to war finance, 84; Russian conquest, 48; 'Sweden's granary', 70; *see also* Provinces

Baner, Gustav Adam (Count), 219

Baner, Johan (Commander), 219, 279

Barley, 62

Baronies, 26; *see also* House of Nobility.

Bible(s), *see* Churches; Clergy

Bielke, Sten, 211, 254
Björko, 71
Björnklou, Matthias, 132, 211
Blekinge, 29, 72, 175
Boëthius, Jakob, 119, 171
Bohuslän, 29, 175
Bonde, Gustav, 2, 210
Botanic Gardens, 231
Bothe, Friedrich, 3
Brahe, Per, 132, 209
Brandenburg, 92; as ally, 32
Breda Peace, 213
Breitenfeld, 63
Bremen, 21, 23, 25
Bremen–Verden, 51, 61, 82; as
    port, 71
Brömsebro Peace, 175
Budgets, see Economic policy;
    Finance
Burghers, attack on nobility,
    110; ennoblement, 112, 114;
    foreign members, 59; v.
    Magistracy, 114; political
    influence, 110; retailer v.
    wholesalers, 112; see also
    Estates
Butter, 70

Calixtus, George, 149
Calvinists, 133, 145, 147; see also
    Clergy
Cartesianism, see Church(es)
Casimir, Johan, 181
Catechism, see Church(es)
Cattle, 62
Charcoal, 66
Charles I (Great Britain), 148
Charles IX, 40; crypto-calvinism,
    133, 141; policy of uniformity,
    40; puritanism, 137; theology,
    132
Charles X, 2, 6, 15, 16, 19, 24, 27,
    28, 31, 38, 42, 65, 135;

accession, 134, 179, 182; and
    constitution, 174–202; as
    generalissimo, 85, 135, 174,
    181, 193; death, 24, 34, 58, 73,
    209; financial policy, 176;
    foreign policy, 185, 189, 201;
    reduktion, 120, 175, 241;
    theology, 132; will, 209; see
    also Army (Swedish)
Charles XI, 2, 3, 15, 16, 18, 19,
    23, 25, 26, 27, 42, 51, 58, 77,
    79, 105, 110, 119, 135, 222;
    accession charter, 128; death,
    73; financial policy, 97; foreign
    policy 277; indelningsverk,
    268; reduktion, 88, 110, 120,
    126, 133, 248; retained native
    tongue, 78; see also Absolutism,
    Army (Swedish)
Charles XII, 1, 6, 19, 21, 27, 28,
    36, 37, 38, 126; death, 29, 37;
    religious policy, 153; see also
    Army (Swedish)
Charles Frederick of Holstein,
    37
Charles Gustavus, 164
Charles Philip, 30
Christina (Queen), 63, 65, 73, 77,
    79, 107, 142, 204; abdication,
    87, 145, 182, 208; accession
    charter, 154; coronation, 205;
    extravagances, 211; Magnus
    De la Gardie favourite, 204;
    Roman Catholic, 145; theology,
    132
Church(es), 8, 10, 11, 17, 142;
    absolutism and, 168;
    Cartesianism, 150, 170;
    catechism(s), 140, 148; church
    v. state authority, 156, 170;
    crypto-Calvinism, 133, 138;
    diocesan courts, 136, 169;
    discipline, 162; discipline of
    people, 133, 163, 168; doctrine,

137; excommunication, 169; Formula of Concord, 141; heresy punished, 146; Law (1686), 168; *Liber concordiae*, 162; Lutheran unity, 132–173; New Philosophy, 151; Norrland Orthodoxy, 138; ordinance (1571), 154, (1650), 142; Pietist movement, 140, 151; puritanism, 137; Quakerism, 144; reformation, 154; sovereign's piety, 133; Swedish Bible, 139; Syncretism, 149; Unionism, 148; *see also* Clergy, Protestant Cause, Religion, Roman Catholicism

Civil Service, ennoblement, 76, 128; salaries, 129, 196; *see also* Estates, Finance, Taxes

Clergy, army chaplains, 136; as crown agents, 115, 134; as rulers, 74; Bible translations, 135, 139; control by Charles XI, 119; crown livings, 168; debates, 169; dislike of absolutism, 119; duties, 134; education, 147; foreign members, 59; friction between ranks, 118, 164; hostility to nobility and peasants, 115, 132; lack of uniformity, 153; ordinances, 153; privileges, 167; spiritual authority, 133, 143, 160; support of peasants, 165; taxes, 105; *see also* Churches, Estates, Religion

Clothing, 67; industry, 68

Coalmines, 123

College of Commerce, 47

College of Exchequer, 198

College of *Reduktion*, 198

College of War, 267

'Colonialism', 47

Congress of Nijmegen, 35

Constitution of Sweden, 174–202

Constitutions of provinces, 40, 42; *see also* Charles X

Copper, 90; Falun mine, 65; industry, 110; Swedish monopoly in Europe, 65

Council of State, 119, 127, 133, 179, 191, 197; Magnus De la Gardie in, 205; misrepresented, 194; restrained, 197; *see also* Charles X; House of Nobility; Oxenstierna, Axel

Counties, 86; *see also* House of Nobility

Courland ports, 31, 36, 61, 92

Courts, *see* Churches, Diocesan Courts, Supreme Courts

Cronberg, B., 123

Cronstierna, Henrik, 121

Crops, *see* Agriculture, Grain, etc.

Crown peasant, 106, 239, 257

Customs, *see* Finance

Dahlberg, Erik, 277

Dalarna, 269

Danish provinces, 61, 62

Danzig, 33, 61, 92

De Besche, Gillis, 115

De Geer, Louis, 115, 123

De la Gardie, Axel Julius, 54

De la Gardie, Gustav Adolf, 217

De la Gardie, Jakob, 41, 123, 203

De la Gardie, Johan, 41

De la Gardie, Magnus Gabriel, 14–16, 41, 118, 120, 122, 132, 203–37; *A Short and Plain Remonstrance*, 225; army commander, 205, 208; arts patron, 21; banished by Christina, 207; educational system, 23; employed by Charles X, 208; estates, 205, 233; favourite of Christina,

De La Gardie—*cont.*
204; financial policy, 212;
governor-general, 205, 209;
v. Gyllenstierna, 218 *et seq.*; in
regency, 209, 211; libel against,
220; losses in *reduktion*, 235;
peregrination, 204; state
chancellor, 209; *Synopsis
physica*, 151; university
chancellor, 204, 208, 231;
Vindiciae Veritatis, 225
De la Gardie, Maria Sophia, 123
Denmark, 21, 25, 33, 36, 75
Diets, 25, 41, 45, 51, 87, 89, 102,
103, 107, 110, 116, 117, 125,
128, 221, 239; influence of
'Army Command', 127, 269;
reduktion resolution (1680),
237; *see also* Council of State,
Estates, *Riksdag*
Diocesan Courts, *see* Churches
Dorpat, supreme court, 43;
University, 8
Drakenhielm, W., 123
Duchies, 68; *see also* Bremen–
Verden, etc.
Durie, John (Calvinist), 141, 148
Dvina river, 36, 47
Dynastic quarrels, 30, 37;
Succession Act, 144

Economic policy, 5, 20, 84; effect
of wars, 13, 25, 58 *et seq.*; 72,
241; effect of regents and
aristocracy, 73; importance of
Finland, 65; *see also* Finance
Economic potential, 59, 90; *see
also* Resources
Edict of Lusuc, 153
Education, 8, 134, 147, 233;
monopoly by Church, 160
Ehrensteen, Edward, 197
Ekman, Olof, 152
'Elephant, The' (Stockholm), 81

Empire (Swedish), *see* Swedish
Empire
Enander, Samuel (Bishop), 116,
136, 164
England as mediator, 37, 38; *see
also* Charles I, Great Britain,
Iron
Eric XIV, 4, 18, 75; Calvinism,
138
Estates (Nobles, Clergy, Burghers,
Peasants), 43, 49, 51; and
constitution, 178–202;
combined in *reduktion* (1680),
242; courts, 134; ennoblement,
76, 112, 114, 127, 128;
entrepreneurs, 114; excluded
persons, 104; immigrants, 114;
peasants *v.* nobility, 107; plea
for fifth Estate, 128; *v.*
regencies, 219, 242; representation in *riksdag*, 192; taxes,
105; *see also* Clergy, House of
Nobility, Peasants
Estimates Office, 97
Estonia, 2, 6, 8, 23, 41, 46;
counties and baronies, 86;
feudal structure, 68; finances,
83, food production, 70;
history, 142
Excommunication, 169
Exports, 60, 67, 71, 82, 87, 90,
114; *see also* Flax, Grain, Iron,
Tar
'Extraordinary revenues', *see* Poll
tax

Falun, 104
Famine, 46
Farming, *see* Agriculture
Fehrbellin, 218
Feudal structures, 68
Fiefs, 86
Finance, 22, 23, 176; *Blue Book*,
213; budgets, 177, *see also*

National Balance Sheet; cash
v. kind, 249; constitutional
aspects, 188–202; court
expenses, 84, 211; customs
directors, 130; customs dues,
82, 90, 97, 187; financiers, 188,
189; French subsidies, 59, 81,
84, 94, 95, 215, 241;
indelningsverk, 238; in
regencies, 211; land tax, 97,
176; liquidity, 97; loans from
nobles, 115; militia levies, 99,
186, 195; moneylenders, 91;
National balance sheet, 80, 82,
90; national debt, 88, 90;
necessity for reduktion(s), 241;
ordinary v. extraordinary
revenue, 177; pawning Crown
property, 196; secret accounts,
80; ship tolls, 84, 90, 92; state
debts, 189, 196; treasure
reserve, 81; war v. peace, 99,
186; see also Army, Counties,
Economic policy, Fiefs, Taxes,
Wars
Finland, 20, 23, 61, 63; counties
and baronies, 86; losses in wars,
64; see also Army (Swedish)
Finnish language, 61
Flax, 47
Fleet, see Navy (Swedish)
Fleming, Herman, 208, 209,
210
Foreign policy, 20, 32, 34, 37, 38,
59, 73, 189, 192
Foreigners in Sweden, 54, 59, 60,
68, 76, 146
Form of government (1634), 43,
76, 99, 132, 133, 141, 154, 179;
Addition (1660), 210
Formula of Concord, 150
Frälse-peasant, 106, 239
France as ally, 32, 34, 37, 213,
225, 241; influence on Magnus

De la Gardie, 204; see also
Finance (French subsidies)
Frederick I, 19
Frederick of Hesse, 37
French subsidies, see Finance
Frontiers, 27

Galle, Johann, 63
Garrisons, see Army (Swedish)
German princes, 32, 39, 50
German provinces, 39, 49
Germany, 31; see also Wars
Gezelius, Georg, 164
Göteburg, 66, 71, 104
Government by regents and
nobility, 73, 88; see also
Regencies
Governors-general, 42, 54, 68,
190, 205, 209
Grain exports, 5, 67, 92; imports,
68; see also Barley, Rye,
Wheat, etc.
Grand tour, 147
Great Britain–Sweden defence
treaty, 100
Great Northern War, 24, 45, 55,
72, 97, 126, 274
Gripenhielm, Edmund, 121
Gripenstierna, Joel, 123, 126
Grundel-Hemfelt, Simon
(Field-Marshal), 121
Gulf of Bothnia, 87
Gulf of Finland, 87, 278
Gustavus Adolphus, 1, 3, 4, 6, 8,
19, 22, 26, 31, 58, 64, 65, 79,
96, 132, 136; accession, 29,
133; army organisation, 265,
279; death, 73, 265, indelnings-
verk, 268; policies, 38; religious
policies, 133, 135, 141
Gustavus Vasa, 137, 154, 237;
death, 63

Gyllenstierna, Johan, 211, 218; enemy of Magnus De la Gardie, 220

Gymnasia, *see* Education, Schools

Halland, 29, 175
Hanover peace, 37
Heckscher, Eli, 60
Helmstadt University, 149
Hemp, 47
Hesse, 37
Holstein, 37
Holstein-Gottorp, 36, 61, 82
Hospitals, 134
House of Nobility, 16, 41, 43, 45, 63, 74; army officers, 126; as moneylenders, 126; bureaucratic, 89; *v.* clergy, 157; creation of counts and barons, 86; customs directors, 123, 129; economic power, 120; ennoblement of civil servants, 76, 128; ennoblement of Clergy, 76; exemption from tax, 120; expansion by Crown donations, 122; geographical origin, 76; grades, 76, 121, 123; high *v.* lower, 128, 252; hostility to De la Gardie family, 204; hostility to Herman Fleming, 123; income, 122; industrialists, 123; in regencies, 210; investors, 124; land lost in *reduktion(s)*, 124, 251; provide cavalry, 266; provincial members, 59, 68, 76, 146

Imperialism, *see* Swedish Empire
Imports, 67, 70, 71
Indelningsverk, 14, 15, 18, 25, 98, 110, 248, 268 *et seq.*
Ingria, 21, 23, 30, 40, 42, 43, 61, 70, 83; social structure, 69

Instruction for Provincial Governors, 170
Invasions by Sweden, 6, 28, 32, 34, 36, 85, 193; of Sweden, 5, 33, 222; *see also* Wars
Iron, 60; English market, 65; exports, 66, 82; foundries, 66, 110, 123; mining, 65; 'Walloon iron', 65

John III, attempt to reconcile with Rome, 133, 154

Kagg, Lars, 210
Kardis Peace, 21
Karlskrona, 72, 74
Kexholm, 30, 42, 61, 69; counties and baronies, 86; social structure, 69;
King, James (General), 279
Knight-service, 68, 267
Kock-Conström family, 115
Königsmarck, Hans Christopher von, profits from wars, 85
Kopparplåtar, 65

Land grants, 63
Land Law, 17, 133, 180, 182
Land tax (ordinary revenue), 79, 105; in kind, 96
Language policy, 46, 78; *see also* Charles XI
Languages, 61, 68
Larsson, Erik (van der Linde), 112
Latifundia, 63, 89
Law, *see* Swedish law
Leijonsköld, Mårten, 121, 123
Liber Concordiae, 168
Livonia, 4, 6, 8, 17, 23, 36, 41, 42, 46; feudal structure, 68; finances, 83; food production, 70; nobility, 45, 86
Loccenius, Johannes, 132
Louis XIV (France), 35, 213

Lund, 63, 64; University, 231
Lüneburg, as ally, 36
Lutheranism, 132 *et seq.*
Lützen, 265
Magistracy *v.* Burghers, 114
Malt, 70
Maritime Powers, 36, 37, 213
Matthiae, Johannes, 118, 139, 141, 152
Mercenaries, 22, 73, 185, 196; *see also* Army (Swedish)
Merchant navy (mercantile marine), 71, 90, 111; effect of frozen sea, 72; in wars, 72
Metals, trade, 71, 114; *see also* Copper, Iron, Silver
Militia levies, 99, 186, 195
Minden, 85
Momma-Reenstierna brothers, 115
Moneylenders, 9, 126; crown servants, 130
Mylonius, Matthias (Björnklou), 204

Narva, 48, 58
Navy (Dutch), 33
Navy (Swedish), 3, 31, 33; defeat, 241; numbers, 72, 74; power, 72; protection of, 35; strategy, 72; *see also* Merchant Navy
Nijmegen, 35
Nördlingen, 85
Norrköping, 104; resolution, 240; succession act, 144
Norway, 21
Norwegian provinces, 62
Nyen (Leningrad), 87, 278
Nystad Peace, 20, 38, 56, 70

Oats, 62, 70
Oliva Peace, 21, 209
Ordinary revenue, *see* Land tax

Osel, 23
Osnabrück treaty, 51
Osterbotten, 71
Oxenstierna, Axel, 2, 4, 40, 41, 58, 84, 86, 109, 117, 142, 148, 154, 161, 184; chancellor, 120, 204; theologian, 132; *see also* Charles X
Oxenstierna, Erik, 190, 198
Oxenstierna family, 69

Parish units, 134, 163, 169
Parliamentarism, 17
Patkul, Johan Reinhold, 45
Peace, 22, 24, 176; *see also* Breda, Brömsebro, Kardis, Nystad, Oliva, Roskilde, Russia, Stolbova, Westphalia
Peace treaties, 21, 37, 56, 175, 190
Peasants, 46, 59; conscription, 260; crown-, 106, 239, 257; *frälse-*, 106, 239, 257; freeholders, 262; landless, 106; opposition to nobility, 107; *reduktion*-effects, 110, 239, 257; *rusthållare*, 105; tax-, 106, 239, 257; taxes on, 259; upper class, 105; *see also* Estates
Penance, 169; *see also* Churches, Clergy
Peter the Great, 36, 53
Petition of Nobility (1719), 128
Pietist movement, *see* Churches
Pitch exports, 67
Poland, 29, 31, 36, 75
Polish truces, 21
Poll tax, 79
Pomerania, 21, 23, 28, 37, 49, 50, 61, 82; finances, 83
Poor Laws, 106, 134
Pork, 70
Postulata Nobilium, 166

Prague, 85, 205; Silver Bible as booty, 231
Precious metals, see Copper, Silver
Prisoners of war, 136, 153
Privilegia quaedam doctorum, 166
Protestant cause, 1, 40, 135
Protestation of Three Estates, 117
Provinces, 22, 73; constitutions, 40, 43; governors, 170; military contracts, 26; reduktion in, 250; see also Bremen, Estonia, etc.
Prussia, 28, 31, 57, 83; peace, 37; ship tolls, 90, 92
Prytz, Andreas (Bishop), 117
Pultava, 58, 63, 136, 274

Rålamb, Clas, 211, 215, 218
Reduktion(s), 6, 9, 15, 16, 25, 43, 44, 55, 62, 71, 87–90, 96, 110, 120, 125, 168, 176–8, 196, 210, 227–63; allodial tenure lands, 240; college of, 198; defensive necessity, 247; demands for, 187, 240, 256; economic necessity, 241, 244; effects on nobility, 239, 251; 'inalienable areas', 240; indelningsverk, 248; political motives, 250; Roman Catholic estates, 237; see also Charles X, Charles XI, Riksdag
Regencie(s), 17, 63, 65, 73, 120, 125, 209, 241; attacks on; 89, 242; foreign policy, 213; religious proclamation, 132
Religion, freedom of conscience, 144; unity in Sweden, 132; see also Churches, Clergy
Reval (Tallinn), 18, 30, 47, 48
Revenue, see Finance
Revolution (1719), 172

Riga, 1, 4, 6, 18, 30, 47, 71; conquest by Russia, 48
Riksdag, 6, 16, 17, 59, 88, 113, 146, 170, 172, 176, 186, 192, 218; nullified, 197; representation in, 192
Riksdagsordning (1617), 102
Roads, 73
Roman Catholic(s)(ism), 40, 133, 154; non-tolerance, 145; Statute of Orebro, 145; see also Christina (Queen), Churches
Roskilde Peace, 175, 191
Rudbeck, Olof, 231
Rudbeckius (Bishop), 166
Russia, 29, 36, 38, 57; see also Wars
Russian Peace, 38
Rusthållare, 105, 270
Rye, 62, 70

Salt, 70
Salvius, Johan Adler, 121, 127, 132
School Ordinance, 168
Schools 8; see also Education
Scriver, Christian, 152
Ship-owners, 71, 91, 111
Ship tolls, see Finance
Short and Plain Remonstrance, A, 225
Sigismund, 40, 155
Silver, customs dues, 90; Sala mine, 65; treasure hoard, 81
Silver Bible, 231
Sjaelland, 193
Skåne, 29, 175
Skytte, Johann (Johan Bengtsson Schroderus), 40, 121, 127, 132
Skytte, Lars, 145
Slave trade, 124
Småland, 269
Spanish succession, 58
Stade, 72

Stålhandske, Torsten, 63
Statute of Orebro, 145, 147
Statutes of Labourers, 106
Steinberg, Anton von, 121
Stettin, 47, 49
Stockholm, as port, 66, 70, 71, 90; population, 104
Stolbova Peace, 3, 4, 21, 30, 69
Stralsund, as port, 71
Strategy, see Army (Swedish)
Stuhmsdorf truce, 4, 93, 94
Succession Act, 144
Supreme courts, 9, 43, 51, 133, 169
Sventjänare, 270
Swedberg, Jesper, 133, 164
Swedish Army, see Army (Swedish)
Swedish Bible, 139
Swedish Empire, 1, 3, 5, 6, 9, 20, 42, 52, 58, 174; chessboard analogy, 74; constitution, 167, 178–202; differences from others, 61; economic pressures, 83; end, 38, 56, 58, 100; expansion, 2, 4, 6, 47, 79, 86, 119, 175; geographical divisions, 59; 'French satellite', 94; 'immigrants', 60; military strength, 24; morality, 163; neutrality, 71, 90; population numbers, 21, 60, 74, 104; poverty, 73; weaknesses, 38, 55; see also Army (Swedish), Economic policy, Estates, Finance, Foreign policy, Merchant Navy, Navy (Swedish), Provinces, Wars
Swedish law, 43; religious unity, 132
Swedish navy, see Navy (Swedish)
Swedish succession, 144
Syncretism, see Churches

Tar, 60, 67; exports, 67, 82
Taubenfelt, G. H., 128
'Tax peasant', 106, 239
Taxes, and constitution, 180, 195; exemptions, 88, 106, 120, 239, 257; see also Army (Swedish), Finance, Land tax, Poll tax
Terserus, Johannes, 140, 150
Tessin, Nicodemus (elder and younger), 114
Textile industry, 111, 114; see also Clothing
Thegner, Olof, 110, 122
Theologians, 132; see also Churches, Clergy
Thirty Years War, 20, 21, 28, 31, 49, 55, 61, 63, 75, 84, 181; finance, 84
Timber, 47; exports, 67
Tithes, 105, 157
Tobolsk, 137
Tolls, 5, 6, 90, 92; see also Finance
Tönningen, 274
Trade routes, 47, 48
Treason, 45
Triple alliance, 213
Truce(s), see Altmark, Polish, Stuhmsdorf

Ulrica Eleonora (Dowager Queen), 152
Uniformity, 40, 42, 44
Unionism, see Church(es)
Universities, 8; see also Helmstedt, Lund, Uppsala
Uppsala council, 138; University, 147, 150, 152, 204, 231

Viborg, 71
Vindicae Veritatis, 225

Wachtmeister, Hans, 74, 243
'Walloon iron', 65
Walloons, 141, 147
War economy, *see* Army
  (Swedish), Economics, Finance
War efforts, 59
'War sustains War', 26, 29, 73, 85
Wars, 11–14, 20, 22, 24, 25, 28,
  30, 31, 33, 34, 58, 59, 63, 64,
  75, 84, 215; *v.* Austria, 175,
  191; *v.* Brandenburg, 75, 175,
  191, 241; *v.* Denmark, 58, 75,
  175, 176, 191, 241, 277; *v.*
  Germany, 94, 100, 277; *v.*

Poland, 75, 175, 185, 191, 203,
  277; *v.* Russia, 100, 175, 191;
  see also Finance, Great
  Northern War, Thirty Years
  War
Westphalia Peace, 20, 31, 86, 95,
  181; satisfaction, 95
Wheat, 62, 70
Wismar, 21, 23, 82; port, 71;
  supreme court, 51
Wittstock, 279
Wrangel, Karl Gustav, 209

Zweibrücken, 61